Truth's Ragged Edge

Truth's Ragged Edge

The Rise of the American Novel

PHILIP F. GURA

FARRAR, STRAUS AND GIROUX *New York*

FARRAR, STRAUS AND GIROUX
18 West 18th Street, New York 10011

Printed in the United States of America
First edition, 2013

A portion of this book first appeared, in slightly different form, in *New England Review*.

LIBRARY OF CONGRESS CATALOGING-IN-PUBLICATION DATA
Gura, Philip F.
    Truth's ragged edge : the rise of the American novel / Philip F. Gura. — 1st ed.
      p.   cm.
    Includes index.
    ISBN 978-0-8090-9445-5 (hardback)
      1. American fiction—History and criticism.   2. Religion in literature.
  3. Religion and literature—United States—History.   I. Title.

PS374.R47 .G87 2013
813'.309382—dc23

                                                            2012029936

www.fsgbooks.com
www.twitter.com/fsgbooks • www.facebook.com/fsgbooks

10 9 8 7 6 5 4 3 2 1

For Larry Buell

*"I shall leave the world, I feel, with more satisfaction
for having come to know you."*

"Truth uncompromisingly told will always have its ragged edges."
—Herman Melville, *Billy Budd*

Contents

Preface

*A*n American born late in the eighteenth century and blessed to live past the midpoint of the next would have witnessed a series of changes, by turns heady and bewildering, to the world of her youth. Between 1800 and 1850, twenty-one new states were admitted to the Union, for a total of thirty-four; the national population exploded, going from around 4 million to 31.5 million, in part due to rapidly increasing numbers of immigrants, from 5,000 in 1790 to 600,000 in the 1830s and 2.6 million in the 1850s; the nation launched its first imperialistic adventures, in Central America and the Caribbean; the national legislature paved the way for the extension of slavery into new territories in the South and the West; and the economy swiftly modernized and expanded as a result of the advent of water- and steam-powered manufacture and the construction of roads, canals, and railways that linked distant producers and consumers.

Other changes marked the era in less visible and quantifiable ways. The invention and dissemination of steam power, telegraphy, photography, and other new technologies changed people's perception of time and space, while the widespread religious upheavals of the period and the fracture of American Christianity into scores of denominations placed many believers in new relations to God and to one another. Late in his career, as Ralph Waldo Emerson recalled this religious tumult, he identified what was to him the defining transformation of the age: by 1850 "the mind had become aware of itself." He wrote that beginning in the 1830s, there arose "a new consciousness" based in the belief that "the individual is the world." This perception cut like "a sword . . . never drawn before" and led to an age "of severance, of dissociation, of freedom, of analysis, of detachment." The youth were "born with knives in their brain [*sic*], a tendency to introversion, self-dissection, anatomizing of motives."[1]

The trajectory Emerson hinted at can be fleshed out. In the late eighteenth century, most Americans lived in a world defined primarily by an individual's relation to divine otherness. A quarter century later, the reigning notion was that of free will, though the expectation that the individual would conform to agreed-upon religious and social models still prevailed. In the two decades preceding the Civil War, another shift occurred, this time toward the self-consciousness that Emerson recognized. Cultural commentators less optimistic than he, pining for a world and way of life that was fast slipping away, saw not freedom but solipsism in this latest turn.[2]

Not incidentally, the first American novels appeared at the start of this transformation, and both reflected and helped make possible the movement toward free will and then Emersonian self-consciousness and self-reliance. A narrative form imported from Europe, the novel took on a distinctively American cast in the hands of native writers. Owing to the fundamental religiosity of American life and to a fractured spiritual landscape, the early novel was often an author's means for articulating her theological position and her prescriptions for her fellow citizens. But, especially deeper into the century, many novelists began to espouse areligious and even antireligious ideas. The novel was frequently a proselytizing tool, but not always for religious ends. In the 1850s, a reviewer for Philadelphia's *Graham's Magazine*, intending merely to comment on the ubiquity and variety of the novel, revealed the contemporary assumption that most novels had such a purpose. He wrote that there are "political novels, representing every variety of political opinion—religious novels, to push the doctrines of every religious sect—philanthropic novels, devoted to the championship of every reform—socialist novels . . . philosophical novels, metaphysical novels, even railway novels [that is, those suited, in topic or length, to be read as one rode the rails]."[3] In the same decade, a reviewer in *Putnam's Monthly Magazine* wrote, "Novels are one of the features of our age . . . we would not know what we would do without them."[4]

To understand how religion determined the nature of the early American novel, we need look no further than the eighteenth-century theologian Jonathan Edwards. On May 30, 1850, the Reverend Edwards Amasa Park addressed the Convention of Congregational Ministers of Massachusetts in the venerable Brattle Street Meeting House in Boston. The assembly was eager to hear an important member of the influential group known as Consistent Calvinists—those who preserved and refined Jonathan Edwards's theology.[5] Yet Park's sermon, titled "The Theology of the Intellect and the Theology of the Feelings," only fanned a controversy smoldering within American Christianity since Edwards's time. No religious address since Emerson's at the Harvard Divinity School fourteen years earlier had so captured the public's attention.[6]

Park asked the question of the era: Were the great truths of Christianity apprehended through the head or the heart? Put another way, were men's actions motivated by rational analysis or emotional impulse? In 1790 the answer had been uncontroversial: by the power of man's reason. But by 1850 some theologians had started to question the divine origin of the Bible, and to argue that the truth of Christian doctrine should be felt rather than understood. The German theologian Friedrich Schleiermacher, who declared that true religion consisted of "feeling" rather than "knowing," was particularly influential in American religious circles. To the chagrin of conservative theologians, Schleiermacher's ideas, at first confined to radical religions such as Transcendentalism, began to spread more widely, so that one's emotional life—how one was affected—often took precedence over what one thought.[7]

Park, drawing on a lesser-known aspect of Edwards's thought, had his own ideas about how one should interpret Scripture. His premise was simple: The theology of the intellect and that of the feelings both had a role to play. He saw that his namesake had recognized the value of the theology of the feelings, a fact de-emphasized by Edwards's logic-chopping acolytes. "In order to reach all the hiding-places of emotion," Park explained, great theologians occasionally had to strain a word "to its utmost significancy," and in so doing seemingly contradicted other parts of their theological system. Such had been the case with Edwards. He was not "a mere mathematician" but gave "his feelings a full, easy, and various play."[8] Because his writings on what he termed "the religious affections" lent themselves to the nineteenth century's understanding of the theology of the feelings, Edwards remained relevant through the antebellum period.[9] Between 1800 and 1860 his hortatory volumes, particularly his narratives of the eighteenth-century revivals, *A Treatise Concerning the Religious Affections* and *The Life of David Brainerd*, were among the most frequently reprinted American books; their primary competition was Benjamin Franklin's *Autobiography*.[10]

Edwards's insistence on both the religious affections and the mind greatly influenced a number of the best-known early novelists. In his *Pierre; or, The Ambiguities* (1852), Herman Melville opined, in a way that Edwards and Park would have understood, that God's truth was one thing and man's conception of it another, yet "by their very contradictions they are made to correspond."[11] Harriet Beecher Stowe, daughter of the Edwardsian clergyman Lyman Beecher, recalled that when she was a child, Edwards's works were still "discussed by every farmer, in intervals of plough and hoe, by every woman and girl, at loom, spinning wheel, or wash-tub."[12] In *The Minister's Wooing* (1859), she used one of Edwards's chief disciples, Samuel Hopkins (who famously argued that a Christian should be willing to be damned for the glory of God), as a sounding board for her characters' conflicting religious views. Stowe's brother Henry Ward Beecher, the most famous and highest-paid preacher in post–Civil War America, wrote in his historical novel of New England, *Norwood; or, Village Life in New England* (1867), "I think we owe everything to her theologians, and most to the doctrinal."[13]

* * *

If the arc from traditional religion to self-consciousness helps us understand how the early novel evolved, the contest between civic duty and individualism, the most consistent trope of the early novel, religious, blasphemous, agnostic, or otherwise, shows that in important ways the novel retained certain features throughout the period. Moreover, this contest was more often than not embedded in the sentimental genre, which traces its origins to Great Britain—to Laurence Sterne's *A Sentimental Journey* (1768) and Henry Mackenzie's *The Man of Feeling* (1771). A reaction to the neoclassical values of restraint and order, the sentimental novel, like Parks's theology, made room for the emotions alongside rational analysis. It took as its primary concern the feelings of its characters, tended to focus on moral behavior, and featured weaker, neglected members of society—women struggling for acknowledgment and self-determination as well as orphans and the poor.

With these constants in mind, let us explore some of the many ideas, settings, and forms that characterized the early novel. Around the turn of the century, William Hill Brown and Charles Brockden Brown (no relation) explored the limits of rationality, emphasizing the random irruption of the irrational into even the most settled lives; their target was the young nation's emergent ethos of liberal individualism. Beginning in the 1820s, some novelists, inspired by the fiftieth anniversary of American independence as well as the bicentennial of New England's settlement, began to write historical fiction, evincing a concern for the public good; in novels by James Fenimore Cooper, William Gilmore Simms, and others, readers encountered characters whose altruistic behavior signaled not only their virtue but also the success of the country's democratic experiment.

Less remembered but just as significant were Catharine Maria Sedgwick and Lydia Maria Child, who questioned the legacy of their Puritan forefathers in light of newer liberal religious denominations, like the Quakers or Unitarians. Moved by debates over the controversy of Indian removal—particularly the expulsion of the Cherokees, Seminoles, and others from their ancestral lands in the Southeast—as well as the budding abolitionist movement, they and other writers approached race in startlingly complex and progressive ways. The Philadelphia novelist Robert Montgomery Bird's *Nick of the Woods* (1837) later pushed this liberal religious bent to its limit with a main character who was both an exemplary Christian and a cold-blooded killer. There were also novelists—the incomparable John Neal most memorably—who questioned the very efficacy of historical knowledge to inform behavior in a time of transformative change. Neal's proselytism was about the form of the novel itself; he thought that novelists who truly confronted contemporary challenges had to conceive of new kinds of narratives, as he did throughout the 1820s.

Neal was ahead of his time; most novelists remained firmly within a religious and sentimental mode. Countering centuries-old narratives that presented humankind as fallen, sinful creatures, they held optimistic views of man's capabilities and believed that no matter what one's circumstances, rather than awaiting religious conversion he or she could achieve moral perfection through self-sacrifice and the power of individual will. For many writers, concern for humanity thus replaced Scripture as the standard against which to judge godliness. As a result, their characters, often beset by severe hardships, struggled against ironclad doctrine in order to fully realize nondenominational piety. In America such fiction reached its apogee in works like Susan Warner's *The Wide, Wide World* (1850) and Maria Cummins's *The Lamplighter* (1854), whose main character, Gerty, inspired millions of readers to emulate her Christian humility.

Yet other authors had already begun to reject what they viewed as the sentimental novelists' shallow assessments of character and motivation. They derided the emergent middle-class consensus about how to be and do good by turning for inspiration to European gothic novels. George Lippard and George Thompson shocked readers with graphic depictions of the violence and sexuality of the city. For them, the formation of Christian character was hardly the issue. They questioned not only the economic system that created flagrant social inequity but also whether in such an environment individuals could maintain any sense of communal responsibility.

Still, the sentimental mode, more malleable than is often recognized, proved enduringly useful. American novelists set sentimental novels in mill villages, for instance. An alternative to working in the city, the mill village provided another opportunity for people seeking wage labor. But life in these communities often was as impersonal as city life; company-owned tenements threw together young, unattached people from different communities, and work spaces filled with the deafening noise of gears, wheels, and belts, as well as health hazards like insidious cotton or wool fibers that lodged in the lungs, and poisonous dyes. Novelists endeavored to draw attention to the plight of the worker, in their estimation a major social problem, through wrenchingly emotional stories.

Accelerating economic and territorial expansion in the 1840s and 1850s brought slavery to the fore, and here, too, American novelists deployed sentimental tropes in new and significant ways, particularly to illustrate the humanity of the enslaved. Slavery in the South spawned a literature of social reform in the North, and by the 1850s African American novelists, including some runaway slaves, added their own testimony to that offered by Stowe and a host of other white antislavery writers who gave dignity and agency to a population that novelists had previously disregarded. Notably, among black novelists there were dissenters from abolitionism. Frank J. Webb questioned the intent of whites who crusaded for emancipation but could not abide living or working alongside a free black, while Martin R. Delany variously advocated revolution and repatriation to Africa or Cuba.

A small number of novelists of utopian fiction created plots that centered on an even more radical reorganization of American society,

North and South. These writers portrayed ideal communities, often based on the socialist ideas of the early-nineteenth-century French utopian thinker Charles Fourier (1772–1837), who was widely read at the time for his vision of a harmonious world devoid of social and economic competition, where gratification of one's passions was assured. Others imagined faraway kingdoms untouched by the corruption of European or American civilization and so offered yet different models of the good society.

By the 1850s novelists had begun to write as much about the individual's consciousness of his behavior as of the behavior itself. They followed the lead of Continental Romantics, who believed that self-examination was central to one's humanity. But they fused secular ideas with the language and concerns of American religion, which now included the ultra-liberal, virtually post–Christian Transcendentalism promulgated by Emerson and his disciples, whose ideas of self-reliance, the primacy of mind over the material world, and the centrality of conscience in directing morality had begun to permeate many aspects of American thought. Even evangelical religion did not escape the influence of the Romantic belief in the limitless power of the mind. The famous revivalist Charles Grandison Finney, for example, a key figure in the Second Great Awakening and an example of Romanticism's reconfiguration of the American religious landscape, accounted for his conversion as follows: "I had no where to go but directly to the Bible, and to the philosophy or workings of my own mind as they were revealed in consciousness."[14]

How to convey such views of mind and personality became the project not only of such well-known novelists as Nathaniel Hawthorne in *The Blithedale Romance* (1852) and Melville in *Moby-Dick* (1851) and *Pierre* (1852), but also of Donald G. Mitchell ("Ik Marvel") in his immensely popular *Reveries of a Bachelor* (1850), Lillie Devereux Blake in *Southwold* (1859), and Elizabeth Stoddard in *The Morgesons* (1862). In these mid-nineteenth-century novelists one sees the halting emergence of a style that in 1890 William James would call a "stream of thought, of consciousness." The novel had entered a new phase, and as subjectivity gradually replaced sentiment as the novelist's donnée, we soon arrive at the doorstep of William's brother Henry and literary modernism.

Just as certain novelists began to represent the mysteries of the interior life, however, some of their contemporaries challenged hyperindividualism as a threat to the nation. The new self-indulgence needed its own counterweight, one provided by a reaffirmation of the nation's democratic bases, the supposed willingness of individuals to live for the commonwealth. In Rebecca Harding Davis's work, particularly *Margret Howth: A Story of To-Day* (1862), and in several of Elizabeth Stuart Phelps's novels of the 1870s, self-indulgence is the chief reason for the country's moral decline. Self-knowledge, Davis believed, should end not in self-absorption but rather in the realization of the nation's founding principles. Hers was one of the first secular arguments for civic duty over individualism to appear in the American novel.

* * *

This book is organized more or less chronologically, moving from the late eighteenth century to the early 1870s, ending with novels written shortly after the war years but not indelibly affected by the cataclysm, which, as a number of historians have argued, American writers took years to assimilate.[15] The emphasis is on the period after 1820, when the publishing industry modernized and expanded, making possible the novel's emergence as the country's most popular literary form. I attempt as much as possible to put every novelist in his or her historical and biographical context, though some remain insufficiently knowable to us. The focus is on authors whose works marked significant turning points for the novel. By my lights, the most popular novelists at the time were not always the most influential, and the work for which an author was best known was not necessarily the most significant in her œuvre.

Three debts make the goals of this book clear. The title is borrowed from Melville's last work, *Billy Budd, Sailor (An Inside Narrative)* (1891). Late in this novella, Melville admits that his narration of Billy's story is not as "finished" as readers might hope, because "Truth uncompromisingly told will always have its ragged edges." I take him to mean that it is difficult to comprehend, let alone write of, truth in any fullness because of its complexity and ultimate ambiguity. My reading of early American fiction is attentive to authors who made an honest attempt to capture that fullness.

My subtitle is likewise borrowed, though not, as is surely evident, from a novel. Alexander Cowie's 1948 history *The Rise of the American Novel* still remains, along with Richard Chase's 1957 classic *The American Novel and Its Tradition*, one of the most thorough and well-regarded studies of its kind. Though I review my book as a revival of a dormant tradition, I hope to recapture only the earlier books' ambition, not their content. After all, much has changed since Cowie and Chase's time. The rediscovery of writers forgotten or ignored because of their gender or race has upended the history of the novel, and stands as an important thread in the rewriting of early American history over the past few decades to make it more inclusive and attentive to the powerless members of society. My hope is that bringing women and African American novelists into the discussion will result in the fullest understanding yet of the early American novel.

The final and greatest debt is to the late Alan Heimert, for the approach to the history of ideas I learned from his work early in my career. As he put it, "An understanding of the significance of any idea, or of a constellation of ideas, requires an awareness of the context of institutions and events out of which thought emerged, and with which it strove to come to terms." But full comprehension, he continued, "depends finally on reading, not between the lines but, as it were, beyond and through them."[16] My intent is to read beyond and through the lines of early novels, to find and examine the constellation of ideas that defined American life in the first half of the nineteenth century and that drove citizens to pick up their quills and write fiction.

PART I } 1789–1850

I } Beginnings

Historians of the English novel point to John Bunyan's *Pilgrim's Progress* (1678) as a progenitor of the form. The American version of this tale is Joseph Morgan's *History of the Kingdom of Basaruah* (1715), a minister's allegory of the Calvinist view of man's fall and redemption.[1] Though uninspired, the book is a testament to the centrality of Christian allegories in eighteenth-century British North America.[2] But with the circulation in the newly independent United States of popular English novels like Samuel Richardson's *Pamela* (1740) and *Clarissa* (1747–48), Laurence Sterne's *A Sentimental Journey* (1768), and Henry Mackenzie's *The Man of Feeling* (1771), novelists began to revise and sometimes challenge allegorical narratives of the pious Christian life. Rather than provide road maps through the Delectable Mountains, they heralded the triumph of individual virtue and urged the cultivation of sentiment in contemporary settings readers would recognize. They often based their novels on the kinds of stories heard from neighbors or read in the weekly newspapers—tales, in other words, populated not by pasteboard archetypes but by real people. Appropriate for earlier times, accounts of a pilgrim's progress lacked the texture and complexity of everyday experience in the late-eighteenth-century United States and particularly its moral ambiguity.

Fictional works that directed an individual through this sinful world emerged first as handmaidens and then as rivals to the sermons, religious allegories, and wonder tales that hitherto had dominated native literature. In his *Algerine Captive* (1797), one of the earliest American novels, Royall Tyler, Vermont superior court judge, playwright, poet, and novelist, noted this shift. His character Updike Underhill, following six years of captivity in the Barbary States, remarks how on his return from his forced absence from the United States he "found a surprising alteration in public taste," for now everyone read novels. "The worthy farmer no longer fatigued himself with Bunyan's Pilgrim up the 'hill of difficulty,' or through the 'slough of despond,'" and "Dolly, the dairy maid, and Jonathan, the hired man, threw aside the ballad of the cruel stepmother, over which they had so often wept."[3] A character in another early American work commented on the same shift in reading habits. "We fly from the laboured precepts of the essayists," he observed, "to the sprightly narrative of the novelist."[4]

This comment appears in what is widely recognized as the first bona fide American novel, William Hill Brown's *The Power of Sympathy*.[5] Brown (1765–1793) was born in Boston, the son of a prominent clockmaker.[6] Educated locally, he displayed a penchant for classical and English literature and by his early twenties was publishing patriotic poetry, thereby contributing to the city's nascent cultural nationalism. In one poem, "Shays to Shattuck: An Epistle," Brown imagines a conversation in prison between a despondent Daniel Shays, fomenter of Shays's Rebellion, and one of his foot soldiers, in which the former tries to justify his rebellion. In another, "Yankee Song," Brown celebrates the state's recent ratification of the Federal Constitution. The poem contains the refrain "Yankee Doodle keep it up, Yankee Doodle dandy" and upon republication the following year carried the now-familiar title "Yankee Doodle." In his early twenties, Brown came to the attention of the prominent printer and publisher Isaiah Thomas, who encouraged regional authors by publishing them in his newspapers and a periodical titled *The Massachusetts Magazine* (1789–1796), whose contributors eventually included Benjamin Franklin, the New Hampshire essayist Joseph Dennie, the poet Sarah Wentworth Apthorp Morton, and the early women's rights advocate Judith Sargent Murray. Thomas was not particularly interested in publishing native fiction, however, finding children's books and almanacs, as well as reprints of popular English titles, more lucrative. But his good nose for profit led him in 1789 to publish Brown's *The Power of Sympathy*, no doubt thinking that its thinly veiled references to recent sensational events in Boston guaranteed its success.[7]

For almost a century this novel was mistakenly attributed—Thomas had issued it anonymously—to another Boston writer, the poet Sarah

Wentworth Apthorp Morton, because she was intimately involved in the scandal that had inspired it. This sordid tale unfolded in two of Boston's most prominent families. Sarah Apthorp married Perez Morton, a prominent state politician who counted the Revolutionary patriot James Otis among his friends. The Mortons graciously allowed Sarah's unmarried sister Frances (Fanny) to live with them in their Beacon Hill home, but she proved too tempting to Perez; a surreptitious affair led to the birth of their child. Sarah and Fanny's father, James Apthorp, was outraged and demanded that Morton openly acknowledge the baby girl. Morton refused, and just before a meeting at which Apthorp planned to press his demand even more forcefully, Fanny poisoned herself and died.[8]

"THIS TYRANT CUSTOM"

Brown used the scandal to explore the vagaries of human passion in a young republic that extolled free will. *The Power of Sympathy*, an epistolary novel, alternates between scenes of overt moralizing and outright melodrama. It begins in a way familiar to contemporary readers, with Thomas Harrington writing to his friend Jack Worthy about his attraction to Harriot Fawcet, whom he plans to seduce. But she successfully resists his intentions, whereupon Brown includes his first surprise: Harrington, now admiring her virtue as well as her beauty, eventually falls in love with her, and she with him. However, some in their circle disapprove of their marriage plans. In particular, Mrs. Holmes, a family friend, urges another of Harrington's friends to dissuade him. Before long, the secret comes out: the couple cannot marry because they are siblings. Harriot is the result of Harrington's father's illicit affair sixteen years earlier with a young woman, Maria. When Harrington's father learned that his mistress was pregnant, his interest cooled, and he abandoned Maria to her fate. The Reverend and Mrs. Holmes took her in, and the family soon included Maria's young daughter, Harriot; Maria revealed the identity of the girl's father to her benefactors. After Maria becomes gravely ill and dies, the Holmeses, to protect their friend Harrington's reputation, place young Harriot out to service. The news of her early years shocks and dismays both Harrington and her, and before long she dies of sorrow and despair. Learning of her death, Harrington shoots himself, an end that borrows from Goethe's book *The Sorrows of Young Werther* (1774).

Much of the novel consists of secondary characters moralizing on this tragic course of events. Worthy's epistles, for example, and those of Mr. and Mrs. Holmes read like didactic essays or sermons on character formation in young women, the dangers of reading fiction, and proper republican marriage. But the characters also punctuate their moral lessons by alluding to other events at least as troubling as the dilemma in which the Harringtons and Harriot find themselves. One subplot concerns a young man, Henry, who after his lover, Fidelia, is kidnapped just before their marriage, takes his own life. Her abductors release her; but on hearing of Henry's fate, she despairs and becomes deranged. Another tangential tale, again centering on the vagaries of passion, details the affair of the senior Mr. Harrington and the young Maria. And in a brief textual reference and lengthy footnote, Brown alludes to yet another contemporary story making the rounds in New England. Elizabeth Whitman, a Connecticut clergyman's unmarried daughter, had died alone in childbirth at a tavern near Boston, the baby's father unknown, a scandal that later became the basis of another early American novel, Hannah Webster Foster's *The Coquette* (1798).

As these stories indicate, in *The Power of Sympathy* Brown was chiefly interested in the wages of excessive passion, both socially approved and illicit. Henry's love for Fidelia is so great that once she is abducted, he kills himself because he cannot imagine life without her. Ophelia and Maria are unable to resist the advances of men who they believe are willing to marry them but in fact are rakes. Harrington and Harriot's affection is so deep that the impossibility of their marrying leads to one's suicide and the other's premature death. Brown implies that love, hatred, and fear cannot be easily controlled and often push one to irrationality. Recounting Ophelia's story, Brown writes that when Martin turned on her, "she awoke from her dream of insensibility, she was like one . . . deluded by an *ignis fatuus* to the brink of a precipice, . . . abandoned . . . to contemplate the horrours of the sea beneath him, into which he was about to plunge."[9]

That terrifying moment, standing at the edge of an abyss and peering over, fascinated Brown, as it did other early American writers. Famously, it became the subject of Edgar Allan Poe's story "The Imp of the Perverse," his name for the impulse to look over the edge, fascinated by the thought of one's extinction. In *The Power of Sympathy*, Harrington and Harriot continue to feel more than familial love even after they realize that their love is illicit. He wonders why "this transport" is a crime, for his affection for Harriot is "most pure, the most holy . . . Here," Harrington exclaims upon learning his dilemma, "was all the horrour of conflicting passions."[10] What precisely *does* one do about such a love? The rational Mrs. Holmes cannot help them. "GREAT God!" she cries to Harrington's sister, Myra. "Of what materials has thou compounded the hearts of thy creatures! Admire, o my friend, the operation of NATURE—and the power of SYMPATHY!"[11] Even the elder Harrington is at a loss to comprehend his son's and Harriot's plight. He asks the Reverend Holmes, "How shall we pretend to investigate the great springs by which we are actuated, or account for the operation of SYMPATHY?" His son, he continues, had "accidentally seen [Harriot], and to complete THE TRIUMPH OF NATURE—has loved her."[12]

Brown, too, stands at the verge of such an abyss but refuses the plunge. He does not pretend to know why such things as Harrington's and Harriot's love occur and ends his novel the "easy" way, with the death of one of the lovers. Harriot's demise drives Harrington to despair, even as his suicide serves a higher purpose: soon he will join her in heaven, where their love "will not be a crime," although the reader never learns why not.[13] In their earthly lives, the problem resides in society's arbitrary rules, in particular an insistence on the supremacy of reason over passion. "Why did I love [this] Harriot?" Harrington ruefully asks. "Curse on this tyrant custom that dooms such helpless children to oblivion and infamy!"[14]

Brown's characters' failings indicated his allegiance to the ideals of republican virtue, selfishness at odds with their privileged position in society. The elder Harrington's dalliance with Maria, his inferior in social class, betrays a social hierarchy that exists even in a supposedly democratic nation. "I am not so much a republican," the younger Harrington tells Worthy early in the novel, "as formally to wed any person of this class. How laughable," he thinks, openly to acknowledge as his wife a "daughter of the democratick empire of virtue."[15] To his surprise, "the power of sympathy" prevails, for he does fall in love. But once the couple's true relationship is known, to formalize it would only fray, if not sever, the still-fragile bonds of republican virtue. Brown thus postpones their happiness until heaven.

SUSANNA ROWSON'S EMERGENCE

The revolutionary nature of the U.S. government was not explicit in *The Power of Sympathy* but in various degrees was the focus of other early

American novels, particularly Hugh Henry Brackenridge's *Modern Chivalry* (1792–1815), set in western Pennsylvania after the disruption of the Whiskey Rebellion, and Tyler's *Algerine Captive*, which drew on the United States' conflict with the Barbary States. These are loose and baggy picaresque novels that through satire probe the country's new social order, in particular the still-uncomfortable notion that the most plebeian citizen should be afforded the same respect as a person of wealth and influence. Thomas Jefferson voiced this ideal when he famously wrote John Adams in 1813 that there is a natural aristocracy among men based in virtue and talent that should trump any inherited or honorary rank.

But these picaresque novels were never as popular as other contemporary novels, such as *The Power of Sympathy*, that center on the vagaries of human passion, typified by seemingly omnipresent tales of seduction. One historian attributes this genre's popularity in part to the "dramatic slackening" of laws against moral offenses like prostitution and adultery. In this climate women "began to experience unprecedented social and sexual freedom," even as didactic novels and other moralistic literature warned of the dangers of female sexuality.[16] Perennially the most popular novel of passion was Susanna Rowson's *Charlotte: A Tale of Truth*, first published to an indifferent reception in England in 1791 by William Lane at his Minerva Press and issued in Philadelphia three years later. In the United States, however, *Charlotte Temple*, as it was retitled in 1797, became one of the bestselling novels before Harriet Beecher Stowe's *Uncle Tom's Cabin* (1852), appearing in scores of editions, most commonly as *Charlotte Temple: A Tale of Truth*. What was its appeal to an American readership?

One answer lies in the way Rowson's biography gave the book an air of undeniable veracity, for just as William Hill Brown's life was brief and relatively uneventful, Rowson's was the stuff of contemporary fiction.[17] She was born Susanna Musgrove Haswell in 1762 in Portsmouth, England, the daughter of William Haswell, a career naval officer, and Susanna Musgrove Haswell, who died when her daughter was only ten days old. When Rowson was a year old, the English navy sent Haswell on assignment to New England as a customs official, and relatives in England cared for her until he brought her over in 1767. Having landed in Boston Harbor on a frigid and stormy midwinter day (a scene she later re-created in her novel *Rebecca; or, The Fille de Chambre* [1792]), Rowson found a new home at nearby Nantasket, a peninsula just south of the city. There she faced many adjustments, for she had to live not only with a parent she hardly knew but also with a stepmother, whom Haswell had married two years earlier. Although Susanna never warmed to Rachel Woodward Haswell, she later looked back fondly on these years, filled as they were with seaside and country walks and fine literature from her father's library, not to mention spirited conversation with the future patriot James Otis, who gave her, according to one early biographer's account, "particular notice and favor."[18]

But the 1760s and 1770s were increasingly difficult times for the Crown's officers. As the imperial crisis escalated, Haswell attempted to stay neutral, but his situation grew tenuous. Finally, in 1775, he and his family were placed under house arrest and relocated, first to nearby Hingham and then inland to Abington, this second move occurring because none other than Perez Morton had accused Haswell of "frequently making such false representations among the inhabitants, as tend to cause divisions, to strengthen our enemies, to intimidate and weaken our friends."[19] During these difficult years Susanna played a large role in staving off the family's privation, often securing food and other necessities from sympathetic friends, both English and American. The family was finally able to return to London in 1778, after Haswell requested an exchange for an American prisoner, a trade completed in Halifax, Nova Scotia, between British and American authorities.

But in England the family's economic difficulties only mounted. After a succession of unremarkable jobs, Rowson found her way to the stage and then, after a modicum of success, began a prolific career as a songwriter, playwright, and novelist. In 1786 she published *Victoria*, and three more novels followed. None, however, drew much attention. During this period she married William Rowson, a hardware merchant, handyman on theater sets, and occasional actor and musician who brought an illegitimate son to the union. William Rowson never attained anything like his wife's success and reputedly was a drunk, but the two remained together until her death in 1824.

In the early 1790s Rowson caught the attention of the prominent American actor and playwright Thomas Wignell, who enticed her across the Atlantic to work in his New Theater in Philadelphia. Arriving at the end of the great yellow fever epidemic of 1793, the family decamped to Baltimore almost immediately. When it was safe to return to Philadelphia, Rowson resumed acting, filling important secondary roles in several of Wignell's productions. She tried her hand at playwriting, penning the relatively popular *Slaves in Algiers; or, A Struggle for Freedom* (1794). She also convinced the city's major publisher, Matthew Carey, to reissue *Charlotte*, the last of the quartet of novels she had written in England in the 1780s. Its publication proved a better business decision for him than it had for Lane, and he issued three subsequent editions in the next few years. But frustrated because on the stage she remained in the shadows of more prominent leading ladies, in 1796 Rowson moved to the Federal Street Theatre in Boston, where her two stepbrothers lived. There she briefly continued her acting career and then, recalling the difficulties of her own teenage years, reinvented herself one more time, as the preceptor of a female academy. She abandoned fiction altogether upon completion of the ambitious but not overly popular historical novel *Reuben and Rachel* (1798). For the next twenty-five years Rowson devoted herself to her Young Ladies' Academy.

SEDUCTION AND BETRAYAL

Rowson's career was transatlantic in scope and achievement, yet surprisingly she is mainly remembered for *Charlotte Temple*. The book's plot is straightforward and, to a late-eighteenth-century reader, would have been familiar. Charlotte is an attractive fifteen-year-old at an English boarding school, placed there by loving parents who have done little to prepare her for adulthood's trials. On one of her walks, she catches the eye of John Montraville, an English officer who is about to go to America and who, after losing interest in marrying the girl when he learns that she has no great wealth, decides he still wants her as his lover.

In the brief dalliance that ensues, Mademoiselle La Rue, a French teacher at the school who herself plans to elope with Montraville's associate Belcour, convinces Charlotte to see the lieutenant one last time before he leaves the country. Told by Madame Du Pont, the preceptor, that her parents soon will arrive to take her home for her birthday, Charlotte has one last chance to turn from her folly. "The irrevocable step is not taken" yet, she reasons; "it is not too late to recede from the brink of a precipice, from which I can only behold the dark abyss of ruin, shame, and remorse!"[20] But La Rue convinces her that it would be cruel not to see Montraville a last time, and caught between love and reason, Charlotte capitulates. Montraville sweeps her into a waiting carriage and seals her fate. Immediately remorseful, Charlotte writes to her parents to alert them to her whereabouts, but Montraville, who has promised to mail her letter, instead destroys it. As their ship embarks for New York, the abductors show their true colors. The fortune hunter La Rue, realizing that Belcour has no money, instead sets her eyes on one Colonel Crayton, a wealthy but simple soul who quickly succumbs to her wiles. For his part, Belcour, aware that Montraville does not intend to marry Charlotte, decides to woo her as soon as opportunity permits.

After disembarking in New York, where Montraville is stationed, he installs Charlotte, now pregnant, in a small home just outside the city. His increasingly infrequent visits do little to alleviate her growing depression, as she finally understands the severity of her plight, as well as the pain her precipitous behavior has caused her parents. Still looking for marriage to a lady of means, Montraville begins to court Julia Franklin, a wealthy heiress. Though he seems genuinely guilty about his treatment of Charlotte, he jumps at an excuse to break with her, an opportunity that arises when Belcour (still trying to advance his prospects with her) convinces him that Charlotte has been with other men, including himself. Having discovered Belcour with her in a deceptively compromising situation (of Belcour's contrivance), Montraville marries Julia but leaves Belcour money for Charlotte and her unborn child. Despondent, she again writes to her parents. Her health continues to decline, and Belcour, too, loses interest in her, stops his visits, keeps the money Montraville earmarked for her, and marries a wealthy farmer's daughter.

Charlotte's only happiness comes when her father, having received her missive, travels to the United States and finds her on her deathbed. She begs his forgiveness and makes him promise to care for her recently born daughter, Lucy. Distraught after he has made a visit to the cottage and not found Charlotte, Montraville frantically searches for her and comes upon her funeral. Meeting Mr. Temple, he confesses his part in his daughter's downfall; he will go on to lead a melancholic life punctuated by frequent visits to his former lover's grave. Mr. Temple and little Lucy return to England. Ten years later Temple and his wife find on their doorstep a destitute woman, none other than La Rue. Separated from her husband for seven years and mired in vice and misery, she asks forgiveness for her part in the family's tragedy. Ever compassionate, the Temples place her in a nearby hospital, where a few weeks later she dies, completing the wreckage begun at the girls' school years earlier.

Charlotte Temple thus has all the markings of a morality tale that warns young women of seduction. But what is one to make of its wildly different reception in England and the United States? Did its subject matter resonate differently because of the younger nation's distinctive political and social ideals? The answer lies not in the reader's sympathy for Charlotte but in Rowson's carefully wrought depictions of other characters' reactions to her plight.

"THE IMPULSE OF A YOUTHFUL PASSION"

Belcour is the novel's only truly unrepentant soul and presumably ends the tale enjoying his gentleman's life in the country. Rowson makes clear that he is a villain and from the outset distinguishes him from Montraville, who is "generous in his disposition, liberal in his opinions, and good-natured almost to a fault." In contrast, Belcour "paid little regard to moral duties, and less to religious ones," and did not think twice about the misery he inflicted on others. In short, "Self, darling self, was the idol he worshiped."[21] So why does Montraville seduce and abandon Charlotte? It is because he lacks virtuous friends who could point out the cruelty of his actions. He is oblivious of the consequences of his unchecked passion: infamy and misery for her and his own "never-ceasing remorse." Had someone informed Montraville of what lay ahead, Rowson writes, "the humanity of his nature would have urged him to give up the pursuit."[22] Instead, Belcour, his ostensible friend who is lost to selfishness, only made the situation worse.

La Rue's story is more complex. Early in her life she is placed in a French convent, from which she elopes with a young military officer, the first of many lovers. In England she continues her debauchery, living with several different men "in open defiance of all moral and religious duties."[23] With La Rue, Rowson, an avowed Federalist, confirms her contemporaries' suspicion that the French Revolution, which while taking its inspiration from the American, descended into what most Federalists believed to be anarchy and madness and has spawned an attendant libertinism. The result, as the Yale president Timothy Dwight warned in a lecture on infidelity to the college's students: "its great object is to unsettle every thing moral and obligatory, and to settle nothing."[24] Rowson's book spoke directly to such fears that in the United States, where the effects of its own revolution were not yet completed, such transgressions as Charlotte's would become all too common.

After another lover abandons La Rue and she is "reduced to the most abject want," she gets a chance at rehabilitation. An acquaintance of Du Pont's generously takes her in, and after La Rue displays what her benefactress takes as sincere penitence, she brings her to the preceptor's attention. La Rue did, after all, have "a pleasing person and insinuating address," as well as "liberal education and the manners of a gentlewoman." But she could not govern herself and had "too much of the spirit of intrigue to remain long without adventures."[25] Unlike Belcour, though, La Rue finally cannot live with herself and finds her way to the Temples to ask for forgiveness. "I am the viper that stung your peace," she exclaims. "I am the woman who turned the poor Charlotte out to perish in the street."[26]

Rowson intended *Charlotte Temple* as a guide or even a warning. She addresses the "young, volatile reader," who she guesses is bored at her novel's frequent depictions of "fainting, tears, and distress." "I must request your patience," she writes. "I am writing a tale of the truth" and intend to "write it to the heart." Do not throw the novel aside, she pleads, "till you have perused the whole."[27] Such perusal, however, does not bring the reader to a simple moral but to Montraville's and Charlotte's welter of conflicting emotions. Uncertainty and remorse complicate the novel; with a little more maturity, Montraville might have made a worthy match.

The message of *Charlotte Temple* is that capitulation to one's feelings without proper rational reflection could lead not only to personal tragedy but to a breakdown of social mores of the sort that Federalists believed had followed the Reign of Terror in France and that would visit the United States if Jefferson were elected president. Once again Timothy Dwight, along with the Charlestown, Massachusetts, minister Jedediah Morse, most typified the hysterical alarm among conservatives. Dwight opined that if Americans did not combat France's infidelity, "those morals which protect our lives from the knife of the assassin, which guard the chastity of our wives and daughters from seduction and violence, defend our property from plunder and devastation and shield our religion from contempt and profanation" would be trampled upon, and "our wives and daughters [would become] the victims of legal prostitution."[28] Charlotte's melancholy death after her abandonment by those whom she, in her naiveté, thought trustworthy was a political as well as a moral lesson for the new nation.

The only American book to approach *Charlotte Temple* in popularity was another tale of seduction and betrayal, Hannah Webster Foster's *The Coquette*, a complex work that, like *The Power of Sympathy*, emerged from the ideas and mores of post-Revolutionary Boston. Although upon publication it did not sell as rapidly as Rowson's novel, it was reprinted throughout the nineteenth century, including a remarkable eight times from 1824 to 1828.

We know less about *The Coquette*'s author than we do of Rowson or Brown. Foster was born in 1758 in Salisbury, Massachusetts, the daughter of a prominent merchant, Grant Webster, and Hannah Wainwright Webster, after whose death four years later the widower sent his young daughter to a women's academy. In 1785 she married John Foster, a young Dartmouth College graduate and minister of the Congregational church in Brighton, Massachusetts. They had six children, three sons and three daughters, two of whom themselves became notable writers.[29] During this busy period Hannah Foster found time to publish two books, *The Coquette; or, The History of Eliza Wharton: a Novel Founded on Fact* (1797), whose title page identified her only as "A Lady of Massachusetts"; and *The Boarding School; or, Lessons of a Preceptress to Her Pupils* (1798), based in part on her own experiences. Aside from some anonymous essays published a decade later in *The Monthly Anthology or Magazine of Polite Literature* (later the *North American Review*), Foster left no other writings, in large part because of her deep engagement in Brighton's religious and social life, which accompanied her station as a minister's wife.[30] After her husband's death in 1829, Foster moved to Montreal to live with her daughter Elizabeth (known as Eliza), the wife of Dr. Frederick Cushing, a physician in that city, where Foster died in 1840.

Like Brown, Foster based her most popular work on a widely discussed current event first reported in the *Salem* (Massachusetts) *Mercury* for July 29, 1788. It was an account of the death four days earlier of a young woman at the Bell Tavern in nearby Danvers, shortly after she had delivered a stillborn child under circumstances to "excite curiosity, and interest [one's] feelings." Someone engaged for the purpose had brought her there in a chaise and then left. The woman's demeanor marked her as from "a respectable family and good education," the report continued, but she "was averse to being interrogated concerning herself or [her] connexions" and kept mainly to herself, anxiously awaiting the arrival of someone (presumably, the father of her child). After her child's and her deaths, kindly townspeople gave them a decent burial.

Within days other papers copied the story, and soon it was the talk of the region, particularly after the woman was identified as Elizabeth Whitman, the daughter of the Reverend Elnathan Whitman, a prominent Hartford clergyman.[31] Though the story was not in itself extraordinary—after the Revolution rates of illegitimate births skyrocketed—the fact that a prominent person had met so sad and mysterious an end caught the public's interest and led many to ask why she had been at the tavern and for whom she had been waiting. A decade after these events, Foster published her novel based on them, changing Elizabeth Whitman's name to Eliza Wharton.

In 1855 Jane E. Locke introduced a new edition of *The Coquette* with a lengthy biographical introduction that included significant new information about Whitman, her family, and the stillborn child's father. Although all of Locke's facts cannot be verified, she did at least help the reader understand just how Foster transformed Whitman's tragic tale for her own purposes.

Elizabeth Whitman had an impeccable New England pedigree. Her great-grandfather had married one of the daughters of Solomon Stoddard, a prominent minister in the Massachusetts Bay Colony and the grandfather of Jonathan Edwards. She seemed destined to unite with a clergyman, and when she was still quite young, such a match was proposed—arranged, really—with one Joseph Howe, minister to Norwich, Connecticut. A considerably older man, Howe died suddenly. At some point in the next few years Whitman, a society belle, entertained another offer, from a recent Harvard graduate, Joseph Stevens Buckminster, minister to an important church in Portsmouth, New Hampshire, and one of the most prominent young "liberal Christians" of the day. But Whitman rejected him and, remaining single, eventually met the untimely death described in the newspapers. Locke offered a crucial but unsubstantiated fact: the father of Elizabeth's child was none other than the Honorable Pierpont Edwards, Jonathan Edwards's youngest, wayward son and thus her second cousin.[32]

Locke intended her biography to rehabilitate Whitman's image. Exceedingly beautiful, highly intelligent, and accomplished, Whitman was always the center of attention. She was extraordinary in other ways, too: very moody, "as the truly gifted ever are, and of a wild incomprehensible nature, little understood by those who should have known her best." In Pierpont Edwards she met someone who presumably understood her and could satisfy her emotional needs. Between them there was "a close affinity of spirit," a "marriage of the soul . . . that overshadows sin." Then the bombshell: the two lovers had not only such a marriage of spirits but also "one [that], though secret, [was] actually sanctified by the law of the land," a fact Whitman was "known to have declared" prior to her death.[33]

Why, then, was she left alone at the tavern to die? Locke repeats the story of Whitman's lonely isolation as she waited in her room, passing the time writing and occasionally playing a guitar, "the only companion of her solitude." Then, one night after about two weeks, a chaise appeared. Someone got out, paused at the door as though looking for something but, evidently not finding what he sought, drove away. In daylight, one could see, in chalk over the lintel at which he had peered, the scrawled letters "E. W.," too faint to see in darkness. Pierpont Edwards, Locke believed, had returned for Whitman, only to miss the agreed-upon symbol by which she marked her location.[34]

More than *The Power of Sympathy* or *Charlotte Temple*, *The Coquette* places the reader in a world in which what passed as moral rectitude conflicted with the national belief in individual freedom. *The Coquette* begins with Eliza's scarcely disguised relief at the death of the Reverend Haly (Howe), an older clergyman whom her parents approved of as an ideal spouse. Free to enjoy more time in genteel society, Eliza draws the attention first of Boyer (Buckminster), who is soon to be installed as the minister over an important church and who thinks that she will make an ideal spouse, and then of Peter Sanford (Edwards), an attractive and self-centered rake who wishes to seduce but not marry her. Boyer presses his suit, but Eliza, unwilling to give up her newfound freedom, asks for time. Boyer grows increasingly impatient because Eliza sees more and more of Sanford, even after friends pointedly warn her of his promiscuity. So pressured, she finally decides to marry Boyer, but because she promised Sanford first to inform him of her decision, she agrees to meet him. By chance, Boyer stumbles on the two in the Whartons' garden and precipitously breaks off the engagement. Sanford is now free to pursue his pleasure. Eliza is mortified at the misunderstanding.

Sanford, who views Eliza as a coquette, knows that he now has the advantage. To prolong his titillation, he announces a lengthy business trip to the South. Genuinely distraught over the breakup with Boyer,

Eliza has no outlet for her affection. After a year, Sanford still has not returned, and she writes Boyer to confess her shortsightedness and to ask if despite her faults, he still might accept her. But he is about to marry his friend Selby's sister, whose personality and character he believes more suited to the sober and important career on which he has embarked. Though still fairly young, Eliza has no more suitors, presumably because they, too, question her judgment and consider her a mere flirt. She falls into a deep melancholy.

Sanford returns to the area married to a wealthy woman, yet Eliza more and more depends on him for attention. He craftily (and perversely) establishes a friendship between his wife and her, so he can regularly see his old amour. Then, as his finances and marriage begin to fail, almost in desperation he again pursues Eliza, needing her attention as much as she does his. He persists, and a dalliance becomes outright seduction. When Eliza realizes that she is pregnant, Sanford deposits her at a tavern, promising to return. Delivering a child that dies after only a few hours, Eliza, too, perishes, leaving her friends and family (and Sanford) in despair. As in *Charlotte Temple*, the wreckage is complete.

"THE VERY SOUL OF PLEASURE"

The Coquette is more than a retelling of the Elizabeth Whitman story. The reader would have sympathized with Eliza very differently than she would have with Whitman or Charlotte Temple. For one, Foster's narration takes a sophisticated epistolary form, with central episodes retold from various points of view. Eliza corresponds most often with her friend Lucy Freeman; Boyer, with his friend Selby; and Sanford, with his friend Charles Deighton. There are also letters among Eliza's friends Lucy Freeman Sumner and Julia Granby, the Richmans, and Mrs. Wharton.

More to the point, Eliza is complex. Unlike the immature and insipid Charlotte Temple, she is attractive and prepossessing. Her unwillingness to abide by conventional norms and to engage in the self-regulation demanded by society tears her apart psychologically. Foster registers how attributes that should be regarded as Eliza's strengths—her honest self-scrutiny and fierce independence—instead cause confusion and depression. Attentive contemporary readers of *The Coquette* would not have merely condemned her folly but rather would have considered the nature and consequence of her desire to exercise her free will.

Part of Eliza's appeal is her willingness to say what she thinks and to declare who she is. Writing to Lucy after the untimely death of the Reverend Haly, she does not hide how she welcomes the opportunity to again indulge her "accustomed vivacity" and playfully complains that she disagrees with Lucy's deeming her ways "coquettish." They deserve "a softer appellation," she argues, because they proceed from "an innocent heart, and are the effusions of a youthful, and cheerful mind."[35] Having escaped what from her standpoint clearly would have been a loveless marriage to an older man, all Eliza wants is "that freedom which [she] so highly prize[s]."[36]

Her dilemma is clear: she does not yet want to marry, even if an acceptable suitor appears and even though her parents and friends think that in this she is dangerously bucking common sense as well as morality. Eliza notes the Richmans' insular and private happiness. It saddens her that "[t]hey have no satisfaction to look for beyond each other."[37] Eliza seeks something else, "some amusement" beyond what she can supply by herself, by which she means attendance at the social occasions at which she is the center of attention.[38] Sanford, who prides himself in his judgment of women, notes her "agreeable person, polished manners, and refined talents," all of which make her "the toast of the country around." He registers as well, however, her tendency to flirtation. This makes him want to "avenge [his] sex, by retaliating the mischiefs she meditates" against men. At this point, he has no "ill designs" but wishes only "to play off her own artillery."[39]

What young woman, beginning to entertain thoughts of the other sex, would not identify with Eliza or wish to emulate her freedom and savoir-faire? Or fantasize about companionship with such a man as Sanford, "a professed libertine" who already had "but too successfully practiced the arts of seduction"? Not ready to accept a comfortable but staid life with Boyer, or wanting to become "an avowed prude at once," she continues to flirt with Sanford, who can easily distinguish between "a forbidding, and an encouraging reception." "His person, his manners, his situation, all combine to charm my fancy," she tells Lucy.[40] But although Sanford is lured to the table, he has more experience at the game. "I am," he tells Deighton, a "Proteus, and can assume any shape that will best answer my purpose."[41]

After Lucy reminds Eliza of Sanford's reputation as a rake, she adds that no person of Eliza's "delicacy and refinement" should ever consider connection to such a man and so believes that Eliza must only wish to exhibit "a few more girlish airs" before she "turn[s] matron."[42] Urging Eliza to accept Boyer, Lucy advises that it is time to "lay aside those coquettish airs which you sometimes put on." But Eliza bristles at Boyer for continuing to press his suit before she is ready to make a decision and recoils "at the thought of immediately forming a connection, which must confine [her] to the duties of domesticity." "You must either quit the subject, or leave me to the exercise of my free will," she tells him emphatically, wanting to claim in the sphere of personal behavior the kind of personal freedom to choose that theologians offered in the religious.[43] Trapped in a culture in which marriage was normative, many readers identified with Eliza's frustrating dilemma as a young woman simply "too volatile for a confinement to domestic avocations" yet having no socially sanctioned alternative.[44]

Even Sanford is surprised at Eliza's continued attention. Knowing that her "sagatious [*sic*] friends have undoubtedly given her a detail of [his] vices," he asks, "[w]hy does she not act consistently, and refuse at once to associate with a man whose character she cannot esteem?"[45] Still, unable to help himself, Sanford takes every opportunity to point out to Eliza the dissimilarity of her disposition and Boyer's, knowing that if he can separate them, he will be more likely to succeed in his "plan." "Not that I have any thoughts of marrying her myself," he writes Deighton; he simply desires Eliza too much "to see her connected with another for life." In fact, Sanford thinks so much of her that he has not yet even decided to seduce her, although "with all her pretensions to virtue," he certainly thinks it possible. "She is," after all, "the very soul of pleasure," he notes.[46]

Thus, Boyer and Sanford seek to entrap Eliza, whose only refuge is to remain single, disapproved of by friends and family. When Lucy marries George Sumner, Eliza does not partake of the general happiness. Why? The idea "of an alienation of affection, by means of entire devotion to another," appalls her.[47] To Eliza, the sacred bond of matrimony promises too short a tether.

After Sanford leaves town to make his fortune, Boyer marries, and attention from other suitors ends, Eliza tumbles into depression. "Health, placid serenity, and every domestic pleasure, are the lot of my friend," she writes to Lucy, while she, "who once possessed the means of each, and the capacity of tasting them, has been tossed upon the waves of folly" until "shipwrecked on the shoals of despair! . . . What have I now to console me?" Eliza exclaims. "My bloom is decreasing; my health is sensibly impaired," and all those talents "with the possession of which I have been flattered" were "of little avail when unsupported by respectability of character!"[48] Lucy's retort stings: "Where is that fund of sense, and sentiment[,] which once animated your engaging form? Whence that strength of mind, that independence of soul, that alacrity and sprightliness of deportment, which formerly raised you superior to every adverse occurrence?"[49] Eliza cannot explain it, and to her other close friend, Julia, she can only invoke the imp of the perverse. "In many instances," she writes, "I have been ready to suppose that some evil genius presided over my actions, which has directed them contrary to the sober dictates of my own judgment."[50]

Sanford's return momentarily delivers Eliza from her melancholia. He renews their flirtation, confessing that his has been a marriage of convenience. Soon enough after his renewed attentions, her friends notice a change in Eliza, a rapid return to her "former cheerfulness," her taste for "company and amusements" again evident. But they believe these only "indications of a mind not perfectly right," as is her irrational defense of Sanford.[51] She tells her friends that she has forgiven his past. To Lucy, who warns her against any reinvolvement because "the world would make unfavorable remarks upon any appearance of intimacy" between her and Sanford, she replies coldly, "I care not for that." It is, she continues, "an ill-natured, misjudging world; and I am not obliged to sacrifice my friends to its opinion."[52] Even at the age of thirty-seven, she rejects social convention and particularly Lucy's notion that "we are dependent beings" and "must feel the force of that dependence."[53]

Eliza's mother expands on the same sentiment, at one point counseling her daughter that we "are all links in the great chain of society, some more, some less important, but each upheld by others, throughout the confederated whole."[54] Here Foster locates one pole of what in the new nation has become a central problem: the relation between individual freedom and social obligation. Mrs. Wharton continues to believe in a reciprocal relation between these two duties, even as her daughter wishes to claim a personal liberty and attendant self-fulfillment that to some was not only morally problematic but also unpatriotic, detrimental to the good of the commonwealth that the Revolutionary generation enshrined as the greatest good. Could it be, Foster asks, that liberal democracy thus contains the seed of that which might destroy common purpose?

Eliza's end comes quickly, narrated by Julia Granby in a letter to Lucy. One night, staying with her friend, Julia awakens to see a man stealing from the house, after which she hears Eliza's footsteps on the stair. Soon enough, Eliza becomes pregnant. Sanford installs her at the tavern, and readers of the many newspaper articles about Elizabeth Whitman knew the rest.

The Coquette is not a simple morality tale like *Charlotte Temple*. It depicts an attractive, intelligent, independent woman meeting an end she does not deserve. For all the patriotic rhetoric and talk of freedom in the air in 1798, many of the country's citizens—women in particular—remained fettered. Eliza Wharton, like others who bristled under such restrictions, learned the length of her chain, and readers registered this as much as Sanford's perfidy.

The Coquette thus explores the national mind-set roiled by inflated notions of freedom and equality beginning to circulate in the late eighteenth century. The novel's continuous republication during the 1820s, when the New Haven theologian Nathaniel William Taylor famously championed free will and thereby fueled much theological bickering, is understandable. But its popularity depended as well on its trenchant presentation of what were becoming more and more complex questions. What was the Revolution's legacy in the realm of personal behavior? When did the pursuit of individual happiness, guaranteed as much as life and liberty, conflict with the greater good of the social organism? Or should the latter even be considered as more than its individual constituents? Foster had transformed a sad tale of frailty and human sorrow into a parable about democracy and its incipient discontents.

A FEMALE QUIXOTE

One of Foster's implicit laments is that a man's sexual transgressions are often excused or forgotten, while a woman's stay with her for life. "It has ever been my opinion," Sukey Vickery, another novelist from this period, wrote, "that the world has been too rigid, much too rigid, as respects the female sex."[55] Other writers noticed such inequalities but handled them differently, sometimes with humor or satire. Such was the case with Tabitha Tenney, author of the popular *Female Quixotism, Exhibited in the Romantic Opinions and Extravagant Adventures of Dorcasina Sheldon* (1801), the title of which, a conflation of Miguel de Cervantes's *Don*

Quixote (1605) and Charlotte Lennox's *The Female Quixote* (1752), points to Tenney's comedic thrust. Readers loved it; four editions, some with illustrations of more humorous scenes, appeared before mid-century.

Tenney was born in Exeter, New Hampshire, in 1762 to Samuel Gilman and Lydia Robinson Gilman. At sixteen she married Dr. Samuel Tenney, a surgeon in the Revolutionary War, who afterward returned to Exeter. An ardent Federalist, he was elected to the U.S. House of Representatives from 1800 to 1807, the years of Jeffersonian ascendency and thus an uncomfortable time for him politically. Both Tenneys liked Washington, however, and remained there until Samuel's death in 1816, after which Tabitha returned to Exeter, where she died in 1837.

Just before her husband's first term as a representative, she published *The New Pleasing Instructor; or, Young Lady's Guide to Virtue and Happiness* (1799), a text that Rowson might have used in her academy, and shortly thereafter began writing *Female Quixotism*. She completed the novel in the nation's capital and sent the manuscript to Boston, where Thomas & Andrews, the same firm that had brought out her first book, issued it. Occupied with family and social life, Tenney wrote nothing else.

Female Quixotism is frequently compared with Brackenridge's *Modern Chivalry*, but Tenney's satire has an edge that could only have been honed by a woman's experience. Her point is that in the new country's free market economy, a highly transient population animated by the prospect of social advancement relied on outward signs to judge a person's inner being. *Female Quixotism* thus presents a vivid example of a culture increasingly reliant on a presentation of self or of various social selves and the accompanying perils of traversing an increasingly impersonal economic and social landscape. Good conservative that Tenney was, she yearns for a vanishing social stability, when through face-to-face interaction one simply *knew* who another person was. It is no accident that many of Dorcas's suitors are transients, products (and, in some cases, casualties) of a country literally and metaphorically on the move. Dorcas's absorption in romantic fictions has impaired her ability to judge its inhabitants' sincerity. As George and Evert Duyckinck noted in their pioneering *Cyclopedia of American Literature*, "[l]eft by a fond [widowed] father to follow her own wishes," Dorcas takes "to reading novels, and so saturates her mind with their wishy-washy contents, that she determines herself to be a heroine," styling herself Dorcasina and seeking romantic love.[56] The novel's ribaldry derives from the fatuousness of a woman whose head is filled with romantic claptrap as she searches for a suitable spouse.

Dorcasina's inflated notions of courtship and marriage lead to a series of comedic encounters with men who pretend to express an interest in her but really value her estate. Accompanied (and sometimes foiled) by her serving woman, Mary, who aptly plays the Sancho Panza part, Dorcasina bumbles through a series of misadventures until her attractiveness fades. She does not die a terrible death, like Eliza Wharton, but becomes a spinster, an end that to many readers must have seemed equally abhorrent.

In her preface Tenney tells the reader that she first heard part of Dorcasina's story in Philadelphia and thought it "so whimsical and outré" that she sought out the rest of it.[57] Dorcasina pursues or is pursued by many suitors, real and imaginary: Lysander, who courts her when she is a blooming twenty-year-old and who really does love her but whose language and demeanor are not romantic enough for her; the Irish-born convict Patrick O'Connor, by turns a scholar, a gambler, and a highwayman, who convinces her that he is a gentleman; Philander, who knows the romantic lexicon but is revealed to be a buffoon; Mr. Cumberland, an older merchant whom her father convinces to consider Dorcasina (already long in the tooth) for her inheritance; the dashingly romantic Captain Barry, who is fresh from Indian wars in the West where he has been wounded and who is young enough to be her son; his servant James, whom Barry convinces to play the suitor with his hostess after he realizes how old and unattractive Dorcasina is; Dorcasina's servant John Brown, who she thinks is a nobleman in disguise and so outfits him in her recently deceased father's wardrobe; Captain Montague, really Dorcasina's friend Harriot Stanley in disguise, who wants to rescue Dorcasina from further misadventures and so kidnaps and hides her; and finally, when she is fifty, Seymore, a villain who has lost his fortune in France and now hopes to recoup it, and who is blunt enough to tell her that she is old and ugly.

There are a plethora of moments that, viewed one way, make Dorcasina seem comic; another, worthy of the reader's sympathy; and yet another, repulsively pathetic. In turn, she is accosted by young ruffians who think she is a prostitute because she has disguised herself to meet O'Connor at his room in town; has midnight assignations, with and without her servant, at which, given the darkness, the principals often misidentify each other, so that at one point she lovingly embraces her African American servant, Scipio, and at another is stripped of most of her clothes. Dorcasina's only respite comes at the end, when, in her spinsterhood, she writes to her friend Mrs. Barry and offers the advice she wishes she had followed. "Suffer not [your] daughters' imaginations to be filled with the idea of happiness," she counsels, "particularly in the connubial state, which can never be realized." Describe life to them, she adds, "as it really is."[58]

Tenney's humor masks the dark aspects of her tale. Dorcasina has indeed read too many "romances," for they make her confuse appearance and reality. She wants her suitors to propose in certain proper words (the episode with Lysander), to dress in particular ways (her infatuation with the recuperating Captain Barry), and to meet her at suitably romantic times and places (her trysts with O'Connor); but she is unaware that these men do her bidding only because they seek her fortune. In other words, she does not truly "know them."

Sally Wood's *Dorval; or The Speculator* (1801), Caroline Matilda Warren Thayer's *The Gamesters; or, Ruins of Innocence* (1805), Samuel Relf's *Infidelity* (1797), James Butler's *Fortune's Football* (1797): the very titles of these other early American novels indicate that their authors dealt with the same themes as Tenney did. In those years, counterfeiting, lotteries, gaming of all sorts, disguise, hypocrisy, and seduction were rampant in the public imagination.[59] Federalists like the Tenneys were quick to blame this topsy-turvy, seemingly immoral world on the Democratic-Republicans whom Jefferson brought to the capital. Jefferson's predecessor John Adams in 1804 warned that democracy was "a young rake who thinks himself handsome and well made, and who has little faith in virtue." "Democracy," he continued, "is Lovelace, and the people are Clarissa."[60]

"ONE OF THE BRIGHTEST ORNAMENTS OF HIS COUNTRY"

The one early novelist who has achieved lasting critical acclaim is Charles Brockden Brown. Nathaniel Hawthorne, Edgar Allan Poe, and John Greenleaf Whittier all later praised his works. The pioneering feminist Margaret Fuller, a great admirer of the best European literature, wrote in the 1840s upon the reprinting of two of his novels, *Ormond* and *Wieland*, that she had "long been ashamed that one who ought to be the pride of our country, and who is, in the highest qualities of mind, so far in advance of our other novelists, should have become almost inaccessible to the public."[61] Brown met with similar approval in Europe. John Keats, Percy and Mary Shelley, William Hazlitt, and William Godwin (with whom he was often compared) held his novels in high regard. No other early American fiction writer was accorded such respect.

What made Charles Brockden Brown stand out among his contemporaries? Marveling at the rapidity with which he wrote and published his novels—he issued four in a three-year period—the anonymous author of a biographical sketch of Brown wrote that they constituted "a series of the most original, powerful, and masterly . . . works of fiction, of which American literature could then, or perhaps even now, boast." This writer also distinguished Brown's readers from those who enjoyed works like *Charlotte Temple* or Isaac Mitchell's American gothic *The Asylum* (1811). Brown wrote "for those who indulge in the deep and powerful emotions; for those who think and feel strongly; who delight patiently to trace every action to its appropriate motive; and to mark the ebbs and flows of passion, and follow them out to their farthest consequence."[62]

Brown's roots lay in Quaker Philadelphia, where he was born in 1771 into a family that traced its American ancestors to the seventeenth century. He was unusually delicate and frail and took readily to the world of books. In his later years, Brown's gauntness made his appearance "remarkable," so much so that "it was impossible to pass him in the street, without stopping to look at him." He had a "pale, sallow, strange complexion," one acquaintance recalled, straight black hair, and a "melancholy, broken-hearted look" in his eyes—"altogether an extraordinary face" that, once seen, "was never forgotten."[63]

In his teens Brown's parents placed him under the tutelage of Robert Proud, future historian of the state of Pennsylvania, at the Friends Latin School, where Brown remained until he was sixteen. He displayed a literary bent, writing poetry and sketching grandiose, though unrealized, plans for no fewer than three poetic epics on the discovery of America and the conquests of Peru and Mexico. His parents, however, steered him toward law, which he studied with Alexander Willcocks, one of the city's prominent attorneys. When it came time to commit fully to such work, Brown rebelled, unable to stomach having to defend guilty clients as well as innocent.

This precipitated a psychological crisis of several years' length that gradually became more severe. "From some dark hints" in Brown's correspondence, one of his biographers, the historian William Hickling Prescott, wrote that "the rash idea of relieving himself from the weight of earthly sorrows, by some voluntary deed of violence, had more than once flitted across his mind."[64] Fortunately, Brown's depression lessened in 1790, when he met Elihu Hubbard Smith, a recent Yale graduate studying medicine in Philadelphia and part of a coterie of writers and intellectuals in New York City and Connecticut. Among Smith's friends were the lexicographer Noah Webster; the poets John Trumbull, David Humphreys, Lemuel Hopkins, Richard Alsop, and other Connecticut Wits; and William Dunlap and his drama circle in New York. Brown felt right at home among these like-minded young intellectuals, delighting in meetings of their Friendly Club at which they frequently read one another's works in progress. He began to ponder the idea of becoming a writer.

For several years Brown moved between Philadelphia, New York, and New England, most often staying with Smith in New York, where he had established a medical practice. In 1798, however, the same year in which Brown published his first novel, *Wieland; or, The Transformation*, Smith's untimely death of yellow fever in an epidemic that struck New York shocked Brown and his friends. Brown contracted a milder case of the disease and, after he started to recover physically and emotionally, began to write at a blazing pace, publishing in rapid succession *Ormond; or, The Secret Witness* (1799), *Arthur Mervyn; or, Memoirs of the Year 1793* (1799–1800), and *Edgar Huntly; or, Memoirs of a Sleep-Walker* (1799). He also assumed editorship of a new journal, *The Monthly Magazine and American Review*, fulfilling Smith's dream of a New York magazine devoted to literary, not religious or political, topics. In addition to publishing essays, stories, and poems, as well as notices of new books and miscellaneous articles reprinted from foreign sources, Brown used the journal as a vehicle for his own stories and novels in progress, most notably his "Memoirs of Stephen Calvert."

After Brown returned to Philadelphia permanently in 1801, he published two more novels, *Clara Howard; In a Series of Letters* (1801) and *Jane Talbot, a Novel* (1801). Three years later he married Elizabeth Linn, who was the daughter of a Presbyterian minister in New York City and whose brother John Blair Linn had become a good friend. Extant correspondence reveals that Brown took part in the business affairs of his brothers while he continued to edit, this time the semiannual *American Register or General Repository of History, Politics, and Science*; to write, primarily political pamphlets of an anti-Jeffersonian stripe; and even to translate from the French C. F. Volney's important *View of the Soil and Climate of the United States* (1804). Prone to bouts of physical illness and melancholy throughout his life, after his marriage Brown continued to repair to the country for health reasons, but to no avail. Late in 1809 he fell seriously ill and never again left his bed. He died of "pulmonary consumption" the following February. Lamenting his early passing, one of Brown's eulogists said, "He seemed destined to become one of the brightest ornaments of his country."[65] Dying so young, Brown would never know that another generation of American writers recognized his prescient insights into democracy's psychological toll.

THEODORE WIELAND'S TRIALS

Brown accomplished much in his thirty-nine years, not the least of which was his participation in one of the country's first literary coteries devoted to cultural nationalism. And unlike, say, Rowson or Tenney, he self-consciously fashioned a career in American letters and in his various editorships helped others with similar aspirations. He also had the satisfaction of seeing his works reviewed, for the most part favorably, on the other side of the Atlantic, where American novels were usually dismissed. Through Smith's good offices, for example, the French émigré bookseller Hocquet Caritat, who also ran one of New York's early lending libraries, published *Wieland*. Caritat took copies of it (and, later, of others of Brown's titles) to London and Paris on his book-buying ventures, making it available to reviewers in the influential European quarterlies. Concomitantly, some of Brown's works appeared in pirated overseas editions. *Ormond* was brought out in London in 1800, and *Arthur Mervyn* and *Edgar Huntly* in 1803. Caritat probably also was the source for the appearance there in 1802 of four of Brown's stories, in *Carwin, the Biloquist, and Other American Tales and Pieces*. French and, eventually, German editions of his novels followed.

Although recent scholarship has brought attention to all of Brown's fiction, as well as to his work as editor and pamphleteer, *Wieland* remains his most important accomplishment. Coming as it did only a year after *The Coquette*, it heralded a new kind of American novel that, while borrowing from and extending certain aspects of earlier American fiction, set new standards for the form, particularly through its emphasis on the religious sources and implications of Wieland's heightened emotional state and subsequent crimes. That *Wieland* was so well received, even though its assessment of human nature is so disconcerting, makes it all the more worthy of attention, as does its status as one of the few early American novels to tackle religious belief directly.[66]

Like many other American novels identified as "tales of truth" or "based on fact," *Wieland* probably owed its inspiration to a contemporary incident, reported in July 1796 in *The New-York Weekly Magazine* and republished a month later in *The Philadelphia Minerva*.[67] The story concerned a father's brutal murder of his entire family—a wife and four children—in rural New York. James Yates, a pious, God-fearing man who never had evidenced any unbalanced behavior, one evening, when reading the Bible, saw a bright light in the room. Two angels appeared on each side of him, one urging him to destroy all his worldly idols, including his Bible, the other urging him to refrain from such blasphemy. Yates tossed his Scripture into the fire and hacked apart his sleigh and killed one of his horses, overt symbols of his vanity and worldliness. After returning inside, he slaughtered his two boys, then chased down his frantic wife and daughters. He dispatched them, too, but not before making one child dance and sing over her dead mother. He then tried to kill his sister, but she managed to escape. Captured, incarcerated, and interrogated, Yates confessed calmly and directly, admitting remorse for his deeds but consoled by having performed the duty to which the "good" angel had directed him. He was imprisoned as a hopeless lunatic, an extreme example of the religious enthusiasm unleashed in the early years of the Second Great Awakening, in which the new Romantic emphasis on self often obscured the lessons of the Scripture, wherein lay commonly discerned and accepted bases of moral virtue.

In his novel Brown condemned such excesses of devotion but also probed the hidden springs of human motivation. His main character, Theodore Wieland, lives in the countryside outside Philadelphia with his wife, Catharine, and their children. His sister, Clara, lives separately in another house on the same property, named Mettingen, and narrates the story as a lengthy missive to a friend who has inquired after her well-being. Catharine's brother, Henry Pleyel, a frequent visitor and an intimate of the family, completes the cast of central characters whose lives will be overturned in the course of the novel. The four have known one another since childhood and live a comfortable, cultured existence: reading poetry, translating classical texts, playing music, and walking the pastoral landscape. The reader never learns the source of the Wielands' wealth that makes possible this genteel lifestyle, but it appears considerable and may be linked to family business in the city.

Family background is crucial to the novel, particularly the story of Clara and Theodore's father, who grew up in Germany. Melancholy and brooding as a young man, the elder Wieland serendipitously discovered the doctrine of the Camisards (a strict French Protestant sect) and became a fervent acolyte. He crossed the Atlantic to evangelize the Native Americans in Pennsylvania but soon turned his attention to land he had purchased on the Schuylkill River. After his large farm became successful, he returned to his religious devotions, building a place of worship on a hill near his home and regularly going there to read and pray. Gradually, his family and friends noticed a peculiar sadness in his demeanor, which he explained by saying that "a command had been laid upon him, which he had delayed to perform."[68] The command had been transferred to another, and he believed that the consequences of his dereliction would be severe.

One evening, increasingly despondent, he went to his hilltop temple to pray. After half an hour a bright light illuminated the building, and his family heard piercing shrieks. Rushing up the hill, his brother found him scorched, bruised, and naked, his clothes reduced to ashes. Still alive, the elder Wieland said that he had seen a person approaching and, when he turned to him, felt a blow on his arm and saw a spark light on his clothing. Whatever happened—the brother thought that his sibling's account had been "imperfect" and that he had suppressed "half the truth"—the elder Wieland's flesh soon began to putrefy, and within hours he was dead.[69]

Clara, then six, said that the impressions upon her brother and her could "never be effaced." Were the events, she continued, "fresh proof that the Divine Ruler interferes in human affairs, meditates an end, selects, and commissions his agents, and enforces[,] by unequivocal sanctions, submission to his will?" Or had her father's death merely been caused by "the irregular expansion of the fluid that imparts warmth to our heart, and our blood, caused by the fatigue of the preceding day"—that is, a sort of spontaneous combustion?[70] Whatever has occurred, the tragedy greatly affects Theodore, who has inherited his father's heightened religious sensibility, which like him, he does not express through traditional services but in private prayer and meditation.

Clara's story proper begins around 1763, "when the Indians were repulsed on the one side, and Canada conquered on the other," and Catharine and Wieland have been married for six years.[71] One evening Wieland decides to retrieve a book he left in the temple on the family estate, which is now devoted to musical and literary recreation. He returns looking troubled and asks Catharine if she followed him on the path. She has not moved an inch, a fact to which Pleyel and Clara testify. "Your assurances," Wieland replies, "are solemn and unanimous; yet I must deny credit to your assertions, or disbelieve the testimony of my senses," for he claims to have heard Catharine call him back from some danger.[72] Not only that: he claims that she spoke these words after he thought he saw a light glimmering in the temple.

Clara is distraught, for she perceives "a shadowy resemblance" between this event and the circumstances surrounding her father's death. She cannot bear to think that her brother's senses might be "the victims of such delusion," for this evidences "a diseased condition of his frame" that might show itself thereafter "in more dangerous symptoms." She then raises one of the novel's central propositions. "The will is the tool of the understanding," Clara observes, "which must fashion its conclusions on the notices of sense." She continues: "If the senses be depraved, it is impossible to calculate the evils that may flow from the consequent deductions of the understanding."[73]

Over the next few weeks, three members of the group have similar experiences. On one occasion, for instance, when Pleyel and Wieland are debating if Wieland should travel to Europe to claim a part of his patrimony, a voice they believe Catharine's dissuades them. It also conveys the erroneous news that Theresa de Stolberg, the woman in Europe whom Pleyel has pledged to marry, is dead. Catharine, however, denies having been anywhere near the men when they heard the voice. More remarkable, a missive subsequently arrives that appears to confirm Theresa's death. Learning of these events, Clara is visibly shaken, for "here were proofs of a sensible and intelligent existence, which could not be denied."[74]

Brown eventually introduces another major character. Francis Carwin appears at Clara's doorstep: a stranger looking like a "clown," his gait, "rustic and awkward," but his voice something "wholly new" and in which "force and sweetness" are memorably merged. His tone is such, she says, "as if an [*sic*] heart of stone could not fail of being moved by it," imparting "an emotion altogether involuntary and incontroulable [*sic*]."[75] Not at all attractive, this man still so influences Clara that she counts their meeting "among the most extraordinary incidents" of her life, so much so that she makes a sketch of the traveler as soon as he leaves. She is surprised and delighted when she learns that Pleyel knows Carwin and that now he, too, will become an inhabitant of the tightly knit—one might say claustrophobic—world of Mettingen.

A series of surreal events now occur involving Clara and Carwin. These culminate when planning to meet Carwin in her home, Clara instead finds a note from him that says that on his arrival he was surprised to find another person in place of her. He also warns her of a horrible sight she is about to see. Entering her bedroom, Clara finds Catharine brutally strangled. Wieland arrives and, seeing Catharine, is overwhelmed with grief, declaring mysteriously, "This is too much! Any victim but this, and thy will be done. Have I not sufficiently attested my faith and my obedience? She that is gone, they that have perished, were linked with my soul by ties which only thy command would have broken; but here is sanctity and excellence surpassing human."[76] As he approaches Clara, he hears noises outside and hastily departs. A crowd gathers, and she soon learns terrible news: Wieland's children have also been murdered.

Clara believes that Carwin is responsible for this devastation, but when she later tells this to her friend Mr. Hallet, he dismisses her speculation by informing her that although Carwin has not been seen since the evening of the murders, the perpetrator has been already brought before the bar and found guilty. Mr. Hallet leaves Clara with a transcription of the trial in which she is astonished to read that the confessor is Wieland and that when he returned to Clara's home, he intended to kill her, too. And why? After admitting his constant desire for closer communion with God, he describes how at Clara's he saw a blinding light, which he thought the luster of the deity, and heard a "shrill" voice, which he took as divine, command him to prove his faith by taking the lives of his wife and children.

Deciding to leave the area once and for all because of its association with such horrific events, Clara returns to her home a last time to retrieve personal papers. There by appointment she meets Carwin, who is to explain his role in the mysterious events at Mettingen. He reveals that he possesses the unusual gift of "biloquism"—ventriloquism. He, for example, mimicked Catharine's voice at the bottom of the hill when Wieland was warned from the temple and convinced Pleyel and Wieland not to venture to Europe. And the more he exercised his gift, the bolder he grew. Because Clara's maid, Judith, with whom he was having an affair, always extolled her mistress's fortitude, to test it, he impersonated murderers in Clara's room. Later, when she again thinks someone is hidden in her closet and inexplicably and irrationally forces the door to find Carwin within, he claims that he had not been there to ravish her but only to pry into her journal to learn more about her. After he had departed and saw Pleyel coming, he decided again to test the strength of his "gift": he impersonated Clara and made it seem as if she and he were having sexual intercourse.

But Carwin insists that he did nothing to encourage Wieland to commit his terrible crimes. "Who was it that blasted the intellects of Wieland?" she asks. "Who was it that urged him to fury, and guided him to murder?" He replies, "If I have memory, if I have being, I am innocent. I intended no ill; but my folly, indirectly and remotely, may have caused it"—that is, his ventriloquism might have disposed Wieland to imagine other, divine commands.[77] But Carwin's "only crime was curiosity." By some "perverse fate," he was led "perpetually to violate" his resolution not to use ventriloquism.[78] Clara, however, still believes that to test Wieland's faith, Carwin had commanded him to kill those he loved most.

At this moment Wieland, escaped from prison and, by another revelation, directed to kill Pleyel as well as Clara, enters her home. She tells him that Carwin is responsible for the recent mystery and mayhem. He has "this moment confessed it," she continues; "he is able to speak where he is not." Wieland asks him if this is so, and Carwin's reply is at best confused and inconclusive.[79] Wieland, possessed, all but forgets Carwin's presence, and as he moves toward Clara, she grasps a penknife to protect herself. At this point, "[a] voice, louder than human organs could produce, shriller than language can depict, burst from the ceiling, and commanded him— *to hold!*" Speaking as the voice of God, Carwin tells Wieland that he has been a fool to think that God would ask him to do evil and commands him to "shake off thy phrenzy [*sic*], and ascend into rational and human. Be lunatic no longer."[80] Now utterly distraught, Wieland seizes Clara's knife and kills himself, compounding the family tragedy.

Three years later some stability has returned to Clara's life. She is living in Europe and happily married to Pleyel, whose beloved Theresa did in fact die shortly after they were married. Clara imparts the novel's moral. The evil of which Carwin was the author, she says, only reveals the "errors" of his victims—that is, their lack of good judgment. "If Wieland had framed juster [*sic*] notions of moral duty, and of the divine attributes," she claims, and if she had been "gifted with ordinary equanimity or foresight, the double-tongued deceiver would have been baffled and repelled."[81]

"LATENT SPRINGS AND OCCASIONAL PERVERSIONS OF THE HUMAN MIND"

Clara's moral, however, is at odds with the tale, and here Brown's genius for probing the depths of religious enthusiasm and human consciousness is most evident. Two matters in particular need further consideration: the nature of Clara's and Wieland's relationship and Carwin's culpability. In delineating each, Brown borrows from and yet dramatically extends the stock tropes so prevalent in other, less ambitious contemporary fiction.

In his preface Brown writes that to understand the novel, the reader has to appeal to those who are "conversant with the latent springs and occasional perversions of the human mind."[82] Some of these matters are related to religious belief, and in *Wieland* Brown draws from the emotive spirituality that emergent groups like the Methodists, Freewill Baptists, and Universalists encouraged.[83] And even though for most Protestants such direct communication with God had ended with the apostles, in the post-Revolutionary period certain ecstatic sects revived the notion. The United Society of Believers in Christ's Second Appearing (the Shakers), for example, believed that their leader, Mother Ann Lee, was the second incarnation of Christ, and they claimed to transcribe spiritual songs received during divine revelation. Universalists, too, though more restrained in their outward practice, promulgated a creed that others could easily misunderstand. If a benevolent God would never condemn frail humans to eternal punishment and thus all were eventually to be saved, as the Universalists believed the Bible proclaimed, why should one live any longer on this troubled earth? A pious mother, following this logic and distraught over her temporal circumstances, might drown her children in a well rather than have them see any more earthly privation.

Wieland also touches on more individual psychological matters, most prominently, an abnormally close relationship between brother and sister that recalls the comparable obsession in William Hill Brown's *The*

Power of Sympathy. Charles Brockden Brown makes much of the similarities between Clara and Catharine: they are the same age, they grew up within sight of each other's houses, their tempers are "remarkably congenial," and their teachers prescribed the same pursuits and allowed them to cultivate them together.[84] Wieland has chosen the only appropriate spouse, but Brown suggests that his relationship to his sister, virtually his wife's double, is unusual and that she understands this. When Clara, for example, hears that her brother is to marry Catharine and the affianced ask if she would like to live with them, she politely declines yet could "scarcely account" for her refusal, "unless it were from a disposition to be an economist of pleasure." Why? For "self-denial, seasonably exercised, is one means of enhancing our gratifications," an odd way to speak about enjoying one's sibling.[85]

Clara's unusual relationship to her brother helps explain a remarkable dream she has of his beckoning her to come quickly to him, not realizing that there is a deep pit that separates them and into which she would tumble. Later, when Clara approaches the closet where she believes murderers have lurked and again thinks someone "whose purposes were evil" is within, she tries to compose herself, only to become more confused.[86] "In my dream," she thinks, "he that tempted me to my destruction, was my brother ... What minister or implement of ill was shut up in this recess? Who was it whose suffocating grasp I was to feel, should I dare to enter it? What monstrous conception is this? my brother!"[87]

She cannot dismiss this "strange and terrible chimera" and is "irresistibly persuaded" that Wieland is there to harm her.[88] Against all common sense and all the conventions of the sentimental novel that would have the heroine thereupon beat a hasty retreat, Clara inexplicably goes *toward* the door to open it. "The frantic conception that my brother was within, that the resistance made to my design was exerted by him, had rooted itself in my mind."[89] But this sexual fantasy ends with her terrifying discovery that it is not her brother but Carwin in the closet.

Still, if the effect of her actions here is not catastrophic—Carwin intends her no harm—this and other disconcerting events initiate her descent from rationality and sanity to mental instability. As she begins her tale, she is deeply depressed and tells her correspondent, "Futurity has no power over my thoughts." For to all that is to come she is "perfectly indifferent ... Fate has done its worst." Throughout the novel she repeatedly describes herself as confused and panic-stricken, and Brown recurs to the gothic metaphor of tumbling headlong into the pit or chasm. Clara insists, however, that despite her frightful memories, she will persist in telling her tale. "My narrative may be invaded by inaccuracies and confusion," she says, but even if it destroys her, she will continue to write it as best she can, given her debilitation. "What but ambiguities, abruptnesses, and dark transitions," she remarks, "can be expected from the historian who is, at the same time, the sufferer of these disasters?"[90] Traumatized, Clara no longer can discern the boundary between reality and imagination.

She even begins to suspect a possible underlying cause of her deterioration. When her friend Mr. Cambridge tries to convince her that the murders were the work of a madman, he tells her details of her grandfather's death. He lived a normal, contented life until the death of his brother, which brought on depression. One day, with his family on the cliffs at Cornwall, England, he began to tremble, "threw himself into the attitude of one listening," and told his companions that he had just heard a "summons, which must be instantly obeyed." He then precipitously hurled himself into the ocean below. This story, compounding those of her father and of Wieland, prompts Clara to wonder if madness does not run in her family and, further, if so, whether she is succumbing to it. "What was my security against influences equally terrific and equally irresistible?" she asks. She is stupefied "with ten-fold wonder" as she thinks about life's fragility. "Was I not likewise transformed from rational and human into a creature of nameless and fearful attributes? Was I not transported to the brink of the abyss?"[91] With so unreliable a narrator describing the novel's central scenes, how is a reader to judge Carwin's culpability? Clara is right to ask whether her brother was "a maniac, a faithful servant of God, the victim of hellish illusions, or the dupe of human imposture."[92]

ON THE CUSP OF CHANGE

The questions Brown raises in *Wieland* and the ways in which his characters grapple with them demonstrate remarkable intelligence and ambition. And while one cannot talk of schools of influence on the pioneering novelists except in the most general terms—that English novels such as *Clarissa*, say, influenced Rowson or that William Godwin's *The Adventures of Caleb Williams* was in the back of Brown's mind—we have the attestations of later writers like Hawthorne, Poe, Neal, and others that of the first wave of American novelists, Charles Brockden Brown made the most lasting impression.

He wove the threads of the sentimental and gothic into a wholly new fabric, a type of fiction whose main texture came from his interest in the roots and branches of human motivation, particularly as they were bent by religious experience in the United States. As his biographer Prescott put it, Brown's great object was to exhibit the mind "in scenes of extraordinary interest. In the midst of the fearful strife," he continued, readers "are coolly invited to investigate its causes and all the various phenomena which attend it."[93] Thus, Brown was interested not only in man's soul but also in his will and the behavior that flows from it, measured against the larger claims made for freedom in the American experiment. The course of a life is not eternally decreed, Brown suggests, but molded by intentions and actions, heredity and fate, coincidence and accident, time and place.

He treated such matters most powerfully in *Wieland* and the three novels that followed in rapid succession: *Ormond, Arthur Mervyn*, and *Edgar Huntly*—sprawling, often untidy creations, each with a plethora of characters and subplots. All display his fascination with a social order disrupted not only by fraud and imposture but also by seduction, poverty, disease, dissimulation, counterfeiting, land speculation, unusual psychic states like somnambulism, and above all a loss of meaningful religious faith. He explores the psychological confusion of individuals who are caught between certainty and contingency, belief in providential decree and individual freedom, American citizens who try to negotiate between the demands of self and society, of personal morality and social expectations.

Through the first two decades of the new century, few other novelists rose to Brown's standard, but many similarly linked themes of sexual seduction and betrayal to the emergence of a sense of the primacy of the individual, typified in *Female Quixotism* but evident as well in *The Gamesters*, and *The Lottery Ticket: An American Tale*, and Rebecca Rush's *Kelroy*. Other novelists introduced different but equally significant themes. Leonora Sansay, another Philadelphian, had been in Saint-Domingue (Haiti) in the last days of French colonial rule. Her epistolary novel *Secret History; or, The Horrors of St. Domingo* (1808) describes life among the embattled ruling class and directly confronts Haiti's slave-based economy as well as the nature of colonial oppression, topics that subsequently informed American fiction during the period of Indian removal and the rise of abolitionism.

For the most part, however, in the first two decades of the nineteenth century most American novelists relied on well-worn tropes in play since the early 1790s and in England before that. This changed in 1821 with the publication of James Fenimore Cooper's second novel, *The Spy*, set during the American Revolution, which unleashed a deluge of historical fictions that did not take English novels such as Richardson's *Pamela*, Godwin's *Caleb Williams,* or Ann Radcliffe's gothic *The Mysteries of Udolpho* as models. Rather, the major influence was Sir Walter Scott, whose tales of the Scottish border, beginning with *Waverley* in 1814, brought him extraordinary success.

But despite Cooper's success and the advent of American historical fiction, Brown's effect was lasting. Brown suggested that if the individual's experience, not social norms, was the arbiter of moral behavior—a proposition implicit in a culture that enshrined each person's right to liberty and the pursuit of happiness—citizens like Eliza Whitman, Harriot Fawcet, and Theodore and Clara Wieland might become more common than one had thought possible. And as the nation's religious complexion more and more mirrored the confusion that revolutionary ideology had unleashed, the war between intellect and emotion that Emerson later wrote about became inescapable.

2 } *Glimmerings of Change*

A week after the novelist James Fenimore Cooper's death in Cooperstown, New York, on September 14, 1851, his fellow author Washington Irving convened a meeting of friends and admirers at City Hall in New York to plan a memorial for the eminent man of letters. The commemoration took place in Tripler (later Metropolitan) Hall, the city's premier venue for stage events, with Senator Daniel Webster of Massachusetts, considered the nation's finest living orator, as the master of ceremonies. The poet William Cullen Bryant delivered the main address, which he titled a "Discourse on the Life, Character, and Genius of James Fenimore Cooper." Others spoke, too, including the historian George Bancroft, who urged the assembly to support a monument to Cooper. All agreed that the evening was a suitably grand occasion for someone who held so large a place in the still-young annals of American literature.

Cooper wrote thirty-two lengthy novels on a wide variety of subjects. His success began in 1821 with *The Spy*, his first historical fiction, set during the American Revolution; next came *The Pioneers* (1823), the first book in what eventually became the five-volume "Leatherstocking Tales," a paean to Manifest Destiny that described the settlement of the United States from New York to the Great Plains. In his protean career he went on to write tales of the sea, such as *The Pilot* (1823), which featured the naval hero John Paul Jones; novels of manners like *Home as Found* (1838); a quasi-utopian romance, *The Crater* (1847) (discussed below); and, for his very last work, a novel based on a contemporary murder trial, *The Ways of the Hour* (1850).

Then, as now, however, Cooper's reputation rests primarily on the five "Leatherstocking" novels (1823–1841), which follow Natty Bumppo, also known as Deerslayer and Hawkeye, from his youthful days near Otsego Lake in south-central New York to his death on the midwestern prairie fifty years later. Ever since the publication of the literary historian R.W.B. Lewis's *The American Adam: Innocence, Tragedy, and Tradition in the Nineteenth Century*, readers have understood Natty's life on the never-ending frontier as emblematic of the nation's most distinctive experience. But that view is in need of a revision. Cooper is, unquestionably, a major early American novelist, but a number of his contemporaries did more to advance the form, because they were attuned to their times in ways that Cooper was not.

With the raucous triumph of Jacksonian democracy, the disestablishment of state churches (accompanied by an explosion of interdenominational competition), and the advent of unfettered capitalism, Americans grappled with newfound freedoms that were as frightening as they were liberating. They found themselves in an unforgiving world, without recourse to the kinds of higher powers that hitherto had ordered their lives. Terrorized by Indians on the frontiers, hypocritical Christians in their churches, sociopaths prowling the streets of the ever-growing cities, and confidence men preying on their goodwill, they had fewer and fewer places to turn. Cooper addressed some of these problems but used his novels to buttress an older, aristocratic worldview typified in the life of of his father, William. The landed squire of Cooperstown, William Cooper resented common citizens who believed themselves his social and political equals, and James inherited his father's distaste for upstart democrats. His novels demonstrate a belief that the ambition unleashed by liberalism and capitalism needed strong regulation, if not outright elimination. To address such topics, Cooper set his best novels in the expanding, unexplored West, but other writers, such as John Neal and Catharine Maria Sedgwick, explored frontiers closer to home. Their stylistic and thematic innovation set the novel on different paths, those leading to different social concerns and, eventually, introspection.

"THAT DAMNED RANTING STUFF OF JOHN NEAL"
John Neal (1793–1876) was a man in a hurry. Beginning with *Keep Cool: A Novel Written in Hot Weather* (1817), he wrote fifteen other novels as well as poetry and plays, essays, art criticism, and an autobiography. In the 1820s he was Cooper's chief rival, publishing no fewer than seven novels in that decade alone. Unlike Cooper, though, he embodied the

democratic ferment that in the early nineteenth century spawned preachers, populist politicians, and confidence men. Neal was another incarnation of the new American citizen typified at this time by the Methodist circuit rider Lorenzo Dow, who eschewed formal education and decried aristocratic and clerical privilege, appealing to the common people through the colloquial speech of the emergent democrats and their hero, the rising democratic politician Gen. Andrew Jackson. Neal, Dow, Jackson, and their followers took seriously the proposition that all men were created equal and thus deserved respect.[1]

Born and raised in Portland, Maine, self-educated, and always eager to pillory the pretensions of the high-born, Neal moved to Baltimore when he was twenty-one to establish a dry goods business with his good friend the Yale graduate John Pierpont, a budding poet. Neal cut a striking figure, about five feet eight inches tall, one person recalled, "a fine head, light-coloured silky hair, robust athletic, iron built; in short, the man to make a statue of, every limb so well developed." There was, this observer added, "so much manhood in the whole figure," something that probably accounts for Neal's seemingly magnetic sway over women.[2] But Neal's striking looks did not guarantee success in business. When the venture with Pierpont failed, he began simultaneously to study law and to write professionally. With Pierpont and five other like-minded intellectuals, he formed the Delphian Club, at whose meetings (as at Charles Brockden Brown's Friendly Club in New York) members read literary works in progress and formally debated current affairs. The group published *The Portico*, a literary journal of some merit to which Neal contributed, among other things, a lengthy, laudatory essay on Lord Byron, a hint to what kind of writing—and authorial persona—he aspired.

In 1824 Neal left Baltimore for a three-year stay in England to advance his own, and his compatriots', reputation among a British readership. Selling himself as "Carter Holmes," a well-traveled countryman, he convinced William Blackwood, publisher of *Blackwood's Edinburgh Magazine*, to commission a series of essays about the United States; he became something of a curiosity: an American who wrote pseudonymously as an Englishman for insular British quarterlies. Eighteen months later, after Blackwood had learned his identity and after they had quarreled over the publication of Neal's *Brother Jonathan* (1825), Neal was picked up by the equally well-regarded *Westminster Review*.

Neal's pseudonymous essays in *Blackwood's* on the current state of

American literature give a good sense of how he thought of the novel as well as of his contemporaries who wrote them. Just a few years after the Anglican cleric Sydney Smith asked in the *Edinburgh Review*, "[I]n the four quarters of the globe, who reads an American book?" Neal provided a list of more than 130 American authors who he claimed already had made notable contributions to literature in English. But he turned the tables on his intended audience, saying that in fact there was no reason why they should read American books, for most of them were just like those of their English counterparts. "With two exceptions," Neal opined, "or at the most three, there is no American writer who would not pass just as readily for an English writer, as for an American."[3]

The "exceptions" were Charles Brockden Brown, the New York writer James Kirke Paulding (1778–1860), and Neal himself (hiding behind his pseudonym). In his assessment of Brown, Neal described what, in essence, distinguished all three. All of Brown's novels, he wrote, "are remarkable for vividness, circumstantiality, and startling disclosures, here and there," and are "full of perplexity—incoherence—and contradiction."[4] Though not as fulsome in his praise of Paulding, whose tale of frontier Delaware *Koningsmarke, the Long Finne* (1823), appeared in the same year as Cooper's *The Pioneers*, Neal still found in him the same energy he found in Brown. Predictably, Neal reserved the highest praise for his own work. "Neal is altogether too much of a poet," he wrote. "He overdoes everything—pumps the lightning into you, till *he* is out of breath, and *you*, in a blaze." "He is, undeniably," Neal continued, "the most original writer, that America has produced."[5]

But what did "Carter Holmes" think of Cooper? A few years earlier, in his novel *Randolph*, Neal had branded him a failed American version of Sir Walter Scott. If Cooper included "some good Scotch [*sic*] dialogue" in his fiction, he noted, few people "would be able to detect the counterfeit." Cooper lacked "originality—passion—poetry—and eloquence." Neal argued that "nobody would know a work of his, by the work itself," for Cooper's style was "without particularity—brilliancy, or force." Cooper, Neal claimed, thus was "greatly overrated by his contemporaries." He has done much," Neal allowed, but "like a boy, without well knowing what he was about."[6]

Neal sought the opposite effect on his readers, and his own works fit the description he gave Brown's œuvre: full of perplexity, incoherence, and contradiction. Frequently criticized for a lack of discipline and drawing obsessively on the Byronic heroes whom he admired, Neal filled his novels of the 1820s with raw and exhilarating energy. In his struggle to contain his large, unruly imagination, he openly broached topics that few other American novelists would touch, and to do so, broached various stylistic conventions and literary genres. He wrote a bevy of works in an amazingly short period—first, *Keep Cool* (1817), then *Logan: the Mingo Chief* (1822), *Seventy-six; or, Love and Battle* (1823), *Randolph; A Novel* (1823), and *Errata; or, The Works of Will Adams* (1823). Neal described them thus: *Logan* was "*declamation*"; *Seventy-six*, "*narrative*"; *Randolph*, "*epistolary*"; and *Errata*, "*colloquial.*" They are, he continued, "a complete series: a course of experiments . . . upon the forbearance of the age," presaging another renegade, Walt Whitman, who termed his genre-smashing poem *Leaves of Grass* (1855) "only a language experiment."[7]

Keep Cool: A Novel Written in Hot Weather shows Neal's penchant for plumbing a character's darker places; an earlier, working title, "Judge Not from First Appearances," evidenced his interest in the kinds of duplicity that were fast becoming a hallmark of the age.[8] *Keep Cool* concerns one Sydney, who is the victim of an insult and in a duel kills the offender. Neal focuses on the debilitating guilt that follows; in his remorse Sydney moves to the wilderness to live in self-imposed exile among Native Americans, for whom honor consists of more than mere revenge. Neal viewed dueling as an outdated and immoral carryover from an aristocratic order no longer relevant in the United States. Opposing this custom was one of the ways in which he made his democratic sympathies clear.

He did something similar in the remarkable *Logan: A Family History*, which he advised should be "taken like opium. A grain can exhilarate," he explained (as one who presumably knew); "more may stupefy," and "too much will be death."[9] The novel takes on a taboo subject, interracial marriage, when the half-mythical Logan, whom everyone believes to be an Indian chief but who actually is George Clarence, a renegade white man, marries a Native American "queen." Set in the border wars in western Virginia, the novel reveals the difference between Neal and Cooper. The latter always studiously avoided controversial topics, including miscegenation, despite its prevalence on the frontier. In *The Deerslayer*, for example, even though Natty acquires a Native American admirer, he finally leaves her behind and dies celibate, and in *The Last of the Mohicans*, two Native Americans—Magua, an enemy of the English, and Uncas, the last of the Mohicans—both love the Englishwoman Cora Munro. Magua captures Cora and her half sister Alice and tries to force the high-spirited dark-haired sister to marry him, even though she is more attracted to Natty. Uncas and Natty Bumppo save the two women, but in the end, Cora, Magua, *and* Uncas all are killed, preventing any interracial marriage.

For Neal, however, interracial relationships could be the very basis of a novel's plot. After settlers kill his wife and family, Logan runs amok against whites. The handsome raven-haired Harold, who lives among the Native Americans and thinks he is one, is actually the sole surviving child of the Logan family massacre. In an act that borders on rape, Harold impregnates Elvira, the colonial governor's wife, while she is half asleep. The reader subsequently learns that she has long been infatuated with Logan and views the striking, dark Harold as a comely surrogate. Learning of this strange nighttime tryst, the governor banishes Harold to the wilderness, where he meets his father, Logan, and discovers his true heritage.

Nor did Neal shy away from relatively explicit references to sexuality, interracial or not, for he believed that instinctual and irresistible desires informed the behavior of women as well as men. In *Logan*, for example, the reader encounters not only titillating descriptions unique in the literature of that period but excessive, almost gratuitous violence: scalping, murder, hatred, rape, and real and implied incest. Reviewers recognized that *Logan*'s inclusion of sex and violence made the novel unique. One expressed "astonishment that the *still life* of [Cooper's] *The Pioneers*, should be read and applauded in the same age that produced *Logan*," for the two novels could not have been more different.[10]

Neal's next novel, *Randolph*, an epistolary roman à clef set in Baltimore, caused a controversy and led to Neal's temporary estrangement from his closest friend, Pierpont. As Neal recalled years later, the book "was received like a lighted-thunderbolt, dropped into a powder magazine."[11] Ostensibly the story of Sarah Ramsay's attempt to learn the truth about the mysterious, handsome Edward Molton, the novel draws on Neal's experiences in the city as a businessman, an aspiring lawyer, and a young man-about-town. Molton recounts in thinly fictionalized terms Neal's own indiscretion with Pierpont's attractive teenage sister-in-law,

Abby Lord. Living for a time in a room adjoining hers, Neal one night crept in while she was asleep and did or was about to do something—just what he never makes clear—when she awoke and screamed. Embarrassed, Neal told Pierpont of the event, excusing himself by saying he did it while sleepwalking; but after he compulsively aired the matter in the novel, the incident became fodder for widespread, prurient speculation. It is no surprise that the following year Neal decamped from Baltimore for the relative peace of England.

Before he left for England, he published *Errata*, in which, reminiscent of Laurence Sterne's *Tristram Shandy* (1759–1769) in its melange of genres, the central character, Will Adams, holds forth on all sorts of topics, including his insatiable sexual appetite. At a pivotal moment, the parents of a pretty young Quaker girl, Caroline, tell her that she has to stop seeing Will, who has been rooming with the family. Knocking on his door to say goodbye, Caroline is overcome with emotion and deliriously falls into Will. In so doing (evidently in dishabille), she exposes her bosom. Will nervously tries to cover her breast but then impulsively presses his "passionate mouth" to it. "I felt her heart stop, and her head reel," he recalls. In a wonderful twist on *la petite mort*, "she turned cold instantly all over," Will's voice "rattl[ing]" in his throat as if he were dying.[12] He faints and awakens three months later in an insane asylum, in a room next to Caroline's, his story told in the voice of Hammond the Dwarf. Hammond tells that Will survives this encounter with his latest woman, but Caroline does not. Before she dies, however, she tearfully tells her parents that she was innocent of any indiscretion, something that Hammond cannot report of Will.

Neal continued to write feverishly and with similar openness and invention in his next novel, the behemoth *Brother Jonathan*, published in three volumes in London, which he hoped would cement his reputation once and for all as Cooper's superior. But some of the book's scenes, filled as they are with gothic excess as well as bumptious nationalism, so troubled his publisher, Blackwood, that he insisted Neal revise it before publication. Neal barely acceded, and the book, an episodic attempt to catch the flavor of New England language and mores as well as its history, did not fare well, as Blackwood had guessed. This disappointment did not end Neal's career, for before him lay another historical fiction, *Rachel Dyer* (1828), a compelling account of one of the Salem witches, and a remarkable forty more years of writing and editing in his hometown of Portland, Maine. But by 1825 he had done his most important work, that "course of experiments" in his breathless, elliptical narrative style.

Though Neal never garnered an audience comparable to Cooper's, his contemporaries and later novelists recognized his importance. Edgar Allan Poe, the era's best critic, excused the hastiness and unfinished nature of Neal's works in light of his daring imagination. "I should be inclined to rank John Neal first, or at all events second," Poe wrote, "among our men of indisputable *genius*."[13] Nathaniel Hawthorne, in describing the difficulties many American writers faced in establishing themselves, cited the contagious interest excited by "that wild fellow, John Neal, who almost turned my boyish brain with his romances."[14] Hawthorne's Bowdoin College classmate Jonathan Cilley, hearing that Hawthorne had published *Twice-Told Tales*, asked him what sort of book he had written. "I hope and pray," he continued, "it is nothing like the damned ranting stuff of John Neal, which you, while at Brunswick [location of Bowdoin College in Maine], relished so highly."[15]

One could add to these appraisals that Neal's willingness to write about the brutality of frontier life, amorous relations between Native American and European men and women, and people's sexual drives and fantasies, marked him as an innovator, for these taboo subjects within decades became prominent themes of the American novel—not the least in Hawthorne's own work. There is as well—and this, too, marks his distance from Cooper—his willingness to take the side of the American democrat rather than the landed gentry or otherwise privileged citizens. If Neal did not immediately exercise as large an influence over fiction writing as Cooper, whose historical romances had many imitators, his subject matter and approach would eventually find their champions.

THE LITERATURE OF RELIGIOUS TRACT SOCIETIES

Neal bucked many trends, and foremost among them was the rise of explicitly religious fiction in America. In the 1810s, as various denominations realized that they could encourage proper moral behavior through reading as well as by attendance at services or in family scriptural study, they began to publish cheap tracts of fifty or fewer pages in runs in the tens and even hundreds of thousands. Some of these were issued commercially, but most were printed for religious publishing societies, one of the period's distinctive phenomena. One consequence of a publishing revolution that lowered costs as it sped up production and a distribution system that soon included railroads and steamboats, the religious tract was born as well of the democratization of Christianity that ensued as state after state did away with established religion.[16]

Many tracts were abridged versions of evangelical works like Jonathan Edwards's *A Narrative of the Surprising Conversions* or stories populated by a variety of nineteenth-century characters from backgrounds recognizable to large and varied readerships. And even though some of their sponsors carried denominational names—the American Baptist Publication Society, say, or the Congregational Board of Publication—over time they became more markedly nondenominational, defined primarily by their commitment to fostering Christian morals. Organizations such as the American Sunday School Union, the American Bible Society, and, the largest of them all, the American Tract Society sought to create and institutionalize a Christian united front to keep the nation virtuous, not doctrinally sound. To counter the lurid tales issued by secular publishers, the tract societies, bankrolled by successful Christian businessmen, delivered a cheap, edifying product to the masses. They were essentially the nation's first nonprofit organizations, with few American homes not visited by one of the societies' thousands of colporteurs.[17]

Sarah Savage, author of *The Factory Girl* (1814), typifies the ambitions of religious tract writers. Not much is known of her, except that she lived in Salem, Massachusetts, and made her living as a teacher and writer. An early convert to Unitarianism, she fulfilled her Christian duty by writing.[18] Even though *The Factory Girl*, her first book, predates the establishment of most of the tract societies and was published commercially, its story of a young woman who, owing to her strong religious training, resists selfishness and luxury set a standard in the nascent genre.

Her heroine, Mary Burnham, is an orphan who lives with and cares for her aging grandmother. To make ends meet, she reels cotton at one of the new spinning factories sprouting up throughout the New England countryside. Not partaking in frivolous entertainments like most of the other factory "girls," she still catches the eye of William Raymond, another factory worker (but not as pious a Christian as she), and they soon are engaged. For a time, Mary works as a teacher, but after caring for a friend, Mrs. Danforth, who falls fatally ill, she returns home for several months.

William wanders. He breaks the engagement and marries another woman, with whom he has a child. When he wins four hundred dollars in a lottery, he abandons his family. Mary returns to the factory, but when her beloved grandmother falls ill, she returns home and once again cares for a dying elderly woman. For all her good works, Mary is rewarded with marriage to Mr. Danforth and the affection of her stepchildren.

Distinguished by its setting in a factory village, the novel is equally notable for the concept of selfhood Savage presents, one based in virtuous behavior best represented by a woman. If earlier novels like *The Coquette* showed women as weak and vulnerable, in the hands of a new generation of writers, female characters were not victims but, potentially, strong, independent individuals whose faith allows them to resist temptation and survive difficult times. As a reward for being a pious, caring Christian, Mary gains a stable, fruitful relationship that frees her from millwork. Savage's purpose was not to criticize or reform the factory but to show that even in this new, morally challenging environment, those who act primarily for the good of others are rewarded. The story ends with Mary's stepchildren giving her two gifts: a writing desk and a Bible so that she can further her interest in self-culture and religion. The implication was characteristic of the time: one can use the pen to promulgate the teachings of Christianity.

Following a pattern set by popular English authors like Hannah More and Maria Edgeworth, who issued large numbers of such tales, Savage wrote many more books, including *James Talbot* (1821); *Advice to a Young Woman at Service* (1823), which addressed the new and growing profession of housekeepers; *Badge: A Moral Tale for Children* (1824); and *Blind Miriam Restored to Sight* (1833). One of her last, *Trial and Self-Discipline* (1835), was part of a new series begun by the well-known Unitarian minister and Harvard professor Henry Ware, Jr. In a note to Savage, Ware indicated his ambition for the new project. "It is the object of the series of little publications," he wrote, "to present familiar illustrations of some of the important practical principles of religion, and to show, by an intermixture of narrative and discussion, how they operate in the government of the heart and life." Savage offered him a tale that was, like her first, cautionary, for in it she both praised the opportunities that the factories brought women and worried about what came with these opportunities—namely, "a spirit of self-reliance, an earthly spirit" that looked "only to this low world for aid, for support."[19] Here Savage provided her character with a significant degree of agency, made possible by a liberal Christianity whose freedom from doctrine opened new personal and social horizons for its adherents.

CATHARINE MARIA SEDGWICK

Catharine Maria Sedgwick emerged on the literary scene in 1822 with *A New-England Tale*, which she originally conceived of as a religious tract and which followed many of the genre's conventions, as Savage's work did. After the strong reception of her next effort, *Redwood* (1825), she became, like John Neal, a chief competitor to Cooper. Indeed, when *Redwood*, published anonymously, was reprinted in Italy and France, the novel mistakenly carried *Cooper's* name on its title page. Her influence may have been greater than either Cooper's or Neal's, though. In her six full-length novels published over a thirty-year period Sedgwick established patterns that many authors, particularly women, reprised through the 1860s.

Sedgwick split her life between New York and the Berkshire Hills of western Massachusetts.[20] She was born in 1789 in Stockbridge, Massachusetts, the sixth of seven surviving children of Theodore and Pamela Dwight Sedgwick, descendants of the region's pioneers and strong Edwardsian Calvinists. A self-made man, Theodore Sedgwick became one of the state's most prominent attorneys and politicians and a long-serving member of the Massachusetts House of Representatives. He also served as a U.S. representative, speaker of the House, and finally, U.S. senator. He was a staunch Federalist, and after the Jeffersonian ascendency in 1800, he resigned his seat. His third wife and Catharine's mother, Pamela, who descended from well-known New England families, needed much care, a good deal of which fell to Catharine, the only one of her three daughters not to marry. Pamela suffered from bouts of severe depression, instigated in part by her husband's long absences from Stockbridge; but Catharine also linked her mother's debility to her Calvinism, the demanding faith of most New England Federalists like the Sedgwicks that Emerson termed "the soul's mumps and measles." Catharine also was very close to her four brothers, Theodore, Henry, George, and Robert, all of whom held prominent positions in business and politics. After her parents died, she alternated stays between the family's home in the Berkshires and New York City, where Harry and Robert had homes.

Catharine's childhood had been filled with nature and books. Stockbridge and its sylvan surroundings were already a summer retreat for wealthy people from Boston and New York City, and her father's study contained literary and historical works that he shared with his daughters as well as his sons. The family attended the local Congregational church, the same one that Jonathan Edwards had overseen after his dismissal from his pastorate in Northampton, which was then in the hands of the Reverend Stephen West, a staunch follower of Samuel Hopkins, one of Edwards's two chief disciples. Thus, in her youth Catharine heard weekly a strong and little-diluted Calvinism, with emphases on such doctrines as the necessity of one's willingness to be damned for the glory of God and a belief that sin is an "advantage" to the universe and that free will is a self-indulgent fiction.

After their father's death, the Sedgwick children gradually began to move in more liberal political and religious circles, even as socially they retained a sense of noblesse oblige. By the mid-1820s Theodore, the sibling most involved in politics, and Catharine, under the influence of another local minister, Orville Dewey, had taken up the liberal Christian creed becoming known as Unitarianism. Catharine had seen firsthand Calvinism's effect on her mother, as well as on her sisters, Eliza and Frances, both of whom were spiritually troubled.[21] With its stress on the innate goodness inherent in every person, on virtue that consisted in outward morality rather than private piety, and on the individual's free will, Unitarianism greatly influenced the tenor of Sedgwick's fiction. It also brought her new friends, liberal intellectuals from Boston and New York whose praise of her writing helped put her on the young nation's literary map. Among these was the eloquent Unitarian preacher William Ellery Channing, the denomination's most visible spokesperson and also a major influence on the Transcendentalists.

FROM TRACT TO NOVEL

Sometime in the early 1820s, emboldened by a newfound faith in her intellectual powers after her conversion to Unitarianism, Sedgwick decided she wanted "to help others to escape from the chains which she had broken." Her brother Theodore, impressed by her evocative letters, suggested that she try her hand at writing something more substantial. She penned a short story about conversion that grew into the first draft of what became *A New-England Tale; or, Sketches of New-England Character and Manners*. Sedgwick showed it to her brother Harry, who encouraged her to expand it and publish it independently as a novel.[22] She took his advice and, on one of her trips to New York, placed it with the publishers Bliss and White, requesting that they publish it anonymously because she was averse to publicity. Sedgwick dedicated the book to Maria Edgeworth, the best-known Englishwoman writing in the same vein, an indication of the audience she sought.

Although they may not have known who wrote the book, readers of religious tracts would have immediately recognized *A New-England Tale*'s heroine, Jane Elton, who embodies disinterested benevolence. The novel's message is that no matter what one's station in life, moderation, honesty, and sympathy, not blind allegiance to heartless doctrine, are the foundation of a religious life. With more and more of her countrymen rejecting religion that cast the individual as a helpless, lost soul, they easily could fall into the snare of selfishness. Liberal denominations like Unitarianism offered an alternative, a life defined by a self-empowerment held in check through a concern for catholic moral virtue. *A New-England Tale* spoke to a readership that increasingly turned to this sort of literature for guidance in navigating a society in which selfishness seemed not only justifiable but the only sensible ethic. Sedgwick reassured readers of the rightness of simple Christian goodness during a time when old pieties were breaking against shoals of individualism.

A New-England Tale's central plot is straightforward. Jane Elton is orphaned at twelve after her father has entered into questionable speculations that eventually fail, sending the family on a downward spiral that ends in both her parents' deaths. Subsequently, Jane is placed with one of her aunts, Mrs. Wilson, who cruelly uses and abuses her and always compares her unfavorably with her two haughty and deceitful daughters because she presumes Jane to be far below her own family's station. Mrs. Wilson represents both a false sense of social entitlement and a desiccated and corrosive Calvinism of the sort that Sedgwick knew firsthand in the Berkshires. Mrs. Wilson constantly flaunts her supposed piety, but she is a flagrant hypocrite. That no one else in town seems concerned about her behavior is meant to suggest the extent of such hypocrisy in conservative religious life at the time. Jane by contrast is a humble, tolerant, and sympathetic Christian of the sort Sedgwick admired. Jane endures the torments of her aunt and her cousins, particularly Elvira and the wayward David. Mrs. Wilson's children cheat, lie to, and steal from their mother; David's drinking, seduction, and finally grand thievery mark him as the worst of the lot. At the novel's end, Mr. Lloyd, a widowed Quaker and one of the few decent people in the story, marries Jane, even though he is old enough to be her father.

With *A New-England Tale*, Sedgwick more than succeeded in her purpose of writing a "very short and simple moral tale" that might "add something to the scanty stock of native American literature," for she established a set of conventions that greatly influenced subsequent novelists, particularly those who contributed to the popularity of "sentimental" literature.[23] Like Eliza Wharton in *The Coquette*, Jane is tempted by suitors who the author shows are not right for her. Her faith is tested when Edward Erskine, the scion of one of the town's prominent families and a rising attorney, notices her beauty and begins to pay more attention to her than to Elvira. Erskine, aware of Jane's persecution in the Lloyd household, persists in his suit, and in a moment of weakness, she accepts his proposal.

But when the young attorney refuses to be swayed by Mr. Lloyd's plea that the young man gather support for and sponsor a bill to reform the state's poor laws, Jane questions the wisdom of her decision. Further, when she learns that Erskine, "habitually under the dominion of self-love," has taken the plaintiff's case in a suit against John of the Mountain, a kind man who lives on the town's outskirts, for supposedly squatting on private land, and that he successfully defended David Wilson in a paternity suit that left Wilson's lover and illegitimate child destitute, she realizes how unsuited he and she are.[24] To most of her contemporaries, Erskine would be a prize husband, but Jane rejects him for his lack of Christian virtue and is both vindicated and rewarded when Mr. Lloyd proposes marriage. Her patience and principles bring her the spouse she deserves. Thus, Sedgwick implied that religious and social pretension can be combated by faith; Jane Elton is an alternative to Eliza Wharton. Happy endings for fictional heroines are possible, despite the dismal ends *The Coquette* and similar novels presented as inevitable.

A New-England Tale was a surprising success, encouraging Sedgwick to begin work on a much longer, bolder novel, which she called *Redwood*. As she had in her first book, she set it in contemporary New England, believing that her own time and milieu provided the best subject matter for her work. "While the elements of human nature and human society remain the same," she wrote in the preface, their "forms and combinations are changing at every moment." Hence "fictitious narrative" had a simple purpose: "to denote the passing character and manners of the present time and place."[25] Her understanding of the inherent flux that characterized nineteenth-century life is a striking sign not only of her attentiveness to the major social and cultural changes through which her contemporaries were living but as well of her modernity in facing and accepting them rather than casting a nostalgic eye backward to simpler times. In the same way, though she played a vital role in the constantly changing idea of the American novel by overturning old conventions and creating new ones, her innovations would themselves be overturned by later novelists, both men and women.

The events in *Redwood* take place on a farm in Vermont; in Lebanon, New York; and in a Shaker village in Hancock, Massachusetts. Ellen Bruce, a guest of the Lenox family, Vermont farmers, is the novel's Jane Elton. A carriage accident brings two visitors to the farm: Henry Redwood, who has been injured, and his daughter, Caroline, aristocratic southerners on a northern tour to escape the southern summer. Soon enough another southerner, Charles Westall, a friend of the Redwoods', comes to visit during Mr. Redwood's recuperation. Redwood hopes that Charles will eventually marry his daughter, who is haughty and conceited; but Charles, initially so inclined, is taken by the very attractive yet very different—because she is virtuous and selfless—Ellen. The two eventually marry, with Caroline left in the hands of an accomplished gold digger—shades of Dorcasina Sheldon's fate!

Ellen is in fact Redwood's daughter, for in his youth he rashly married and impregnated a servant girl, a backstory reminiscent of William Hill Brown's *The Power of Sympathy*. This union soon was broken by Redwood's forced travel abroad and the young woman's death, but not before she gave birth to Ellen. Raised by pious New Englanders on New Testament principles, Ellen finds happiness with the southern aristocrat Westall, who has enough good sense to realize that she, not the frivolous Caroline, is the right match, a resolution that evinces Sedgwick's belief in the obsolescence of class in the Jacksonian period.

A subplot takes place at the Hancock Shaker village that Susan and Emily Lenox have joined as converts, drawn by the sect's simple and chaste lifestyle as well as by the Shakers' belief that their leader, Mother Ann Lee, was the female incarnation of Christ. One of the Shakers, a man named Reuben Harrington, has not quite subdued his lust, however, and is so taken with Emily that he kidnaps her with the intent to seduce her. Eventually, Emily's friends and family manage to rescue her before any harm is done. Adding much-needed drama to Sedgwick's narrative, this episode also serves as an occasion for the author once again to inveigh against dogmatic religion—in this case, Shakerism—and the hypocrisy that often accompanies it.

Redwood was an immediate success and was quickly published in England and translated into five languages, including French and Italian, an honor not accorded many American writers and a testament to the book's appeal as a strong example of indigenous literature.[26] Many readers made the comparison to Scott, even though in her preface Sedgwick took pains to distinguish between her attempt to capture the region's character and manners and Scott's "historical romance."[27] Harry Sedgwick wrote excitedly from New York with the news that "the sale is constantly increasing, and the booksellers say that it is now better than [Scott's] Redgauntlet [a novel from 1824]." A few months later, readers began to make another inevitable comparison. Harry told her that city booksellers, who found her novels strong sellers, were eager for her next work, for "they say it will go as well [as] or better than one from Cooper or Irving."[28] What no one yet knew was that her next work would challenge the very grounds of the former's success.

RIVALING COOPER

With *Hope Leslie; or, Early Times in the Massachusetts* (1827), Sedgwick took a risk. She rejected her own advice in *Redwood* to use a contemporary setting and attempted to write a Scott-like historical fiction. She took as her subject the early settlement of New England and in particular the combat between Native Americans and white settlers. The result proved to be her most powerful novel, one that though it still relies on heroines representative of liberal Christian virtue, introduced complex new characters, including nonwhites, to her readers as well as challenged both the traditionally patriarchal trajectory of American history and, more particularly, Native Americans' role in it.

Sedgwick's inspiration for *Hope Leslie* came from various sources. One was Cooper's *The Last of the Mohicans*, which had appeared a year earlier and dealt with the incompatibility of Native Americans and European settlers as well the former's seemingly inevitable extinction, a topic that greatly interested Sedgwick. Reviewers, too, thought that she should write historical fiction. William Cullen Bryant, in his *North American Review* notice of *Redwood,* wrote that she should have for her second novel returned to the country's history "to set before us, the fearless and hardy men, who made the first lodgment in its vast forests" and the "savage tribes by whom they were surrounded, and to whose kindness they owed so much, and from whose enmity they suffered so severely." It was an invitation to challenge Cooper on his own ground.[29]

Another source of inspiration was the novel *Hobomok: A Tale of Early Times* (1824), by Sedgwick's friend Lydia Maria Francis Child, which imagined lasting intimacy between a European woman and a Native American man, based in part on the Pocahontas legend.[30] Ironically, Sedgwick had inspired the younger Francis to write. As she put it in a letter, she wanted nothing less than "to *think,* and *write,* and *be*" like Sedgwick.[31] Finally, Sedgwick had been moved by a chance meeting several years earlier on the Iroquois Confederacy's reservation in upstate New York with a descendant of Eunice Williams, the daughter of the Reverend John Williams of Deerfield, Massachusetts, taken captive in a raid in 1705. Eunice Williams had subsequently married a Native American and rejected all entreaties to return to the Christian fold.[32] The dramatic story had a long afterlife in nineteenth-century New England and served as the foundation of Sedgwick's plot.

Although in her preface Sedgwick humbly noted that she did not intend *Hope Leslie* "as a substitute for genuine history" but rather as a stimulus to her young countrymen "to investigate the early history of their native land," she steeped herself in seventeenth- and eighteenth-century sources (many of which had recently been reprinted). She read such indispensable works as Governor John Winthrop's journals, Roger Williams's *Key into the Language of America,* William Hubbard's *Narrative of the Indian Wars in New-England* and *A General History of New England,* and Cotton Mather's *Magnalia Christi Americana* and even less obvious but useful books like Nathaniel Ward's *The Simple Cobler of Aggawam in America.* But at some point she decided—and this was her true innovation—to tell history in part through the voices of those excluded from these narratives—that is, Puritan women and Native Americans. Although in *Hope Leslie* she once again valorized a particular kind of Christian behavior, her methods for doing so broke new ground.

Sedgwick set *Hope Leslie* in a frontier settlement on the Connecticut River—a thinly disguised Springfield, Massachusetts—in the early 1640s. William Fletcher has moved there from England with his wife and two sons, one an unnamed infant, the other named Everell. Hope and Faith Leslie, daughters of Alice Leslie, the Englishwoman whom Fletcher loved but whose parents forbade the match because of his radical religion, arrive in Boston. After her father's death, Alice decides to cast her lot with the Puritan settlement, only to perish on the sea voyage, but not before she names Fletcher the girls' guardian. After meeting them in Boston, Fletcher sends the younger of the two, Faith, on to Bethel, the name of his residence, and remains in Boston with Hope to attend to business. Traveling with Faith is Oneco, a Pequot Indian boy about her age whom Governor Winthrop gave to Fletcher as a ward after the child was captured in a brutal attack on the tribe, as well as Oneco's attractive fifteen-year-old sister, Magawisca. Oneco and Magawisca are the children of the Pequot leader Mononotto, who survived the massacre.

Mononotto has sworn revenge for the loss of his wife and most of his tribe and decides to attack Bethel during Fletcher's absence. In the ensuing battle the Pequots kill several whites, including Mrs. Fletcher and her younger child. The chief rescues his children and takes Everell Fletcher and Faith Leslie captive. As the Native American party retreats into the forest, Mr. Fletcher and Hope Leslie return from Boston to the terrible scene. Sedgwick reveals that during the course of Magawisca's stay with the Fletchers, she and Everell (about the same age) have had a special bond. When she realizes that her father intends to torture and kill her friend, she eloquently pleads for his life. But her father is unmoved, and as he swings his tomahawk downward to kill Everell, Magawisca leaps between him and it. The blow severs her arm, and in the chaos that follows, Everell escapes.

The action jumps ahead seven years. Faith is living among the Pequots and is married to Oneco, and Hope is in Boston. She has been forced to leave Bethel because she defended Nelema, an Indian powwow (medicine man), who used herbs and "magic" to cure a Bethel settler from the effects of a rattlesnake bite but was accused of witchcraft by Jennett, the Fletchers' bigoted housekeeper. Sedgwick also introduces new characters. With Everell on the ship on which he returns to New England is Sir Philip Gardiner, supposedly a recent convert to the Puritan creed but in fact still a Catholic, and his "page," Rosa, a young woman who is Gardiner's mistress and whom he has dressed like a man to avoid suspicion. Also new to the tale is Esther Downing, Governor Winthrop's niece, a pious Puritan sent across the Atlantic for health reasons, who quickly befriends

Hope Leslie. A convoluted love story ensues. Gardiner and Everell vie for Hope's attention, even as Esther pines for Everell's, and Esther believes that Everell loves *her*. At the same time, Faith's fate remains unresolved. Will she return to the Christian fold?

Endeavoring to bring Faith back to Puritan society, Hope succeeds in contacting Magawisca, and they plan a meeting between the sisters on a remote island in Boston Harbor. Gardiner, however, overhears their conversation and alerts the authorities, who, worried about rumors of an imminent Indian attack and believing that Magawisca has information about it, surreptitiously position themselves on the island to surprise the sisters. The meeting is traumatic for Hope. Faith, attired in full Native American garb, no longer speaks English and rejects Hope's attempts to get her to return to civilization. The Puritan authorities capture Magawisca and Faith, but not Hope, whom Oneco pulls into his canoe and flees the island. Eventually, Hope escapes, only to find herself among drunken sailors who know Gardiner. One of them, "Roslin" (that is, Rosa) tells Hope her sad tale and exposes Gardiner's embrace of Puritanism as self-serving pretense.

The penultimate scene takes place in court as Magawisca defends the Native American way of life in the face of Puritan expansionism. Everell's plea for clemency on the basis of her sacrifice for him falls on deaf ears, and Magawisca's eloquence only offends the court more; she is imprisoned. In the course of her testimony, however, she reveals Gardiner's hypocrisy and affair with Rosa, turning the magistrates against him. Everell and Hope again flout the authorities by freeing Magawisca from her cell. Sedgwick ends her tale by having Esther, who overhears Everell say that he loves Hope and not her, relinquish him so that he and Hope can marry, while Magawisca and Faith return to the forest, to remain forever apart from white, Christian society.

REVISING PURITAN HISTORY

With *Hope Leslie,* Sedgwick sought to recover a lost version of Puritan history and to address a range of contemporary questions. Whose version of the relations between Native Americans and whites is the reader to accept—Magawisca's or the Puritans'? What is the reader to make of Everell Fletcher's and Hope Leslie's various challenges to civil and religious authority, particularly in light of the fact that they, along with Magawisca, are the most appealing characters? What of the relationships between

Magawisca and Everell, and Oneco and Faith? Sedgwick leads the reader to think that the first two make a good match and that between the latter there is in fact an admirable love. Does she then counsel racial amalgamation?

Contemporary reviewers found Sedgwick's depiction of Native Americans much richer than Cooper's, or anyone else's, for that matter. Like her white characters, each Native American is a welter of contradictory emotions. This certainly is true of Magawisca, who bitterly condemns the settlers for decimating her tribe yet is capable of the selfless gesture that saved Everell. So, too, with her father, Mononotto. He is the fearless and violent leader of the remnant of his people, but he also genuinely loves Magawisca and Oneco.

To her credit, Sedgwick allows these characters to tell their own versions of history. Most memorable is Magawisca's recital, early in the story, of the history of the Pequot War. As seventeenth-century Puritan historians described them, the Pequots were scheming villains who had to be exterminated if the settlers were to make the surrounding countryside safe for settlement. But Magawisca stresses the unnecessary severity of the Puritan attack on the sleeping encampment. She describes the murder of old people, women, and children: "the piteous cries of the little children—the groans of our mothers, and oh! worse—worse than all—the silence of those who could not speak."[33] "You English tell us," she continues, "that the book of your law is better than that written in our hearts, for ye say it teaches mercy, compassion, forgiveness—if ye had such a law and believed it, would ye thus have treated a captive boy?," an allusion to the Puritans' beheading of sixteen-year-old Samoset, another of Mononotto's children.[34] Everell has heard stories of the war as long as he can remember, but now he realizes that "he had heard them in the language of the enemies and conquerors." From Magawisca's lips "they took a new form and hue."[35]

Even in 1827, almost two hundred years after the events she fictionalizes, Sedgwick was courageous to offer such an alternative history, for the United States was mired in problematic relations with the Native American nations at the time. As she was writing, there was increasing Seminole resistance to Florida's organization into a territory as well as the beginning of troubles over Cherokee lands in Georgia. But even as Sedgwick floats the radical notion of a positive, reciprocal relationship between whites and Native Americans, she, too, finally capitulates to the tenor of the age. At the end of her novel, Magawisca and the remnant of her people begin "a pilgrimage to the far western forests."[36] Rejecting Hope Leslie's plea for her to return and dwell with them, this fiercely proud woman replies that the "Indian and the white man can no more mingle, and become one, than day and night."[37] As progressive as it was, *Hope Leslie* thus contributed to the ever-growing nineteenth-century myth of the "vanishing Indian."

Readers also have to grapple with Everell's and Hope Leslie's challenges to authority, for they frequently are at odds with the colony's magistrates and, by extension, civil society. Here Sedgwick extended her vision of a less restrictive, more ecumenical religion. The book begins with the father of Mr. Fletcher's love, an avowed royalist, forbidding any marriage between his daughter Alice and Fletcher, already a committed Puritan. Everell inherits his father's contrarian nature—it took courage to leave behind family and friends and sail across the Atlantic—but ends up decrying the irrational and unfeeling precepts of Puritanism. Debating with Esther the injustice of Magawisca's imprisonment, Everell tells her that surely

> there must be warrant, as you call it, for sometimes resisting legitimate authority, or all our friends in England would not be at open war with their king. With such a precedent, I should think the sternest conscience would permit you to obey the generous impulses of nature, rather than to render this slavish obedience to the letter of the law.[38]

To Sedgwick's contemporaries, these "generous impulses of nature" were what animated a true Christian, which she sought to extend to Native Americans. Everell's complicity in the plot to free Magawisca from jail, an act for which he and Hope could be severely punished, shows the depth of his commitment to the power of individual conscience.

SEDGWICK'S LATER YEARS

Hope Leslie was popular in its time and had a lasting effect in early American literature.[39] A decade later, when the *North American Review* commented on the historian John Lothrop Motley's *Merry-Mount* (1849), a historical fiction of early New England about the reputed libertine Thomas Morton and his escapades among the Native Americans, it claimed that though many authors had attempted to use the region's early history for background, "the only successful novel" was "Miss Sedgwick's

'Hope Leslie.'"[40] Later, a writer of the introspective novels that defined the 1850s and 1860s, Donald Grant Mitchell (known as Ik Marvel), remembered that *Hope Leslie* "rallied" for Sedgwick "a great army of admirers," particularly because its "pictures of savage life" seemed "more truthful than those of Cooper['s]."[41]

Sedgwick did not rest on her laurels. In 1830 she published *Clarence*, in which she substituted contemporary New York, a city she knew well, for the New England countryside of *A New-England Tale* and *Redwood*. The novel relates the interwoven stories of three families—the Clarences, the Roscoes, and the Laytons—and focuses on the rise and fall of their fortunes in the country's largest and most commercial city. The Clarences are nouveaux riches. They inherit their wealth from a long-lost grandfather whose fortune failed to bring him happiness. The Roscoes begin the story with means but become saddled with debt after Mr. Roscoe dies, forcing them to change their lifestyle and to go to work alongside people they believe are beneath their station. The Laytons are the wealthiest, but because of Mr. Layton's compulsive gambling and his wife's profligacy, they, too, encounter trouble, but of a different kind. A stranger named Pedrillo forces Layton, caught cheating at cards, to give him his attractive daughter, Emilie, as payment for a debt.

The novel's heroine is Gertrude Clarence, a natural target for speculating single men. But unlike other characters, she questions the endless pursuit of wealth and the consumerism and instead tries to persuade the rich to use their money for good causes. *Clarence* thus takes up the debate over disinterested benevolence and civic republicanism that characterized religious and political debate. Sedgwick realized that wealth did not mean happiness, a contrarian view in 1830. The rich in her book languish in boredom, cynicism, or worse. Sedgwick was no Thoreau, bellowing against the economic system itself. Rather, she condemned those who value money excessively and mindlessly subscribe to the notion that goods make the man.

Clarence was unique for its setting. Several years before Cooper wrote the novel of manners *Home as Found* (1838), Sedgwick understood that the modern city represented new moral challenges that greatly affected family life, gender roles, and the individual's sense of worth. In the 1840s, New York, Philadelphia, Boston, and other cities grew by leaps and bounds with the arrival of immigrants from Germany, Ireland, and other European countries suffering various deprivations. These urban landscapes became the setting of a new genre of city fiction, in which American citizens and recent immigrants collided with an unforgiving, secular world that Sedgwick already had glimpsed.

But she chose not to follow the path of city fiction. After *Clarence*, Sedgwick wrote only one more important novel. In *The Linwoods; or, "Sixty Years Since" in America* (1835), she evoked the same era that Neal did in *Seventy-six*, that Cooper did in *The Spy*, and that even the quintessential city novelist George Lippard broached in his *Washington and His Generals* (1847): the period of the American Revolution. The novel relates the story of two families, the stalwart republican Lees of New England, and the Linwoods, a Tory family in New York City. After many melodramatic scenes and predictable cameo appearances by the likes of John Adams, John Hancock, the Marquis de Lafayette, and Tadeusz Kosciusko, Eliot Lee, a New England son and soldier stationed in New York, marries Isabella Linwood, heiress to the family fortune after her father disowns her brother for supporting the American cause. The message of the story is conveyed through that marriage: in the new United States, rank and privilege will matter less than true love and devotion to the new nation.

Inexplicably, after the success she experienced as a popular novelist, Sedgwick did not publish another lengthy fiction for almost two decades. Instead, and at the request of her friend the Reverend Henry Ware, Jr., she returned to penning religious tracts.[42] She first obliged Ware with *Home* (1835), which she dedicated to "Farmers and Mechanicks"—that is, to those who might still need to be enlightened about the virtues of liberal religion in a confusing, secular environment. *The Poor Rich Man and the Rich Poor Man* (1836), whose title was its moral, and then *Live and Let Live; or, Domestic Service Illustrated* (1837) both went through a score of more editions and proved to be her bestselling works. These were increasingly conservative, for as much as Sedgwick emphasized the social inequality so visible in New York, she suggested that disparities in wealth are best compensated for by patience and humility rather than by activism. The popularity of her late fictions suggests the reading public's approval of Sedgwick's evocation of an orderly, well-regulated world.

In 1857, Sedgwick returned to novel writing one more time with *Married or Single?* In the novel she addressed a topic with which she had wrestled all her life: whether a woman should remain single if she wished. But she raised more questions than she answered. In the book's preface, Sedgwick states her own, and for the time, radical, position. "[We] raise our voice with all our might against the miserable cant that matrimony is essential to the feebler sex—that a woman's single life must be useless and undignified—that she is but an adjunct of man—in her best estate merely a helm to guide the nobler vessel."[43]

Despite the title and Sedgwick's own feelings, though, most of the characters in her last novel do marry, for better and worse; she understood that in a culture in which marriage was considered normative, her choice of spinsterhood was still a rare exception. The prospect of marriage determined a young woman's behavior, severely restricting her (as it had Eliza Wharton). To Sedgwick, single women in the 1850s were not that different from those in the 1790s, even though progress had been made in the fight for access to education and to the public sphere of lecturing and writing. But the discourse of women's rights had moved far beyond what Sedgwick and many women were yet willing to sanction. For the great majority of her readers, the significant but difficult and tragic life of Margaret Fuller, before 1850 the country's most advanced feminist, was not as appealing as a heaven-made match like that of Everell Fletcher and Hope Leslie or, in *Married or Single?*, of Frank Esterly and Eleanor Herbert, two intelligent people who marry and thereafter treat each other with mutual respect. Such a "republican marriage," not of equals but of two respectable individuals from separate spheres, still trumped the single life.

COOPER V. SEDGWICK

One sign of Sedgwick's prominence was her appearance in 1834 in James Barton Longacre's *National Portrait Gallery of Distinguished Americans*, one of only four authors so privileged. Similarly, when John S. Hart published his elegant *The Female Prose Writers of America* in 1852, he placed Sedgwick at the head of the volume. He was most impressed by *Redwood* and *Hope Leslie*, not only because they had appeared when there was so little fiction of note by American women but also for their undeniable literary quality. Hart did not, however, mention the novels'— particularly *Hope Leslie*'s—role in centering women's influence in what hitherto had been male-centered historical narratives and in offering Native Americans an important place at the table.

After 1833 Cooper, sensing that he was losing his audience to writers like Sedgwick, began to behave like a bull in a china shop. He had trouble with his audience as early as 1825, with *Lionel Lincoln; or, The Leaguer of Boston*, set in the early months of the Revolution. To his surprise, this novel gained nowhere near the audience of *The Spy*. The next year he and his family sailed for an extended stay in Europe. He had better luck with his next two novels, building on the success of *The Pilot* with works of the sea, *The Red Rover* (1827) and *The Water-Witch* (1830), as well as with *The Prairie* (1827), the novel in which Natty Bumppo, an old man, dies on the prairie. In these same years Cooper also sought to capitalize on *Hope Leslie*'s success by publishing *The Wept of Wish-Ton-Wish* (1829), based, like Sedgwick's novel, on whites taken captive by Native Americans. But it was a disappointment.

In Europe, he took an odd turn and began to write stories set on the Continent, which were very different from anything he previously had done. These years saw *The Bravo* (1831), set in Venice and sharply critical of the oligarchy that controlled the city-state even as it put forth a face of republicanism; *The Heidenmauer* (1832), focused on the emergent class struggle unleashed by the Protestant Reformation in sixteenth-century Bavaria; and *The Headsman* (1833), a convoluted love story set in contemporary Switzerland, another novel dealing with the struggle between aristocrats and republicans and an allegory about the errant course of American democracy.

His American readership, however, wanted novels set in the New World, before or after the Revolution. But on his return in 1833 Cooper found America to be a very different country, not the least because of the reign of "King Andrew" Jackson, who had enlarged the franchise, promising every white male citizen, regardless of his social standing, education, economic status, or commitment to republican virtue, a slice of the American economic pie. Democrats filled governmental positions with the hoi polloi and looked down on wealthy landowners like Cooper; for his part, the author of novels like *The Spy* and *The Pilot*, in which he preached a now-outdated civic republicanism, had nothing but contempt for the new order.

Retreating to his boyhood home in Cooperstown, New York, the setting of *The Pioneers*, Cooper began to attack this new democratic element head-on in his fiction. In so doing, he alienated much of his audience. In *Homeward Bound* and *Home as Found*, both published in 1838, Cooper drew on his experience with settlers who had trespassed on his family land. The novels follow the aristocratic Effingham family, from their return from a stay in Europe—where they are pestered by the democrat Steadfast Dodge, a vulgar busybody whose main concern is his own profit—to their encounter with democrats on their home turf, including Aristabulus Bragg, the epitome of the self-centered, self-made man of this brave new world. Throughout, Cooper's sympathy lies with the Effinghams, whose tradition of civic engagement is now widely disparaged by those in pursuit of personal wealth.

By 1840 the terrain had shifted beneath Cooper, severely curtailing his relevance to both the place of the novel in American culture and his social views. His only triumph in these years was the magnificent *The Deerslayer* (1841), in which he dreamed of a time even before his childhood, the days when white men first saw the region around "Lake Glimmerglass," which bordered Judge William Cooper's town. William Cullen Bryant's encomium at a memorial dinner for the novelist in the winter of 1852 unintentionally relegated Cooper's work to the past. Cooper wrote "not for the fastidious, the overly refined, the morbidly delicate" but, rather, for "mankind at large—for men and women in the ordinary, healthful state of feeling."[44] The trouble was that as the century progressed, most readers had a different understanding of the "ordinary, healthful state of feeling." Sedgwick in her later works, her eye registering the urban environment and her heart attuned to the plight of such hitherto underrepresented groups as women and Native Americans, proved more ready to offer the next generation of novelists a way to negotiate an increasingly complex, impersonal, and often hostile world—Charles Dickens's world, not Sir Walter Scott's. Her novels' counsel of Christian patience and humility in the face of the impersonal enormity of the city and her willingness in her work to tell the stories of neglected kinds of characters were responses to a nation whose forms and combinations were changing at every moment.

A SOUTHERN COOPER

From the mid-1820s through 1840 Sedgwick and Cooper dominated American fiction. In 1835, however, another, similar voice, that of the Charleston, South Carolina, writer William Gilmore Simms (1806–1870), emerged. He broke onto the national scene that year with two novels, *The Yemassee*, set in pre-Revolutionary South Carolina, and *The Partisan*, the first in a string of novels about the Revolutionary War in the South. The prominent New York publisher Harper & Brothers and Philadelphia's Carey & Lea issued his works, and the New York firm of Wiley & Putnam considered him enough of a national figure to publish his essays

Views and Reviews in American Literature, History and Fiction (1845) in its new Library of American Books, alongside works by Poe, Melville, Margaret Fuller, and others. By the 1840s Simms was widely regarded as Cooper's southern counterpart.

One of his most original works, however, was his very first and little-noticed fiction, *Martin Faber: The Story of a Criminal*, published in 1833 and unlike anything Cooper ever conceived. Had Simms continued to work in this vein, his influence on American fiction might have been different, for in style and theme *Martin Faber* most resembles Edgar Allan Poe's work. Poe in fact mentioned it favorably when assessing Simms's career in 1846, maintaining that it indicated a genius "of no common order."[45] A novella, *Martin Faber* takes the form of a first-person criminal confession, a genre of nonfiction that had flourished in the colonies for a century and a half.[46] A gothic tale inspired, as Charles Brockden Brown's works had been, by William Godwin, the novel revolves around its eponymous main character's seduction of Emily Andrews and his murder of her when she becomes pregnant, an act perpetrated so that he might marry another and wealthier woman, Constance Claiborne.

Faber cannot shake the horror of his crime and impulsively confesses it to his closest friend, William Harding, begging him to keep it secret. Harding can't, and he reports Faber to the authorities. But Faber denies his involvement and is exonerated, prompting Harding, now obsessed by the matter, to try to piece together what really occurred. Through astute ratiocination that prefigures Poe, Harding determines the scene of the crime and, bringing Faber there in the presence of the court, dramatically unearths Emily's body, a brooch with Faber's initials still in her hands. Subsequently visited in jail by his betrayed and almost hysterical wife, Constance, Faber tries to stab her but fails. The tale ends with him awaiting the hangman's noose.

In his "Advertisement" to the book Simms explained that it was "an experiment," its design "purely moral." Martin, he explained, had been an overly indulged only child, and as he matured, he developed an ineradicable self-indulgence that led not only to his becoming an "idler" but also to his horrendous crimes. In the preface to a second edition of the work two years later, Simms was even more explicit about his intentions. "Martin Faber is not unnatural," he wrote; "you may see him daily," for he walks in London where "there are five thousand persons well disposed to defy the laws, and cut your throat, for a shilling . . . The mind of the reader is shocked with that man, in his true colors, as a monster, whom he not unfrequently shakes hands with, as a fellow-citizen, in the street."[47]

Simms was describing what Poe later called "The Man of the Crowd," a personality type he also examined in "William Wilson." Faber is in thrall to emotions that push him to horrific deeds but is able to disguise his mania. "I certainly did not intend violence," he explains to Harding as he describes Emily's murder.[48] After Faber is exonerated, Harding asks why he told him of the crime. Sounding like the narrator of Poe's "The Tell-Tale Heart" or "The Black Cat," Martin says that he simply "could not help it."[49] Simms's subject was the corrosive effects of the imp of the perverse that animated Charles Brockden Brown's Carwin. And while Simms did not set *Martin Faber* in the city, he in fact described the sense urban dwellers had that they simply could not "know" another person. In the early decades of the nineteenth century, the lack of moral guidance that resulted from the slackening of religious and civic authority, particularly in the nation's new urban spaces, led to the fear that Martin Fabers would become more common.

After *Martin Faber*, Simms turned to writing the historical romances for which he became best known. And with the growing sectional crisis, he was inextricably drawn to polemic, particularly after 1850, when he became an open apologist for the southern cause. As a consequence, he lost some of his northern readership. His late romances mattered little, for American fiction was headed in other directions. What the editors of *Arcturus*, a literary journal affiliated with the Young America writers in New York, said of Cooper in 1841 applies as well to his southern counterpart. After Scott's success, they observed, in the hands of Cooper, his American double, "the historical novel became a fashion." They added that "the production of a work of this kind" was now "as mechanical as the outpouring of moral commonplaces in an essay after the days of the *Spectator*."[50]

ROBERT MONTGOMERY BIRD AND METEMPSYCHOSIS

Simms's contemporary Robert Montgomery Bird resisted such commonplaces. Born in 1806 in New Castle, Delaware, Bird was raised by an uncle in that town, a center of learning and cultivation.[51] He benefited greatly from its Library Company as well as from the tutelage at New Castle Academy. At fourteen, he moved to Philadelphia to live with his mother, recently widowed again, and at seventeen entered Germantown Academy to prepare for college. He matriculated at the Pennsylvania

Medical School and College of Pharmacy at the University of Pennsylvania to prepare for a career as a physician. In 1827 he established a practice in the city, but just as Charles Brockden Brown had turned away from the practice of law, Bird soon devoted more time to belles lettres. He wrote poetry and short stories for *The Philadelphia Monthly Magazine*, and because the theater was thriving in Philadelphia, he turned his pen to drama.

His first big break came in 1830. Two years earlier the famous American actor Edwin Forrest had begun to offer cash prizes for the best plays written by Americans, and in the fall of 1829 Bird submitted *Pelopidas*, a play set in Thebes. Forrest liked it and awarded it a prize but never produced it because it had no role suitable for him. Bird went back to his desk and penned *The Gladiator*, set in ancient Rome, which had a character that fitted Forrest perfectly. The actor produced it in New York, Boston, and finally Philadelphia, where it garnered accolades and made Bird a literary lion. His fruitful association with Forrest continued for a few years but ended in 1834; by then Bird was wholly devoted to writing fiction.

The two works that merit attention are *Sheppard Lee* (1836) and *Nick of the Woods; or, the Jibbenainosay* (1837). The first, published anonymously, was Bird's most experimental novel and was not well received. *Sheppard Lee* is a sardonic, picaresque tale in which Bird sharply satirizes different social classes—from the wealthiest Philadelphian to the abject southern slave—in the nation's supposedly egalitarian society. Described thus, it sounds like an update of Brackenridge's *Modern Chivalry*, except for one thing: the book relies on the existence of metempsychosis (literally "change of the soul"), the belief that, after death, a soul can pass into another body, human, or animal.[52]

In *Sheppard Lee*, Bird uses metempsychosis to criticize the same America that Sedgwick pillories in *Clarence*, for *Sheppard Lee* is an illustration of how envy pushes an individual to assume different postures or social "selves" to improve his station.[53] The titular character has reasons to inhabit the various bodies he does, from self-preservation to material betterment, but is content in none of them until returning to his own corporality, he discovers who he truly is. With its counsel to accept one's given place in life, the novel is a morality tale as conservative as anything Sedgwick or Cooper wrote, but its premise and narration are unique. Its value lies in Bird's original take on personal identity to forward his cultural criticism.

At the novel's start, in a passage that recalls Benjamin Franklin's *Auto-biography*, Sheppard Lee describes his reason for writing about himself. "It sometimes happens," Lee observes, "that circumstances conspire to elevate the humblest person from obscurity, and to give the whole world an interest in his affairs."[54] Of course, Franklin's various social transformations came through hard work and minding the main chance, not through supernatural happenstance, as Lee's do; but the compulsion for the successful individual to tell his tale is quintessentially American.

Lee is the son of a prosperous New Jersey farmer who "gradually converted his whole estate into a market-farm, raising fine fruits and vegetables, and such other articles as are most in demand in a city [that is, Philadelphia]."[55] Although he is one of eleven children, Lee eventually inherits the property because over a short span of years, all his siblings save one sister die, some in grotesquely humorous ways that foreshadow the dark humor in Lee's various incarnations. One brother, for example, was "killed by attempting to ride a pig"; another brother, who saw the whole episode, "could not cease laughing at it" and "died of the fit within twenty-four hours."[56] But even though Lee is the survivor, he does not put his inheritance to good use, for by his own admission he lacks ambition and is "indifferent" to "the game of greatness which was playing around [him]."[57]

Lee tries to get money in any way but through honest labor. He buys lottery tickets but fails to win. He sinks all his cash in a "southern gold-mining company" but leaves the prospect with one-fifth of what he invested. He tries a dozen other get-quick-rich ventures, none of which is successful, and so finally decides to "turn politician" in the hope of being given some office that might afford him "a comfortable subsistence," a ploy that worked for many in the age of Jackson. Lee finds, however, that politics is "the maddest project" that ever possessed him, for it transforms him from "the easiest and calmest tempered man in the world" into "the most restless and discontented." And even in this game Lee loses, for a better-connected competitor gets the patronage position he seeks.[58]

As a last resort, Lee decides to hunt for buried treasure supposedly left by the pirate captain William Kidd in a swampy area along the Delaware River. Here the story takes a supernatural turn. Digging at midnight at a spot pointed out by his superstitious slave Jumble Jim, Lee seriously injures himself with his mattock and falls into a "trance." When he awakens, he feels "exceedingly light and buoyant, as if a load had been taken, not merely from [his] mind, but from [his] body."[59] When dogs and people he knows run from him, he realizes that he has died and become a ghost. Returning to the scene of his accident, Lee is shocked to find that his body is gone and presumes that he is doomed to a disembodied yet conscious existence.

Soon after, he stumbles across the corpse of Squire Higginson, a wealthy brewer who died while hunting when he tripped on a fence and hit his head. Lee then considers, "Why might I not, that is to say, my spirit" possess a "tenement which there remained no spirit to claim, and thus, unite interests together, as two feeble factions unite together in the political world to become a body possessing life, strength, and usefulness?" He also is prompted by envy of the luxurious life Higginson led. "How much better," Lee thinks, "it would be . . . to inhabit his body than my own!" The words are scarcely out of his mouth before he feels himself "vanishing, as it were, into the dead man's nostrils," and the next moment he *is* the squire.[60]

Six more miraculous transformations occur. When Lee's spirit inevitably gets into some scrape or finds itself disappointed in its current body and life, Lee wills himself into the next available corpse and revivifies that person. As Higginson, for example, he enjoys wealth and prestige but is acutely afflicted by gout and lorded over by a termagant wife. He escapes that fate to become Isaac Dulwer Dawkins, a dandy and rake whose body he takes up after Dawkins has drowned himself in an act of Romantic despair. But Lee finds that because Dawkins lived a lifestyle beyond his means, creditors constantly dun him. In order to escape promises to elope with two different women on the same night, Lee invigorates the body of the recently deceased Abram Skinner, "Old Goldfist," a miser, moneylender, stock jobber, and gambler so mean and despicable that Lee, despite enjoying the man's wealth, quickly yearns for another change.

He then enters the body of a loving Quaker philanthropist, Zachariah Longstraw, tragically murdered by a prisoner he sought to rehabilitate. Lee learns how ungrateful most recipients of charity really are and the darker truth that some who purport to be agents of philanthropy are in fact confidence men. Continuing his peregrinations, Lee is kidnapped by profit-seeking Yankees and shuttled below the Mason-Dixon Line to be sold to bigoted southerners as an abolitionist. To escape lynching, he has to enter the body of the slave Tom, who has a relatively kind master. When an inflammatory pamphlet urging slave rebellion falls into his hands and he shares its contents with his fellow slaves, Lee joins with them to plan a rebellion. They raid and burn a plantation and kill some of the inhabitants, for which Lee is hanged.

Although the reader assumes that Lee's resilient soul finally has met its end, a pseudoscientist who performs galvanic experiments—administering electric shocks to the body—resuscitates him. Lee then inhabits his final body, that of Arthur Megrim, a dissolute, bored Virginian, who, witnessing Tom's miraculous resurrection, promptly drops dead. At another quack performance, at which a German doctor displays a new method of mummification, Lee is surprised to see that the doctor has preserved his *own* body. He enters it and astounds the audience by arising and running off full tilt to his farm in New Jersey, where his prudent sister and brother-in-law have made the property profitable again. They tell him that despite his experiences, for the past two years he has been there, convalescing, in a trance from which he has only recently emerged. Lee does not believe it, of course, and relates his extraordinary adventures, which they then urge him to publish, even if it all has been a dream.

After experiencing everything from being a wealthy businessman to a slave, Sheppard Lee admits that now he is a "changed, I hope, a wiser man—disposed to make the best of the lot to which Heaven has assigned me, and to sigh no longer with envy at the supposed superior advantages of others."[61] Most of his contemporaries were convinced that more or different was better, but in *Sheppard Lee* Bird rejects the pabulum of social mobility on which the majority of his fellow citizens were raised.

The novel asks whether the self is fixed or malleable. If one dreams that he is someone else, how is that different from consciously wanting to become that person? Bird believes that heredity and environment are determinative. In his adventures, Sheppard Lee never relinquishes his own self-consciousness; he always knows who he is. But when he inhabits other people's bodies, he begins to *act* like them. This was a powerful warning to a nation built on the premise of perpetual self-transformation. Unlike the change that occurs in spiritual conversion, which involves a total renovation of consciousness, to become a different person by putting on masks for different occasions (particularly for social or economic gain) is a dangerous act. Bird suggests that a person is better off in the body—that is, in the social position—into which he is born.

This leads him to the problematic suggestion that the slave Tom should have remained such. When Lee (as Tom) meets his master on the plantation at Ridgewood Hill, he is surprised at how kind and caring he is. Realizing that slavery is not as bad as he thought, Lee "was contented with [his] servile condition" and "was so far from looking back with regret to [his] past life of freedom, that [he] ceased at last to remember it altogether."[62] When he reads the abolitionist tract urging masters to free their slaves because they are men and possess the rights of other Americans, he ends up leading an unsuccessful revolt and is hanged for it. Bird thus suggests that maintaining the status quo in the South (as well as in the North) is preferable to revolt. When Lee becomes Tom, for the first time he ceases to remember his previous states of existence. Not knowing what liberty is, he does not desire it. This is, Lee explains, perhaps because the "African" lives so much in the present or because his mind has "sunk beneath the ordinary level of human understanding, and [is] therefore incapable of realizing the evils of [his] condition."[63] Bird believed that to empower the black race was to invite disaster.

There are similarities between Tom and Washington Irving's Rip Van Winkle. Like Lee, Rip has an "aversion to all profitable labor" and would rather escape to the woods than tend his farm. After Rip wanders into the Catskills and falls asleep for twenty years, he returns to a community where even his dog and his children do not recognize him, for he has slept through the American Revolution. He cannot understand the changes that this event has brought and is confused by the "busy, bustling disputatious tone" in the populace, so different from the way that his townspeople lived before the war. When asked on what side he has voted, Rip hasn't a clue what participatory democracy means and declares himself "an honest subject of King George III."

Rip awakens in Sheppard Lee's individualistic world and cannot adjust to it. Instead, he becomes a "chronicle of the old times," a storyteller who recalls the way things were before the ascendance of liberal democracy, not a participant in or an advocate for it. Sheppard Lee does the same by writing his story. Bird's novel was a profound and innovatively expressed critique of its times, but unlike Sedgwick's work, it suggested that a traditional acceptance of one's lot in life was the best solution, not the kind of positive change promised by religious and political liberalism.

THE JIBBENAINOSAY
Sheppard Lee's inquiry into the nature of the self never drew wide public attention, but this was not the case with Bird's next work, *Nick of the*

Woods. Initial sales were weak owing to its publication during the country's first large-scale depression, the Panic of 1837, but the novel eventually became popular, his bestselling work. In *Nick of the Woods* Bird turned to Cooper's frontier, in this case Kentucky, and offered a tale that made *Sheppard Lee*'s considerable violence look tame by comparison. Part conventional love story, part captivity narrative, the novel is memorable for its portrayal of a backwoods trapper, Nathan Slaughter, a devout Quaker whose wife and children have been massacred by Indians but who professes an ethic of love and pacifism. But he is in fact a split personality. At nighttime Slaughter becomes the Jibbenainosay, Nick of the Woods, brutally slaughtering Indians and hacking the sign of the cross on their breasts.

As the story opens, Roland Forrester and his cousin Edith make their way through Kentucky's backcountry to start their lives together. Stopping at Bruce's Station, they meet Slaughter, regularly ridiculed for his pacifism. They also hear the legend of the Jibbenainosay, a creature that mercilessly kills and mutilates Indians. Traveling farther into the forest, the couple is warned that a band of natives intent on violence is nearby. The party does indeed come under attack and, after barricading themselves in a settler's deserted cabin, have to surrender to the Indian chief Wenonga, who carries them off to his camp.

Nathan Slaughter subsequently frees Roland, and joined by blustery Ralph Stackpole, a frontiersman based on the recently deceased Davy Crockett, the three set off to free Edith from Wenonga. They almost succeed, but instead, all three are captured. The Indians prepare to burn them at the stake, but fortuitously, the state cavalry rides in to rescue them. In the ensuing battle Nathan kills Wenonga, who was responsible, it turns out, for the massacre of his wife and children, and recovers his family's scalps. He also reveals that at times he, the peaceful Quaker, enters a trance that transforms him into the Jibbenainosay. After each violent foray against the local Indians, he is overwhelmed by guilt, and he reverts to the peaceful Quaker the community knows. At the novel's end, Nathan acknowledges that the Quaker ethic is an inadequate response to the frontier's violence and with his trusty dog, Peter, walks into the wilderness.

Rejecting the romanticized view of Native Americans found in most contemporary frontier novels, Bird also rejects stereotypes about good Christian settlers. Treachery is commonplace on both sides in *Nick of the*

Woods. Poor Nathan, unable to deal with this reality, succumbs to a mania that transforms him from devout Christian to avenging devil. Bird thus offers another version of what he presented in *Sheppard Lee*, a world in which people think they see a Higginson, a Longstraw, or a Tom but do not realize that inside every person is the soul of someone else, a Sheppard Lee. In *Nick of the Woods* the reader discovers the devil himself, vying with Christ for Nathan's allegiance.

Bird tried to depict the psychic toll westward expansion took on its participants but, with Nathan's renunciation of his pacifism and departure into the wilderness, transforms a very complex and tortured human being into just another frontiersman who prepares the way for the settlers, always a step ahead as he lights out for the territories. Nathan, tortured as he is, becomes the avatar of the progressive settlement of the land and of its consequence, the subjugation and forced removal of Native Americans, the most infamous example of which at the time was the forced removal of the Cherokee from Georgia and North Carolina to the Oklahoma Territory in 1838.

As with his treatment of slavery in *Sheppard Lee*, Bird seems incapable of imagining a viable alternative to the status quo. Among novelists of Cooper's generation, only Neal and Sedgwick provided viable alternatives to entrenched politics and religion, even as they were forced to cloak their radicalism in inherited genre conventions. In the next decade many more fiction writers were to challenge public opinion and traditional virtue in similar ways, even as others continued to follow the paths cleared by the likes of Cooper, Simms, and Bird. Their novels were undeniably popular, but the fiction of the more speculative novelists among their contemporaries proved more truthful as well as more useful to subsequent writers. In particular, novelists whose best work appeared in the 1840s more clearly delineated the racial and cultural fissures that had begun to rend American society. To embody these in fiction and to offer palliatives, however tentative, required more foresight and courage than any of their predecessors had yet displayed.

3 } Preparing the Ground

In the 1840s, new technologies transformed how books were published and sold.[1] Large urban firms like Harper & Brothers in New York, J. B. Lippincott and Company in Philadelphia, and Ticknor, Reed and Fields in Boston brought together under one roof almost every step in the bookmaking process, from copyediting manuscripts to printing, binding, and packing bound copies for delivery. Outside the cities, job printing remained viable, but presswork consisted primarily of locally circulated goods—sermons, almanacs, and other pamphlets, reprints of schoolbooks and religious tracts, and blank forms for legal and business purposes.

The big urban firms built steam-powered flatbed presses capable of producing more copies at a rate that, twenty years earlier, would have seemed impossible. The casting of stereotyped plates from hand-set type meant publishers did not have to wait for type to be reset and could reprint titles on demand. Once published, a title might stay in print for many years, and as firms changed hands, their assets now included the stereotyped books they had in storage. In negotiating their contracts, authors specifically wished to retain ownership of these plates if a firm failed or was sold.

Bookbinding became more mechanized, with hand-operated stabbing machines, rolling presses, and folding machines accelerating a once-laborious process. Cloth-covered boards, designed in-house for each book, became the preferred way to issue books, replacing the time-consuming and expensive leather or morocco bindings of an earlier era. A publisher might bind a title in several different styles, in everything from a simple cloth binding to one highly embossed and gilded, furthering the commodification of books. Railroads, steamboats, and private express companies meant new books would go on sale in Cincinnati, Buffalo, and Cleveland just a few days after they appeared in New York or Philadelphia.

Advertising, too, dramatically changed the book business. Large cities witnessed the first emergence of daily newspapers and the proliferation of weekly newspapers. Trade papers and literary journals carried extensive and detailed advertising sections, enabling customers to learn about titles much more rapidly. *Literary World, Putnam's Monthly Magazine,* and Horace Greeley's *New-York Tribune,* which featured Margaret Fuller and then her fellow Transcendentalist George Ripley as reviewers, became important to how books were noticed and received. *The Knickerbocker Review,* the *Democratic Review, Arcturus,* and other new journals published new literature and book reviews, taking it upon themselves to foster their own notions of a native literary culture.

New print technologies and the rising cultural nationalism came together in a project undertaken by Wiley & Putnam called the Library of American Books. In 1845 Wiley charged one of his editors, Evert Duyckinck, who had helped found *Arcturus,* with developing two new series at the firm: the Library of Choice Reading, a series of European classics in affordable standard bindings, and the Library of American Books, a series of new books, not reissues of Cooper, Irving, or Bryant.[2] Wiley wanted the series to be easily identifiable by its inexpensive binding; paper covers were the rule. The firm decided to treat authors well, paying a sum up front and then guaranteeing a 10 percent royalty after the edition broke even and allowing them to keep the copyright.

In his new role Duyckinck first signed Nathaniel Hawthorne, whose wife was Wiley's first cousin. Hawthorne served the series in a variety of capacities: as editor of its first volume, his friend Horatio Bridge's *Journal of an African Cruiser* (1845); as a contributor, with his collection of stories, the two-volume *Mosses from an Old Manse* (1846); as a sympathetic book reviewer of the library's titles; and as an aide in signing other New England writers.[3]

Hawthorne took this last task seriously, though did not always meet with success. Through him Duyckinck chased Emerson's increasingly popular and significant work. Although Duyckinck very much wanted to secure *Representative Men,* the best he could do was to offer to publish a volume of Emerson's poetry. Negotiations on this project stalled, however, when Emerson realized that the terms of his contract with his Boston publisher were more lucrative. Nor did the Library of American

Books carry any of Henry David Thoreau's works, in part because early in the series' history, Hawthorne had warned Duyckinck of Thoreau's "unmalleable disposition." He was a "most tedious, tiresome, and intolerable" fellow, Hawthorne wrote of his friend, and the only way "he could ever approach the popular mind would be by writing a book of simple observation of nature."[4] In 1848 Thoreau sent him the manuscript of *A Week on the Concord and Merrimack Rivers*, but when Duyckinck offered to publish it only if the author assumed the financial risk, Thoreau took it elsewhere.

Still, the series included a notable collection of essays: the former Concord resident Margaret Fuller's two-volume *Papers on Literature and Art* (1846), William Gilmore Simms's *Views and Reviews in American Literature, History and Fiction* (1845), and John Greenleaf Whittier's *Supernaturalism in New England* (1847). In poetry, Duyckinck famously secured Poe's *The Raven, and Other Poems* (1845). He also published some important, if not pathbreaking, fiction, particularly short stories and tales. In addition to Hawthorne's *Mosses* he brought out Caroline Kirkland's *Western Clearings* (1845), based on her experiences in Michigan; Ohioan James Hall's *The Wilderness and the Warpath* (1846); Simms's *The Wigwam and the Cabin* (1845); and Poe's *Tales* (1845). There were only two lengthier fictions: Cornelius Mathews's *Big Abel and Little Manhattan* (1845), and Duyckinck's most important discovery, *Typee; or, A Peep at Polynesian Life* (1846), young Herman Melville's first book.

Despite the high quality of its publications, the Library of American Books was not lucrative enough for Wiley & Putnam to extend it beyond 1847. But it had served its purpose, securing for its publisher some of the best native literary talents awaiting recognition and publication. Soon after it folded, the Boston house of Ticknor, Reed and Fields (in 1854, Ticknor and Fields) began to assemble its own shelf of authors, primarily New Englanders, whom it considered the best of the day. Its easily recognizable books, sewn in characteristic drab brown cloth bindings stamped in gilt, soon circulated throughout the country. It eventually counted among its authors Emerson, Hawthorne, Thoreau, Oliver Wendell Holmes, Whittier, and James Russell Lowell.

NEW YORK'S CULTURE WARS

In the 1840s, with the publishing industry and the nation's literary culture becoming ever more centralized, writers of any ambition had to find their way to Boston, Philadelphia, or New York.[5] New York was the mecca. It had not only the largest firms but also many important journals that reviewed new fiction, poetry, and essays. The journals were the product of literary coteries of like-minded men and women who banded together around certain political and cultural ideas.[6] In the Boston area, this famously occurred among the intellectuals known as the Transcendentalists. Composed as it was of clergy, reformers, editors, writers, lecturers, and others who first propounded their ideas in the Unitarian *Christian Examiner*, this loosely knit group, in the late 1830s, saw a need for a public mouthpiece. Members soon started their own journals, including *The Western Messenger*, *The Dial*, and *The Boston Quarterly Review*. Transcendentalists espoused specific views of religion and philosophy that spilled over into social activism and, to a lesser extent, literature.

In Manhattan, similar groups were determined foremost by politics, their members supporting either Andrew Jackson and Martin Van Buren's Democratic Party or the newly emergent Whig Party.[7] In the 1840s two of the most prominent of these groups gathered around *The Knickerbocker: or, New-York Monthly Magazine*, the chief organ of the conservative Whigs; and the *United States Magazine and Democratic Review* and *Arcturus*, both Democratic publications. Editors of these journals exercised an inordinate amount of influence on the reception of new literary works; they decided which books to review and frequently selected the reviewers. The resulting tangled web of reciprocal obligation and perceived slights made New York's entire literary world cruel and forbidding, particularly for outsiders.

The Knickerbocker was founded in 1833 by Samuel Langtree, a New York physician with a literary bent, but a year later Lewis Gaylord Clark and his twin brother, William, purchased it. *The Knickerbocker* became Lewis's obsession, and he ran it until its demise on the eve of the Civil War. A native of central New York State, he was one of the city's first bona fide intellectuals, frequently attending theatrical and musical performances and lectures, dining out with authors and artists, and maintaining a literary salon at his home at 139 Nassau Street. Winningly handsome, with a high brow, slim nose, and well-groomed curly hair, he was "vain, feline, vindictive." Bon vivant and boon companion, he could cruelly turn on anyone who doubted his literary judgment or the worth of his journal.[8]

In his desire to make *The Knickerbocker* a truly American journal, Clark eschewed reprints of English authors, the lifeblood of other American periodicals, and beat the bushes to find writers who represented his notion of national literature. Washington Irving was an early contributor, and Clark discovered Henry Wadsworth Longfellow; he was the first to print such popular poems as "The Village Blacksmith" and "Psalms." A superb judge of literary talent, he also secured some of Nathaniel Hawthorne's early stories, including "The Fountain of Youth" (later renamed "Dr. Heidegger's Experiment"), and in 1847 serialized the young Harvard graduate Francis Parkman's account of his journey west, *The Oregon Trail.* He published poems by Bryant, Oliver Wendell Holmes, and Whittier and fiction by Cooper. Such was *The Knickerbocker*'s quality that other journals frequently reprinted pieces from its pages.

Clark's writers, with the exception of Hawthorne, consisted almost to a man (there were few women in the journal's earliest years) of Whigs and High Church Episcopalians. In thrall to Cooper, Bryant, and Irving, writers for *The Knickerbocker* admired English writers like Scott and Wordsworth and deplored German philosophy and what they viewed as the immoral literature of Germany and France, particularly the urban realism of Eugène Sue and Honoré de Balzac and the brave new world of George Sand. This put *The Knickerbocker* circle at odds with Boston's avant-garde, for Emerson, Margaret Fuller, and their cohort embraced precisely these authors and ideas, particularly the German ones. Clark excused New Englanders like Longfellow, Holmes, and Whittier, whom he was proud to publish before their more radical inclinations—Whittier was an abolitionist—became widely known.

The Knickerbocker was also at odds with New York's Democratic intellectuals, who celebrated the common man, first in the *United States Magazine and Democratic Review* and, later, in the more explicitly literary *Arcturus*, which in the 1830s and 1840s challenged *The Knickerbocker* for intellectual supremacy in the city. The first and longer-lasting journal was the brainchild of the remarkable John L. O'Sullivan. Born on a British warship near Gibraltar—his parents were traveling around the still-dangerous Barbary Coast during the War of 1812—O'Sullivan began at Columbia College in New York when he was only fourteen and graduated in 1831. Because of his need for funds (his impecunious upbringing no doubt contributed to his political sympathies), O'Sullivan taught at the Columbia Grammar School, where he might have encountered a student named Herman Melville. O'Sullivan passed the bar but was much more interested in the city's rapidly evolving world of print.

His family's fortunes improved after his mother successfully sued the U.S. government for a claim of more than twenty thousand dollars owed her because of improper seizure in 1823 of the cargo from a ship her husband owned. The windfall enabled O'Sullivan to realize his dream of starting a national journal of politics and culture, a project that he began in Washington, D.C., in 1837. Like other northern Democrats, he believed in "a populistic vision of citizens pulling together, sharing responsibility, and refusing the special privileges attached to extreme individualism."[9] Branding themselves supporters of the extension of freedom in Europe, Texas independence, and the cause of labor, those who gathered around the journal in its early years positioned themselves against selfishness, individualism, and commercialism—against, in short, what they viewed as Whig ideology.[10]

O'Sullivan outlined his expansive cultural vision—he later coined the term "Manifest Destiny"—in his prospectus for the journal. "The vital principle of an American national literature," he wrote, "must be democracy." The problem was that the American mind was enslaved to English literature. "We have a principle, an informing soul—our own, our democracy, though we allow it to languish uncultivated." This had to become the "animating spirit" of a national American literature.[11]

Such an empowering vision had not yet been offered the American writer, and to a remarkable degree O'Sullivan succeeded in attracting talent to the *Democratic Review*'s pages. He encouraged submissions about the city, the plight of the incarcerated, and the westward expansion of democracy. Hawthorne's democratic sympathies found a permanent home under O'Sullivan's tent, as did some early works of a young Brooklyn journalist-cum-poet named Walter Whitman. O'Sullivan also secured work from Catharine Sedgwick, who since the mid-1830s had moved in the Democratic direction. Bryant, another Democrat, was a regular contributor, though he never approached O'Sullivan's radicalism. Whittier, whose "Songs of Labor" fitted the editor's interests, also became a regular. Even Henry Thoreau sold O'Sullivan two pieces, including a review of the utopian J. A. Etzler's *Paradise Within the Reach of All Men, Without Labor, by Powers of Nature and Machinery* (1833). Not surprisingly, the *Democratic Review*'s pages also carried Continental news and literature and welcomed writers like Honoré de Balzac, Eugène Sue, George Sand, Pierre-Jean de Béranger, and others whom *The Knickerbocker* avoided but who represented brave attempts to represent social reality—and the inevitable triumph of liberal democracy—with the kind of honesty O'Sullivan thought too often lacking in the American strand.

YOUNG AMERICA

In the late 1830s some members of O'Sullivan's coterie started a new journal, *Arcturus*, which in its three years of existence greatly enlivened the city's literary scene. Associated with a loosely organized group called Young America, its backers forwarded O'Sullivan's literary goals but cared less for politics. Among *Arcturus*'s prime movers was Evert Duyckinck, son of a successful bookseller and publisher. Duyckinck graduated from Columbia in 1835 and was admitted to the bar two years later. But instead of establishing a practice, he chose to make a grand tour of Europe, pursuing his love of art and literature, learning German, becoming particularly taken with Herder's and Goethe's works.

A fair-haired and blue-eyed Knickerbocker, Duyckinck was much more at ease in the modern city than most in Clark's group. His tastes were idiosyncratic; he held in high regard the French urban realists whom the Whigs despised, and he had no use for writers like Irving, Cooper, and James Kirke Paulding. He wanted to publish someone "original." His younger brother, George, shared his proclivities and later joined Evert in his various literary enterprises.

The other important presence behind *Arcturus* was Cornelius Mathews, whose energy and irreverence recalled John Neal. Born in Westchester County, just north of New York City, he moved to Manhattan as a child and remained there for the rest of his life. He was rotund, wore steel-rimmed glasses, and constantly bounced when he talked. His ego was immense; he considered himself the greatest writer America had yet produced and was not shy about saying it. He published a few pieces in *The Knickerbocker* but, realizing his political sympathies lay elsewhere, soon broke away, collecting some of his early stories and other work in *The Motley Book* (1838). *The Knickerbocker* promptly panned it; Clark was miffed that Mathews had left his group. Although many subsequent literary historians have pilloried Mathews, Perry Miller took his proper measure more than a half century ago. Mathews, he wrote, "was almost the only man outside New England who gave serious thought to the problem of the new directions in which an American artist might develop, who sought for vistas untenanted by Irving, Bryant, and Cooper."[12]

The first issue of *Arcturus* appeared late in 1840. Both Duyckinck and Mathews contributed regularly to its subsequent issues, their work joining that of Hawthorne, Lowell, and Longfellow, among others who previously had published with Clark. In a monthly editorial titled "The City Article," the editors addressed topics of interest and concern to New Yorkers. They avoided the gossip popular in an age of literary celebrity that readers could find in *The Knickerbocker*, and in the *New-York Mirror*, whose editor, Nathaniel Parker Willis, shamelessly fed an insatiable public interest in the lives of the elite.[13]

Through these years Mathews continued to publish his own work. In the narrative poem *Wakondah: The Master of Life* (1841), he wrote about Native Americans, but without critical success. Next came *The Career of Puffer Hopkins* (1842), a novel about the corrupt politics of contemporary New York that, though not popular, represents an important early attempt to capture the unique features of the city. In an address to New York University alumni, Mathews described his ideal of the kind of fiction that could represent the new urban environment. "In the mighty metropolis a man's nature is fed and excited by a thousand sources"; therefore, "[w]e will take our position in the thoroughfare and catch, with a pleased eye, the strange humors, the cunning dealing and actions of common men."[14] In *Puffer Hopkins* he did just that; it was the first American novel to examine the local ward politicians of New York as they oiled their patronage machine, the dupes who worked for them, and a whole American system, from the city slums to the highest reaches of the government, that reeked of corruption and was poisoning American democracy.

Mathews's muckraking continued in his ambitious tale *Big Abel and Little Manhattan* (1845), a story of contemporary New York and two offspring of its earliest inhabitants, Dutch (Big Abel) and Native American (Little Manhattan). Abel Henry Hudson and Lankey Fogle are the last descendants of the first people to live on the island who, fallen on hard times, go to court to try to reclaim their patrimony. Wrongly convinced that they have won their suit, they walk around Manhattan deciding who will keep which parts of the burgeoning city. Through them, Mathews contrasts a rapidly vanishing past filled with heroic men and women of strong moral values with the "busy, bustling, disputatious" society that, by the 1840s, was ascendant.

As proud as he was of New York's centrality, he knew the city well enough to understand that it typified what was wrong in the United States—in particular, how the current generation, in its mad dash for wealth, betrayed the promise of 1776. In "Crime in the Metropolis," a "City Article" in *Arcturus*, after commenting on the city's grandeur, he observed that New York fostered immorality and crime. "Yonder are temptations to vice; the gaudy courtesan invites to the chamber of the grave; the midnight haunt of pleasure is gathering a company for the house of mourning; there the unbridled desire for wealth is reaming in the brain, and dreams of Potosi or El Dorado, of golden anticipation, turn the mind earthward." In New York, as in every great city, the "lust of the eye, the lust of the flesh, and the pride of life are flourishing rankly in citizens' hearts."[15] Singing the city in this key, Mathews hoped to represent a more authentic American experience, and to thereby draw attention to the young nation's failings.

AN AMERICAN MONK LEWIS

Mathews recognized that the rapidly growing cities of the 1830s and '40s were profoundly impersonal but did not truly address the despair of its inhabitants. The first novelist to do so was Philadelphia's George Lippard. Lippard's life was so remarkable that he seems to have stepped out of one of his many novels.[16] He was born in 1822 on a farm in Chester County, about forty miles from Philadelphia, the fourth of six children. After his father suffered a debilitating injury that made him unfit for manual labor, he moved the family to Germantown, to live with George's grandfather and aunts. In 1825 George's parents, unable to care for their family, left him and his siblings with their relatives and moved to Philadelphia. In the interim, Lippard's grandfather's fortunes declined, and he had to sell off much of his valuable land to pay debts. When he died, the aunts sold the remainder of the family land and moved with young George to Philadelphia.

After his mother's death in 1831, his father remarried, but the boy remained with his relatives, a decision that later cost him his inheritance. He toyed with becoming a Methodist minister, and a benefactress offered to pay for him to go to an academy in New York where he could prepare for Middletown College (later Wesleyan University). But George did not like the school's regimen and returned to Philadelphia. He was present at his father's death in the dark year of 1837, soon after learning that his parent had denied him any portion of the two thousand dollars he left behind.

As a child Lippard was physically weak and introverted.[17] While in Germantown, he had found solace in fishing and hunting along the Wissahickon Creek, the emotive preaching of Methodist circuit riders, and books. After his abortive schooling for the ministry, he studied law and from 1839 to 1844 worked as a legal assistant to well-known Philadelphia attorneys, a period punctuated by three violent riots that highlighted the city's social problems: in 1838 an antiabolition and antiamalgamation mob burned Pennsylvania Hall, dedicated three days earlier as a venue for the promulgation of social justice; four years later whites viciously attacked a black temperance parade; and two years after that, there was a nativist riot against immigrant Catholics.[18] These and other events left a deep imprint on Lippard, and within a year after the last, he left the law to begin his first novel, *The Ladye Annabel* (1844).

Fortuitously, while he was struggling to write the book, Lippard met the editor of a penny newspaper, *The Spirit of the Times*, who hired him as a cub reporter. Soon he was reporting on crime (a staple of such papers) and writing daily columns and news stories. His political sympathies are already evident in some of this work: he wrote about trials of corrupt politicians; preachers caught in acts of infidelity; and, in one particular instance, his outrage at the acquittal of Nicholas Biddle, head of the Bank of the United States, on a conspiracy charge. Given the poverty and distress he had known as a child, and the bank closings, unemployment, strikes, and starvation that occurred in Philadelphia during his late adolescence and young adulthood, Lippard empathized with the poor and forgotten. He was a fervent Jacksonian Democrat and viewed the moneyed classes as parasites pulling the nation from its true destiny.

He left *The Spirit of the Times* in 1842, published a few stories and longer serialized fiction in other periodicals, and in 1843, only twenty-one, became the principal writer for the weekly *Citizen Soldier*, contributing both trenchant book reviews—he showed no mercy to pretentious Whig writers and publishers—and compelling tales, including a serialized version of his first novel. His spirit was buoyed when, after he sent *Ladye Annabel* to his friend Edgar Allan Poe for his opinion of it—Poe was working across the street from *The Citizen Soldier*'s offices at the Whig-edited *Graham's Magazine*—Poe replied that he found it "richly inventive and imaginative—indicative of *genius* in the author."[19]

In 1844, Lippard left *The Citizen Soldier* and plunged headlong into reformist activities in the city. He also wrote his best-known novel, *The Quaker City; or, The Monks of Monk Hall: A Romance of Philadelphia Life, Mystery, and Crime*, a macabre satire of the city's upper classes. It elicited criticism and praise in equal measure and sold a phenomenal sixty thousand copies in its first year of publication and ten thousand copies in each year of the following decade, becoming the most popular American novel before Susan Warner's *The Wide, Wide World* (1850) and spawning a host of imitations, domestic and foreign.

Lippard next wrote about the American Revolution, specifically the contrast between the heroism of the commanders of American forces and the self-serving public officials who assumed power once independence was secured. The result was *Blanche of Brandywine* (1846), followed the next year by three more novels: *Washington and His Generals, The Rose of Wissahikon*, and *Legends of Mexico*, which celebrated Gen. Zachary Taylor's recent and successful incursions into Mexico. Lippard also began *The Nazarene*, a sequel to *The Quaker City*, but issued only five of its projected twenty-four installments. In 1848 came *'Bel of Prairie Eden*, set in the American West, and *Paul Ardenheim*, a weird fantasy involving a Revolutionary War setting and medieval alchemists and monks. These astonishingly productive years made him Philadelphia's best-known writer.

Lippard's frenetic pace only increased. In 1849 he published five serialized novels. Toward the end of the year, at the age of twenty-seven, Lippard turned to activism. He founded a reformist journal called the *Quaker City Weekly*, which lasted for two years and reached a circulation of fifteen thousand, and a remarkable organization called the Brotherhood of the Union. This was a semisecret society whose goal was to "espouse the cause of the Masses, and battle against the tyrants of the Social System; —against corrupt Bankers, against Land Monopolists and against all Monied Oppressors." If labor could not attain its goals through normal political means, Lippard wrote, he advised it "to go to War, in any and all forms—War with Rifle, Sword and Knife."[20] He announced the organization's founding in his periodical and soon received requests to start chapters all over the country.[21] The Brotherhood of the Union welcomed all laborers, men and women, regardless of occupation. Lippard named the chief officers of each local chapter after prominent Americans, in descending order of rank, "Washington," "Jefferson," "Franklin,"

"Wayne," "Fulton," and "Girard"; Lippard was elected "Supreme Washington" of the national organization for life.[22]

Over the next few years, Lippard organized the Industrial Union, a cooperative store for seamstresses, who toiled through twelve-hour days at pitifully low wages; worked with the radical Daughters and Sons of Toil, advocates of rights for women, African Americans, and Native Americans, to establish a cooperative of carpetmakers; and supported a German workingmen's league with utopian goals. Lippard's example inspired his fellow Philadelphian Uriah S. Stephens's founding, in 1867, of the Knights of Labor, one of the earliest national labor groups.[23]

In 1851 Lippard's young wife, Rose, died of consumption, prompting him to attempt suicide at Niagara Falls; a friend saved him. He also lost his two young children to disease. Finding himself again in debt, he continued to write novels but never recovered his previous readership. He died early in 1854 of consumption at the age of thirty-one. His funeral, widely reported, was memorable. The Brotherhood of the Union, the Odd Fellows, and the Freemasons led the procession to the city's Odd Fellows Cemetery, accompanied by hundreds of laborers, many of whom were German Americans. Encomiums filled the regional papers. The Transcendentalist Theodore Parker, whose writings on social issues Lippard much admired, may have provided the most probing judgment: Lippard, Parker observed, "[did] not seem at peace with himself or the world."[24] The popularity of Lippard's works suggests that many Americans felt similarly.

MONK HALL

Lippard dedicated the bound edition of *The Quaker City* to "the Memory of Charles Brockden Brown." In 1848, in the periodical *The Nineteenth-Century*, Lippard's friend Charles Chauncey Burr explained that Lippard was attracted to Brown because the latter's novels "were extraordinary creations of the kind, lifting a man beyond himself, anatomizing his very soul, laying bare the secret springs of human action, with as much power and truthfulness as though the author were some invisible spirit, who looked calmly from his superior existence upon the loves and hates of poor mortality."[25]

This describes Lippard's work as much as Brown's. With religious authority diminished and individualism ascendant, readers were beginning to look to novelists for the kind of guidance that in the past they found only in Scripture, and guidance was exactly what Lippard offered, though in titillating dress. "The great object of literature," he wrote in his weekly journal, is "the social, mental, and spiritual elevation of Man . . . When [literature] works without a direct regard for these objects it is either making ropes of sand or playing in a gunpowder magazine with a torch in his [sic] hand. It is silly or it is wicked."[26] Morally impassioned, socially concerned, and, like Brown, interested in probing the motivations for the darkest human actions, Lippard was in many ways as much novelist as preacher.

Lippard's immediate inspiration for *The Quaker City* was a famous trial in Philadelphia in 1843. Singleton Mercer, an upstanding Philadelphian, was charged with murdering another wealthy citizen, Mahlon Heberton, who had lured Mercer's younger sister Sarah to a house of prostitution and seduced her after promising to marry her. A few days later Singleton shot Heberton as he tried to leave the city on a New Jersey–bound ferry. Lippard combined this story with other sordid contemporary tales about the vices of Philadelphia's wealthier and respected citizens (he had a special animus against hypocritical clergy) to write a nightmarish novel based around Monk Hall, a large multistory edifice in the city where supposedly pious and upright citizens met to carry on nightlong orgies. The idea for Monk Hall probably came from exclusive gentlemen's clubs, like the Philadelphia Club and, in New York, The Century Club, that recently had appeared in large cities as private social spaces for the wealthy.

The sinful actions of the large cast of Monk Hall regulars include seduction, rape, incest, cannibalism, murder, counterfeiting, robbery, drunkenness, opium use—all indulged in by Philadelphia's finest and described in graphic terms. Albert Livingstone, a regular visitor at the hall, finds his social-climbing wife, Dora, asleep naked on a divan with her lover, a man masquerading as an English lord. The Reverend F.A.T. Pyne drugs and tries to rape a young woman named Mabel, whom he has raised as a daughter. The reader learns that she is the illegitimate child of Devil Bug, a feral African American who is the chief pimp at Monk Hall.

Lippard's re-creation of the Heberton-Mercer affair is the heart of the novel. Gustavus (Gus) Lorrimer is his Heberton. He brags to Byrnewood Arlington (Mercer) that he can seduce a particular young woman; neither realizes that the woman is Byrnewood's sister Mary. She is infatuated with Lorrimer and wants to stay with him even after she learns his true intentions. Lippard also takes liberties with Lorrimer's death scene, having Byrnewood not just shoot him but drink the villain's blood and dance on his corpse.

Mary's love for Gus is serious but misguided. Her "fluttering fascination" is nothing more than "the blind admiration of the moth, as it floats into the flame, which will at last consume it." For Mary does not understand "that in her own organization were hidden the sympathies of an animal as well as of an intellectual nature, that the blood in her veins only waited an opportunity to betray her." Let a man like Gus play with that animal nature, "let him rouse the treacherous blood, let him fan the pulse into quick, feverish throbbings, let him warm the heart with convulsive beatings, and the woman becomes like himself, but a mere animal."[27] That women might desire sex as much as men excited and shocked readers, as it had when John Neal broached the possibility in the 1820s.

Lippard's larger purpose recalls that of his hero Charles Brockden Brown fifty years earlier. He sought to make people aware of the complexity of their emotional lives, how far they are from the rational beings they presume themselves to be. He exposes the irrational core in every person and shows that liberty and individualism lead to immorality and sin as much as they do to happiness. If people are in thrall to powerful, subliminal forces beyond their control, the very foundations of American life begin to tremble. Absent the strong political or religious authority to govern society and morality, uncertainty, ambivalence, and even chaos ensue, as in contemporary Philadelphia.

There is in *The Quaker City*, too, a significant backlash against popular domestic fiction, of which Sedgwick was the preeminent practitioner. Lippard overturns virtually every one of the conventions of the genre. Like domestic fiction, for example, *The Quaker City* is about a home, but the home is the horrific Monk Hall, and about family, but about its perversion, primarily the seduction of daughters. It describes young women who become unwed mothers and have to raise children alone or abandon them, as well as older maternal women, like Devil Bug's assistants, Mother Nancy and Long-haired Bess, who initiate girls into the wiles of prostitution after promising to take them "home."

In one scene, as Devil Bug is about to enter the hall's basement, filled with the bodies of people murdered there, Lippard sounds off against genteel writers unable to stomach the real stuff of modern American city life.

Shallow-pated critic with your smooth face whose syllabub insipidity is well-relieved by wiry curls of flaxen hair, soft maker of verses so utterly blank that a single original idea never mars their consistent nothingness, penner of paragraphs so daintily perfumed with quaint phrases and stilted nonsense, we do not want you here . . . We like to look at nature and at the world, not only as they appear, but as they are.

When a genteel writer dies, he continues sarcastically, his monument will be of "gingerbread," and the motto, "Here lies the Poet of Twaddledom, whose whole life was characterized by a pervading vein of Lollypopitude."[28]

Lippard also had a vivid sense, as Henry David Thoreau was to express it a decade later, that with the rise of industry men had become mere tools. In an essay in his weekly, Lippard imagines a colloquy with the sort of capitalist who takes his pleasure in Monk Hall. "Do you notice the unnatural position in which [the workers] are forced to work," Lippard asks, "the breast bent, the stomach cramped—no chance for a free breath, no chance for one stretch of muscle—there they sit twelve hours per day . . . How long do you think the *human machinery* will last at this rate?" "O, they must get rich and employ others to work for them," Lippard's capitalist straw man answers. "That is, they who are trampled today," Lippard sneers, "must turn tramplers [*sic*] themselves tomorrow. Such is your [the factory owner's] philosophy and the philosophy of the world."[29]

While most Americans lauded the growth of the steam-powered factory system, Lippard saw and condemned industrialization's dehumanizing aspects. With regard to the railroad, which transformed notions of time and distance, Lippard again presaged Thoreau. "Look at it [the railroad train], as it thunders on! What a magnificent impersonation of power; of brute force chained by the mind of man! . . . All true, but woe, woe to the weak or helpless who linger on its iron track! And woe to the weak, the crippled, or the poor whom the locomotive of modern civilization finds lingering *in its* way. Why should it care? Its work is to move onward and to cut down all whom poverty and misfortune have left in its path."[30]

Lippard's animus extended to groups like the American Tract Society, the American Sunday School Union, and other such quasi-religious organizations that sponsored Sarah Savage, Catharine Sedgwick, and other writers. A devout believer in a religion of humanity with Christ at its center, Lippard viewed such benevolent societies as further manifestations of corrupt capitalism. Reading one of their annual reports, he was reminded that "[a] Sunday School composed of children who are taught the plain principles of Christ by a single-minded teacher is one thing," but "a Sunday School Union with its imposing display of Managers, its complacent Annual Report, its immense concentration of Power," is quite different. "We believe," Lippard thundered, "that the Religion of Christ withers and dies whenever it comes in contact with any Immense Corporation based upon the Money Power."[31]

The historian David Reynolds, who has done more than anyone to bring Lippard to the twenty-first century's attention, writes that "*The Quaker City* is one of the most important popular novels in American history."[32] Indeed, Lippard's vivid realization of man's irrationality leads him to a profound social critique, for he was convinced that once man acknowledges the potential for darkness in the depths of his soul, he will realize that all mankind is equally profound and worthy of respect. Lippard, disappointed at what he viewed as a country rotted to its core, was not the last nineteenth-century American novelist to offer this solution.[33]

"THE ROMANCE OF REALITY"

Of Lippard's many imitators, one stands out. In his largely unverifiable autobiography *My Life: or the Adventures of Geo. Thompson* (1853), George Thompson (1823–ca. 1873), author of approximately sixty books (an estimate because he wrote under a number of pseudonyms), presents himself as an inversion of Benjamin Franklin, having failed where the latter succeeded and carrying throughout his life a visceral hatred of conformity to the establishment.

Thompson, born in New York and orphaned at a young age, became a printer's apprentice and then moved into the city's rapidly expanding world of journalism and fiction writing. In his autobiography, he claims to have been raised on Thomas Street, absorbing the stories of the local brothels and taverns. Growing up, he was a devotee of high culture and debauchery, engaging in theater- and concertgoing, drinking and fine dining, and brawls. He began his writing career in Boston, where he published two of his best-known works, *Venus in Boston* (1849) and *City Crimes* (1849), fairly short novels issued in paper wrappers that sold for twelve and a half cents each, considerably less than other fiction. His forte was writing for "sporting" magazines, which were aimed primarily at men and which, in addition to reporting on horse racing and other gaming, published blatantly sexual—"spicy" was the preferred word—stories and serialized novels, advertisements for "cundums" and other medical paraphernalia, and the addresses of brothels. He returned to New York in 1853, and shortly thereafter his work began to appear in such sporting journals as *Venus' Miscellany* and *The Broadway Belle*. He served as editor of the latter and was once jailed along with its publisher for printing salacious content.[34]

His novels challenged the immensely popular domestic fiction typified by Sedgwick's later works. He subverted standard plot devices and characters prevalent in sentimental writing, shocking readers with depictions of violence, perversion, and pornography. His heroines, unlike those in domestic fiction, act irrationally and without regard for Christian humility. They become helpless victims of an amoral world, and their families are often facilitators in their downfall. In his novels, the home is no haven. In *Venus in Boston*, Sow Nance, a procuress, describes her background in this way. "I came from a first-rate family," she says. "My father was hung for killing my mother—one of my brothers also danced a hornpipe in the air [that is, was hanged], and another is under sentence of death, off South, for beating a woman's brains out with a fire shovel, and choking her five children with a dishcloth."[35] The novel ends with inhabitants of the city's underworld, bent on luring young women to their moral destruction, repeating the injustices visited on her.

Thompson went further than Lippard in his dissection of obsessions and perversions, particularly sexual ones, to which people are prone. In his novels a reader finds adultery, miscegenation, group sex, incest, child sex, rape, gay sex, and cannibalism. To indulge these desires, his characters commit murder and other horrific crimes. Also, Thompson, like Lippard, believed that women have voracious sexual appetites. In *City Crimes* (1849), Julia Fairchild, by all appearances a sophisticated, proper lady, deflects her fiancé's advances so that she can have frequent and lusty sex with her African American servant, Nero, who eventually gets her pregnant. A character in *Venus in Boston* (1849) laments that she is married to an older man who cannot satisfy her sexual appetite. In frustration she exclaims, "'tis slavery—'tis madness, to be chained for life to but one source of love, when a thousand streams would not satiate or overflow."[36]

Most memorable is "Jew Mike's Story" in *Venus in Boston*. The character

Jew Mike brags to some of his working-class friends about his time as butler to the family of a Lord Hawley. He notices that during the husband's frequent absences, Lady Hawley receives visits from Captain St. Clair, a striking young officer in the dragoons. When her husband's loyal valet, Lagrange, stumbles on the couple in the act and refuses to keep silent, she goes to Mike, whom she trusts, and tells him that Lagrange has to be silenced, "*at any cost.*" As she stands before him, "her glossy hair all disordered," her nightdress "but imperfectly conceal[ing] the glories of her divine form, her heaving bosom so voluptuous and fair," Mike knows what she wants and what price to ask: he will murder Lagrange for nothing less than a night with her. Eager to be rid of the pesky valet and to set him at his criminal task, she agrees. Mike keeps his end of the dark bargain. He slays Lagrange and cuts out his tongue to prove to her ladyship that he will never talk.

Mike wishes to collect his "pay" then and there, but Lady Hawley tells him to return at midnight. When he does, she declares him a fool ever to think that she would give herself to someone so base. Instead, she offers him whatever sum he wishes. He threatens to expose her, but she is unfazed and reminds him that if he goes to the authorities, no one will believe someone of his low station. The magistrate will honor her story: that Mike murdered Lagrange of his own free will. Mike then attempts to force her, but Captain St. Clair, hiding in the room, interposes. The enraged butler seemingly keeps to his place and continues to serve the family while he decides to exact his revenge in a novel way: he stuffs Lagrange's body into a cask of some of Lord Hawley's best wine and, after a week, serves a decanter to the lady and her lover!

After one tryst, the two lovers dream aloud about how wonderful it would be if they could continue their antics without worrying about Lord Hawley's imminent return, at which point they turn again to Mike and ask if he will murder his master. Still smarting from Lady Hawley's dismissal, Mike refuses and asks if they haven't drunk "blood enough" yet. Puzzled, they inquire what he means. Mike escorts them to the wine cellar, opens the polluted cask, and pulls out Lagrange's corpse. In the ensuing confusion and horror, Mike flees the country and thus lives to tell his sordid tale. Thompson clearly intends the reader to cheer the servant's escape and his ingenuity.

As this subplot suggests, in *Venus in Boston* Thompson's "heroes" are often criminals or deviants who through outrageous acts make clear their hatred of an unjust, hypocritical society. Thompson despises the wealthy land- or millowner, the pious churchgoer, attorneys and businessmen, corrupt public officials, and others and suggests that "crimes" against them are justified, given what the urban poor daily endure at their hands. His stories are nothing less than the "romance of reality," he says in the preface to *Venus in Boston*, for they depict "the details of common everyday life—the secret history of things hidden from the public gaze, but of the existence of which there can be no manner of doubt."[37] Even as Lippard and Thompson fancied themselves as realists, however, in retrospect they seem like fabulists, embellishing reality in their dark ways in order to further their merciless satire. They offered not only vicious social critique but also moral condemnation redolent of Calvinism's frightening promise of fire and brimstone to unrepentant sinners.

This was a radical position. In the same year that Thompson published *Venus in Boston*, the conservative Boston writer Edwin Percy Whipple decried such literature as theirs as the "romance of rascality," a play on Thompson's phrase. Authors of this genre, Whipple explained, believe that "the world is sadly out of order" and offer as proof that "all the wise men are shut up in insane asylums, and all the heroes are clanking fetters or pounding stone in prisons." These writers contend that "the real virtue of society is to be found in the victims of 'social arrangements'" and that sin is only a socially constructed and sanctioned word "by which bigots express their dislike of great souls and free opinions."[38] Thompson would have responded that Whipple's appraisal was accurate.[39] Thompson, like Lippard, believed that the world was out of order. Both men's novels were attempts to shock readers into recognizing this.

A TALE OF THE REAL AND IDEAL

Other novelists in the 1840s reacted to the problems afflicting American society not through critique or satire, but by imagining utopian alternatives to the overcrowded, corrupt cities. Europe's Romantic Revolution inspired some of these novelists. Romanticism's influence had been apparent in the novel for some time, in, for example, Charles Brockden Brown's indebtedness to William Godwin, John Neal's infatuation with Byronic heroes, Cooper's premise that the grand American theme was the lonely self in dialogue with the grandeur of the natural world, and Sedgwick's treatment of the Native American's innate nobility.

But nowhere was this sense of an individual's self-sufficiency and self-worth more evident than in the Transcendentalist movement of the late 1830s and 1840s. Following the example of Emerson and, in different ways, George Ripley and Orestes Brownson, young men and women, primarily New Englanders, came to believe that the self was part of the divine and had to be cultivated as such, a faith that jibed nicely with the principle that all men (and women) are created equal. Concomitantly, they believed that the increasingly complex urban, industrial environment prevented such self-awareness. This group produced reams of essays, sermons, tracts, and poetry but was notably uninterested in fiction, although the liberal Christianity from which Transcendentalism flowed did produce its share of novelists, including Sedgwick, Lydia Maria Child (for *Philothea: A Romance* [1836]), and the Unitarian minister William Ware, who wrote several romances set in classical times. Among the Transcendentalists proper, though, there was but one novelist, the Maine clergyman Sylvester Judd. His *Margaret: A Tale of the Real and Ideal, Blight and Bloom; Including Sketches of a Place Not Before Described, Called Mons Christi* (1845) garnered praise from a variety of reviewers and represented a different American genre: the utopian romance.

Judd was born in Westhampton, Massachusetts, in 1813 and raised, as Sedgwick had been, in a religiously conservative household. He went to Yale College and after graduation taught school in the Massachusetts hill town of Templeton, whose population was divided between Unitarians and Calvinists. Although the orthodox group had hired him, Judd soon was attending the Unitarian services. He found that minister's sermons more congenial, for, he wrote in his journal, he loved to worship "in Nature's temple" whose "dome is the sky, whose pillars are the mountains."[40] Moving to Northampton, Massachusetts, Judd came to grips with his internal religious conflict. In his autobiography he explained that in his deepest self he had remained unchanged from childhood. He sought to glorify God and perform good works. What *had* changed, however, was his acceptance of consciousness as the "primary, incontrovertible, unequivocal source" of spiritual evidence, a notion that put him squarely in the Transcendentalist camp. Consciousness was nothing less than "the eye of the soul," Judd thought. Through it he saw a beautiful world in which men and women were intrinsically good, not fallen, as he had been taught to believe.[41]

He entered the Harvard Divinity School in the summer of 1837, a time of great cultural ferment—Emerson delivered his famous address "The

American Scholar" at Harvard's commencement that year and his "Divinity School Address" the next—and spent his time not only preparing for the Unitarian ministry but also reading. He wandered in the works of Carlyle and Coleridge, among the English Romantics, and Fichte, Hegel, and Schelling, among German thinkers. Called to the pulpit in Augusta, Maine, he ministered there until his death in 1853, preaching Transcendentalist doctrine while technically a Unitarian clergyman.

In 1845 the Boston publishing house of Jordan and Wiley, which had published a number of issues of the Transcendentalists' journal *The Dial*, brought out *Margaret* in an edition of one thousand copies, half of which the unknown Judd had to subsidize. He told his friend Edward Everett Hale that his was "a New England book," designed to "embody the features and improve the character of our favorite region," but also mentioned his utopian aspirations. He had designed the book, he continued, to show how a life in Christ could lead an entire community to "peace, temperance, and universal freedom."[42]

The novel tells the story of the spiritual growth of the eponymous Margaret, a country girl unencumbered by artificial religion or philosophy and open to the salutary influences of the natural world. She is a Transcendentalist without knowing it, reading nature at every step, always making the right decision because she follows her conscience. Margaret lives in the backwoods, at "the Pond," with the family of Didymus Hart, to which she was brought at a young age by one of its sons, Nimrod, following the death of her parents. Among the Harts, and particularly under the tutelage of their second son, Chilion, she flourishes, even as she confronts what Judd regards as civilization's corruptions, including her neighbors' harsh Calvinism. Because of Margaret's natural piety, she resists attempts to bring her to the "true" faith, although she is deeply interested to learn from her neighbors of the remarkable Jesus.

The second part of the novel, "Youth," finds Margaret in her teens, continuing to resist attempts to bring her into the orthodox fold. She meets Mr. Evelyn, who speaks to her of his religion, which Judd does not name but which is patently Unitarianism. Mr. Evelyn, who appreciates nature and the spirit like a Transcendentalist, deeply moves his young tutee. In the final section, "Womanhood," Margaret and Evelyn, now married, regenerate the community by teaching their Transcendentalist Christianity; a white cross on the summit of nearby Mons Christi marks the town's reformation. *Margaret*, Judd believed, could help initiate spiritual and social transformation on a large scale, making Mons Christi a model for the entire nation's salvation from the evils of commercial society and the selfishness it had unleashed.

Margaret Fuller, Greeley's book reviewer at the time, at first gave *Margaret* a rather brief, dismissive notice; but as the book picked up steam, she revisited it and declared it "full of genius, profound in meaning, and of admirable fidelity to Nature in its details." Her friends, she added, "drew from it auspicious omens, that an American literature is possible even in our day," by which she presumably meant a day so much devoted to the market.[43] Writing in the Unitarian house organ *The Christian Examiner*, the clergyman Frederic Dan Huntington called *Margaret* "the most emphatically American book ever written."[44] It was—James Russell Lowell chimed in—"one of the most original books yet written in America."[45]

In his second effort in this vein, *Richard Edney and the Governor's Family, A Rus-Urban Tale* (1850), Judd turned his attention to the city, as many other writers were doing. The novel narrates Edney's move from the Maine countryside to the city, where there is more work but also more challenges to his piety. By dint of moral and physical courage Edney finds favor with the governor's family and eventually wins his daughter. In so doing, he resists the undeniable appeal of Plumy Alicia Eyre, a beautiful, intelligent, aspiring factory operative who, dressing herself in cheap finery, seeks to rise above her class. The book champions the rural work ethic of honest farmers and artisans against the shrewd manipulations of capitalists and consumers and urges those newly arrived to the city to maintain the nation's virtues, as had the inhabitants of Mons Christi. Utopia, Judd implies, was not in Concord or Boston but in a place where a different social ethic reigned.

OTHER UTOPIAN DREAMS

Although Judd's dreams remained unrealized, the 1840s witnessed a remarkable number of utopian experiments. These arose in the Northeast and the Midwest as concern grew about the nation's headlong rush into industrialization, its tolerance of southern slavery, and its colonialist expansion into the Southwest, as well as about Christianity's fragmentation into scores of competing denominations and sects. Proponents of utopian communities believed that Americans were trampling the principles on which the nation had been founded. Some novelists directed the same anger and frustration that animated dystopian novelists like Lippard and Thompson into suggesting alternative dispensations of American society quite different from Mons Christi.

The utopian scheme on Judd's mind when he wrote *Margaret* was the Transcendentalist community at Brook Farm in West Roxbury, Massachusetts, begun four years earlier under George Ripley's leadership. Ripley had founded Brook Farm "to insure a more natural union between intellectual and manual labor than now exists" and to "combine the thinker and the worker, as far as possible, in the same individual" so that they could "prepare a society of liberal, intelligent, and cultivated persons, whose relations with each other would permit a more simple and wholesome life, than can be led amidst the pressure of our competitive institutors."[46]

After two years at Brook Farm, Ripley saw the need for a more structured community and adopted the ideas of the French social theorist and visionary Charles Fourier. Fourier argued for renovation of all facets of existence, from personal matters such as sexual preference to the very composition of the universe. He believed that he had discovered the underlying principle of the cosmos, the law of "attraction," which over millennia humanity had ignored or repressed, most recently in its enthusiastic and uncritical embrace of an inhumane economic system.

According to Fourier, to restore universal "Harmony," society had to build and divide into "phalansteries," cooperative communities of 1,620 residents in which all aspects of life were organized by the "passions"— the instinctual, nonrational parts of the self that demand gratification. He settled on the number 1,620 because he had observed that there were 810 personality types. With twice that number of people in a phalanx, everyone would at some time or other be attracted to at least one of his or her fellow phalansterians. As their desires changed, inhabitants rotated through different kinds of labor, aspects of education, and even sexual partners.[47]

As fantastic as Fourier's ideas sound, by the 1840s they had many followers, and scores of phalansteries were built east of the Mississippi River. Although few of these communities adopted every aspect of Fourier's plan—many could not tolerate true sexual freedom—they accepted his critique of capitalism and his basic premise of "association." Several novelists set fictions in these radical, experimental communities. Nathaniel Hawthorne's *The Blithedale Romance*, based in part on the author's own experience at Brook Farm in its earlier, pre-Fourierist phase, remains the best known.

An earlier example, coincident with the height of interest in Fourier's scheme in the United States, was the anonymously issued *Henry Russell; or, The Year of Our Lord Two Thousand* (1846), one of the few American novels to describe life in a Fourierist phalanstery. As its full title indicates, *Henry Russell* is a futuristic novel, imagining a Fourierist community in rural New York at the turn of the twentieth century. The chief dramatic personae are Mr. S. John, an artist called to work at the community; his beautiful eighteen-year-old daughter, Mary; her two friends Kate Templeton and Julia Watrous; Kate's handsome brother, William; and Henry Russell, all of whom walk the idyllic countryside surrounding their community and discuss the utopian venture.

The novel is uncomplicated, as are most works in the utopian vein, for their purpose is not deep analysis of characters or motive but the depiction of the reformation of an unfair social system. The characters in *Henry Russell* spend the novel discussing society and philosophy. The reader learns about the system of "attractive" labor in which there is always employment of "a sufficient variety from which each member [can] select to suit his peculiar tastes and talents."[48] The community's inhabitants treat crime as temporary insanity that can be cured by concern and rehabilitation, not by lengthy incarceration. The author writes that the purpose of such an association is "truly and rightly to live; to live in the full extent and scope of life; to give action and enjoyment to [the members'] whole nature, and to develop and exercise it to its utmost."[49]

Simple as *Henry Russell* is, it illustrates how the anger and disappointment over contemporary social conditions that Lippard and Thompson felt did not move every novelist to despair. Even Lippard allowed himself a utopian moment: in his *New York: Its Upper Ten and Lower Million* (1853), one of the subplots concerns a mechanic's plan to begin a workingman's utopia on the West Coast. At the end of that novel, Dermoyne, Lippard's hero, leads "three hundred emigrants, mechanics, their wives and little ones, who have left the savage civilization of the Atlantic cities, [to] a free home beyond the Rocky Mountains."[50]

The creation of fictional utopias went beyond the nation's borders. Basing their works on books such as Jonathan Swift's *Gulliver's Travels* (1726), a number of novelists criticized the nation's shortcomings through the trope of the imaginary voyage. The immensely popular *Kaloolah; or,*

Journeyings to the Djébel Kumri: An Autobiography of Jonathan Romer (1849) was a purported first-person account like many other works in the genre. Its author, W. S. Mayo (1811–1895), was a medical doctor turned writer who had spent time wandering North Africa and then sought to capitalize on his adventures as Melville had done in his first two novels, *Typee* and *Omoo* (1847), based on his travels to French Polynesia.

Born in rural New York State, Mayo earned a medical degree at the College of Physicians and Surgeons in New York City at the young age of twenty-one. After three years practicing medicine, he succumbed to wanderlust, wishing to venture into the unexplored heart of Africa. He never reached his destination but did spend three years on the Barbary Coast. Upon his return to New York, he returned to his medical practice but also began to place travel sketches based on his adventures in periodicals eager for such exotic fare. George Palmer Putnam, now separated from John Wiley, took a chance on Mayo's immense book-length manuscript of the adventures, but not until he had trimmed it by a third. Mayo balked at this severe editing and was so miffed that he asked that his name not appear on the title page. After the book's success, however, he reconsidered but, keeping up the ruse of its authorship, designated himself only as "editor" of the "found" manuscript that comprised the tale proper.

Kaloolah tells the story of a young "Yankee," Jonathan Romer, whose background is much like Mayo's. The first third of the book details his life in the rural United States, with nods to Cooper's interest in woodcraft as well as to Sedgwick's escape from an orthodox faith. But after Romer's work as an assistant in a local doctor's office finds him on the wrong side of a criminal investigation, the young man absconds to New York, where he runs into his father's old shipmate Captain Coffin. Coffin is about to depart for Málaga on the southern coast of Spain and agrees to take Romer, who knows nothing of sailing and gets a harsh indoctrination to the seaman's life.

When a storm savages the vessel, Romer is knocked unconscious and awakens clinging desperately to the wrecked ship. After six weeks a slave ship en route from Cuba to North Africa rescues him. This experience allows Romer to inveigh against the injustice of slavery, a rant that has no effect on the captain, who changes direction for the Congo, where the slave market is reputedly more profitable. Romer is surprised to see among the enslaved a beautiful, strikingly light-skinned girl with European features. He learns that she is Kaloolah, from Framazugda, an ancient nation in Africa's interior whose inhabitants are white. Romer purchases her and her brother with the intention of freeing them to return to their homeland; but his plans are foiled, and the three have no choice but to run. They reach Freetown, West Africa, where Romer boards a vessel heading for England but not before he locates a native who promises to guide Kaloolah and her brother to their home.

Infatuated with her benefactor, Kaloolah balks at Romer's departure and is only assuaged by his promises to return within a few years. But he is captured and sold into slavery by Bedouins on the dangerous Sahara coast. A year and a half later, he escapes and serendipitously finds Kaloolah, not yet returned to Framazugda. The two decide to make their way to her homeland. Exotic adventures ensue: they battle an immense lion, cross a wide, dangerous river, and finally see in the distance the Djébel el Kumri, the Mountains of the Moon, that mark Framazugda.

Here the book takes its utopian turn, for Romer enters a "primitive" country that makes the United States and Europe seem barbaric by contrast. But Framazugda is not a Christian utopia like Judd's Mons Christi. Rather, its society is based on reason, justice, and a sense of communal obligation—ideals, in other words, within reach of humankind without any need for a divine model or a Fourierist reorganization and seemingly what the United States might still be. In Framazugda, one's physical health is as important as one's moral and intellectual health. The Framazugs are aware of the deleterious effects of industrial pollution and of the hazards of food contamination. They greatly value personal cleanliness and make bathing facilities available to all inhabitants, free of charge. Because they sweep and wash the streets daily, no refuse is ever visible. They set aside much public space for parks and insist on healthful exercise.[51]

If its physical environment stands in stark contrast with the overcrowded, squalid cities of the United States, Framazugda's government is even more extraordinary, harkening back to nation-states administered by an aristocracy of intelligence and merit. The king appoints a "dagash" as the chief administrative officer, who chooses ten assistants from among the city's *literary* men. "Only those who have written a book, or perpetrated something in the literary way, are considered eligible to the office," for the populace believes them best qualified for public service. To guard against autocracy, every five years the people hold a referendum to decide whether the king has executed his office diligently and fairly. If two thirds vote in the negative, he is compelled to resign, but, somewhat strangely, "his heir" takes his place and a new administrator is installed.[52]

The Framazugs' religion also evinces an enlightened worldview. They believe in a range of future states, good and bad, into which one moves depending on one's present behavior. There is no heaven or hell and no elaborate and restrictive doctrines. Their beliefs "offer strong incentives to virtue" in *this* world, making the gateway to any future reward in their own control.[53] Framazugs earn different ranks or positions, but those are not acquired through inheritance or grasped through chicanery or corruption. They have made the transition from piety to moralism. Romer comes to realize that a distant deity has not imposed the evils so prevalent in the "civilized" world as punishment for sin but, rather, that they are the result of men's own foolishness, "of false teaching and bad habits—of imperious fashion—of long continued and assiduous experiments in evil—an industrious training in vice—of a diabolical combination of selfish men to trample their fellow citizens beneath them, to degrade and beggar them, and to crush, with the iron heel of power, their generous impulses."[54]

Mayo points out only one failing of this ideal society: because the Framazugs have been so isolated, they have not experienced war. But while Romer is there, the Jallas, a belligerent tribe from East Africa, begin to mobilize against them. Romer and his Yankee ingenuity save the day. Remembering that as he entered the country, he saw both saltpeter in caves and sulfur on the slopes of a volcano, he manufactures gunpowder and makes wooden guns (anticipating the inventiveness of Mark Twain's Hank in *A Connecticut Yankee in King Arthur's Court*). He arms and organizes a defensive militia of Framazugs that successfully repels the Jallas. The story ends with the promise of fruitful interaction between Framazugda and the United States, sealed by the birth of Kaloolah's and Romer's male child.

In *Kaloolah* Mayo did everything he could to satisfy his American readership, which was drawn to exotic travel narratives and encounters with other cultures. But he also aired his grievances against modern civilization. Not willing to give up all the technological wizardry that accompanies Western civilization, he has Romer "save" the Framazugs with defensive armament. Further, Mayo's detailed description of the country's social, political, and religious organization betrays his sense that if the United States is to continue to prosper, it must return to its formative principles and disavow both liberalism and the slavery it perversely permitted.

COOPER'S VISION

Another utopian fiction came from the pen of none other than James Fenimore Cooper. *The Crater; or, Vulcan's Peak* (1847) was an implicit attack on the insurgents engaged in the Antirent War in upstate New York in the 1840s. Cooper's increasingly conservative politics pushed him to a central role in this agitation.[55] On the one side were impoverished tenants who were not able to pay the rents on their lands, and on the other, the owners of large estates who would not sell to the tenants at the terms the latter proposed. The conflict preoccupied the Albany legislature, where farmers sought the disestablishment of the tenant system while armed bands of their supporters dressed, ironically, as "Indians" and roamed the countryside, intimidating landowners.

Cooper stood squarely on the side of property and law and order. Tenants, who had the luxury of long-term leases, could improve their lands without fear of losing their investments. And if cash was scarce, there were provisions to pay rent "in kind"—that is, with crops or other staples like lumber. To Cooper, stalwart defender of the principles of the American Revolution, right should not be determined by the majority but by recourse to principle and established law. The new American democrats, not the dissipated elites satirized by Lippard, were challenging the very foundation of the new nation. Cooper's mood was not improved when the New York legislature sided with the Antirent Party, which led him to write *The Crater*.

The novel is a powerful indictment of the contemporary United States, and when Cooper's countrymen reviewed it, they condemned its highly politicized ending. *The Crater* tells the story of Mark Woolston, first mate on an American ship, and Bob Betts, one of the crew, who are shipwrecked on a small volcanic reef in the Pacific Ocean. The only survivors, they construct a small raft from the remains of the ship, but before they can use it to escape, another storm washes away Betts and the craft, leaving Woolston the sole inhabitant of the atoll. The nod to Jonathan Swift is evident, in the setting and, less obviously, in the coolheadedness and intelligence that Woolston displays in adjusting to his solitary confinement and the religious experience that stemmed from his ordeal. "Cut off, as he was," Cooper writes, "from all communion with his kind; cast on what was, when he first knew it, a barren rock in the midst of the vast Pacific Ocean, Mark found himself, by a very natural operation of causes, in much closer communion with his Creator."[56]

One night a severe earthquake rocks the reef and, rather than sinking it, raises an archipelago from the sea, lorded over by the immense Vulcan's Peak and soon lush with plant and animal life. All the land lacks is people, a fact remedied by Betts's return in a ship carrying many of Woolston's concerned friends and relatives. Enchanted by the islands' beauty and bounty, the group decides to remain and elects Woolston governor because of his survival skills, his knowledge of the islands, and his strong moral character. He establishes a society in which all have equal rights but in which only those who share his virtues hold positions of authority.

But as news of the colony gets out, the dream begins to fade. Swayed by the wealth they attain through trade, the inhabitants abandon their humility, particularly after emissaries from the outside world appear: attorneys, a newspaper editor, clergy of competing denominations— Presbyterian, Methodist, Baptist, and Quaker (in the colony's early years it had gotten along with one Episcopalian priest). As Cooper puts it, because of the islands' natural bounty, now there was "more danger of their inhabitants falling into the common and fatal error of men in prosperity . . . of their beginning to fancy that they deserved all the blessings that were conferred on them, and forgetting the Hand that bestowed them."[57]

Demagogues (like those in upstate New York) begin to shout that all men are equal—Woolston "was much too sensible a man to fall into any of the modern absurdities on the subject of equality," Cooper notes—and that the majority should rule.[58] Merchants and their lawyers litigate for financial gain. Law, Cooper writes, "which had been used for the purposes of justice . . . now began to be used for speculation and revenge."[59] Clergy of different denominations bicker over what God intended for the colonists. "The next-door neighbors hated each other most sincerely," because they took different views of regeneration, justification, predestination and all the other subtleties of doctrine.[60] "Whole communities," Cooper sneers, "degenerate into masses of corruption, venality, and cupidity, when they set up the idol of commerce to worship in lieu of the everliving God."[61] The islands become the state of New York, writ small.

Shorn of his power by the new settlers, fed up with the bickering and chicanery, Woolston leaves for a visit to the United States. On his return he learns that again God has spoken: another earthquake has *sunk* the islands. "The terrible truth flashed on [Woolston's] mind"; "that spot which had almost as much of Heaven as of earth about it" was now a hundred fathoms under the Pacific.[62] Years later Woolston remembers these events and expresses Cooper's sentiments:

> For a time our efforts seem to create, and to adorn, and to perfect, until we forget our origin and destination, substituting self for that divine hand which alone can unite the elements of worlds as they float in gasses, equally from His mysterious laboratory, and scatter them again into thin air when the works of His hand cease to find favour in His view.[63]

This is not the view of a spirited reformer but that of a disillusioned conservative. Cooper's invocation of the "divine hand" in the plot of *The Crater* is a sign of his continuing desire to return to the security of religion and God's providence at a time when more and more Americans were deifying what the Transcendentalist minister Theodore Parker called "the great god, Mammon."

In the 1840s, novelists' responses to the social concerns that had informed the work of Child, Sedgwick, and other early domestic writers began to take new, and often opposing, tracks. While conservatives like Cooper and Simms continued to propound the idea that only the guiding hand of divine Providence could steady the Republic, social critics like Lippard and Thompson despaired of the Republic's salvation unless democracy was extended to the lowest rungs of society. At the same time, utopian novelists envisioned radically new societies—Judd's depended on the model of Christ, Mayo's on a benevolent monarch, and Henry Russell's on Fourier's agnosticism—and thereby counseled a wholesale rethinking of the American experiment. Given the country's seeming reluctance to engage in any such large-scale renovation, what counsel could the next generation of novelists provide? In particular, how could one adapt Christianity to address the continuing failure of the power of sympathy that earlier writers had so celebrated as the core of republican virtue?

PART II } The 1850s

4 } The Conventions of Sentiment

In the spring of 1849 George Palmer Putnam received a hefty manuscript from Henry Warner, a prominent New York attorney who had fallen on hard times during the Panic of 1837. Warner already had shown the manuscript to two other publishers, but both had passed on it. Putnam was not immediately convinced of its merit. He took it to his summer home on Staten Island, where his mother was visiting. Putnam asked her opinion, and the next day she told him: "If you never publish another book, publish this."[1] He put the book into production and invited Susan Warner to stay at his home through the summer and early autumn to correct the proof. She and her family—her father, Henry, and her younger sister, Anna, who had come up with the novel's title, *The Wide, Wide World*—eagerly awaited the published book, her first literary effort, which finally arrived in mid-December and carried on its title page her pseudonym, Elizabeth Wetherell.

Sales started slowly. Putnam's mother remained confident and reminded him that "the book was so good, she was sure that Providence would aid him in the sale of it."[2] She was right. By February the first edition of fifteen hundred copies had almost sold out. In April Putnam printed another thousand copies and told the author that "your book has been received with remarkable interest in various quarters, and I consider it . . . 'a hit' in a special and emphatic sense of the word."[3] Indeed it was, for within two years *The Wide, Wide World* was in its fourteenth edition. It eclipsed Lippard's *Quaker City* as the most popular book in the nation, a position it held until the publication of Harriet Beecher Stowe's *Uncle Tom's Cabin* in 1852, and it remained in print into the early twentieth century. Other authors envied this success. Nathaniel Hawthorne wrote his publisher, William Ticknor, that "America is now wholly given over to a d[amne]d mob of scribbling women, and I should have no chance of success while the public is occupied with their trash." A bit disingenuously he added, "and should be ashamed of myself if I did succeed in the same way."[4]

Warner's book changed the dynamic of the publishing industry. Publishers began to search for the next bestseller. In trying to re-create *The Wide, Wide World*'s financial success, they began to invest large sums in advertising campaigns in papers and periodicals with large circulations. And often women wrote these books. The popularity of Warner's novel inaugurated an era when women writers, following Warner's formula, dominated the publishing world.

Two aspects of Warner's novel made it a distinctively American example of the novel of sentiment. The first was its basis in, and evocation of, Christian life. *The Wide, Wide World* descended from religious tracts and the stories and novels of Sarah Savage and Catharine Maria Sedgwick. What set it apart from its predecessors was that it embodied the larger shift in American religious life from the soul-searching and theological basis of earlier works to ideals of Christian behavior and service.[5] It proposed that a woman's character and life were now up to her and not divinely ordained at creation—that she should align her behavior as much as possible with the virtues exemplified by Christ.[6]

The implications of this idea suggest the second aspect. *The Wide, Wide World* was empowering. Because women were still excluded from politics and the market, they had to turn elsewhere to exercise their will and intellect.[7] While their fathers, husbands, and brothers were out of the home, building reputations and adding to their worldly gains, women remained in the home, becoming adept at conquering themselves with the goal of entering the kingdom of heaven. Hence they found ways of exercising that vaunted American value: free will. From invisibility to prominence, from disregard to respect, from religious tract to lengthy fiction, women writers made enormous strides during the 1850s through the sentimental novel.

SUSAN WARNER

Warner was born in 1819 in New York, the second of five children, three of whom died in childhood; she was close to the other survivor, her sister,

Anna, born in 1827. Their father, Henry, a New England farm boy who made good, had graduated from Union College, studied law with a well-known New York attorney, established his own practice in the city, and married Anna Marsh Bartlett, stepdaughter of a wealthy and prominent New Yorker. She died in 1828, and his sister Frances—beloved maiden Aunt Fanny—moved in to help her brother care for his young children.

For the first twenty years of her life, Susan lived comfortably. The family resided at first in Brooklyn and, after 1830, on Broome Street, near Broadway, in Manhattan, then at St. Mark's Place, one of the best addresses in the booming city. During this period Henry Warner purchased Constitution Island, a square mile of land in the Hudson River across from West Point, as a picturesque location for a future country home. In 1836, the Warners were well on their way to becoming one of New York's most fashionable families, one of the city's "upper ten," as George Lippard would soon put it.

But the Panic of 1837 crushed Henry Warner as it did countless others. He had to sell the home on St. Mark's Place as well as all the family's furniture and many other belongings. He was able to keep Constitution Island, where the family now spent summers, but during the rest of the year he was relegated to renting only a few rooms in Manhattan. He tried unsuccessfully to reestablish his law practice. As he got older, he and his two daughters, neither of whom married, moved permanently to the island, where he unfortunately got involved in costly lawsuits with neighbors when he tried to drain some marshland on the riverbank. He almost lost the property to foreclosure. Fortunately, a friend stepped in and assumed the mortgage until Warner could pay it off.

In an attempt to stave off that financial crisis, in 1849 Susan began writing *The Wide, Wide World*, and thereafter, she and Anna (who also wrote fiction) supported the family through their novels and stories. After Henry's death, the sisters spent the rest of their lives together in the old farmhouse, still writing novels—Susan a remarkable twenty-seven and Anna four—along with four coauthored books. Still, they struggled to remain solvent, often transferring the copyright to their work outright rather than wait for royalties. Susan died in 1885, but Anna stayed on, selling the island with stipulations that she be allowed to live the rest of her life on it and that it eventually be given to the federal government (it was made part of West Point). During the last years of her life, Anna wrote a memoir of her beloved sister that remains the best source of information about her.

The Wide, Wide World tells the story of Ellen Montgomery, a young girl who grows up in comfortable circumstances in New York until her father, an attorney, loses an important lawsuit. The family's fortunes spiral downward. Montgomery accepts a job in Europe and asks his wife, already in poor health, to accompany him, thinking that the climate will be conducive to her recovery. Because her mother is too weak to care for Ellen, her parents send her to live with her aunt, Miss Fortune Emerson, who lives in Thirlwall, in the country, and is not pleased to have to take charge of a presumably spoiled city girl who knows nothing of farm life. Ellen's separation from her mother is terribly painful, though both submit to Mr. Montgomery's will, which they treat as an extension of God's. This is Ellen's first lesson in female resignation.

Subsequent lessons come at Miss Fortune's, where she suffers indignities and humiliations because of her "fancy" upbringing. Her aunt, for example, dyes all her expensive white stockings a drab color more suitable to farm life and withholds Mrs. Montgomery's letters to Ellen until her behavior "improves." Again someone absolutely controls Ellen, just as her father did. Her recourse is to her faith and the belief that God intends her suffering for some good, a lesson whose logic derived from the eighteenth-century theologian Samuel Hopkins's controversial notion that one must be willing to be damned for the glory of God.

Finding little solace in this harsh doctrine, Ellen becomes resentful, angry, and dispirited, until a woman named Alice Humphreys befriends her. Alice, a minister's daughter, instills in Ellen the ethic, not doctrine, of Christian love and urges her to fill her new household with it. Ellen tries sincerely. She pays more attention to her grandmother (whom Miss Fortune neglects) and obeys her aunt to a fault, until she has no reason to berate or belittle her niece. Ellen also learns the worth of honesty and hard work when Aunt Fortune and Bram van Brunt (a neighbor who tends the farm during Fortune's illness and whom she later marries) assign her various household tasks that earlier would have baffled her.

After her marriage, Miss Fortune allows Ellen to board at the Humphreyses' home, enlivened by the return of Alice's brother, John, who is studying for the ministry. This happy time for Ellen soon ends, however, because of first Alice's untimely death and then that of her father in

Europe. Unhappily acceding to the last of her father's demands, Ellen moves to Scotland to live with her mother's family, the Lindsays. They are strict but more in a social than a religious sense; they are aristocratic types who "know" what is right and try to mold their ward. Again Ellen submits, even though she yearns for independence and to return to America and John Humphreys, thus to be independent of her family's influence. At one point Mr. Lindsay takes away a book that John has sent Ellen, prompting her to exclaim, "But it is mine." Her uncle's chilling rejoinder sums up a nineteenth-century woman's plight: "And you are mine."[8] A visit from John gives Ellen the will to endure until she is of age, and the novel ends with the reader believing that soon enough Ellen will be rewarded with marriage to John Humphreys, who will not "own" her in the way others have, even if she must love and obey him.

ONLY SUBMISSION MAKES ONE FREE

Anna knew something of Susan's own religious struggle, and in her invaluable reminiscences, she relates much about the solace she and her sister found in Christianity, especially after 1836, when Henry Warner purchased a pew in the Mercer Street Presbyterian Church, near the family's home on St. Mark's Place. Administered by the Reverend Thomas Harvey Skinner, a theologian of some note and later a founder of Union Theological Seminary, the church became a haven for the Warner sisters, with Skinner's sermons the highlight of their week. In April 1841, Anna and Susan were admitted to church membership and devoted themselves to good works. Susan's writing was a part of this effort.

Skinner was prominent in New School Presbyterianism and counted as close friends Albert Barnes and Edward Beecher, both of whom in the 1830s were tried by the General Assembly of the Presbyterian Church for heresy. The trials ended in acquittal but also in a severely split denomination, with opposing parties debating the importance of revivalism to faith. Skinner's New School welcomed and encouraged a congregant's emotional reinvigoration through revivalism, a theology of the feelings; the Old School emphasized a probationer's strict adherence to doctrine and the central role of sacraments, a theology of the intellect that reinforced the clergy's rather than the church member's responsibility in salvation. Even the parishioner Henry Warner weighed in on the debate. In 1838 he published *An Inquiry into the Moral and Religious Character of the American Government*, an anti-Jacksonian tract in which he looked to those of strong religious faith to resist the Democrats' descent into folly and evil, exemplified by, among other developments, Jackson's insistence on Sunday mail delivery. Warner thought the Whigs, many of whom strongly supported Skinner's kind of evangelical fervor, measured up to his own standards.

In Skinner's thought, conversion did not always come instantly and overwhelmingly, as it did to Saul on the road to Damascus, but was an individual's choice. Conversion was "an intelligent, voluntary, invisible act of the mind, in which it ceases to rebel against God, submits to his authority, and accepts his mercy."[9] In a passage that derived from Jonathan Edwards's notion of true benevolence (Skinner had trained at Princeton Theological Seminary, where Edwards's works still informed the curriculum), Skinner defined the effects of such conversion. "The offering up of prayer and praise," he wrote in *The Religion of the Bible* (1838), "meditation on the Scriptures, attendance upon ordinances, liberality toward the poor, the utmost exactness and irreproachableness of life"— none of these meets the requirements of "spiritual religion" unless there is "a correspondent sensibility in the heart." There must be "a feeling of the divine Presence" and a "relishing of the Divine excellence." "God must be enjoyed," he concluded, "or there will be disquietude of soul."[10] A Christian need not master the intricacies of Protestant theology. He ought only to study the Bible and align himself with Christ's teachings. This is what Ellen Montgomery does in the course of *The Wide, Wide World*.

Another famous theologian, in this case a Congregationalist, also influenced Susan Warner's novel. In 1846, Horace Bushnell (1802–1876), pastor of a church in Hartford, Connecticut, published his highly controversial but influential *Christian Nurture*, a book that, like the trials of Barnes and Beecher, rocked American theology. Even more than Skinner, Bushnell downplayed the significance of conversion and argued instead that an individual becomes a Christian over time through strong religious education, particularly in the family. If religious virtue is to prevail, parents have to inculcate it in their children by teaching and through the example they set. The family unit is the key to Christianity's power: "How trivial, unnatural, weak, and, at the same time, violent, in comparison, is that overdone scheme of individualism, which knows the race only as mere units of will and personal action." "Our over-intense individualism," he continued, "carries with it an immense loss of feeling, affection, sentiment, which hardens the aspect of every thing, and dries away the sweet charities and tender affections." Individualism thus "makes the church a mere gathering of adult atoms."[11]

Parallels with *The Wide, Wide World* are many, for Bushnell's notion of a young person's growth toward grace fits Ellen precisely. Christian education, he wrote, "is not to break, but to bend rather, to draw the will down, or away from self-assertion toward self-devotion, to teach it the way of submitting to wise limitations."[12] Thus Ellen cares for Aunt Fortune, even though this relative treats her harshly, because she knows that it is right. Likewise, she endures (though with many tears) her time with the Lindsays, unsympathetic and unsentimental Scots Calvinists (as well as prissy aristocrats) to the core. As the reader learns in what Warner intended as the novel's final, though originally unpublished, chapter, Ellen will be indeed rewarded by marriage to John Humphreys.

John S. Hart, in his pioneering *Women Prose Writers of America* (1852), wrote that *The Wide, Wide World* was the only novel in which religion as understood by "Evangelical Christians" was "exhibited with truth." He also marveled at the novel's rapid rise to prominence. Its "readers soon began to multiply," he wrote, "and every one who read the book, talked about it, and urged its reading upon his neighbors, until, within a year from the time of its publication, it had reached a circulation almost unprecedented." Perhaps even more unusual, this occurred without advertising by the book's publisher. "It was one of the most signal instances in recent times," Hart wrote, "of a popularity reaching almost to fame, and springing up spontaneously, and entirely in advance of all the usual organs of public opinion."[13]

The most interesting notice of the novel appeared in a remarkable nineteen-page review in the *North American Review* by another successful woman novelist, Caroline Kirkland (1801–1864), who had moved from New York to the wilds of Michigan. Her first work, *A New Home, Who'll Follow?* (1839), based on her experiences after her relocation, made her so well known that Wiley and Putnam issued her second work, *Western Clearings* (1845), in its Library of American Books. In her lengthy essay Kirkland reviewed not only *The Wide, Wide World* but also Warner's more recent *Queechy* (1852), set in early-nineteenth-century New York and based in part on the experiences of her parents' generation; and Anna Warner's *Dollars and Cents* (1853), a novel set in Philadelphia that, like her sister's first book, deals with a wealthy family's difficulties after the father's ill-considered investments.

Kirkland's essay was a lament about the current state of the American novel, which she divided into two main types: "the philosophical, political, sectarian, or philanthropic novels" and those "which are essentially essays on the condition of the poor, with hardly a fiction to soften the sharp outline."[14] Nowadays, she wrote, "There is no truth but literal truth," and "heroes, who do not interest themselves in political economy and the condition of the masses, are unworthy of good fortune."[15] As a result, the novel had become "a *quatrième état* [fourth estate]; something considerable in government; a power formidable to evildoers; but not particularly lovely or cheering to those who resort to it merely to delight or exalt the imagination, suggestive of possibilities of happiness, or as counter-agent to the disenchanting tendencies of our wayward, blundering experience."[16]

But *The Wide, Wide World* was something new. The book, originally "bought to be presented to nice little girls, by parents and friends who desired to set a pleasant example of docility and self-command before those happy beginners," soon found mothers, fathers, and older brothers and was even "under the pillows of sober bachelors," who read it with tears in their eyes.[17] Kirkland believed that the Warner sisters, though they had not so intended, had created "new rules" for the novel, moving it beyond the didactic religious tract. Their books had a "character of their own—humane, religious, *piquant*, natural, national," for they paint "human nature in American type"—that is, they reflected the country's democratic promise—and "appeal to universal human sympathy." Above all, they recognize the heart as "the strong-hold of character and religion as the ruling element of life; religion—no *ism*, however specious or popular" but defined as being of "one mind with Christ"and thus ecumenical, not bound to the restrictive dogma of any one denomination. Kirkland knew "of no prototype of such books" except for the Bible.[18]

GERTY'S PLIGHT

Susan Warner's *Queechy*, the name of a fictional country village based on Canaan, Connecticut (where Warner's Aunt Fanny had lived), appeared in 1852 and was well received, though not as well as its predecessor. The novel was about life among New York's fashionable citizens in the 1820s and 1830s, before the panic, so had neither the immediacy of *The Wide, Wide World* nor an appealing universal character like Ellen Montgomery. Two years later another runaway bestseller, Maria Cummins's *The Lamplighter*, eclipsed Warner's first novel. The book sold forty thousand copies in its first two months of publication and seventy thousand in its first year.[19] Cummins achieved not only popular success but also a kind of literary celebrity that Warner never experienced.

Cummins was born in 1827 in Salem, Massachusetts, into a prosperous family. When she was small, her father, David, became the judge of the court of common pleas of Norfolk County, and the family moved to Dorchester, a few miles from Boston. He took a strong interest in her education and, when she was a teenager, sent her to Mrs. Charles Sedgwick's Young Ladies School, in Lenox, Massachusetts, overseen by Catharine Sedgwick's sister-in-law. The writer herself was a frequent visitor. Sedgwick's effect on the young woman is unknown, but *The Lamplighter* was thematically similar to *A New-England Tale*, and Cummins, like Sedgwick, never married. Also like Sedgwick—and unlike Warner— Cummins never wrote from financial need. She did not have much in common with the heroine of her novel.

The Lamplighter opens in the kind of squalid urban setting made vivid by Lippard. The reader meets eight-year-old Gerty, an orphan living with Nan Grant, who is cruel to her young charge, the child of her husband's friend, who is presumed drowned at sea. At one point Nan drops Gerty's pet kitten, her only joy, into a pot of boiling water, prompting the young child to throw a piece of firewood at her. At another, she locks Gerty in her garret when she learns the child is afraid of the dark.

After several fights, Nan throws Gerty out of the house, and soon enough the aptly named Trueman Flint, an old "lamplighter" whose job it is to illuminate the city's gas streetlights, takes Gerty under his wing. In his tenement Gerty meets Mrs. Sullivan, a kind woman caring for her elderly father, and her son, Willie, who is five years older than Gerty and boards with a city pharmacist to learn his trade. Trueman introduces Gerty to someone called "God" and a thing called "prayer." The two Sullivans educate Gerty in more prosaic ways. Mrs. Sullivan teaches her how to keep house, and soon Gerty has cleaned and rearranged Trueman's room, making it a place of comfort and love.

Through Trueman, Gerty meets Emily Graham, a young blind woman.

Trueman worked for Emily's wealthy father until he sustained a serious injury that reduced him to his current job. Because of his misfortune, Emily feels obliged to help Trueman whenever she can, even though he holds no grudge and is thankful for whatever odd jobs Mr. Graham provides. Emily assumes responsibility for Gerty's Christian education. Her first task is to tame the young girl's furious temper and to replace it with an ethic of patient love. Emily's own life offers the strongest argument for such a change: although blinded several years earlier—the reader does not learn how until late in the novel—she bears the tragedy without bitterness and ministers to those in need.

Gerty is tested often during her transformation. Trueman suffers a stroke from which he never recovers; Gerty, twelve years old, nurses him through his final illness but harbors no anger at a God who could allow her friend to die in such a manner. Later, while living at Emily's family's home, she finds herself persecuted by Mrs. Ellis, the Grahams' housekeeper of many years, who resents the addition of another family member. Emily counsels that Gerty must "learn to bear even injustice, without losing [her] self-control."[20] Soon enough, Willie Sullivan goes to India for several years to pursue a career in the merchant trade, leaving Gerty at the mercy of Mrs. Ellis. Gerty decides to leave the household to assume a teaching position in the city, hoping to move in with Mrs. Sullivan to care for her and her father, both of whom are ill. But when the two die, Gerty moves to a city boardinghouse.

Within a month she is back in Mr. Graham's country home, for Mr. Graham has married a fashion-hungry widow who brings along two insufferable daughters, Isabel (known as Belle) and Kitty, and Emily needs Gerty by her side. With their mother's tacit approval, both stepdaughters, but especially Belle, treat Emily with indifference and are overtly cruel to Gertrude (as she now is called), who has blossomed into an attractive young woman. Emily's example finally takes hold in Gertrude. Boiling with anger over another slight, in a moment of startling self-consciousness she looks out the window at nature's beauty and is transformed. "A delicious composure" steals into her heart, extinguishing any desire for revenge. "She had conquered; she had achieved the greatest of earth's victories, a victory over herself." [21]

The trials do not end, however. Emily's health begins to fail, while Willie Sullivan returns. He seems infatuated with Belle, a lapse in judgment that makes Gertrude question her high opinion and continued affection for him. Now a stoic Christian, she keeps her composure and accepts this disappointment. Complicating matters is the appearance of an older man named Mr. Phillips, who accompanies the Grahams on a tour along the Hudson River. He seems particularly interested to hear as much about Gerty's early life as she can remember.

On this trip, Gertrude makes what readers at the time would have understood as the ultimate Christian sacrifice. In a steamboat accident and fire, with Belle in mortal danger, Gertrude risks her own life to rescue her tormentor. Both survive, and Gertrude's good deed is rewarded. Mr. Phillips turns out to be Philip Amory, not only her long-lost father but also Emily's onetime lover, who had accidentally blinded her after her father banished him. The novel concludes with the reconstitution of Gertrude's family. Amory and Emily marry, as do Gertrude and Willie.

The complexity of its characters and plot sets *The Lamplighter* apart from *The Wide, Wide World* and many other sentimental novels. Like Warner's novel, it instructs the reader to acquiesce rather than to resist, yet Gertrude never resigns herself to her fate. She begins in combativeness and self-consciously transforms herself into a Christian but never relinquishes her powerful personality. Empowering rather than passive, Cummins's ideal of womanhood grew from her religion, which, unlike Warner's, did not involve submission.

Like Sedgwick (and perhaps as a result of her influence), Cummins joined a Unitarian church. *The Lamplighter* reflects that denomination's broadly ecumenical stance as well as its emphasis on Christ as the only necessary moral exemplar, another way Cummins's religious views differed from Warner's. As opposed to Bushnell's doctrine of self-abnegation, Cummins's Unitarianism emphasized self-realization. Gertrude controls her own life in ways that Ellen does not. She has the courage to stand up to Mr. Graham, for instance, when after she tells him that she is going to return to the city to work, he virtually orders her to remain at Emily's side. As she mulls over his outburst, she wonders if he considered "that my freedom is to be the price of my education, and I am no longer able to say yes or no."[22] Independence and grace go hand in hand. Cummins's emphasis on a woman's free will accounts in part for the appeal of *The Lamplighter*, for it shows that however divorced a woman might be from political and economic life, she can retain her agency and self-worth.

Gertrude, like Ellen, settles into marriage, but surely Willie's and her relationship becomes one between equals rather than protector and protected.

MILL GIRLS

Of course, the harshness of Ellen Montgomery's and Gerty's early lives might have appeared less so in comparison to the drudgery of factory life. Alongside the rise of the modern city, the opening of lands west of the Mississippi River, and the proliferation of railroad track and telegraph wire, the development of large-scale industries was one of the period's most significant economic and demographic developments. Sarah Savage's *The Factory Girl* (1814) was just the first of many novels set in this new environment.

When Charles Dickens made his American tour in 1842, he stopped at the great factories in Lowell, Massachusetts, which seemed to be one of the seven wonders of the modern world. He was struck by Lowell's newness; factories, churches, merchants' shops, roads, hotels: all seemed to have sprung up the day before he arrived. He was also surprised at the appearance of both the workers and their workplaces. Well dressed and clean, the female workers "had the manners and deportment" of "young women," not "degraded brutes of burden." In the factories' well-organized and clean workrooms he was amazed to see plants "trained to shade the glass" from excessive sunlight. He found the city's boardinghouses, segregated according to sex, similarly neat. He noted that the landlords looked after their charges' morals.

Dickens also marveled at the "joint-stock pianos" in many of the boardinghouses, the fact that most of the young ladies belonged to circulating libraries, and, most amazingly, that they issued their own literary magazine, *The Lowell Offering*. The contrast with the squalor, poverty, and ignorance of the Manchester mills in England was stark. Dickens attributed the better conditions in America to the young nation's seemingly endless opportunities for economic opportunity and, hence, geographic mobility. "Many of the circumstances whose strong influence has been at work for years in our manufacturing towns have not arisen here," he observed, because Lowell's workers did not constitute a permanent population. "These girls," he wrote, primarily the "daughters of small farmers," come from other places, "remain a few years in the mills" to earn their wages, "and then go home for good."[23]

American observers offered less enthusiastic takes on factory work. A story in *The Lowell Offering* of a mill girl's introduction to her work did little to entice others to follow her:

> She went into the Mill; and the sight of so many bands, and wheels, and springs, in constant motion was very frightful. She felt afraid to touch the loom, and she was almost sure that she could never learn to weave . . . the day appeared as long as a month at home . . . There was a dull pain in her head, and a sharp pain in her ankles; every bone was aching; and there was in her ears a strange noise, as of crickets, frogs, and jewsharps [Jew's harps] all mingling together, and she felt gloomy and sick at heart.[24]

A writer for the *Olive Leaf and New England Operative* found the constant din the most oppressive aspect of the mills. When the heavy waterwheels began to turn and move other wheels in the building, she wrote, the sound "deepen[ed] at every revolution, until the confused hum of spindles and the discordant clang of looms filled the air, and the very earth seemed to tremble under the combined operations of these giant powers."[25] Lucy Larcom, who had worked in the mills in the 1840s and who became one of the factory world's most articulate chroniclers, thought it ironic that "hours passed in the midst of monotonous noise, which drowned the sound of human voices, brought with them a sense of isolation as one feels in the loneliest wilderness."[26]

Whatever the physical or psychological effects of factory work, however, Americans unsurprisingly focused on its moral consequences. One mill girl's lament brimmed with moral anxiety: "Thrown into company with all sorts and descriptions of mind, dispositions and intellects, without counselor or friend to advise, and surrounded on all sides with the vain ostentation of fashion, vanity and light frivolity—beset with temptations without, and the carnal prosperities of nature within, what *must*, what will be the natural, rational result?"[27] In his introduction to Dorus Clarke's *Lectures to Young People in Manufacturing Villages*, which typified many such books published in the 1830s and 1840s for the new laboring population, the Lowell, Massachusetts, minister Amos Blanchard similarly observed that just as "a new direction has been given to a large amount of American genius, capital, and labor" and "every village of New England resounds with the din of machinery," so "a corresponding change has come over the character and habits of a large portion of the people."

Multitudes, especially the youth, once scattered "among the farms and smaller workshops of the country," now were "congregated in compact masses" and subject to "all the influences, good and evil, which attend a dense and busy population." The once-pervasive influence of family, "restraining from vice and stimulating to good behavior with all the secret magic of a charm," had virtually disappeared.[28]

Novelists took up the task of re-creating and commenting on factory life as well. Aside from Savage's work, Catharine Williams's *Fall River: An Authentic Narrative* (1833) was one of the earliest and most narratively distinctive examples.[29] Williams retells the tale of the murder in the factory city of Fall River, Massachusetts, of the young millworker Sarah Maria Cornell, purportedly by the Methodist minister Ephraim Kingsbury Avery. Several months pregnant, she was found hanged from a farmer's haystack roof in a nearby town shortly after she had met with Avery; other marks on her body and the type of knot used on the rope suggested foul play rather than suicide, and Avery was apprehended and indicted. The trial played out over several months, captivating public attention, and Avery finally was acquitted. Williams, author of several other books, clearly thought the judgment erroneous and tried to recover as much of Cornell's story, sad as it was, as she could. Using published accounts of the trial as well as other primary materials (including some of Cornell's letters), Williams created a hybrid narrative, half fact, half conjecture or outright fiction. *Fall River* spoke to Cornell's hardships as a poor weaver in the new industrial economy, with much about the tenor of life in factory villages.

The book did not immediately produce many imitators. Within months of Lippard's success with *The Quaker City*, however, city mysteries set in the new factory environment quickly appeared: titles like Bradbury Osgood's *Mysteries of Lowell* (1844) and the anonymous *The Mysteries of Nashua; or, Revenge Punished and Constancy Rewarded* (1844). In these novels, unscrupulous millowners, agents, and overseers replaced Lippard's corrupt and depraved attorneys, bankers, and clergy.

Warner's and Cummins's formulas lent themselves to the same setting. Tales of girls who leave behind the comfort and virtues of home to test their independence in the factories became common. Ariel Cummings's *The Factory Girl; or, Gardez la Coeur* (1847) was a typical sentimental mill novel. Calliste Barton leaves her country home for "the City of Spindles" to make money to send her brother to college. Once at the factory, she must avoid such frivolous entertainments as dancing school and cotillions, which only abet temptation. Raised a good Christian, Calliste resists sin and, after she has put her brother through divinity school, returns to the country to marry her local swain, now a doctor.

The eponymous and impressionable heroine of a novel by "Miss J.A.B.," *Mary Bean, the Factory Girl* (1850), meets a different fate. A good country girl, she is swayed by the attention of George Hamilton, who pretends to be wealthy and, telling Mary that he loves her, convinces her to go with him to the mill city of Manchester, New Hampshire. Once there, installing her in a women's boardinghouse, he promises to marry her. Hamilton confesses that he is impecunious, and she, still infatuated, vows to work in the mills to support them. Worse than poor, though, he turns out to be a villain. He gets her pregnant, commits robbery and murder, and leaves her for another mill city, Saco, Maine. Mary tracks him down; they reconcile and go to Boston, where she once again begins to work in a factory. Because her pregnancy is now apparent, Hamilton sends her to a doctor for an abortion; she dies during the procedure. Indignities continue, for her lover dumps her body in a millstream, and after it is recovered, her loving sister returns it to the country and erects a marble tablet on Mary's grave. *Mary Bean* reads like *Charlotte Temple* updated for the factory world.

Pointing out the abyss was one thing; proposing an alternative required greater imagination and resolve. Of novels from the 1850s devoted to the worker's plight, Martha W. Tyler's *A Book Without a Title: or, Thrilling Events in the Life of Mira Dana* (1855), a plea for the rights of women as well as the first American novel to depict a labor strike, stands out.

The novel's first section details the title character's experiences in Lowell, where her brother Warner, a boardinghouse supervisor, secures her a job as a factory worker, even though she is only sixteen years old. A country girl, a tomboy whose family nicknames her Dick, Mira is the "wildest, merriest being, that ever rambled over clover meadows, or danced gypsy-like" through the woods.[30] For her, going to Lowell is part of growing up, for she has a "wild vague yearning for education and fame, that ever sweeps over the soul of the young and hopeful."[31] Although she finds the city a "perfect heap of houses, and people, too," and is surprised that she has to sleep with seven other girls in a room in one of the company's boardinghouses, Warner tells her that she will soon get used to the change and must strive to "tame down that high, wild spirit."[32] Because she does not want a life of mere "selfishness and ease" like many of her coworkers but instead to help "lift the pall" of suffering she sees in the world, rechanneling her exuberance is not difficult. She resolves not to be swayed by frivolity and "to lay aside a sum of money for the purpose of attending school" when she leaves the mills.[33]

A natural leader, attractive, articulate, and brave, Mira emerges as the organizer of a "turn out," or strike, after the company cuts its employees' wages. Urging her coworkers to stick together, Mira leads four thousand young women out of the city. She stays behind to make sure that the pay-masters honor the wages already owed and becomes the target of retalia-tion by the company's agents and overseers. The strike is widely reported in regional papers, bringing Mira to the attention of an American ship captain in Europe, who, fascinated by news of the remarkable young woman, decides he wants to marry her after he returns to the United States.

Mira does marry the captain; even Tyler could not envision her hero-ine's remaining single. The author thus shifts her focus from factory life to family life and then from the joys of this first marriage to the trials of a second. Mira hints at her domestic troubles. She asks why if crime de-mands a "retributive act," one should not build a "scaffold for the hanging of men's reputations, and suspend them before the public gaze [as] a warning to others to follow in their footsteps."[34] The subject of her anger is Edward Tyrell, her abusive second husband (her first, happy marriage ends when her spouse dies at sea). "If this little book should be instru-mental in saving a single sister from sorrows like those which befell the heroine of these pages, then my labor is not in vain, and I shall hear con-tentedly the fault-finding of the critic, and the murmur of dissenting voices."[35]

Mira becomes so desperate for financial independence that she decides to write a book about her trials. She shows it to a publisher in Boston, who offers her a thousand dollars for the manuscript, but she wisely holds out for more. The novel ends with her achieving her independence from Tyrell and buying a cottage for her family, which now includes her aged mother. Her anger in the preface seems much justified, even as she feels blessed to have fulfilled her youthful promise and ambition.

Within a year, Tyler self-published a second edition of her book, with telling revisions. In her preface she admitted that the story's ending had been "merely imaginative" because Mira (Tyler?) did not regain custody of her children. Moreover, she described the unenthusiastic response to the book. Her readers were not as sympathetic as she had hoped. Tyler's heroine, who takes charge in the factory as well as in her family life, may have been too radical for readers accustomed to the more biddable heroines of Warner and Cummins.

FANNY FERN'S DYSFUNCTIONAL FAMILY

Or perhaps Tyler's prose, rather than her main character's radicalism, was the problem, for a similar character in another novel from the time became a cultural sensation. She was Ruth Hall, the thinly fictionalized alter ego of Sara Payson Willis Parton, popularly known as Fanny Fern. Parton's stories and first novel, *Ruth Hall: A Domestic Tale of the Present Time* (1854), made her one of the most widely read authors of the 1850s. In some ways she hewed to the formulas of the sentimental novel but at the same time challenged the foundations of the American version of the genre, foremost in her avoidance of Christian didacticism—and of Christianity altogether, for that matter. Her bold self-assertion at a time when submission of one kind or another was expected of women appealed to readers, many of whom found her work salutary and inspirational.

Parton was born in Portland, Maine, in 1811, the fifth of Nathaniel Willis and Hannah Parker Willis's nine children. Her father was a printer and editor, first of the *Eastern Argus*, a Portland newspaper, and later, in Boston, where the family moved a few weeks after Sara's birth, of both a religious paper, the *Boston Recorder*, and a children's paper, the highly successful *Youth's Companion*. Her parents sent her to female academies, including Catharine Beecher's Hartford Female Seminary. There she met Sedgwick and the popular poet Lydia Sigourney, the "sweet singer of Hartford." She also encountered Catharine's sister, Harriet Beecher Stowe, who remembered her as "a bright laughing witch of half saint half sinner," a girl with "a head of light crêpe curls—with a jaunty little bonnet tipped to one side, & laughing light blue eyes," who excelled at writing compositions and hated arithmetic.[36]

In 1831 Parton returned to Boston and began to work for her father. In 1837 she married Charles Eldridge, a Boston bank cashier with whom she had three daughters, the first of whom died in 1845. The next year tragedy struck again: her husband died of typhoid fever, leaving her with two young children, little cash, and considerable debt. Neither Charles's parents nor hers offered to support her in any significant way; instead, they urged her to remarry. She did so in 1849, to Samuel P. Farrington, a widower with two daughters of his own. The match was a disaster. Farrington was jealous and abusive, and two years into the marriage Sara took her daughters and left him. Farrington spread ugly rumors about why she had gone and, two years later, obtained a divorce from her for "abandonment." Influenced by these false rumors, her parents and parents-in-law again refused her any significant aid.

Sara found it difficult to find work and so to support her family. She tried unsuccessfully to get into teaching and worked as a seamstress for pitiful wages until, recalling how some women made money from publishing in newspapers and journals, decided to see if she could sell some of her writings. She asked her brother, Nathaniel Parker Willis, one of the best-known New York writers and editors, if he would publish her, a reasonable request given that in his *Home Journal* he regularly included the work of Lydia Sigourney, Lydia Maria Child, "Grace Greenwood" (Sara Jane Clarke Lippincott), and "Fanny Forrester" (Emily Chubbuck), among the country's most popular women writers. Unsettled by the rumors surrounding her second marriage, though, he refused. Reminding his sister that every day brought in the work of "dozens of starving writers" trying to make it in New York, he told Parton that her writings showed "talent" but "overstrain[ed] the pathetic," while her humor "[ran] into dreadful vulgarity sometimes." He was embarrassed that other editors might know that his own sister had even written such things, for "in one or two cases they trench very close on indecency." He saw "no chance" for her.[37]

Such a cruel response would have crushed a less independent woman. But it only fueled Parton's ambition. She sold some work to the *Olive Branch* and William Moulton's popular *True Flag*, and by the end of 1851, having adopted the pseudonym Fanny Fern, her work—trenchant commentary on city life and personal relationships—was appearing in many other city papers and journals (including her brother's) as readers speculated about their author. Moulton's subscriptions picked up, too, but he continued to pay her next to nothing. In September 1852, Oliver Dyer, editor of the *Musical World and Times*, approached her with a lucrative offer to write exclusively for his paper, which she accepted.

An enterprising publisher, James Derby, of the firm Derby & Miller, published a book-length collection of Parton's articles that appeared in 1853 as *Fern Leaves from Fanny's Portfolio*. Within a year the book sold close to seventy thousand copies in the United States and a remarkable twenty-nine thousand more in England. Later that year Derby published a collection of her writings for children, *Little Ferns for Fanny's Little Friends*, and a year later, *Fern Leaves, Second Series*. By then Sara Willis Parton was making enough money to support herself and her daughters quite comfortably.

Early in 1854 Mason Brothers, a relative newcomer in New York's publishing circles, convinced her to sign a contract for a novel that included the unusual stipulation that she not publish anything else until the book appeared. This proved to be a brilliant public relations ploy, for while her audience clamored for more of her short pieces, Mason Brothers filled newspapers and journals with announcements of the forthcoming novel. When *Ruth Hall* finally appeared late in 1854 (it carries an 1855 publication date), it was an instant hit, reportedly selling seventy thousand copies in its first year, fewer than Cummins's *The Lamplighter* and Stowe's phenomenally successful *Uncle Tom's Cabin* (1852) but still enough to make waves in the literary world.

Within the year Parton followed with *Rose Clark* (1855), which did not do as well as *Ruth Hall* but still added to her reputation as a writer. She also signed another exclusive contract, with Robert Bonner, to write weekly columns for his *New York Ledger*, as she did until her death. In 1856, at the age of forty-four, she married the editor and writer James Parton, best known as Horace Greeley's biographer, and together they kept one of New York's best-known literary salons. The Partons' marriage was happy. Interestingly, though, at Sara's request, the two had signed a prenuptial agreement, guaranteeing her the income from her books and articles should she choose to remarry; by statute law, the income was his. Fortunately, she never had to invoke the clause. The couple remained together until her death in 1870 from cancer.

Parton used the autobiographical *Ruth Hall* to settle scores with her unsympathetic parents and in-laws, her brother, and the New York editors who had grown rich from her work while paying her little. One of the earliest reviews, a negative one in *The New York Times*, labeled Fern's style "masculine," a telling remark. "If Fanny Fern were a man," the reviewer wrote, "a man who believed that gratification of revenge were a proper occupation for one who has been abused, and that those who have injured us are fair game, *Ruth Hall* would be a natural and excusable book." But, he continued, "[w]e cannot understand how a delicate, suffering woman can hunt down even her persecutors so remorselessly."[38]

Hawthorne made an observation in the same vein in response to Parton's astonishing success, which he envied. Early in 1855 he wrote his publisher, William Ticknor, that he had been reading *Ruth Hall* and wished to except it from his blanket condemnation of other women writers. "I must say I enjoyed [the novel] a good deal," he told Ticknor. "This woman," he continued, "writes as if the devil was in her; and that is the only condition under which a woman ever writes anything worth reading . . . Generally, women write like emasculated men, and are only to be distinguished from male authors by greater feebleness and folly." But when they "throw off the restraints of decency, and come before the public stark naked, as it were—then their books are sure to possess character and value." He ended by asking if Ticknor knew anything about Parton and requested that if the publisher ever met her, to "let her know how much I admire her book."[39]

What about Parton's writing made Hawthorne separate her from the novels written by that "damned mob of scribbling women" that he despised? In her preface Fern noted that her book would undoubtedly puzzle some, for it was "entirely at variance with all set rules for novel-writing," having no "intricate plot," "startling developments," or "hair-raising escapes." She noted its verbal economy, for she had "compressed into one volume" what she could have expanded "into two or three," a skill honed on her short stories and essays. Finally, she admitted that in the novel she had "entered[,] unceremoniously and unannounced, into people's houses, without stopping to ring the bell."[40]

"THE DEVIL WAS IN HER"

At the start of *Ruth Hall*, its title character seems to be a typical domestic heroine. Parton skims through Ruth's early life in a chapter. The second chapter, less than a page long, recounts her wedding to the good Harry Hall, the only child of a rural doctor and his termagant wife. The newly-weds start life together and try to avoid Harry's prying and hypercritical parents, who regard Fanny as a spoiled young girl and an incompetent housekeeper. Parton's tone is genial and facetious as she writes of Ruth's giving birth to a young girl she and Harry name Daisy.[41]

The book takes a dark turn when one winter little Daisy falls ill with the croup. After putting off a visit to the ailing child, Dr. Hall, Harry's father, finally appears and pronounces matter-of-factly that "the child is struck with death." He counsels the shocked parents to "let her drop off quietly" and to refrain from seeking a second opinion, which would be a waste of money.[42] Daisy dies within the day. Ruth's depression following her child's death is only partially relieved by the arrival several years later of two more daughters, Katy and then Nettie.

Eight years later Harry, summering with his wife and daughters at a northeastern beach resort, falls ill with typhus and dies, but not before Daisy's deathbed scene is essentially repeated: Dr. and Mrs. Hall arrive before the end, and the former informs Ruth, "It is all up with [Harry]; he's in the last stage of the complaint; he won't live two days."[43] Parton paints an equally vicious portrait of Ruth's family. When her foppish brother Hyacinth Ellet appears at the hotel after Harry's death, all he thinks of is how unkempt his sister, who has just fainted, looks. "It is really quite dreadful to see her in this way," he says. "It is really quite dreadful. Somebody ought to tell her, when she comes to, that her hair is parted unevenly and needs brushing sadly."[44]

The Halls and Mr. Ellet (Ruth's mother is deceased) bicker after they realize that Harry recently lost money in a poor business deal and has left his wife and child with virtually nothing; neither party wants to extend help. Instead, each family wants to take one of the little girls, but Ruth insists that she will find work instead to support them. The Halls consent to providing a pittance only after they learn that some of their fellow parishioners are talking about how stingy they are. Mr. Ellet follows suit, agreeing only to support his daughter and grandchildren for a limited time.

With her children, Ruth moves to a truly hellish environment: New York City. As they enter the city, they meet people out of George Lippard's world: "a low-browed, pig-faced, thick-lipped fellow, with a flashy neck-tie over a vest," says of Ruth, "prettyish, is n't she?" "Deuced nice form," his friend replies, as he lights a "cheap cigar." "I should n't mind kissing her."[45] Parton's description of the boardinghouse district, which replaces the idyllic country cottage in which the family once lived so happily, similarly recalls Lippard and Thompson:

In a dark narrow street, in one of those heterogeneous boarding-houses abounding in the city, where clerks, market-boys, apprentices, and sewing-girls, bolt their meals with railroad velocity; where the maid-of-all-work, with red arms, frowzy head, and leathern lungs, screams in the entry for any boarder who happens to be inquired for at the door; where one plate suffices for fish, flesh, fowl, and dessert; where soiled table-cloths, sticky crockery, oily cookery, and bad grammar, predominate; where greasy cards are shuffled, and bad cigars smoked of an evening...

At the summer resort, Ruth met a despairing woman named Mrs. Leon, who warned her never to allow one of her daughters to marry someone whom she did not truly love, for she herself had made that fateful error. Now, as Ruth, Katy, and Nettie pass an insane asylum in the city, Ruth hears that Mrs. Leon has just perished inside, her husband having committed her. She and the children are led past chained inmates to Mrs. Leon's corpse, while the cries of "maniacs over [Ruth's] head echoed through the stillness of that cold, gloomy vault." The attendant hands Ruth a letter that Mrs. Leon addressed to her in her last days but never sent. "I am not crazy, Ruth, no, no—but I shall be; the air of this place stifles me; I grow weaker—weaker. I cannot die here; for the love of heaven, dear Ruth, come and take me away."[46]

Pressured by Harry's parents, Ruth consents to let Katy visit them, without realizing that they intend to keep her. Further reduced to desperation by her failure to find a livable wage, Ruth finally decides to try the literary world and encounters the disapproving Hyacinth. Just as Parton's brother had done to Sara, he dismisses her and her abilities. Yet in the very issue of his journal, he pleads "for public favor for a young actress, whom he said had been driven from the sheltered privacy of home, to earn her subsistence upon the stage" and whose acting he believes should have received a better welcome. Ruth must take her writing elsewhere, but how, she thinks, "can I ask of strangers a favor which a brother's heart has so coldly refused?"[47]

Soon enough, Ruth is a regular contributor to the story papers under the pen name Floy, whom everyone is discussing. There are all sorts of rumors about her identity—for example, that she is a man, "because she had the courage to call things by their right names, and the independence to express herself boldly on subjects which to the timid and clique-serving were tabooed." Others think she is "a disappointed old maid," a "designing widow," a "moon-struck girl," or a "nondescript." Some try to imitate her and, "failing in this, abused and maligned her." The "hypocritical denounced the sacrilegious fingers which had dared to touch the Ark," and the "fashionist [sic] voted her a vulgar, plebeian thing"; "the earnest and sorrowing," however, "to whose burdened hearts she had given voice, cried God speed her."[48]

Floy becomes a literary celebrity. Fan letters start to arrive at her editor's office. Some ask for advice; others are marriage proposals. A college professor writes her to complain about her violation of "all established rules of composition," for in her writing she was "as lawless and erratic as a comet."[49] The composer Louis Jullien publishes "The Ruth Hall Schottische," sheet music whose cover pictures a young woman representing Ruth. Another enterprising musician, G. F. Wurzel, issues a popular song, "Little Daisy." Underneath the veneer of fame, though, lurks discontent. Nettie asks her mother, "When I get to be a woman shall I write books, mamma?" "God forbid," Ruth replies. "No happy woman ever writes. From Harry's grave sprang 'Floy.'"[50]

Hyacinth is livid, for he has learned Floy's identity. He forbids any of his sister's articles from appearing in his paper and refuses to read positive reviews of her book. Still, he pathetically clings to her success. He points out to a friend a steamboat on the Hudson River named *Floy* and admits that it is named after his sister, but when the friend wonders how it could be so, for he has heard that Floy was "in very destitute circumstances" and wandered "from one editorial office to another in search of employment," Hyacinth becomes apoplectic.[51] Mr. Ellet is less ambivalent about claiming a role in Ruth's phenomenal ascent. He self-servingly tells a friend that he just had been reading some of his own daughter's sketches and "thinking what a great thing it is for a child to have a good father."[52]

The novel ends with Ruth's assuring her permanent financial security through her purchase of a bond for one hundred shares in the Seton Bank, a document that Parton reproduces in the book as a tangible symbol of Ruth's (and her own) remarkable diligence and talent. In the last chapter, Ruth, her children, and her beloved editor, Mr. Walter, visit Harry's grave. As they turn away, a bird "trilled forth a song as sweet and clear as the lark's at heaven's own blessed gate." "Accept the omen, dear Ruth," Mr. Walter says. "Life has much of harmony yet in store for you."[53]

Ruth Hall had indeed made Parton wealthy, but reviewers differed on what she had accomplished. The harshest notice came from the *Southern Quarterly Review*, in which the reviewer used the occasion to assess Parton's readership. "The almost universal ability to read," he wrote, "and the consequent love of reading, have developed in this nation of readers especially, an immense middle class of ordinary readers of average intelligence." He then speculated on what precisely this audience sought in novels. "Flat insipidity is not tolerated even by the middle class," he noted. "Until the advent of 'Ruth Hall,'" no writer "had hit the nail precisely on the head; the small intelligences were yet without a pet book." Parton had written a book for the great, unwashed middle-class readership, for *Ruth Hall* was, in this reviewer's snide opinion, "a miracle of *inspired mediocrity*." He went on in this condescending tone, explaining that a typical middle-class reader like "Nancy" never wanted to go "beyond her depth. She is quick and sensitive too," he added sarcastically. "She knows that Hawthorne's Psychology was never meant for her," for when she encounters it, she has "a disagreeable sense of insecurity," presumably of the sort with which she has plenty of experience in her own restricted role as wife and mother.[54]

The reviewer for *The Pioneer; or, California Monthly Magazine* attacked the novel on different grounds. He pilloried the cult of celebrity and all "those false enthusiasts who gather autographs, portraits and anecdotes without any idea of the worth and character of the objects of admiration." Gossipmongers were even worse. "Why should the world care about anything" in writers, except "what is really uncommon? What have we to do with their private lives, petty sins, or family quarrels?"[55]

"You have perverted the good your covert hints of reform might have accomplished," he wrote, addressing Parton and the high quality of her previous writing. He accused her of a "petty, vindictive spirit," something "sprung from a malignant heart," and was outraged at Parton's attack on domesticity. "The family circle had always been considered sacred," but Parton had exposed to the entire world what should have been kept private. She had "violated the sanctity of the fireside." And to what end? The book was nothing less than Parton's "glorification of herself."[56] *The Knickerbocker* agreed with this last judgment. "There is one thing that militates against the idea that [*Ruth Hall*] is an entirely authentic and veritable history," its reviewer noted: "the praise that she is all the while awarding the heroine."[57]

Writing in the early feminist journal *The Una*, Elizabeth Cady Stanton, one of the country's foremost advocates of women's rights, understood that the novel was a breakthrough. Its great lesson "is that God has given to woman sufficient brain and muscle to work out her own destiny unaided and alone." Further, with regard to the depiction of an unloving family, Stanton thought that "the censure more justly belong[ed] to the living subjects," not to Ruth herself.[58]

In *Ruth Hall*, Parton worked through and beyond the conventions of the sentimental novel. The novel is about family, domesticity, and womanhood, but Parton had little interest in Christian submission and morality. Like the heroines in other sentimental novels, Ruth endures one defeat after another and the cruelty of those who should be protecting her. But she never resigns herself to her fate. Rather, Ruth fights for herself and her children at every turn, succeeding in a man's world without much help at all. She becomes wealthy and famous because of her innate talents and ambition. The latter, notably, grew in part out of her desire for revenge. The novel simultaneously fought against the pervasive sexism of American society and exemplified American values—namely, individualism and self-reliance. No wonder it upset so many critics.

Not insignificantly, Parton created an unorthodox, fragmentary style for *Ruth Hall* that was perfectly suited to her subject. Her ninety chapters are often very brief—some less than a page—and consist of evocative vignettes, rapid shifts in scene, and overheard conversations, as though the reader were walking Manhattan's streets and piecing together what she could of Ruth's story as it unfolded. Some readers would find the same experience in Whitman's contemporaneous long poem *Leaves of Grass* (1855). The reader observes Ruth's growing self-consciousness, and Parton comes close to revealing the workings of consciousness itself.

BREAKING THE MOLD

Parton was not alone among women novelists at the time who came up with new ways of presenting character and selfhood in their fiction. Among the most innovative was Caroline Chesebro'. Born in 1825 in Canandaigua, New York, she was the daughter of Nicholas Cheseborough, a hatter, wool merchant, and postmaster, and Betsey Kimball

Cheseborough. Her father acquired some notoriety when, with two other Freemasons, he was charged in the kidnapping and disappearance of William Morgan, who had planned to publish a book revealing Masonic secrets. Cheseborough and his coconspirators served a year in jail, but because Morgan's body was never positively identified, he escaped further punishment.

Cheseborough sent his daughter to the local Canandaigua Seminary. A few years later she began to write stories for *Graham's Magazine* and *Holden's Dollar Magazine*—she shortened her family name at this time— which were later collected in her first book, *Dream-land by Daylight* (1851). Encouraged by positive reviews—one reviewer found in its stories "unmistakable evidence of originality of mind"—she wrote her first novel, *Isa, a Pilgrimage* (1852).[59] Next came *The Children of Light* (1853), the story of two strong women, Asia Phillips and Vesta Maderon, who, when they are rejected by the men they love, move together to the city, where Vesta fulfills her ideal of service by supporting Asia in her budding acting career. Like Sedgwick in *Married or Single?*, Chesebro' bemoaned the indignities suffered by women in heterosexual relationships. Unlike Sedgwick, she ventured an alternative.

Chesebro' followed *Children of Light* with a long, sprawling novel, *Getting Along: A Book of Illustrations* (1855), focused on various couples' relationships. Assuming marriage as the norm, Chesebro' judges the soundness of each marriage by the partners' fidelity to their original commitment. The novel is about the varied and complex nature of commitment and is proof that the search for a suitable spouse was just as compelling a fictional trope as it had been in *The Coquette* fifty years earlier. Finally, in 1863, Chesebro' published *Peter Carradine; or, The Martindale Pastoral* (1863), an innovative novel, about three heroines and their differing versions of the same events. For reasons unknown, she then abandoned writing, even though *The Knickerbocker* had opined that "among the numerous candidates for literary same," Chesebro' had "few or no superiors."[60] She took a position teaching English composition at the Packer Collegiate Institute in Brooklyn, where she remained until she moved to Piermont, on the Hudson River, to live with her brothers. She died there in 1873 and was buried next to her parents in Canandaigua.

Chesebro' was interested in the plasticity of gender roles—she had an expansive view of womanhood—and this interest sets her novels apart. Her heroines are not trapped by society's expectations, but rather experience more of themselves and the world as they challenge the limits of propriety. This approach found a memorable expression in her first novel, *Isa*, which Chesebro' dedicated to Grace Greenwood (1823–1904), the pen name of Sarah Jane Lippincott. The choice is significant, for by 1852 Greenwood, who had started out writing children's stories and poetry, was well known not only as an author and editor but as an outspoken advocate of women's rights and abolition. Given the plot, characters, and politics of *Isa*, Greenwood was the proper muse.

The novel relates Isa Lee's story, which begins in conventional sentimental fashion. She is raised in a poorhouse but is rescued by Mrs. Dugganne and her son, Weare, who, on a charitable mission to the house, recognize that she possesses intelligence and spirit. Isa flourishes in their home, a place of love and stability. She is deeply impressed by Mrs. Dugganne's kindness and forbearance, particularly during the periodic visits of her husband, an alcoholic. She admires Weare, in all respects Mr. Dugganne's opposite, who is a strongly moral and religious young man (of orthodox faith); the reader learns that he had his clerical education in Richmond, presumably at the Presbyterian seminary in that Virginia city.[61] Isa grows remarkably, soon surpassing Weare, the divinity student, in knowledge and ability.

Isa's studies open new vistas, and she begins to write philosophical essays on the power of the human will. As Weare describes her unorthodox belief, "Will, human will, is next to, it leans up close against God—God first—yes, he is the first of all powers, and mortal will next."[62] Her essays so impress Mr. Warren, the owner of *The Guardian*, that he invites her to live with him and his wife and to work as an assistant to his editor, Alanthus Stuart. Isa accepts, even though it means leaving Weare, but soon enough she begins to delight in the company of Stuart, also an author, "though neither a popular nor even an acknowledged one," because his views are too "transcendental" and "demand too much of a reader's thought and investigation." When she learns his nom de plume, though, she realizes that he is the author of a book that she admires but that Weare has banished from the family library for its supposed theological radicalism.[63]

When Mrs. Dugganne falls ill, Isa returns to her home but, after the benevolent old woman recovers, leaves once again feeling that her ideas about religion, morality, and woman's place in society have made her incompatible with the people who raised her. Debating Weare about God's sovereignty, for instance, she shocks him by declaring that belief in it is "cowardly" at best, for "there is no limit given but that which our own will regulates. No other voice," Isa writes, "than man's mental capacity, ever said, *thus far, no farther.*"[64] It also dawns on her that Alanthus Stuart is her intellectual match, and after Mr. Warren sells *The Guardian,* the two turn exclusively to their writing. Isa's works are "curious and powerful" and "singular enough to enchain attention" so that "it became a fashion to read them, and for a time, among certain classes, those who longed and labored for the progress and advancement of their kind, to praise them."[65]

Isa receives a proposal of marriage from an older man, General S., with whom she discussed women's rights at one of Mr. Warren's soirees. He offers her "his name, his fame, his fortune." Isa refuses, for she wants no restrictions in her life. She and Alanthus move to Europe, where they can live together unmarried without breaking societal taboos. Isa reveres his "originality, daring, and power," while Alanthus admires her confidence, for that was the "keystone of Power, Love, and Knowledge."[66] He beholds in her nothing less than "the completion of himself."[67]

They have a child, who tragically dies young. Isa then becomes gravely ill, and in her last days, as her sickness becomes widely known, Weare Dugganne visits her. "Do you anticipate annihilation?" her husband asks in front of Weare. No, she replies, "THERE IS NO ANNIHILATION. I have never for a moment imagined that there is. I am going within the veil—and you will follow me."[68] To Dugganne's horror and despair, Isa dies without returning to the Christian faith, and he curses Stuart for "ruining" her immortal soul. But she dies peacefully, having wagered that if there is an afterlife, Stuart will meet her there.

In *Isa,* Chesebro' broached subjects few other American novelists at the time, men or women, dared to: the relationship between orthodox religious faith and personal fulfillment, between the demands of the soul and the demands of society, and between love and marriage as well as the possibility of living a life of the mind, inhabited by radical philosophical and political ideas. *The American Whig Review* took notice. "Somebody has remarked that this is an age of skepticism" in which there is a tendency to "mistrust all old faith and creeds, to disregard the old landmarks in almost every thing." But "amid the Babel of creeds and beliefs," the male reviewer asked, "is there one that in any measure does or can compensate for those so perseveringly sought to be overturned?" And can "the new fill and take the place of the old in the human mind?" *Isa* is "the embodiment of these questions," the reviewer continued, but he criticized the eponymous heroine's progress toward what he thought of as "self-deception." The fault of the novel is that "Isa makes her self-will, her intellectual progress, and her ambition, a three-fold deity."[69] In this sense, Chesebro' had not surpassed traditional religious belief; she had merely fashioned a personal religion out of secular values and ideas.

The reviewer for *Harper's New Monthly Magazine* similarly pointed out Chesebro's skepticism but thought that her novel left the reader bewildered. Instead of proposing a coherent religious or intellectual alternative to traditional Christianity, the novel exemplified "the perils of entire freedom of thought" during "the state of intellectual transition between attachment to tradition and the supremacy of individual conviction."[70] The author's thought was in fact coherent, though it was rooted in a variety of contemporary (and secular or at least non-Christian) ideas: Emerson's Transcendental idealism; Margaret Fuller's pathbreaking *Woman in the Nineteenth Century* (1845); and the women's rights movement, particularly Elizabeth Cady Stanton's Declaration of Rights and Sentiments, issued at the Seneca Falls Convention of 1848 (an event that occurred not far from Canandaigua). Fuller's trajectory was not so different from Isa's, in fact. The former went to Europe as a correspondent for Horace Greeley's *New-York Tribune* and there conceived a child out of wedlock; like Isa, she could not find emotional comfort in her own country.

Significantly, the reviewer did praise the interiority of the author's approach. "The scene is laid in the interior world—the world of consciousness, of reflection, of passion. In this twilight region, so often peopled with monstrous shapes, and spectral phantasms," Chesebro' trod "with great firmness of step." When Isa discovers a volume of essays that "canvassed without mercy, without reverence, even mock-reverence . . . the belief of Christians, the laws of society, the standard of morality, the principles of duty," she was most taken by the author's treatment, "wholly, or principally," of the internal life.[71] "With rare subtlety of discrimination," Chesebro' brings "hidden springs of action to light, untwisting the tangled webs of experience," as she reveals "some of the darkest and most fearful depths of the human heart."[72] This was the thread connecting Chesebro' to Charles Brockden Brown and George Lippard, who likewise plumbed the depths of human motivation, as well as to her contemporaries Hawthorne and Melville, who, like she, "risked the uncertain chances of success in resting a popular tale upon a purely psychological foundation."[73]

"AN INFINITESIMAL OUTBIRTH OF THE INFINITE"

Isa was reformist and feminist fiction, in which Chesebro' advocated allegiance to the voice within over the demands of traditional faith. Another important novelist, reformer, and feminist, Mary Gove Nichols (1810–1884) was a restless believer and seeker of truth who championed such causes as dietary reform, enlightened physiology, hydropathy or the water cure, and free love. Nichols was born in 1810 in Goffstown, New Hampshire, a small town in the southern part of the state. Her parents, William Neal, who farmed the area's rich river bottom, and Rebecca Neal, held unusual religious views. William was an avowed freethinker and atheist while Rebecca was his opposite, a professing Christian who insisted that parents should curb children's willfulness. More influenced by her father, Mary was not broken by her mother's discipline or attracted to her religion; she found her way to Quakerism, through an uncle. She met a fellow believer, the thirty-one-year-old bachelor Hiram Gove, who fell in love with her, eleven years younger than he was.

Mary realized that she did not love Gove but, yielding to social pressure, accepted his proposal. To make matters worse, during her engagement she did fall in love, with another Quaker about her own age. Gove discovered their dalliance and was enraged, prophesying that if Mary did not marry him, she would burn in hell. Confused, she went through with the nuptials, only to realize very quickly that she had made a terrible decision. For all his outward piety Gove was a possessive, cruel, and unscrupulous man, always bending her will to his, and so paranoid and violent that to Mary his lovemaking came to seem like rape. She remained in this horrific situation for years. Finally, when she was thirty-one, she left him, taking their daughter, Elma, with her (she had lost several other children to miscarriage or stillbirth). Because state law mandated that only men could initiate divorce proceedings, technically she remained Gove's wife.

During the years she suffered with Gove, Mary was the main breadwinner, lecturing and teaching classes as a public advocate for various health reforms. She advocated dietary reform, influenced by the vegetarianism of Sylvester Graham (of graham cracker fame) and then by the new fad of hydropathy, or, as it was known, the water cure, which involved a regimen of cold bathing, wrapping oneself in wet towels, and drinking great quantities of water. She also read much about women's physiology and began to lecture on this subject; she was so well regarded that in 1842 Harper & Brothers published her *Lectures to Ladies on Anatomy and Physiology*. After her experience with Gove, she wanted women to learn about their bodies so that they could control their sexual lives, a topic that drew crowds to her lectures. During this period she also fell in love with Henry Gardiner Wright, a young English reformer who shared many of her passions. Sadly, he soon died of cancer, at only thirty-two years of age.

Shortly after his death, Mary's father died, putting her child in jeopardy because Gove had owed him money; holding this debt over him, Neal had pressured Gove not to claim his granddaughter, as under the law he could. After Neal's death, Gove did just that. To reclaim Elma, Mary hired lawyers and eventually devised a plan, ultimately successful, to kidnap her daughter. The two moved to New York City to escape her husband and boarded at the home of Joel Shew, a well-known hydropathist. Marx Edgeworth Lazarus, a charismatic reformer and an advocate of Charles Fourier's social reforms, was another guest. Mary was won over to his cause after listening to him expatiate on Fourier's hope to make labor attractive, to eradicate the boredom associated with it, and to allow full expression of the human passions in the service of self-fulfillment.

Mary next fell in love with Thomas Low Nichols, five years her junior, whom she met at the poet Frances Osgood's well-known New York soiree. At Osgood's one was likely to encounter such representatives of the city's intelligentsia as Albert Brisbane, Fourier's chief American disciple; Edgar Allan Poe and Herman Melville; and Horace Greeley. At first she thought Nichols foppish and too forward, but the more he pursued her, the more drawn to him she became. Nichols pressed his case with the Swedish mystic Emanuel Swedenborg's notion of conjugal love, that a true marriage of souls is spiritual. Nichols believed that he and Mary were made for each other, and before long, she agreed. But Mary was still married to Gove.

Fate intervened. At the age of thirty-eight Hiram Gove fell in love with someone else and told Mary that he would grant her a divorce. Mary and Nichols married in a Swedenborgian ceremony and from then on worked together for their various causes. He, too, was interested in physiology—he earned a medical degree at the New York University Medical College—and in 1852 published his *Esoteric Anthropology*, which combined his interest in physiology with dietary reform, the water cure, and Fourier's social theories into what Mary Nichols's modern biographer calls, for its period, "an outrageously sexual book."[74]

The following year the Nicholses joined the anarchist Josiah Warren's Modern Times utopian community on Long Island, hoping eventually to garner support for their own plan for Desarrollo, an "educational and industrial institute" based on Fourier's system of association rather than on Warren's hyperindividualism. The couple remained at Modern Times for two years but had a falling-out with Warren over the degree of sexual liberty in the community; the Nicholses favored mandating free love in the community rather than leaving it to personal choice, a principle with which Warren did not agree. They then traveled into the Ohio Valley, visiting other communes, and after briefly becoming spiritualists—and insisting that they could contact spirits from beyond the grave—they converted to Roman Catholicism.

Thomas was horrified when the Civil War broke out, so they decided to leave the country, making their final pilgrimage by ship. They lived the rest of their lives in England. In the course of their time together, both Mary and Thomas published frequently, including fiction. Mary wrote stories (some under the pseudonym Mary Orme) that appeared in *Godey's Lady's Book* and other prominent journals, and a number of novels, including *Uncle John; or, It Is Too Much Trouble* (1846) and *Agnes Morris; or, The Heroine of Domestic Life* (1849). In 1855, she published a third, autobiographical novel, titled *Mary Lyndon; or, Revelations of a Life: An Autobiography*. It was as remarkable as *Isa*. The big difference between the two was that Nichols believed she could bring a new world into existence in the United States rather than simply escape the current one.

The title character says at the beginning of her story, "I have resolved to write the real and actual Life of a Human Being, so far as I can. Nobody ever did it, though many have tried and more have pretended."[75] Yet she recognizes the inadequacies of language. It is impossible, she says, to describe in words those who have "blasted our lives deeply," for "it is only at a distance that we can describe the burning prairie with calmness, and only through the long vista of years that we can see our lives, cleared from the mists and clouds of feeling, and describe them as they really were."

"A description of sorrow is not sorrow," she laments, for "what is felt can never be described." Yet she must try: "I shall go on, and, simply and truly as I *can*, I shall tell my story," presumably for the benefit of other women who suffer as she had.[76]

What Mary Lyndon relates closely parallels Nichols's own trials during her journey to self-consciousness and self-fulfillment. Shortly after her marriage to a man named Hervey, she falls into a deep depression. She entertains frequent thoughts of suicide until she retreats into "piety and resignation." She reflects "long, and deeply, and bitterly, on marriage" and comes to the conclusion that without love it is only "legalized adultery."[77] The first part of the novel ends with Lyndon's achieving her freedom and kidnapping her daughter, Elva, from her husband, but also with the heroine's experiencing a terrifying hemorrhage that incapacitates her for weeks.

Part 2 details her intellectual and moral self-development, which begins at the town lyceum. A moderately progressive Unitarian minister allows women to read compositions at the meetings he conducts, assuming that they will not read their own work but rather the work of men. But Lyndon reads an essay she had written entitled "The Sphere and Condition of Women." Unnerved by the large crowd, she persists and describes the woman's sphere "as that undefined, and seemingly undefinable, thing; that space which has no center, and can have no circumference" because man has never allowed any "fair and free trial" of all of woman's powers. And no woman has even dared ask the question, "What can I do?" because marriage remains her "annihilation," destroying not only her heart but also "her health and usefulness."[78] After she finishes and experiences the applause, she knows she has found her life's work.

At a picnic sponsored by the lyceumgoers, Lyndon meets an attractive Englishman, Mr. Lynde, and with great interest listens to a brief speech he makes. He talks of Earth "as an infinitesimal outbirth of the Infinite; as being created from the Uncreate [*sic*]; beautiful, because the soul of beauty was informing, and from hour to hour from year to year, through all time, harmonizing this bud and blossom of the Eternal, which men call earth." Sounding almost like a parody of a New England Transcendentalist, Lynde goes on about "the inmost definition of Faith, even our oneness with divinity—and thus we came to a self-reverence, and all things were sacred, not alone what men had written in the Bible, but what the spirit had written in all nature."[79] To Lyndon, at least, it all makes sense. In Lynde's presence, she feels that "the omnipotent Love" lives in her spirit, "to sustain, to control, to direct" her.[80]

At an evening symposium, two of Lynde's reformist friends, Mooney and Lang, discuss a planned utopian community (clearly Fourierist but described as "communist"), a public event to which "all the literary, and transcendental, and radical aristocracy of the place" (including Mary Lyndon) are invited. In the projected utopia, no one will own the land, only the use of it, and "and no government but self-government" will be recognized. Further, the members are to use no violence "toward man or beast," and so no criminal can be so punished, no flesh eaten, and no woolen garments worn.

But it is more dream than possibility, the suddenly skeptical Lynde reminds after the two have finished their presentation. He says "that cold, hard theories are not life" and "cold, hard intellectualities about universal love are not love."[81] Further, Lynde disagrees with their wish to subjugate individual will. The chief questions for anyone interested in the projected community, Lynde suggests to Lang at a subsequent meeting, are, "Will I live my own life in my own freedom, or will I be subjected to you, or others?" and "Will I enslave others in my turn?"[82] Lynde finds what he wants in Lyndon, for they become lovers. These months are the happiest in her life, for Lynde is a fount of wisdom. But their joy is brief, for Lynde confides that he has a serious illness. The section ends with Mary's beloved traveling to England, escorted by friends who have crossed the Atlantic to bring him home to die.

Part 3 begins with news of Lynde's death, Hervey's assumption of Elva's guardianship, Mary Lyndon's plan to rescue her daughter yet again, and their escape to New York. Mary, alone, moves from one boarding-house to another. She eventually finds work as a teacher and lecturer on health reform and sells some articles to Sarah Josepha Hale's *Godey's Lady's Book* as well as a novel to Harper's. She meets an impractical but obviously brilliant Transcendentalist, Ellery, and accepts his generous invitation to move into a large home to live alongside a diverse group of boarders. Vegetarianism, water cure, and calisthenics are the rule. Mary flourishes in this environment of like-minded souls, teaching classes on physiology to forty women, giving four lectures a week on different reform issues, and writing for magazines, aware that she has indeed found her purpose: "to rouse an enthusiasm for health and human culture that will never die."[83]

At a Christmas holiday party, she meets Mr. Vincent, who has "an air of crystalline precision" that at first she does not like. Still, she is drawn to him, and after an extended epistolary courtship, the two realize that they are each other's destiny. Hervey's wish for a divorce soon follows, and when she finally is free, she tells Vincent on what terms he may have her. "In a marriage with you," she tells him, "I resign no right of my soul. I enter into no compact to be faithful to you. I only promise to be faithful to the deepest love of my heart . . . If my love leads me from you," she warns him, "I must go." She also makes what then were two odd requests. "I must keep my name," she says, "the name I have made for myself, through labor and suffering." And second, "I must have my own room, into which none can come, but because I wish it."[84] Vincent accepts her terms, and the novel ends with the birth of their unnamed child.

Mary Lyndon is the most radical women's novel of the pre–Civil War period, owing to Nichols's insistence on the limit of language in conveying lived experience, the assertiveness of her alter ego, and its depiction of unconventional life philosophies that seem to have little to do with Christianity. The distance between Warner, Cummins, and Parton, on the one hand, and Chesebro' and Nichols, on the other, is negligible in one sense: all wrote within the sentimental genre, incorporated religion into their novels, and wrote in order to empower women. Yet compared to the last two, the formers' conservative Christian values and commitment to marriage and the home as women's sphere make them appear utterly traditional. Their popularity, however, made possible the acceptance of the work of their more radical female contemporaries. This was their most lasting legacy.

5 } On the Color Line

In his charming memoir of youth, *A Small Boy and Others* (1913), Henry James recalled the impact of Harriet Beecher Stowe's *Uncle Tom's Cabin* (1852) on the America of his childhood. "We lived and moved at that time, with great intensity, in Mrs. Stowe's novel. Its appeal was universal," for "that triumphant work [had] no classified condition; it was for no sort of reader as distinct from any other." The novel "knew the felicity of gathering in alike the small and the simple and the big and the wise, and had above all the extraordinary fortune of finding itself, for an immense number of people, much less a book than a state of vision, of feeling and of consciousness in which they didn't sit and read and appraise and pass the time, but walked and talked and laughed and cried and, in a manner of which Mrs. Stowe was the irresistible cause, generally conducted themselves."[1] James's was only the most eloquent reminiscence. *Uncle Tom's Cabin; or, Life Among the Lowly* was the nineteenth century's bestselling novel, with ten thousand copies sold the first week, one hundred thousand copies sold within two months, and three hundred thousand the first year. Its influence on American culture was pervasive: Stowe's work appeared as a children's book and a play, and scenes from it appeared on ceramics, sheet music covers, cartes de visite, and advertising cards for a variety of products.[2]

Today the novel is best remembered as the vade mecum of the abolitionist movement, as the book that set the nation on the path to civil war. It is a well-known anecdote that when Lincoln greeted Stowe at the White House during her visit in December 1862, he quipped, "So you are the little woman who wrote the book that started this great war."[3] Given the novel's political importance, Stowe's influence on the development of the form is seen as secondary, if it is considered at all. But *Uncle Tom's Cabin*, though conventionally sentimental in many respects, had a profound effect on the American novel. Above all, Stowe brought the sentimental novel into conversation with fugitive slave narratives, and if the novel's origins were partly in this inchoate African American genre, its success made possible fully realized novels by African Americans, the first of which were greatly affected by Stowe's characters and plot.

Harriet Beecher was born in 1811 in Litchfield, Connecticut, the seventh of nine children of Lyman Beecher and Roxana Foote Beecher.[4] Her father, a prominent Congregational clergyman, was educated at Yale and along with its president, Timothy Dwight, Jonathan Edwards's grandson, played a prominent role in the revivals that became known as the Second Great Awakening. Roxana was the daughter of a well-known Connecticut family; she died in 1816 at the age of forty-one, leaving her husband with a home full of children. Lyman eventually remarried, but Harriet spent much of her girlhood with her aunt Harriet Foote. Several of Stowe's siblings went on to live remarkable lives: Henry Ward became one of the country's best-known preachers; Charles and Edward also became clergymen and were active in abolitionist circles; Catharine became a pioneer women's educator, and Isabella a leader in the women's suffrage movement.

Both Harriet and her eldest sister, Catharine, attended Miss Sarah Pierce's Female Academy in Litchfield, a bucolic town in northwestern Connecticut and a regional center of culture.[5] In addition to the academy, the town was home to Judge Tapping Reeve's law school, the first in the country.[6] Lyman Beecher had a successful career in Litchfield, initiating many revivals in his church and throughout the state, the crucible for the initial phase of the Second Great Awakening.[7] In 1827, after attending Hartford Female Academy, Harriet remained at the school, which her sister Catharine had established, as a teacher of rhetoric and composition.

In 1832, Lyman took his battle against slackening faith to the gateway of the American West. He uprooted his large family—his wife, five children, and Aunt Harriet—and moved to Cincinnati, Ohio, to take over as president of Lane Theological Seminary. Harriet Beecher soon met a young instructor in theology, Calvin Stowe, whom she married in 1836. She gave birth to twins, Eliza and Harriet, and eventually five more children, one of whom, Charley, died of cholera in his first year. In this same period, Stowe began to publish stories based on her experiences in New England and her travel to the West, which she collected and published as *The Mayflower* (1843).

Cincinnati at the time was a bustling, growing city. In 1840 it counted 46,000 residents, a number that included many German immigrants. A decade later it was home to more than 150,000 people, many of them Irish immigrants who had fled the potato famine. Located just across the Ohio River from the slave state of Kentucky, the city also had a significant African American population, both free and fugitive, and so attracted bounty hunters. During her years there, Stowe frequently encountered the institution that was legal across the river, and her exposure to slavery's indignities greatly strengthened the abolitionist sympathies she had inherited from her father.

By 1846 Stowe was not well and near exhaustion. Debilitated by the burdens of childbearing and housekeeping, she traveled to the new water cure establishment in Brattleboro, Vermont, that the German immigrants Robert and William Wesselhoeft had founded. For fifteen months Beecher followed its strict regimen, which included homeopathic rather than allopathic medicine. She and her husband then traded places, his stay at the spa lasting a year while she tended to the family in Cincinnati. Then, in 1850, Calvin was invited to assume a teaching position at Bowdoin College in Brunswick, Maine. Stowe was pleased to move back to the Northeast, even though her husband's tenure at the college was comically brief. While he was trying to extricate himself from Cincinnati—Stowe already had settled the family in Brunswick and was quite happy there—he was offered the chair of sacred literature at Andover Theological Seminary, one of the most prestigious positions in the country. Stowe did not want to leave Maine, but Calvin won out; the chance to teach at his denomination's chief educational institution was impossible to pass up.

With the passage of the Fugitive Slave Law, part of the Compromise of 1850 that made it illegal for any American to aid a runaway slave and empowered commissions to force citizens into fugitive-hunting posses, Stowe was outraged. Talk of abolition was common in her family, and this latest political development prompted her sister Isabella to say, "Now, Hattie, if I could use a pen as you can, I would write something that would make this whole nation feel what an accursed thing slavery is."[8] Drawing on her experiences in Cincinnati as well as on accounts she had read in newspapers, periodicals, and books, Stowe began work on what would become *Uncle Tom's Cabin*. As she wrote in the preface to a later edition, she had help. "I did not write it. God wrote it. I merely did His dictation."[9]

In 1851 and 1852, *Uncle Tom's Cabin* appeared (with the subtitle *The Man That Was a Thing*) in forty-one weekly installments in *The National Era*, an antislavery journal for which Stowe had previously written a number of stories. Her editor, Robert Bonner, had been behind Sarah Parton's initial success. Even before Stowe had completed the novel, she offered the whole to the publisher Phillips, Sampson, & Company, which had published her sister Catharine. But the firm passed on it, thinking a book by a woman on such an inflammatory topic was too great a risk. John P. Jewett's firm snatched it up, offering a 10 percent commission on sales, which Stowe accepted, later to realize, however, that the arrangement still favored her publisher. Released in book form in March 1852, *Uncle Tom's Cabin* soon outpaced Susan Warner's *The Wide, Wide World* and by September was so popular that one newspaper reported Stowe's receipt of "the largest sum of money ever received by an author, whether American or English, for the sale of a single work in so short a period of time."[10]

The majority of southerners detested the novel, which they thought was riddled with exaggerations and outright errors. Defending her work, a year later Stowe published *A Key to Uncle Tom's Cabin* (1853), in which she documented her sources for significant episodes in the novel. Southerners answered with fiction of their own, such as Mary Eastman's *Aunt Phillis's Cabin; or, Southern Life as It Is* (1852). The controversy only fed the book's sales, in the United States and abroad. Stowe's tour through England and Scotland thrust her into the vanguard of the transatlantic antislavery movement; immense crowds greeted her at every stop. Several enterprising English firms published the book, paying Stowe no royalties because there were no international copyright laws at the time.

Another national crisis provided the background for Stowe's subsequent novel. In May 1854 Congress passed the Kansas-Nebraska Act, which allowed the inhabitants of the large Kansas/Nebraska territories, both above the Mason-Dixon Line, where slavery had previously been outlawed, to decide by popular sovereignty whether they wished to allow the institution within their borders upon achieving statehood. The passage of the act set off border wars between pro- and antislavery settlers, who poured into the territory to boost their side's vote, and launched the national career of "Captain" John Brown. During these years of tumult and bloodshed on the frontier, Stowe wrote *Dred: A Tale of the Great Dismal Swamp* (1856), a flawed work that nevertheless presented the complexity of African American culture through a fierce rebel based on Nat Turner, a character quite different from the pious Christian slave Uncle Tom.

On her return to Andover in 1857, Stowe received the news that her son Harry, a Dartmouth College student, had drowned while swimming in the Connecticut River. His death precipitated a crisis of faith in Stowe. The clergyman who offered her consolation was none other than Andover's Edwards Amasa Park, whose sermon on the theology of the intellect and of the feelings had rocked New England's religious world a decade earlier. His concept of "disinterested benevolence" was of little help to a grieving parent like Stowe. Park's inability to lighten her soul led Stowe to abandon the orthodoxy to which he, her father, and her husband adhered.

She did not wait long to make her decision public. Disconsolate over the state of the nation, Stowe wrote *The Minister's Wooing* (1859), in which Jonathan Edwards's disciple Samuel Hopkins figures as a major character. In the novel, Stowe put her father's theology on trial and found it wanting. Purging this poison from her soul, she then retreated to half-fictionalized memories of New England's past, particularly in *Oldtown Folks* (1869) and *Sam Lawson's Oldtown Fireside Stories* (1871), based on her early years in Litchfield. She continued to write novels, now in the vein of other emerging New England women writers like Mary Prescott Spofford, Mary E. Wilkins Freeman, and Sarah Orne Jewett, who, writing in the realist vein championed by William Dean Howells and Henry James, focused on the distinctiveness and idiosyncrasy of rural New England's life and character. Although well received, these novels did not burnish Stowe's reputation. Her greatest effect on American literature had come much earlier, when she had probed African American experience through her depiction of Uncle Tom, Dred, and a host of other memorable characters.

THE RELIGION OF DOMESTICITY: A TEXTBOOK CASE

In *Uncle Tom's Cabin*, Stowe surpassed Warner and Cummins in her advocacy of a religion of the heart to replace a theology of intellect.[11] She also gave black characters a dignity and self-consciousness that paved the way for other writers, including African American writers, to explore the question of race in America.

When the novel opens, Tom lives in comfortable circumstances for a slave. He serves the Shelby family on their Kentucky plantation, where he has worked for decades. He has a wife and children and is beloved by his extended plantation family. But Mr. Shelby is near default on his mortgage and must do what a few months earlier would have seemed unimaginable: sell off some of his faithful slaves. The slave trader Haley bargains for those he considers the most valuable for resale: the trustworthy Christian, Tom, and the young son of the beautiful mulatto slave Eliza, Mrs. Shelby's son's favorite. Eliza overhears the plans for her son's sale and escapes with Harry, and, after an abortive attempt to recover the two runaways, Haley hauls off a stoical Tom in chains, despite Mr. Shelby's assurance that Tom would never try to escape.

The narrative splits in two. One plot traces Eliza's and Harry's trials as they escape across the Ohio River; reunite with George Harris, Eliza's husband and Harry's father, who also has escaped; elude the pursuit of "slave-catchers"; and finally reach freedom in Canada. The other details Tom's tribulations. Tom's new master is the humane but cynical Augustine St. Clare, who purchases him as a favor to his young daughter, Evangeline (known as Eva), after Tom saves her when she falls off a steamboat heading down the Mississippi River to New Orleans, where the St. Clares live. Believing that slavery is an evil but ineradicable part of southern culture, St. Clare indulges his slaves even though he thinks that they are too feebleminded to live as free people.

His precocious Little Eva, by contrast, is the epitome of goodness, insistently questioning why blacks are enslaved. She extends her Christian love to all of the family's charges, even the seemingly intractable Topsy, a girl the same age who was abused and neglected earlier in her life. But Eva contracts tuberculosis, and when it becomes clear that it will kill her, she makes her father promise to free his own slaves, especially Tom, to whom he confides his intentions. As Eva nears death, she calls her Christian family, black and white, to her, giving each individual a lock of her golden hair as a remembrance and begging them to pray. This lachrymose deathbed scene is one of the iconic moments in the American sentimental literature.

But before St. Clare can draft Tom's emancipation papers, he is fatally stabbed while trying to break up a fight at his gentlemen's club. His neurasthenic, self-centered wife has no intention of honoring Eva's request to free Tom and the other slaves. Instead, she sends them to auction, setting in motion the novel's last section. The cruel Simon Legree, a transplanted New Englander who has come to the South to make his fortune, purchases Tom and carries him to his ramshackle plantation on the Red River. Tom meets two slaves, the magnetic and mysterious mulatto Cassy, Legree's onetime mistress, and the beautiful fifteen-year-old Emmeline, whom Legree buys at the same time as Tom and whom he sees as Cassy's replacement.

On Legree's plantation, Tom is unwilling to assume an overseer's position because it would involve whipping his fellow slaves, for whom he becomes an inspiring example of stoicism and love in the face of violence. When Cassy and Emmeline escape and Tom refuses to give them up, Legree beats him to the brink of death. On his deathbed, just like Little Eva, Tom displays the transformative power of faith. And before he passes, he has the joy of seeing young George Shelby, who promised to purchase Tom and return him to his family in Kentucky. After Tom's death George vows to manumit his slaves, including Tom's wife and children. Stowe ends the novel with upbeat, sentimental flourishes: Cassy discovers that she is Eliza's long-lost mother—together with George Harris they find freedom in Canada—and that Madame de Thoux, a steamboat passenger whom Shelby befriends, is Harris's sister.

The novel's two main characters, Tom and Little Eva, embody *imitatio Christi*: both strive for patience and humility in the face of suffering, and both love all humanity unconditionally. There is no interdenominational bickering or sterile logic chopping but rather a wholesale acceptance of the gospel message, whose consolation is available to all. When Eva, close to death, speaks with her father, he asks, "What is being a Christian, Eva?" "Loving Christ most of all," she replies. But "You never saw him," St. Clare responds. "That makes no difference," the child says. "I believe in Him, and in a few days I shall *see* Him."[12] Stowe writes that the "child's whole heart and soul seemed absorbed in works of love and kindness," an incontrovertible sign that through her faith she has become Christ's emissary.[13]

Similarly, after Legree has severely beaten Tom, in his debilitated state the latter has a vision "of One crowned with thorns, buffeted and bleeding." Tom gazes "in awe and wonder at the majestic patience of the face; the deep, pathetic eyes thrilled him to his inmost heart; his soul woke, as, with floods of emotion, he stretched out his hands and fell upon his knees." The vision then changes. "The sharp thorns became rays of glory," and the face bends toward him and says, "He that overcometh shall sit down with me on my throne, even as I also overcame, and am set down with my father on his throne."[14] Tom briefly assumes the power of a prophet.

> Gradually and imperceptibly the strange, silent, patient man, who was ready to bear every one's burden, and sought help from no one,—who stood aside for all, and came last, and took least, yet was foremost to share his little with any who needed—, the man who, in cold nights, would give up his tattered blanket to add to the comfort of some woman who shivered with sickness, and who filled the baskets of the weaker ones in the field, at the terrible risk of coming short in his own measure . . . this man, at last, began to have a strange power over them . . . and many would gather together to hear from him of Jesus.[15]

Legree's two overseers, Sambo and Quimbo, realize how wicked they have been and ask, "O Tom! Do tell us who is Jesus anyhow?" "Jesus, that's been a-standin' by you so, all night! Who is he?" Tom, as injured as he is, speaks in "a few energetic sentences of that wondrous One—His life, His death—His everlasting presence, and power to save." "Why didn't I never hear this before," exclaims Sambo, "but I do believe!! Lord Jesus have mercy on us!"[16] Sambo and Quimbo become Christians as a result of seeing the power of faith in action.

Uncle Tom's Cabin was not the first instance of a white author trying to portray black experience. In 1836, for example, the historian and journalist Richard Hildreth had written *The Slave: or, Memoirs of Archy Moore*, in which he used the runaway Archy's voice to tell a story of bondage and freedom; in 1852, with the success of *Uncle Tom's Cabin*, Hildreth reissued the work as *The White Slave*. Moreover, for decades American readers learned of slavery from an increasing number of first-person slave narratives, some of which were redacted stories told to and written by white interlocutors (often associated with the abolition movement), while others—most famously, *The Narrative of the Life of Frederick Douglass* (1845)—were in their subject's own words.

But because she centered her novel on a diverse group of slaves and allowed them to speak about their lives, Stowe's indictment of slavery had a panoramic authenticity, though one blurred slightly by the gauze of sentiment.[17] Apologists for slavery might argue that a particular slave narrative or journal article was biased, but the immense reach of Stowe's setting—it encompassed virtually the whole United States of the time—was proof of slavery's deleterious effect on the nation. Stowe showed that there was no single, paradigmatic experience of slavery. Rather, the institution pervasively dehumanized both blacks and whites, in the South and the North.

In addition to Tom, Eliza, and Cassy, Stowe's cast of distinctive African American characters included Eliza's handsome young child, Harry (already adept in the dances and trickery of the minstrel shows); Eliza's husband, George, "high-skinned" and highly intelligent, who wants for himself the rights the Constitution guarantees white men; Sam and Andy, two of the Shelbys' slaves, plantation jokesters whose shenanigans delay the pursuit of the escaped Eliza; Adolph, St. Clare's pretentious mulatto valet, who dresses incongruously like a gentleman; and, of course, Sambo and Quimbo, Legree's thuggish overseers who are converted by Tom's example. Taken individually, the characters can appear to be stereotypes. Taken together, they represent a remarkable cross section of the slave's experience.

"A MUCH MORE STRIKING STORY THAN DOUGLASS'S"
In May 1853, at the meeting of the British and Foreign Anti-Slavery Society in London, Stowe met the African American antislavery lecturer and author William Wells Brown.[18] He had been in Great Britain for four years, having left the United States after the passage of the Fugitive Slave Law. While there, Brown lectured, wrote for London newspapers, and published a travel book, *Three Years in Europe; or, Places I Have Seen and People I Have Met* (1852). Meeting Stowe held special meaning for him, for he was at work on a novel of his own, which was to be published in London the next year as *Clotel; or, The President's Daughter: A Narrative of Slave Life in the United States*. It was the first novel by an African American.

Brown himself was already well known. Second only to Douglass as a writer and lecturer, he was a major draw on the antislavery lecture circuit. He was the author of *Narrative of William W. Brown, A Fugitive Slave* (1847), which by the time he went to England had passed through four American and five British editions and was frequently compared with Douglass's narrative, published two years earlier. After the British philanthropist Ellen Richardson bought Brown's freedom in 1854 for three hundred dollars, he returned to Boston and the lecture circuit and began to speak against the Kansas-Nebraska Act. He was indefatigable. In 1856, he developed a one-man play, *Experience, or, How to Give a Northern Man a Backbone,* which he performed himself, and in 1858 he published *The Escape; or, A Leap for Freedom: A Drama in Five Acts.* Before his death in 1884, he revised and republished *Clotel* a number of times and wrote several more books, including histories of the achievements of the "Colored" race during the Civil War and in American history more generally.

Brown was born into slavery in 1814 on Dr. John Young's plantation near Lexington, Kentucky, to a white father and a slave mother. When Brown was two, Young moved to the Missouri Territory, in what is now St. Charles County. In 1827 Young relocated to a farm just outside St. Louis. He sold Brown's mother and several siblings for financial reasons and hired out Brown to local businesses. Brown worked at a tavern, at a hotel, and on a steamboat, bringing his salary to Dr. Young but enjoying a modicum of freedom. He also served for two years as a handyman to James Walker, a slave trader, and with him made trips to the infamous New Orleans slave market; on one such trip he witnessed the sale of an African American reputed to be one of Thomas Jefferson's daughters. In 1830 he worked in the printing office of the Reverend Elijah Lovejoy, an abolitionist and the editor of the *St. Louis Times.* In 1836, after Lovejoy had published an exposé of the lynching of a St. Louis African American, proslavery agitators burned his office, and a year later, in 1837, in Alton, Illinois, he was murdered during another raid on his establishment. Brown was hired out to a slave trader and then, after returning to Young's plantation and trying to escape, was sold to a merchant and finally to a steamboat owner, who made Brown his coachman.

In 1834 Brown successfully escaped, traveling northeast from Cincinnati to Cleveland, receiving aid along the way from the Quaker family of Wells Brown, whose name he later assumed out of gratitude. That same year he married the free black Elizabeth Schooner. They had two daughters but then became estranged. For the next nine years, Brown worked on Lake Erie steamers, often assisting fellow slaves to escape to Canada, and eventually settled in Buffalo, which had a large black population and where he was active in the Underground Railroad. He attended antislavery meetings and in 1843 met Douglass, who encouraged him to speak for the cause. At the annual meeting of the Western New York Anti-Slavery Society in 1846, Brown gave a well-regarded speech in favor of African American voting rights, and the following year he was invited to lecture at the Massachusetts Anti-Slavery Society, of which Douglass was a member.

The success of Douglass's *Narrative* encouraged Brown to write his life story, the frequent subject of his lectures, and in June he sent the manuscript to the prominent Massachusetts antislavery advocate Edmund Quincy. Quincy, whose condescension here suggests his difficulty in dealing with Douglass, found it "a much more striking story than Douglass's & as well told" and noted that Brown had been a slave longer than Douglass. "I do not know that his intellectual power is equal to that of Douglass," Quincy wrote a friend, "but he is of a higher cast of character," with "no meanness, no littleness, no envy or suspicion about him."[19]

After the publication of his narrative, Brown emerged as a national figure, even though his estranged wife tried to sully his reputation by accusing him of abandoning her and their children. For a few months he lectured jointly with William and Ellen Craft, runaway slaves from Georgia who became known for the daring way they had escaped: Ellen was light skinned and masqueraded as a wealthy southern lady; William was dark and posed as her valet. Brown spoke several times at the New England Anti-Slavery Convention in Boston in 1849 and afterward was elected as a delegate to the International Peace Congress in Paris. From there he traveled to London, setting in motion his British career and the publication of *Clotel*.

MR. JEFFERSON'S DAUGHTERS

Although *Clotel* was the first African American novel, Brown makes clear in his preface that he wrote it for a British audience. "The great aim of the true friends of the slave should be to lay bare the institution, so that the gaze of the world may be upon it, and cause the wise, prudent, and the pious to withdraw their support from it."[20] That the British had introduced slavery into the American colonies provided "sufficient reason why Englishmen should feel a lively interest in its abolition." If the incidents Brown described "should add anything new" to the British public's understanding of slavery and "thereby aid in bringing British influence to bear upon American slavery, the main object for which this work was written will have been accomplished."[21]

At its beginning, *Clotel* inverts the reader's expectations. Often, particularly for a posthumous work, someone closely associated with the author wrote an account of his life for the introduction. Brown, though, introduced his own book with a "Narrative of the Life and Escape of William Wells Brown," an abridged version of his story, published several years earlier in the third person. He also undercut another long-standing convention of the slave narrative, which usually had a white abolitionist introduce the work; William Lloyd Garrison and Wendell Phillips, prominent New England abolitionists, had vouched for the authenticity of Douglass's *Narrative*.

In his introduction Brown states the novel's premise: "Were it not for persons in high places owning slaves, and thereby giving the system a reputation, and especially professed Christians, Slavery would long since have been abolished."[22] The novel itself relates the story of Currer and her daughters, Clotel and Althesa, who are the mistress and children of none other than Thomas Jefferson. By the 1850s the idea that Jefferson may have fathered children with his slaves was not new; it had been around since 1802, when rabid anti-Jeffersonians circulated rumors about a slave named Sally. In Brown's hands Jefferson became an example of the prevalence of miscegenation throughout the slave states and even among the country's political and moral leaders.

Clotel consists of several entwined plots. One involves Currer, a forty-year-old laundress who is the property of John Graves. Currer lives in Richmond and for two decades has, with Graves's permission, hired out her time. Her time at Jefferson's left her with two daughters, Clotel, sixteen years old, and Althesa, fourteen. Graves dies, and to settle claims against his estate, the three women are sold at auction. Dick Walker, a slave trader, buys Althesa and her mother and takes them down the Mississippi River to resell them at a profit. Clotel remains in Richmond, the mistress of Horatio Green, who purchases her for the considerable sum of fifteen hundred dollars.

Brown describes the disintegration of Currer's family. The Reverend John Peck, a Methodist minister, buys Currer, giving Brown the opportunity to inveigh against the hypocrisy of the clergy. Peck, an absentee landlord with a home in Natchez, Mississippi, places her, now irrevocably separated from her daughters, in the family of his overseer, Ned Huckleby, whose inhumane treatment of her Brown describes in stark terms. James Crawford, a native Vermonter and local bank teller, purchases Althesa as a domestic. Because she is so fair skinned, the family's boarder, Henry Morton, has difficulty believing that she is a slave. Smitten, he purchases and then marries her. By moving to another part of the city where no one knows Althesa's heritage, the two are able to live happily as man and wife and to raise two children, Ellen and Jane. The Mortons become financially successful and try to purchase Currer, but Peck refuses the offer. After he dies from cholera, his daughter Georgiana and her husband convert to the abolitionist cause and intend to free all of Peck's slaves. Before this occurs, though, Currer dies in a yellow fever epidemic. The thwarted plans, a hallmark of sentimental novels, recalls the similar event in *Uncle Tom's Cabin* when Augustine St. Clare decides to free Tom but, before he draws the papers, is killed in a fight at his gentlemen's club.

Althesa and Henry soon die of yellow fever, too. Because the latter never formally manumitted his wife, his creditors, discovering that Althesa was black, seize her daughters and auction them to help pay Morton's debts. Ellen commits suicide the night after her purchase. Jane's new owner keeps her under lock and key until she capitulates to his sexual advances. When Jane's lover finds and tries to free her, her master kills him, and she descends into a profound depression and dies of illness soon after.

Meanwhile, in Virginia, Horatio Green installs Clotel as his mistress in a cottage outside Richmond; he seems genuinely affectionate, and eventually they have a daughter, Mary. But Green harbors political ambitions and cynically marries a wealthy and influential man's daughter, Gertrude. He reveals this to Clotel and begs her to allow him still to see her on the same terms as before. She is devastated. Still in love with her, Green sends money for her and Mary. But Gertrude eventually discovers her husband's arrangement with Clotel and insists that he sell his slave out of state. Gertrude takes Mary as a house slave and mistreats the girl, a constant reminder of her husband's infidelity.

The slave trader Dick Walker returns to the narrative, purchasing Clotel, as he had her mother and sister, and selling her at auction in Vicksburg to a plantation owner. After a short period, she and a fellow slave, William, plan to escape, using the same hoax as William and Ellen Craft did. They succeed and reach freedom in Cincinnati. Clotel then surreptitiously makes her way to Richmond to try to recover Mary. But she is identified; her last owner is notified of her whereabouts, and she is transferred at his request to a slave prison in Washington, D.C. Clotel escapes and tries to cross a bridge over the Potomac River. Trapped between her pursuers and approaching Virginians, she leaps over the railing to her death—in plain sight, Brown notes, of the White House.

Brown devotes the remaining chapters to Mary. In the Greens' home is a "white" slave named George, whom Mary loves. After his participation in a failed slave revolt, which Brown modeled on Nat Turner's rebellion, George is captured and sentenced to be hanged. But three nights before his execution Mary helps him escape, and he makes his way to Canada. He tries to purchase Mary's freedom but learns that the Greens have sold her to a New Orleans trader. Distraught, he crosses the Atlantic and settles in Manchester. Ten years later, while he is vacationing at Dunkirk, a veiled widow and young child approach him as he reads in a cemetery; seeing George, the woman faints. The next day Monsieur Devenant, the woman's father-in-law, calls and invites George to dinner. When George sees the woman, without her veil, *he* faints, for it is Mary! Devenant's son saw her in New Orleans, fell in love, and tried unsuccessfully to buy her freedom. The young Devenant followed her, wooed her, and then convinced her to escape to France with him. There they married and had a child, but Devenant died soon thereafter; she was visiting his grave when she saw George. They marry and, with Mary's child, live out their lives in France, where their race is not a stigma.

What did Brown accomplish in *Clotel*? How should the reader understand this ungainly novel, a hodgepodge of fact and fiction? For one, it suffers from inevitable comparison to *Uncle Tom's Cabin*, a clear influence on Brown. The London *Literary Gazette* noted that he did not have "the literary art and dramatic skill which have gained for the story of Uncle Tom its world-wide popularity" but did possess the "force and earnestness" befitting a writer who himself was still technically a slave.[23] A month later a reviewer for *The Athenaeum* of London called Brown's "a voice to swell the chorus which Mrs. Beecher has raised" but observed that the book's "literary merits" were "such as can only claim a local—as distinguished from a general—success."[24]

No contemporary reviewer commented on the novel's source material or genre mixing. For epigraphs at the head of each chapter, Brown had selected quotations from his own anthology, *The Anti-Slavery Harp: A*

Collection of Songs for Anti-Slavery Meetings (1848). He borrowed details of Clotel's and Althesa's stories from Lydia Maria Child's story "The Quadroons," printed in another antislavery compilation, *The Liberty Bell* (1842). His description of a burning of a runaway slave in Natchez depended on a report in the *Natchez Free Trader*.[25] William's and Clotel's escape to freedom derived from the story of William and Ellen Craft, with whom Brown was personally familiar. Clotel's dramatic death paralleled that of a woman in Grace Greenwood's poem "The Leap from the Long Bridge: An Incident at Washington."[26] Nor was Brown averse to recycling his own material. In 1852, *The Anti-Slavery Advocate* published his "True Story of Slave Life," essentially an earlier version of Clotel's sale at auction. The story of Henry and Althesa Morton is an expansion of a tale in his *Description of William Wells Brown's Original Panoramic Views of the Scenes in the Life of an American Slave, from His Birth in Slavery to His Death or His Escape to His First Home of Freedom on British Soil* (1849[?]), a catalog issued to coincide with an exhibition of artists' depictions of slavery he had commissioned while in England.[27] Later sections depend on his "Narrative of American Slavery" from a letter in his *Three Years in Europe* (1852).

The variety of sources served Brown's purpose: to compose not a novel but, rather, as his title page has it, "a narrative of slave life in the United States." He mixed and inverted popular discourses—of sentiment, politics, reform—to show how, when it came to slavery, the best intentions mean nothing. He urged the reader to consider the utter incongruity of white America's rhetoric about freedom and equality in light of its sanctioning of slavery and, effectively, rape. He wanted readers to go to the roots of the nation's problems. By indicting Jefferson, he wanted Americans to acknowledge the sins of the fathers and to move forward by committing a kind of national patricide.

TRUTH STRANGER THAN FICTION: HARRIET JACOBS

Like Brown, African American authors, particularly if they were not well known and wrote fiction, did not have an easy time finding a domestic publisher. Antislavery societies were always interested in first-person testimonies, which usually were fairly brief and thus inexpensive to produce. The talented and unique Harriet Jacobs could not find a publisher for her *Incidents in the Life of a Slave Girl. Written by Herself,* completed in 1857, for four years. *Incidents* is an autobiographical novel notable for Jacobs's forthrightness about sexual harassment and rape. Not only must her alter ego, Linda Brent, escape bondage to rescue her children, but at the same time, she has to fend off the persistent advances of her white master. How she finally does so was a source of everlasting shame. Hers was certainly not the kind of story with which many northern white readers were intimately familiar.

Born in Edenton, North Carolina, around 1813, Jacobs was the child of a carpenter, Daniel, and his wife, Delilah, slaves owned by a tavern keeper. In the same town she had a maternal grandmother, Molly Horniblow (Aunt Martha in the novel), a freed black and baker who owned her own home. Jacobs was orphaned at a young age, and at eleven she moved in with the Norcom family, for she had been willed to Mary Matilda Norcom, then three years old. Margaret's father, Dr. James Norcom, Jacobs's de facto master, harassed her sexually. Soon enough she had two children, Joseph and Louisa Matilda, though not by Norcom. Their father was a young white attorney named Samuel Tredwell Sawyer, who treated her well and to whom she gave herself in part to foil Norcom's advances.

Norcom continued his pursuit of Jacobs into her late teens. When she would not yield to him, he sent her to one of his plantations and placed her young children with her grandmother. When Jacobs learned that he also planned eventually to send her children to the plantation as field slaves, she decided to run away, believing that Norcom would find the children too troublesome and leave them with her grandmother. It worked. Jacobs hid in a seven-by-nine-foot garret storeroom in her grandmother's home, sewing, reading, and writing to pass the time, communicating with family members only at night. Sawyer bought their children and let them continue to live with Mary Horniblow. He did not free them but did take Matilda north to a free state.

Incredibly, Jacobs lived for seven years in the storeroom, finally escaping to the North and finding her way to Brooklyn.[28] She located her daughter, Matilda, and asked Sawyer to send her son to her as well. Working as a domestic across the East River, Jacobs served the family of none other than Nathaniel Parker Willis, Sara Willis Parton's haughty brother. In this instance, at least, he made a decent show of himself. After Norcom began making frequent trips north to try to reclaim her, Jacobs informed the Willises of her plight and moved, first to Boston and then to Rochester, New York, where her brother John lectured for an abolitionist society.

John paid Matilda's way through two years at the Young Ladies' Domestic Seminary in Clinton. Jacobs began to work in the bookstore of the Rochester abolition society, above the office of *The North Star*, Douglass's newspaper. There she met the Quaker reformers Isaac and Amy Post and lived with them when her brother was on the lecture circuit. She confided in Amy Post, who urged Jacobs to publish her remarkable story for the antislavery cause. Thus, sometime after 1852, and after Mrs. Willis bought Jacobs's freedom for three hundred dollars, she began to commit her life story to paper. At Post's suggestion, she contacted Stowe to see if she might be willing to turn her narrative into an "as told to" story that, given the novelist's fame, would garner the backing of the abolitionist societies. Stowe's response was not overly generous. She looked at the manuscript and asked Mrs. Willis if it all was true. If so, she intended to use it in her *A Key to Uncle Tom's Cabin*, essentially purloining Jacobs's life story.

Jacobs prevented this by beating Stowe to the press, publishing a "Letter from a Fugitive Slave" in Greeley's *New-York Tribune*. After completing the manuscript of her book but still lacking a white sponsor, she began the search for a publisher. She went to England but met with no luck. She approached Phillips, Sampson, & Company of Boston, but it wanted her book only if it came with Stowe's endorsement, which Jacobs at this point refused to pursue. After further inquiries, she found a publisher that would issue the novel if Lydia Maria Child endorsed it. Jacobs did not know Child; but the latter obliged, and her name appeared on the title page as "editor."[29] Still, there were more delays, brought on by the vagaries of the publishing world.[30]

The book finally appeared in 1861 under the pseudonym Linda Brent. It did not sell particularly well but elicited good reviews in the abolitionist press. A letter in *The Liberator* noted that *Incidents* described the reality of life under slavery because "in contrast with [the] mingling of fiction with fact" in Stowe and Brown, it was the "record of complicated experience in the life of a young woman" that did not need "the charms that any pen of fiction, however gifted and graceful, could lend."[31] The *National Anti-Slavery Standard* concurred, contrasting the novel with Stowe's and approving of its avoidance of sensationalism.[32]

But the book had a limited impact on American culture at large and on Jacobs's career. At the start of the Civil War, she went to Washington to devote her time to relief work behind the Union lines among freed blacks and escaped slaves. In later stages of the war and after its end, she continued this work in Alexandria, Virginia, and Savannah, Georgia. She reported on her activities in antislavery publications but published no fiction or narrative comparable to *Incidents*. Jacobs died in Washington in 1897, she and her book all but unknown.

But she had offered a serious challenge to both sentimental conventions and contemporary slave narratives. Sentimental fiction was set in the home, where mothers cultivated family virtue as a counter to the immorality of society. Yet the southern homes Jacobs lived in were a source of, not a buffer against, that immorality. And although Douglass and Stowe had made readers aware of slave masters' licentiousness, in *Incidents* the public encountered a thorough first-person account of the slave woman's life: the "foul words" whispered to a fifteen-year-old by a man forty years her senior; the physical and psychological brutality; the master's plan to build a cottage in the woods where he could violate his slave undisturbed. "What could I do?" Linda, Jacobs's heroine, asks.[33] "I thought and thought, till I became desperate, and made a plunge into the abyss," using a metaphor to which women in fiction had turned since Charles Brockden Brown's Clara Wieland.[34]

Linda took a white lover to stave off Dr. Flint's advances. Mr. Sands heard of her tribulations and "expressed a great deal of sympathy" to her. She knew "whither all this was tending" and "the impassible gulf" between them, but by choosing and willingly submitting to Sands, she exercised her agency. "There is something akin to freedom in having a lover who has not control over you," she thought, "except that which he gains by kindness and attachment." The "painful and humiliating memory" of her choice haunts her, yet she reasons "that the slave woman ought not to be judged by the same standard as others," presumably the strictures of true womanhood.[35]

What was a reader accustomed to the conventions of the sentimental novel to do when asked to identify with Linda not as a suffering black but as a woman subject to the unwanted advances of a powerful man? The black woman's experience of motherhood prevented any sense of "sympathy" a white reader might claim she had in reading the text. Reading *Incidents* thus was not, as Stowe said of her novel, an exercise in "feeling right" about the slave's plight. It upended the entire moral framework of white society. What white woman had ever been in Jacobs's position? As Linda explains, "the condition of a slave confuses all principles of morality, and, in fact, renders the practice of them impossible."[36] "I have placed myself before you," she continued, "to be judged as a woman whether I deserve your pity or contempt."[37]

FRANK J. AND MARY WEBB

By the 1860s there were many firsthand testimonies from African American women and men who had experienced the bonds of slavery. But what of free northern blacks, some of whom were educated, ran profitable businesses, and aspired to the same virtues as the white people in their communities? What was the nature of their experiences in pre–Civil War America? Frank J. Webb's *The Garies and Their Friends* (1857) offered a remarkable answer, one that anticipated the direction African American literature took after emancipation, as it addressed prejudice and segregation rather than slavery.

How Webb came to write his novel remains a mystery, for nothing in his background prefigures its appearance. He was born a free black in Philadelphia in 1828. He may have worked in a clothing store and in the printing trade, although the details of his youth are lost to us. In 1845, he married Mary "E."; they both were seventeen at the time, and both appeared in the 1850 U.S. Census as "Mulatto."[38] Webb's business ventures did not go well, and around 1855 Mary, who, like her husband, was well educated, decided to try to support them by giving performances of famous poems and scenes from plays. She studied with A. A. Apthorp, a "Professor of Elocution" in Philadelphia who took "a warm interest in her success," and soon traveled as far as New England for her recitals.[39] Mary became well known; Stowe even wrote a short drama based on *Uncle Tom's Cabin* called *The Christian Slave* for her performances. An audience favorite was her rendition of Henry Wadsworth Longfellow's "Hiawatha," which she recited while "arrayed in the picturesque costume of the North American Indians," which added "greatly to the effect."[40]

In 1856, carrying letters of introduction from the likes of Longfellow and Stowe, the Webbs sailed to England, where Mary's shows continued to garner attention. It was there that Webb wrote *The Garies*, which was published by the London firm G. Routledge & Company, with prefaces by Stowe and Lord Henry Brougham, who had been instrumental in the passage of the British Slavery Abolition Act of 1833. The book sold well in England on the eve of the Civil War. Surprisingly there was no American reprint and only a single notice of it in the contemporary American press: *Frederick Douglass' Paper* republished a review that had appeared in the London *Daily News*.[41]

Mary Webb suffered from a chronic pulmonary condition, and in 1858 the couple left England for the more favorable climate in the south of France. From there they traveled to Jamaica, where the Duke of Argyll had appointed Webb to the post office in Kingston. Mary continued her popular performances. She died the next year, and in 1864 Webb married Mary Rosabell Rodgers, a Jamaican. They had four children in Jamaica and two more in the United States after they returned in 1869. Frank took courses at the Howard University Law School, worked as a clerk for the Freedmen's Bureau, and wrote for the weekly *New Era*, in which he published two novellas along with poetry and essays. Around 1870 the Webbs moved to Galveston, Texas, where Frank did postal work for another decade. He ended his working life as a teacher and then as the principal at the Barnes Institute School, an elementary school for black children. He died in Galveston in 1894.

BEING BLACK IN THE CITY OF BROTHERLY LOVE

The particular events in Webb's experience in Philadelphia that led him to write *The Garies* are unknown. In the memoir of his wife added to the English edition of *The Christian Slave*, he did note that Mary had been greatly upset by the death of her mother, "who fell victim to anxiety produced by the passing of the infamous Fugitive Slave Law." He concluded the memoir by anticipating the end of slavery, when his "oppressed fellow countrymen" would prove that they were not inferior and genius was no longer considered "the exclusive attribute of one race or another," suggesting his sympathy with, if not involvement in, the abolitionist cause.[42]

But the memoir does not prepare the reader for the complexity and power of *The Garies and Their Friends*. Slavery is in the background. Except for the first chapter, the novel takes place in Philadelphia. As Stowe noted, African Americans in that city formed a "large class" and "have increased in numbers, wealth, and standing," constituting a "peculiar society of their own" and "presenting many social peculiarities worthy of interest and attention."[43] Stowe understood that Webb's book was of interest because it posed a question that vexed even abolitionists: "Are the race at present held as slaves capable of freedom, self-government, and progress?" That Webb relied on understatement and an accumulation of telling details further set his novel apart. Twenty years later his style would have been described as realist, in the same vein as William Dean Howells and Henry James.[44]

The Garies and Their Friends is an account of the relationships among the Garies: Clarence, a wealthy white plantation owner turned abolitionist, and Emily, his mixed-race slave, and their two children; a black middle-class family, the Ellises; Charles, a hard-working carpenter, his wife, Ellen, a laundress and seamstress, and their three children, Esther, Caroline (or Caddy), and Charlie; and Mr. Walters, a wealthy black businessman. The Philadelphia it evokes was a longtime center of abolitionist sentiment and home to a large population of blacks, both free and fugitive, who for decades had built discrete communities, next to but separate from white neighborhoods.

As George Lippard had shown, however, Philadelphia was not immune to problems between blacks and whites and between classes. Though the kinds of civil disruptions so prevalent in the 1830s and 1840s abated in the next decade, the situation for Philadelphia's sizable black population remained tense. In good measure, this was because its modest economic success bred resentment in its poorer white neighbors, particularly recent immigrants with whom it competed for jobs. Webb's subject was not the experience of slavery, nor was it national policy regarding slavery, such as the Supreme Court's 1857 *Dred Scott* decision declaring that people of African descent were not protected by the Constitution nor could ever become citizens. It was, rather, the simple but pervasive hatred of whites for blacks.

The novel opens in the early 1840s on the Garie family's Georgia plantation. Clarence Garie hears about black life in the North from his light-skinned childhood friend, Mr. Winston, just returned from the region. The latter relates that in New York he easily passed for white and thus had a delightful time yet would never settle there; he has seen enough of white and black life to convince him that among whites he "could not form either social or business connections, should his identity with the African race be discovered." At the same time, he knows that he could find "sufficiently refined association" among people of color "to satisfy his social wants" but laments that he could not "bear the isolation and contumely to which they were subjected."[45]

When Winston visited another friend, Mr. Ellis, in Philadelphia, he came to understand that should he settle there, he would "have to be either one thing or the other—white or coloured. Either you must live exclusively amongst coloured people," Ellis told him, "or go to the whites and remain with them." Should Winston choose the second option, his friend continued, he had to bear in mind that it must never be known that he had "a drop of African blood" or he would be "shunned" as if he had a "pestilence," no matter how fair he looked.[46]

Emily Garie, pregnant with the family's third child, urges her husband to move the family north so that her newest child can be born free. At Winston's suggestion Clarence writes to Mr. Walters, a black real estate magnate who owns and rents out "one hundred brick houses" in Philadelphia. The action then moves to that city, with Mr. Ellis and his family readying the Garies' new home. An imposing figure, "above six feet in height, and exceedingly well proportioned," with a "jet-black complexion, and smooth glossy skin," "wooly hair" combed back, and an "aquiline nose, thin lips, and broad chin," all the "very reverse of African in their shape," Walters is the picture of an aristocrat. Yet even though he is "worth half a million dollars," he is discriminated against. To cement his racial solidarity, over his mantel he has a striking oil painting of Toussaint l'Ouverture, the hero of the Haitian Revolution, which very much impresses Garie.[47]

Before long, the Garies begin to experience racial prejudice. They live next door to the Stevens family, who at first do not recognize Mrs. Garie as black. Mrs. Stevens tells the Garies about her fear that Walters "would put a family of niggers next door," not realizing yet to whom she was speaking. When Mr. Garie tells her that Emily is black, she is rendered almost speechless. To her husband she says that it is "sickening" to see the Garies together, with Mr. Garie being "as tender and affectionate to her [Mrs. Garie] as if she was a Circassian—and she nothing but a nigger—faugh! It's disgusting."[48]

When Mr. Garie plans to wed his wife legally (as he was not able to do in Georgia), the minister whom he enlists to perform the ceremony refuses to do so because he despises "amalgamation" and believes that God has marked out "the negro race" for "servitude" to whites. The Ellises then have to find a black minister to perform the ceremony.[49] The Garies' children do not escape the ubiquitous race hatred, for not only does the son, Clarence, overhear Mrs. Stevens disparagingly calling his mother a "nigger," but the miserable woman also mobilizes other families with children at the same school as the Garies' children and threatens to withdraw them if the teacher does not expel the black children. The teacher never guessed the truth.

Mrs. Stevens's husband, an unscrupulous attorney, makes inroads with minor ward politicians and tawdry real estate brokers, hoping to gain control of large sections of the city occupied by black families by inciting riots against their communities and thereby forcing them to move to safer areas. "We can render the district so unsafe," Stevens tells his co-conspirator, Morton, "that property will be greatly lessened in value," after which it would sell for less, presumably to Stevens and his cronies. Stevens asks McCloskey, one of the plotters, to attack the Garies' home and, when Garie appears at the door, to shoot him dead. Why? Because "he is one of those infernal Abolitionists, and one of the very worst kind; he lives with a nigger woman—and what is more, he is married to her!"[50] Stevens makes a list of houses to be attacked and singles out that of Mr. Walters. Walters is alerted to the plot, however, when a friend of his finds the list.

Walters converts his home into a fortress and invites other black families to join him, as the Ellises, among others, do. Walters has long prepared for such an event; he has a store of guns and ammunition. When the mob attacks, the defenders first shower them with heavy stones. The mob fires on the home. The blacks return fire, and several from the mob are hit. When the blacks learn that the crowd intends to go to Mr. Garie's home, Mr. Ellis ventures out of Walters's house to warn the family, only to be caught and badly beaten. The rioters cut two of his fingers off, to prevent him from ever doing carpentry again.

The riot escalates. The mob assaults the Garies' home, even though it is far from the city's black neighborhoods. Mr. Garie is shot in the head at close range and killed, and the rioters ransack the house while his terrified wife and children hide in a woodshed. The mob eventually retreats, but Mrs. Garie, too, dies, from "premature confinement" (that is, premature delivery), "brought on by fright and exposure."[51] The coroner's inquest (involving the vicious Stevens) into the Garies' deaths provides a "very unsatisfactory and untruthful verdict" that does not "at all coincide with the circumstances of the case, but such a one as might have been expected where there was a great desire to screen the affair from public scrutiny."[52] To add to the tragedy, the Garies cannot be buried in the beautiful Ashgrove Cemetery because white Philadelphians "won't even permit a coloured person to walk through the ground, much less to be buried there."[53]

As Mr. Walters helps settle the Garies' estate in favor of their children, he and his attorney are surprised to receive a letter informing them that a first cousin of Clarence Garie's exists who wishes to claim the inheritance, because the children had a mother who was a slave and so cannot, "except under certain circumstances," inherit the money. When this mysterious individual appears, it is none other than Stevens, for his mother and Mr. Garie's father were brother and sister. Stevens claims that the two children are his property and that he can take them south to sell, but fortunately, Walters and Mr. Balch, an attorney, have evidence that links Stevens to Mr. Garie's murder and to the incitement of the riots. Steven is forced to make some provision for the children from Mr. Garie's legacy and in the end accepts a monetary settlement instead of the children.[54]

As Balch and Walters discuss the offer to assist the children, they broach another topic. Balch suggests that given the children's light complexion, they be raised as white. Walters acknowledges how much better he could have done for himself if he had been taken for white and that he is "almost tempted to curse the destiny" that made him black. Though he admits "that in our land of liberty it is an incalculable advantage to be white," he initially balks, insisting that he would rather be sneeringly called "the nigger millionaire" than worry about being exposed for what he is not, for someone who is passing "is never safe."[55] Finally swayed by Balch's argument, however, he gives in, and Balch arranges for Clarence Garie to live with a widowed friend and attend a fine boarding school. The boy understands that he has to keep secret his mother's race.

The narrative shifts ahead to the mid-1850s. Mr. Walters marries Esther Ellis, and Emily Garie weds Charlie (now Charles) Ellis, an accomplished young man. Clarence, however, is engaged to a white woman, Birdie Bates, and agonizes over whether he should reveal his heritage. All this becomes moot, however, when Stevens's son, George, a man cut from the same cloth as his father, exposes Clarence, ending the couple's marital plans. As Mr. Bates exclaims to Clarence, "you have been acting a lie, claiming a position in society to which you had no right, and deserve execration and contempt."[56] Three deaths punctuate the novel's final passages. On his deathbed, the Irishman McCloskey confesses that Stevens ordered Mr. Garie killed, and Stevens's fear of exposure and trial drives him to suicide. And even though the children's patrimony is restored to them, Clarence, humiliated and without any future prospects, moves in with his sister, Emily, and soon thereafter dies of consumption.[57]

The Garies and Their Friends was startlingly ahead of its time. The Garies, Ellises, and Mr. Walters care less about slavery than they do about class. When Mrs. Ellis tells Mr. Walters that they plan to put their son, Charlie, out "to service," Walters argues against it, for "it begets a feeling of dependence to place a boy in such a situation" and would spoil him for any more meaningful or lucrative work. Where, he asks, "would I or Ellis have been had we been hired out all our lives at so much a month?"[58] Yet as Walters realizes, the white people whom he surpasses in wealth will never accept him. No black character mentions that a few years before the events in the first part of the novel, Pennsylvania passed a law disenfranchising black men, a privilege they long had enjoyed.

A comparison between Webb and Lippard is instructive. Both wrote of Philadelphia and its problem, but they did so in quite different modes. Lippard was a vicious satirist; Webb, an anatomist. In *The Quaker City*, the reader learns little of Lippard's Devil Bug; he is less a character than a symbol. It's never apparent how he thinks of himself as a free black among whites. In contrast, Webb's characters exhibit a liberating but also problematic self-knowledge. They choose their own lives, but when a light-skinned black decides to "pass" as white, the result is confusion and despair. If Lippard wanted to shock readers into recognizing the immorality of the American city, Webb wanted to prod readers, white and black, toward a new self-consciousness about race and American values. And since his cause was not abolition, Webb's *The Garies* best comparison is not the novels of Stowe or Brown, but the African American literature during Reconstruction and under Jim Crow, of which Frances Ellen Watkins Harper's *Iola Leroy* (1892) is perhaps the most powerful example.

THE LURE OF REPATRIATION

Like Webb's *The Garies*, the white sentimental novelist Sarah Josepha Hale's *Liberia; or, Mr. Peyton's Experiments* (1853) and the black radical Martin R. Delany's *Blake; or, The Huts of America; A Tale of the Mississippi Valley, the Southern United States, and Cuba* (1859–1862) explored black self-consciousness, but in settings farther afield. Both novels are about black emigration, to Liberia and Cuba, respectively. The novels could not have been more different. Hale believed that blacks were inferior and therefore could not be peacefully or fruitfully integrated into white society; Delany, that the continued dilution of the black race through miscegenation sapped its inherent power and beauty.

Hale (1788–1879), a New Englander, headed the *Ladies' Magazine* of Boston for two years before becoming the inaugural editor of *Godey's Lady's Book*, a monthly Philadelphia journal whose popularity soared during the antebellum period. In this position she sought only unpublished work and avoided controversial topics; more than any other periodical, hers became a widely recognized emblem of sentimental culture. Although Hale supported abolition, her views of blacks were like those of many northerners (including Stowe)—that is, she believed that they were human beings deserving of respect, but at the same time that they were inferior to whites. Hale supported the American Colonization Society's plans to repatriate blacks in the West African region that became Liberia, an effort that had begun in earnest in the mid-1820s, when the first shiploads of free blacks left the United States, bound for the region south of Sierra Leone.

In 1853 Harper & Brothers published Hale's *Liberia*, the only American novel of the period to treat this episode in African American history. No doubt influenced by the widespread interest in utopian schemes like Charles Fourier's, Mr. Peyton, a Virginia plantation owner, attempts to ameliorate the conditions of his slaves by establishing a quasi-socialist collective. His effort fails because of a lack of interest and commitment on the part of the slaves, and Mr. Peyton sees "that matters could not be much worse" and would improve only "when each one felt himself individually responsible."[59] Peyton next considers resettling his slaves in Canada, a project that he finally rejects when he realizes that the kinds of prejudice free blacks encounter from American whites would likely be present there, too, and that in a remote settlement there would be little opportunity for the regular religious instruction of his former slaves.

This leaves Liberia, which he learns of at a meeting of a "Colonization Society." The second half of the book is set in the new African nation, as black emigrants try to convert the native tribes not only to Christianity but also to American principles of self-government. For the settlers, this is not a return to African roots but a neocolonialist enterprise. Hale depicts the settlers' economic, political, and social institutions, foreign relations with European powers bent on enlightening the "dark continent," and combat with indigenous tribes who sell captives to the traders in West African ports. Hale sincerely believed that Liberia had a transforming effect on those who emigrated. "I can tell a man that's been raised in Liberia from America as soon as I see him," Nathan, a repatriated black, tells his friend Ben. "Why, they seem more like men. You know, Ben, you never felt like a man in America." "No," Ben replies. "I used to try mighty hard, but I could never feel like anything but a nigger."[60] Because the Africans are so benighted, American blacks cannot help feeling superior. Hale concludes the book with documents that support her observations, as Stowe had done in *A Key to Uncle Tom's Cabin*.

Martin Delany was less sanguine about the Liberia enterprise. From his reading—particularly William Nesbit's damning *Four Months in Liberia* (1855), for which he provided an introduction—he believed that Liberia was doomed, for two reasons: first, because the settlement project was undertaken by American blacks who thought of Africans as inferior, and second, because many of the settlers were of mixed, not pure, black heritage. Oddly, Delany himself was not pure, though he claimed to be descended from African chieftains. He was born in Charleston, (West) Virginia, in 1812, to a slave father, Samuel Delany, and a free mother, Pati, who traced her heritage to what is now Angola. Early on his mother moved the family to Chambersburg, Pennsylvania, supposedly to protest a Virginia law prohibiting blacks from learning to read. At nineteen Delany went to Pittsburgh, where he married Catherine Richards, daughter of a merchant, and devoted himself to newspaper editing and the cause of abolition; his *The Mystery* (1843–1847) was one of the earliest black newspapers. From 1847 to 1849 he coedited *The North Star* with Frederick Douglass and often lectured for the antislavery cause.

In 1850, having studied medicine with several doctors in Pittsburgh who provided testimonials to his education and ability, Delany was admitted to Harvard Medical School, along with two other blacks. They were the first African Americans to be admitted, but administrators dismissed all three a few months later after white students complained of their presence. Infuriated by the experience and others like it, in 1852 Delany published *The Condition, Elevation, Emigration, and Destiny of the Colored People of the United States, Politically Considered*, a powerful polemic in which he challenged the economic and social discrimination he found rampant even in liberal northern circles. In these years, he also began to advocate black emigration to Central or South America.

Delany soon began to look across the Atlantic as well. In 1859, he traveled to Africa to assess the possibilities for repatriation. He and Robert Campbell, a Jamaican who had been teaching school in Philadelphia, went to Lagos and then Abeokuta (both now in Nigeria), where they signed a treaty with local (Yoruba) chiefs for a parcel of land that later was abrogated because of tribal infighting, ending Delany's dream of a black republic there. The journey inspired him, however, for during this period he wrote and published serially in *The Anglo-African Magazine* and then in *The Weekly Anglo-African* pieces that were republished as *Blake; or, The Huts of America*. The work dealt with blacks in the Caribbean and Africa as well as in the United States. Unfortunately, because key weekly issues of the latter paper have not yet been located, there is no complete version of the novel (about six chapters are missing).

With one exception, the first half of *Blake* follows a trajectory familiar to readers of slave narratives. It tells the story of Henry Holland (later Blake), a pure black West Indian stolen and sold to one of Louisiana's Red River plantations, the same region where Uncle Tom meets his death. Henry "marries" another slave, Maggie, but while he is absent on business for his master, Stephen Franks, Franks sells her to a northerner who takes her to Cuba. Henry then escapes and travels through the South as a fugitive, spreading—and here is where *Blake* deviates from the usual narrative—his dream of slave rebellion wherever he goes.

The second part of *Blake* takes place in Cuba and Africa. Henry travels to the Caribbean island as a servant of American filibusters intent on annexing Cuba to the United States.[61] Henry is fortunate enough to locate his wife, and he purchases her freedom. He is here transformed into "Blake," the "Commander in Chief of the Army of Emancipation," the leader of black insurgents whose goal is the overthrow of the Spanish-backed Cuban government and the establishment of a black state based on an economy of cotton production that would rival the South's (Delany believed that political economy was inextricably linked to black liberation). His army seeks to repel the incursions of American filibusters who want to make the island another slave state and who fear that any liberalization of legal codes against blacks might lead to their eventual supremacy.

In Cuba, the liberation poet Placido gives Blake and his followers advice and inspiration. Through him Delany champions black pan-nationalism. "Colored persons," Placido says at one meeting of the conspirators, "whatever their complexion, can only obtain an equality with whites by the descendants of Africa of unmixed blood." He explains his logic. "The instant that an equality of the blacks and whites is admitted, we, being the descendants of the two, must be acknowledged the equal of both."[62] Unlike Webb, who doubted the final efficacy of amalgamation, Delany saw true revolution as possible only through those who took pride in every drop of their black blood. But the latter could be trusted in the all-important work of nation building only if they became self-reliant and independent, free of the subservience that too often marked their lives among whites. With the overthrow of their Spanish rulers and the foiling of filibusters' plans to annex their land, Cuba's blacks would set an example for the rest of those enslaved in the Americas. "I am for war," Blake declares at one point, "war upon the whites."[63]

But Placido also understands Africa's place in this grand project: it is where blacks can build an economy that will lead to true political and psychological independence. After another central African character among the revolutionaries, Madame Cordora, hears Placido extol the virtues of Africa, she says, "I never before felt as proud of my black as I did of my white blood." Now she sees that "blacks compose an important element in the commercial and social relations of the world."[64] For such a revolution to succeed, enlightened leaders like Blake had to take the lead so that "the more ignorant slaves" who returned to Africa would "have greater confidence in, and more respect for, their headmen and leaders."[65] As one of the nation's leading black intellectuals, Delany believed that he was destined to fill such a role.

And fill it Delany did, but in ways that he did not anticipate, for the revolution he sought never occurred. During the Civil War he led efforts to recruit black soldiers and was commissioned as a major, the highest military rank attained by an African American. He served in the Freedmen's Bureau on Hilton Head in South Carolina before being mustered out of the army in 1865. He subsequently held appointments as a judge and ran, unsuccessfully, for political office in South Carolina. Later in life he worked as a doctor in Charleston. He continued to write political pamphlets and completed his ambitious *Principia of Ethnology: The Origin of Races and Color, with an Archaeological Compendium of Ethiopian and Egyptian Civilization, from Years of Careful Examination and Inquiry,* published in 1879, in which he argued that since time immemorial there had been original, uncorrupted races that had to be preserved, a position that pitted him against "assimilationists" like Douglass. When Delany died of tuberculosis in Wilberforce, Ohio, in 1885, his dream of a racially pure society was farther from reality than ever.

LIVING "FREE" IN NEW HAMPSHIRE

Even more unusual in the history and development of the American novel than Delany's work was Harriet E. Wilson's *Our Nig; or, Sketches from the Life of a Free Black, in a Two-Story White House, North by "Our Nig"* (1859), which appeared in the same year Delany began to serialize *Blake*. Like Jacobs's *Incidents*, it is largely autobiographical; and like Webb's *The Garies and Their Friends*, *Our Nig* was written by a free black but, in this case, one from New England and a much lower economic stratum.

Scholarly detective work has filled in the rough outlines of Wilson's difficult but remarkable life, to add to what is known from the testimonial letters appended to her novel. She was born Harriet Adams, a free black, in the small town of Milford, New Hampshire, in 1825. At an early age she was orphaned and put out to service with local families. She led a harsh existence, her friend Margaretta Thorn recounted in one of the appended letters, "both in the house and field," and "was indeed a slave, in every sense of the word."[66] Another letter, from "Allida," reports that Adams was rescued from this fate by "an itinerant colored lecturer" who brought her to an "ancient" town in central Massachusetts (probably Worcester), where she lived with a Mrs. Walker and made palm-leaf hats, popular in the period.[67]

Through the "colored lecturer," Adams then met a fugitive slave, "young, well-formed, and every handsome." After a brief courtship, in 1851 Adams took her beau, Thomas Wilson of Virginia, back to New Hampshire, where they married. It was not a good choice, for within a year he left to go to sea and never returned to her. In mid-1852 their son, George Mason Wilson, was born, in nearby Goffstown, and, weak in health, Harriet Wilson had to take her child "to the county farm, because she could not pay his board every week."[68] This presumably was Goffstown's "Hillsborough County Farm," a "poor farm," which a family or supervisor, reimbursed by the town, would run for the indigent. This institution was quite large, and according to local histories, it was overcrowded and rife with disease.[69]

Here Wilson's story takes an unusual turn, testifying ironically to the promise of American opportunity and initiative. One day a stranger, "moved by compassion" for her and her child, "bestowed" on her "a recipe for restoring gray hair to its former color." Wilson promptly began to manufacture the product and sell it in southern New Hampshire and northeastern Massachusetts as Mrs. Wilson's Hair Regenerator. This business did well, but ill health continued to plague her, and to support herself and her son, she penned *Our Nig*. In the summer of 1859, she registered the copyright at the District Clerk's Office in Boston, where she was then living, and enlisted the printers Rand & Avery to print the book "for the author."

Our Nig was a mendicant's tract, not a slave narrative. Such works were common in the period and often played on a distinctive trait of their authors. (A book in the same genre, for example, was *Life of Maj. Joseph Howard, an American Dwarf, Thirty-eight Years of Age, Thirty-six Inches High, and Seventy-two Pounds in Weight, Written by Himself* [1855].) "Deserted by kindred," Wilson explained in her preface, "disabled by failing health," she had no choice but to write a book. She appealed not to sympathetic whites but to her "colored brethren universally for patronage, hoping they will not condemn this attempt of their sister to be erudite, but rally around me a faithful band of supporters and defenders." She realized that her description of the northern treatment of blacks might work against the abolitionist cause, and she did not wish in any way to "palliate slavery at the South." Toward this end, she had "purposely omitted what would most provoke shame in our good anti-slavery friends at home."[70]

Wilson probably sold her book as she peddled her hair restorative, but *Our Nig* did not sell well; it went unnoticed in the abolitionist press. It thus did little to alter her financial situation, and her son, George, died in Milford of a "fever" within six months of its appearance. Wilson continued to sell her hair product. By 1867 she was living in East Cambridge, and she later moved to Boston's South End. She had changed her profession; she was now Hattie Wilson, a trance medium and spiritual healer. She was also active as a public lecturer on such topics as labor reform, human brotherhood, and the threat of the "money power." She even appeared onstage with the celebrated women's rights advocate Victoria Woodhull and on one occasion reportedly spoke before an audience of sixteen thousand. Her life came to an end in 1900 in Quincy, Massachusetts, where she died at the age of seventy-five.

In *Our Nig*, Wilson tells the story of Frado, a mulatto child, and under-cuts the conventions of the sentimental novel on every page. As the story opens, the reader learns of Mag Smith, an orphan who, "early deprived of parental guardianship, far removed from relatives," is left to "guide her tiny boat over life's surges alone and inexperienced."[71] Trusting and naive, she falls in love with someone of higher social standing, believing he will change her life. After "she surrendered to him a priceless gem," however, "which he promptly garnered as a trophy, with those of other victims," the wily seducer leaves her to face the condemnation of her community.[72] For years she lives as an outcast in a hovel on the edge of town, doing low-paying work, for which "foreigners who cheapened toil and clamored for a livelihood, competed with her . . . Every year her melancholy increased" as her means diminished.[73] These opening passages are unusual because despite the impression given by the book's title, Mag is white.

No one cares for Mag, except "a kind-hearted African" named Jim. Eventually, Jim begins to wish that she will marry him, for "she'd be as much of a prize to me as she'd fall short of coming up to the mark of white folks."[74] He musters the courage to propose. He "knew well what were her objections." "You's had the trial of white folks, any how," he says. "They run off and left ye, none of come to see if you's dead or alive," he reminds her. Demonstrating the power of racism to warp its targets, Jim subcon-sciously inverts the idea of "passing" in white society when he states, "I's black outside, I know, but I's got a white heart inside." Jim prevails, and they marry; Mag descends another step down "the ladder of infamy" and has "sundered another bond which held her to her fellows." "You can philosophize, gentle reader," the narrator observes, "upon the impro-priety of such unions, and preach dozens of sermons on the evils of amalgamation."[75]

The couple has two "pretty mulattos," but Jim falls ill of consumption and dies. Mag returns to her hovel and struggles to make ends meet. Then, with no other recourse, she begins to live with Seth, Jim's black partner, and "enter[s] the darkness of perpetual infamy" because the union is not blessed by "civilization or Christianity." Mag and Seth be-come so desperate they decide that if they are to find decent work, they must move and leave behind their children. At the age of six, Frado, "a beautiful mulatto, with long, curly black hair, and handsome roguish eyes, sparkling with an exuberance of spirit almost beyond restraint," is left at the doorstep of the Bellmonts, a well-to-do white family who live in the "large, old-fashioned, two-story white house" of the novel's subtitle and whose mistress is widely known as a bigoted shrew.[76] During the family's walk to the Bellmonts' house, a dozen children chant as they pass by, "Black, white and yeller [yellow]."[77]

In the Bellmont family, the daughter, Mary, wants to "send her [Frado] to the County House," but the son Jack says to keep her because "she's real handsome and bright and not very black, either." They begin to call her "*our* nig."[78] Mrs. Bellmont accepts her as free labor, and within a year Frado is "quite indispensable" to the family. When school approaches, they argue about whether she should go, the mother thinking "people of color" are "incapable of elevation," but Jack counters that his little favorite should have the opportunity.[79] Mr. Bellmont sides with his son, even though Mary is upset that she will have to attend the same school and is ashamed to be seen "walking with a nigger."[80] After the teacher berates her charges for making fun of Frado, their attitudes change, and, owing to Frado's wit and good nature, she becomes the school favorite.[81]

Jealous of Frado's popularity, Mary finds every opportunity to persecute her. When Mary dirties her dress crossing a stream, she blames Frado for causing her to fall, and when Frado denies it, Mrs. Bellmont, always siding with her daughter, props open her young servant's mouth with a stick for "lying."[82] The abuse escalates, with Mrs. Bellmont brutally kicking Frado for not following an order precisely enough.[83] Occasionally, Frado finds solace with Aunt Abby, Mr. Bellmont's sister, and an older son, James, who, working elsewhere, occasionally visits his family home. Jack continues to side with Frado, writing his brother about the "pretty little nig" in the house.[84] Mrs. Bellmont reacts to the attention her family members bestow on Frado by selling her dog, Fido, one of Frado's few joys, and then cutting off Frado's beautiful hair.[85]

Aunt Abby cares enough about Frado to bring her to religious meetings, even though Mrs. Bellmont, sharing the opinion of most of her neighbors, thinks it a waste of time. Abby, though, believes that Frado has a soul like anyone else and is distressed to hear the child sobbing, "Why was I made? Why can't I die? Oh, what have I to live for? No one cares for me only to get my work." Frado continues, "No mother, father, brother or sister to care for me, and then it is, You lazy nigger, lazy nigger— all because I am black! Oh, if I could die!"[86]

As when the still-enslaved Frederick Douglass sits on the shores of

Chesapeake Bay and watches the boats skimming freely over the water, prompting a remarkable address to the liberty for which he yearns, at this moment Frado becomes fully aware of herself. There are echoes, too, of *Uncle Tom's Cabin*, for when James, one of Frado's strongest supporters, falls ill, she heeds a clergyman's injunction to accept a compassionate savior and has a religious experience similar to Tom's. "Come to Christ," the minister urges. "All, young or old, white or black, bond or free, come all to Christ for pardon."[87] Frado begins to avidly read a Bible that Abby has given her, prompting Mrs. Bellmont to tell her sister-in-law that she has "caught" Frado reading it "as though she expected to turn pious nigger, and preach to white folks."[88] In a scene reminiscent of Little Eva's death, on his deathbed James urges Frado to believe as he does so that she, too, will have "a *heavenly* home" to replace the terrible one in which she finds herself.[89]

Following a talk with Mr. Bellmont, who assures Frado that she does not deserve the punishments his wife inflicts, Frado stands up to her mistress when threatened with another beating. "Stop," she shouts; "strike me, and I'll never work a mite more for you," as she stands "like one who feels the stirring of free and independent thoughts."[90] Remarkably, Mrs. Bellmont, rather than fly into a rage, drops her "weapon" and carries out the task she had set for Frado.

Frado completes her service to the Bellmonts and begins work for another local family. But soon she requires a doctor, who pronounces her very ill. Frado is put out at public expense, going to the home of "two maidens, (old,) who had principle enough to be willing to earn the money a charitable public disburses."[91] Frado remains there three years but never fully recovers. She then is placed with the less solicitous Mrs. Hoggs and gets even sicker. When she finally rebounds, she makes a semblance of a living with her skillful sewing, until she hears of an opportunity to move to a central Massachusetts town where the girls make straw bonnets, setting in motion the next phase of her life.

In the town there often appeared "professed fugitives from slavery, who recounted their personal experiences in homely phrase" to win recalcitrant northerners to the antislavery side. Wilson's use of "professed" was meant to suggest that some of these speakers were impostors or, at the least, would embroider their tales to meet their audience's expectations. Frado meets Samuel, "a fine, straight negro, whose back showed no marks of the lash, erect as if it never crouched under a burden," who nevertheless styles himself an escaped slave. In her infatuation, Frado, like many a sentimental heroine, is blind to his lie and plunges ahead, marrying him. Samuel often leaves to "lecture" for weeks at a time and has "little spare money." Eventually, "he left her to her fate—embarked at sea, with the disclosure that he had never seen the South, and that his illiterate harangues were humbugs for hungry abolitionists." He also leaves her pregnant. The story ends with a friend's giving her the "recipe, from which she might herself manufacture a useful article for her maintenance."[92] As we know from Wilson's life, illness compelled her to write in the hopes of alms. Frado "has felt herself obliged," her friend Allida says, "to resort to another method of procuring her bread—that of writing an Autobiography."

Our Nig is less about a woman betrayed by her heart than it is about the determinative power of culture. The novel challenges the sentimental novel's correspondence with reality or, at least, with the reality of black Americans. In one sense, at least, the novel is firmly sentimental: it is in part about how religion builds self-worth and provides a blueprint for surviving intolerable conditions. But its lesson is that, among free blacks, there is little hope for a better life, even through religion. Mag went with her first "love" because she was poor and took another step downward when out of dire economic need she married a black man. Though aware that her revelations of northern white prejudice could hurt the antislavery cause, Wilson wanted the reader to understand that ending slavery would do little for northern blacks, who would continue to be the victims of discrimination that kept them poor and hopeless.

Stowe was essential to the rise of African American literature; *Uncle Tom's Cabin* made a novel featuring black characters a viable proposition for publishing houses. A fervent reformer, she envisioned a better world for blacks after the end of slavery. Douglass described the prejudice of white workers with whom, on free soil, he competed for jobs, but his criticism was tempered by the generally upward trajectory of his *Narrative*. In *Our Nig*, however, there is no better world on the horizon, for Frado is subject to the vagaries of the free black's life. Brown, Jacobs, Webb, Delany, and Wilson, perhaps most of all, saw little hope for blacks in America. Contingency, not hope, is the primary theme of their works. For all the noble causes that spurred Americans to write novels in the first half of the nineteenth century, it is worth pointing out that Wilson did not write hers to counter prejudice but to merely stave off poverty.

6 } Discovering Self-Consciousness

In 1854 *Putnam's Monthly Magazine* ran a lengthy article on "Novels: Their Meaning and Mission," in which the writer observed that the last quarter century had "had the effect of completely revolutionizing" the form. While some attributed the changes in the genre to a single writer—William Godwin, whose *Caleb Williams* had so large an influence on Charles Brockden Brown, or Henry Fielding—"the true secret of the new impulse" was "with greater probability the more profoundly earnest spirit of the age," the movement toward "a radically stronger and nobler theorem of life and literature in all their departments—by a deeper theosophy and a more transcendent philosophy."[1]

By "transcendent" the writer gestured to the German idealism that had fertilized the American Transcendentalist movement.[2] He observed that the philosophy responsible for the new novel had already given us Emerson, Carlyle, Goethe, and Schiller, part of the splendid "fabric" woven by Kant, Fichte, Novalis, and Jean Paul Richter. An influence on all areas of thought at the time, the "idea" of the transcendent now had "taken possession of the field of imaginative writing—of novels," a product of an "era when there is such a fecundity and . . . overflowing of mental and psychological life."[3]

One of Transcendental philosophy's effects was (as Emerson put it so well) to make the mind aware of itself. In fiction this meant attention to the "deeper psychology" that Henry James appreciated in Hawthorne.[4] *Putnam's* essayist wrote that because "the domain of the novel ranges over the entire field of the real and the ideal," it "touches every point of man's consciousness."[5] In the 1850s, such interest in consciousness, particularly self-consciousness—the relation of the "me" to the "Not-Me" that Emerson had written about in his seminal *Nature* (1836)—began to inform fiction in a variety of ways. As sentimental novelists replaced piety with moralism, other novelists, influenced by their interest in the "transcendent," moved toward a faith based in internalized religious experience. Neither adherence toward a faith of abstract doctrine nor good works satisfied their characters' spiritual hunger, and thus they imagined a close relationship to God and particularly to Christ. In this private space, one discovered the true self. But because of the way such faith was conceived and realized, it was not easily accessible to others and could encourage solipsism.[6]

THE ETERNAL BACHELOR

Donald G. Mitchell's pseudonymously issued *Reveries of a Bachelor; or, A Book of the Heart* (1850) was the most popular example of the new self-consciousness of American fiction, even though in some ways it still epitomized the culture of sentiment in its portrayal of a bachelor yearning for the domestic life. Mitchell's novel consisted of extended "reveries" that together paint a portrait of a young, aimless bachelor, the author and Mitchell's alter ego, Ik Marvel (from two of Mitchell's favorite English authors, Isaac Walton and Andrew Marvell). Within a year of its publication, *Reveries* had sold fourteen thousand copies, and each year thereafter it enjoyed a "steady and widely extended circulation." It was quickly translated into French and German and into many more languages later in the nineteenth century.[7]

Mitchell never expected such success and later lamented that for the rest of his life, no matter what else he wrote, he would always be the dreamy bachelor Ik Marvel. Born in 1822, Mitchell was the son of a rural Connecticut minister who died when Mitchell was eight. In the following decade, he lost his mother and several siblings to tuberculosis, which he also contracted but survived. After his father's death Mitchell was placed in a boarding school in Ellington, Connecticut, and thus knew little of family life; that may explain his obsession with it that marks his immersion in the sentimental. In 1837, the year of the country's first major depression, he entered Yale College, where several relatives had matriculated and where he flourished, particularly enjoying his work on *The Yale Literary Magazine*. He graduated as valedictorian of his class and, to satisfy his relatives' wish that he soon find a profession, chose to read the law, even though his heart was not in it.

Through the good offices of a family friend, in 1844 Mitchell went to Liverpool as secretary to the U.S. consul in that city. The damp climate did not help his delicate lungs, and he spent much time wandering through France and Italy, seeking drier air and gathering material for a series of travel sketches. On his return to the United States, Mitchell placed some of these in the *American Whig Review*. Using the name Ik Marvel for the first time, he wrote more satiric sketches about Washington, D.C., where he had spent two months, for the New York *Courier and Enquirer*. Hearing of the democratic revolutions in Europe, Mitchell returned and witnessed some of the violent events in Paris in 1848. Back in America, he published *The Battle Summer* (1849), based on his first-hand observations of the upheavals.

In 1849 Mitchell published "A Bachelor's Reverie" in *The Southern Literary Messenger*. *Harper's New Monthly Magazine* reprinted it a few months later, to considerable praise. Mitchell then proposed a volume of such "daydreams" to Charles Scribner, who published *Reveries of a Bachelor* in late 1850. "Ik Marvel" was soon the talk of the literary world, and Mitchell brought out a sequel, *Dream Life: A Fable of the Seasons* (1851), which also sold well. A year later, *Harper's New Monthly Magazine* offered him a regular column on miscellaneous topics of his choice, and Mitchell thereafter sat for two years in what became the famed "Editor's Easy Chair" at the magazine.

Given his continuing financial success, Mitchell made plans to realize his dream of owning and cultivating a farm, which finally came to fruition in 1855 with his purchase of Edgewood, not far from New Haven. In the interim, he married Mary Pringle, the daughter of a South Carolina rice planter, and accepted a post as consul to Venice, which he secured with the help of Nathaniel Hawthorne, who had written a presidential campaign biography for his college classmate, the Democrat Franklin Pierce, then president.

On their return from Venice, Mitchell and his wife took up residence at Edgewood. Settling into life as an amateur agriculturalist and landscape gardener, he began to write what he called "rural" essays, although, as some scholars have pointed out, such writing is more accurately termed "suburban," for Mitchell, like Andrew Jackson Downing, among others, articulated a landscape and lifestyle halfway between the city and the country.[8] Mitchell collected some of these essays in *Rural Studies, with Hints for Country Places* (1867), a volume that typifies the incorporation of the kinds of sentimental tropes about spouses, children, and the home itself in such rural, idyllic settings.

He also began to write less autobiographical fiction. His major effort, first serialized in *The Atlantic Monthly*, was *Dr. Johns: Being a Narrative of Certain Events in the Life of an Orthodox Minister* (1866), which bears comparison to Stowe's *Oldtown Folks* (1869) as an evocation of New England life half a century earlier but which met with little success. In 1883 Mitchell revisited his popular works, writing new prefaces for *Reveries* and *Dream Life*, even though he considered these inferior to his later writing. Still widely known as Ik Marvel, Mitchell lived out his days at his beloved Edgefield, where he died in 1908, but not before he saw the beautiful fifteen-volume "Edgefield" edition of his works that Scribner published in 1906, which ensured that future generations also would enjoy *Reveries of a Bachelor.*

DAGUERREOTYPING THE HEART

Why did readers find *Reveries* so delightful and enthralling? A reviewer for *The American Whig Review* wrote that the key to the book's success was "the very ingenious form into which [the book] is thrown."[9] As another put it, in *Reveries* "all is vague, sliding, unfinished," its chapters "limpid, pellucid streams of thought."[10] The book was written in a style that was later called stream of consciousness. In his preface Mitchell called his work "a collection of those floating Reveries which have, from time to time, drifted across my brain." If he had imposed on them "more unity of design," he continued, he "might have made a respectable novel." He chose instead "the honester [*sic*] way of setting them down as they came seething from [his] thought, with all their crudities and contrasts, uncovered."[11]

Putnam's compared Mitchell's prose to one of the era's technological wonders, photography. Mitchell's book succeeded because "his nature is, as it were, iodised [*sic*], and registers, with the sensitive accuracy of a daguerreotype, every passing light and shade" of whatever comes into "his sphere."[12] That reviewer paid Mitchell another compliment by saying that in *Reveries* he had also succeeded in capturing the *interior* of his subject: it was a "book of the heart," just as the daguerreotype memorably recorded the exterior. Indeed, the reader shares Marvel's deepest secrets.

The book comprises four interrelated "reveries" or parts, each in a different way dealing with two of the standard topics of the sentimental:

love and marriage. The opening reveries find Ik musing on the desirable and undesirable aspects of marriage. On the negative side, he worries about giving up his independence. "Shall a man who has been free to chase his fancies over the wide world, without lett [obstruction] or hindrance, shut himself up to the marriage-ship, within four walls called Home, that are to claim him, his time, his trouble, and his fears, thenceforward forever more, without doubts thick, and coming to Smoke?"[13] Eliza Wharton had considered the same thing, but a half century earlier life without marriage, for a man or a woman, had been socially unacceptable. In 1850, however, a single *man*, while still raising an occasional eyebrow, was more common, although Ik's questioning of the worth of "Home," a central idea in the culture of sentiment, would have immediately seized the reader's attention.[14]

Ik considers the joy and satisfaction of having a wife always at your side and caring for you, a "sweet-faced girl" "suffer[ing] your fingers to play idly with those curls that escape down the neck," providing sympathy when family or friends die, comforting you should you fall ill, and at your bed as your last moment approaches.[15] But then comes the thought that the joy is transient. Inevitably, the fire burns down until "there was nothing but a bed of glowing embers, over which the white ashes gathered fast." Ik "was alone, with only [his] dog for company."[16] He thinks of tasting such ashes if a child should die or his wife should pass away. He imagines tending to his beloved through her last illness and enduring her funeral and grows almost hysterical at the prospect of such a loss and the loneliness that would follow. Finally, he decides that a wife is better than a coquette, even though he cannot help admitting his attraction to and fascination with the latter.

The final and longest reverie, titled "Morning, Noon, and Evening," features a different voice—he calls himself Paul—speaking directly to the reader as he relates a melancholy series of events in his own experience of love. He thinks back to his paradisiacal youth on a farm with his cousin Bella, three years younger. "Morning brings back to me the Past," Paul says, and "the past brings up not only its actualities, not only its events, and memories, but—stranger still,—what might have been."[17] He leaves Bella behind when he goes to college and then to Europe, where Carry, whom he has met on the ship and then reencounters in the bucolic English countryside, catches his interest. Then he is on to Rome, where he meets Enrica, the beautiful teenage daughter of his housekeeper, who is home after time spent in a convent. She clearly finds the American attractive and immediately goes out of her way to please him: when introduced, "she steals up behind, and passes her arm around me, with a quick electric motion, and a gentle pressure of welcome—that tells more than a thousand words."[18] But he finally realizes what a friend tells him, that her "southern nature with all its passion" is not suited to his, and he leaves her, and Rome, behind.

Later Paul meditates on the relation between past and present and wonders what has become of all the people whom he has known and loved. He returns to the farm and then decides to inquire after Bella. He trembles as he goes to her family's door, "for it flashed on [him], that perhaps,—Isabel was married." The news is worse. "Bella is dead," he learns.[19] Moreover, he finds when he reads through her unsent letters that she never lost her feelings for him. These heartfelt missives lead to an epiphany for Paul: "I loved Bella. I know not how I loved her,—whether as a lover, or as a husband loves a wife; I only know this,—I always loved her." He had shared everything else with her, he realizes, but had "never told her how much I loved her."[20] This regret haunts him like nothing else he has experienced.

But the letters also reveal something else remarkable: Bella and Carry had been intimate schoolmates. With the former gone, Carry means even more to Paul. He has to find her, for she is "doubly dear" to him, now "that she is joined with [his] sorrow for the lost Isabel."[21] Five years later, by chance he encounters Carry on a train. After they part, he writes her proposing marriage. Her reply is not what he had hoped, for her parents have already arranged for her to marry her godfather's ward, Laurence. Paul is despondent, but the hand of fate intervenes. Traveling in Europe, Laurence falls in love with another woman, and Carry's godfather finally permits him to break his betrothal to Carry, freeing her to marry Paul. A last turn of fate's windlass: on their wedding trip to Europe, they meet Laurence and find him married to—Enrica! The families end up living near each other, close to the farm where Paul and Bella had played, enacting the idyll of which Paul had often dreamed.

Mitchell's reliance on the tropes of the sentimental novel might seem to counteract his innovative style. But his ambitions were different. Toward the end of *Reveries*, Paul makes his way back to the old farmhouse and recounts, "I dreamed pleasant dreams that night for I dreamed that my Reverie was real."[22] In other words, it *all* has been a dream. Paul is the same lonely bachelor whom the reader met on the first page of the book, even though Mitchell led the reader to believe that this final "reverie" was in fact no reverie at all, but a remembrance. All along, Paul was living a dream life, trying to escape his loneliness. Sentiment informed Paul's dreams, yet one lesson of *Reveries* is that the escapism offered by the sentimental mode can have the pernicious effect of prolonging an individual's youthful unhappiness.

It should not be surprising that Emily Dickinson and her family read *Reveries* with pleasure, for Mitchell's willingness to "tell the truth but tell it slant," as she put it, can account for the book's popularity even among such sophisticated readers. *Reveries* appeared when Dickinson was an impressionable nineteen years old, and as her letters to her sister Susan and others indicate, it was a favorite. Indeed, it is possible that she acquired her love for her trademark dashes from Mitchell's compulsive use of them, for in his eddying prose as well as in her elliptic verse, this diacritical mark indicates spontaneity and helps capture the flow of consciousness.[23] And like Marvel, she, too, would work within and beyond the boundaries of the culture of sentiment in which they both thrived.

"THE OBSCUREST MAN OF LETTERS IN AMERICA"

By 1850 another writer was being lauded for writing fiction—to that point, short stories—that similarly probed his characters' hearts and minds. In that year, James T. Fields, the junior partner in the ambitious Boston publishing firm of Ticknor and Fields, solicited the work of a reclusive Salem, Massachusetts, author, Nathaniel Hawthorne, some of whose stories he had read. He showed Ticknor a lengthy short story, and he encouraged Hawthorne to turn it into a novel. The aspiring author did just that, adding, among other things, a lengthy autobiographical preface about his recent stint as a customshouse inspector in his native port city. The resulting novel was *The Scarlet Letter* (1850), which, while not a financial success compared with that year's bestsellers, Susan Warner's *The Wide, Wide World* and Mitchell's *Reveries of a Bachelor*, quickly sold out its first printing of twenty-five hundred copies and was immediately reprinted. Reviewers—admittedly, some of whom were friends of the publisher—promptly anointed Hawthorne the country's most important novelist and its best prose stylist since Irving.

But Hawthorne's road to acclaim had not been as direct as this brief summary suggests. His ship captain father, Nathaniel Hathorne, had died on a voyage to Surinam (Dutch Guiana) when his son was only four, prompting his widow and their children to move in with her family, the Mannings, in Salem. When Hawthorne was in his teens, the family settled in what was still wilderness in Raymond, Maine, where the Mannings had land; but a year later he returned to Salem, to prepare for college under the guardianship of his uncle. He entered Bowdoin College in Brunswick, Maine, in 1821; his classmates included Horatio Bridge, a future naval officer, Franklin Pierce, a future president; and, in the class behind him, Henry Wadsworth Longfellow, the future poet, translator, and professor.

After graduation in 1825 Hawthorne again returned to Salem, without a set goal but interested in the new profession of authorship. In his preface to *The Scarlet Letter* he humorously alludes to the low status of such ambition when he imagines his Puritan forebearers learning that their descendant is "a writer of storybooks." "What kind of business in life," a dour relative exclaims, "what mode of glorifying God, or being serviceable to mankind in his day and generation,—may that be?"[24] But Hawthorne was nothing if not persistent. He had completed some short stories while at Bowdoin and worked on a novel, *Fanshawe*, which he published anonymously and at his own expense in 1828. It went virtually unnoticed, however, one reviewer calling it evidently "the first effort of a Collegian," and another summarizing it pithily, if a tad sarcastically, as a "love story," which, "like ten thousand others, [has] a mystery, an elopement, a villain, a father, a tavern, almost a duel, a horrible death, and—Heaven save the mark!—an end."[25] The novel's reception so embarrassed Hawthorne that he burned many of the unsold copies. (Around this time, too, he added the *w* to his family name.) He had trouble getting noticed beyond Salem and Boston and claimed that he had the "distinction" of being, "for a good number of years, the obscurest man of letters in America."[26]

In 1831 Hawthorne began to publish stories anonymously in a popular Boston gift book annual called *The Token*. Several years later he collected these, many based in New England's colonial history, as *Twice-Told Tales* (1837) and put his name on the title page. He republished the tales in 1842, and in 1846 brought out another collection, *Mosses from an Old Manse*. This book met critical, if not popular, success. Some reviewers suggested that he was a potential successor to Irving, Cooper, and Sedgwick, a writer who could finally bring respectability to American literature.

One reviewer who believed that was his old schoolmate Henry Wadsworth Longfellow, who lavishly praised *Twice-Told Tales*. "When a new star rises in the heavens," Longfellow wrote, "people gaze after it for a season with the naked eye, and with such telescopes as they may find. In the stream of thought, which flows so peacefully deep and clear through the pages of this book, we see the bright reflection of a spiritual star, after which all men will be fain to gaze 'with the naked eye, and with the spyglasses of criticism.'" The book could have come only "from the hand of a man of genius."[27]

Other early notices similarly enhanced Hawthorne's reputation. Some reviewers latched on to the unusual serenity and inwardness of Hawthorne's fiction. Poe claimed that the prominent feature of the stories was what a painter would term "*repose*," for "all is quiet, thoughtful, subdued," and "we are soothed as we read."[28] In *The Knickerbocker*, Lewis Gaylord Clark observed that Hawthorne had no superior "as a quiet yet acute observer and most faithful limner of Nature. His mind," Clark wrote, using the same metaphor applied to Mitchell's works, "reflects her images like the plates of the Daguerreotype."[29] Nathan Hale, Jr., observed that Hawthorne's tales never contained much "external action." Rather, he unveiled "the movements of the inner man, and the growth of motive and reflection."[30]

The young author's next collection, *Mosses from an Old Manse*, while again well received, also elicited some telling criticism. Poe, perhaps seeing no improvement or growth in Hawthorne's work, wrote that he was "peculiar" but also predictable; there was "sameness" and a "monotone" to Hawthorne's works, which too often inclined toward allegory that would keep him from both true greatness and wide popularity.[31] Hawthorne himself recognized as much when, in his introduction to "Rappaccini's Daughter," he deprecatingly described an alter ego, M. de l'Aubépine (the hawthorn tree, in French), as occupying

> an unfortunate position between the transcendentalists . . . and the great body of pen-and-ink men who address the intellect and sympathies of the multitude. If not too refined, at all events too remote, too shadowy and unsubstantial . . . to suit the taste of the latter class, and yet too popular to satisfy the spiritual or metaphysical requisitions of the former, he must necessarily find himself without an audience.[32]

In the *Democratic Review* in 1845 Duyckinck alighted on the quality that Poe and perhaps even Hawthorne himself could not explain: "a power of fascination which is exercised over the mind by the occasional gloom and pale glimpses as it were of fiends starting up on the page." For him, the "novel and original element" in Hawthorne was "the shadow which Sin and Death in their twin flights are forever casting upon the world; shadows which fall alike upon the so-called evil and the good, which darken all that is pure, and defile all that is sacred, but not more than in actual life."[33] Melville later called this Hawthorne's "power of blackness ten times black."[34] Hawthorne was content to rest among these shadows, and his reticence prevented him from imagining the kind of spiritual freedom Transcendentalists promised their followers.

If he did not seek to dispel gloom in his fiction, Hawthorne did at least try to do so in his life, as one of the original participants in George Ripley's communitarian experiment at Brook Farm. He had become engaged to Sophia Peabody—sister of Elizabeth, a spinster Transcendentalist, and Mary, a teacher who married the educational reformer Horace Mann—and intended to bring her to Brook Farm after their marriage. Hawthorne curtailed his stay, however, returning to Boston in November 1841, after about seven months; the environment, for a variety of reasons, had not been as conducive to his writing as he had hoped.[35] The experience was not fruitless, though; it was to provide the background to his third novel, *The Blithedale Romance* (1852).

Hawthorne and Peabody were married in July 1842 and took up residence in Concord at the bucolic "Old Manse," previously the home of the Reverend Ezra Ripley, where his grandson Ralph Waldo Emerson had written *Nature*. In 1845 the couple, now with a young daughter, returned to Salem to live with Hawthorne's mother, and the following year, with the help of his old classmate Pierce, now president, Hawthorne assumed the position of surveyor at the Salem Custom House, where he conceived *The Scarlet Letter*.

"A TALE OF HUMAN FRAILTY AND SORROW"

Like the earliest American novels, *The Scarlet Letter* deals with seduction, but the event—the climax in works like *The Coquette* and its progeny—occurs prior to the novel's action proper. In Hawthorne's depiction of Hester Prynne's desperate attempt to keep her daughter, Pearl, when the magistrates threaten to make her a ward, and in Pearl's desire to hold the hands of both her mother and her father in daylight and so to be acknowledged as their child, it similarly draws on sentimental tropes, particularly the idea of the sanctity of family bonds. The novel's innovation lies elsewhere, in its psychological dissection of the emotional lives of its three central characters, Hester; the Reverend Arthur Dimmesdale, her lover; and Roger Chillingworth, her husband. With the novel Hawthorne finally broke allegory's hold on his imagination.

The Scarlet Letter was widely reviewed. One of its most trenchant evaluations appeared in *The Universalist Quarterly and General Review*, where the minister Amory Dwight Mayo recognized the acuteness of Hawthorne's characterizations but in the service of what he considered a flawed religious vision.[36] Mayo related the novel to one of the most hotly debated theological propositions of the age: whether the mind was "free, acting from volitions self-suggested or voluntarily adopted," or was "subject to influences which encompass it and insinuate themselves into its structure." The former view, affirming free will, assumed in man "a definite individuality" that allowed him to stand "apart from nature, or other souls, or the Deity," and by "sheer will and energy" to create a world of his own, a position that in its extreme form ended in the subjectivism that Emerson championed. The latter view posited that God, "in some way inexplicable to man, lives in his universe, and causes his will to be done through all modes and qualities of finite action." In this view, "individuality has less distinctness of outline" and is less significant, for man is subject to the same unswerving force and aware of forces that "circumscribe his activity and interfere with the assumption of his omnipotent individuality."[37]

There are times in every man's life, Mayo argued, when this riddle of freedom and fate becomes painfully manifest and his natural reaction is to deny his cosmic dependence. "Now and then," though, a man is born who can "look straight down into the spirit without searing his eyeballs, witness this conflict of law and will, trace its results," and "not lose his balance of mind." Hawthorne was one of these, Mayo asserted, for he concentrated the reader's interest upon the raging battle between human will and spiritual law.[38] Unlike Emerson, however, who posited a healthy balance between an individual's "Power" and divinely established "Fate," Hawthorne dwelled so much on the latter that he became "an unfit medium" for the proper interpretation of man's relation to God. Thus, in *The Scarlet Letter*, powerful as it was, Mayo found a "certain ghastliness about the people," a result of the author's obsession with sin. "No puritan city ever held such a throng as stalks" through the book, Mayo observed, and "even in a well conducted madhouse, life is not so lurid and intense."[39] In portraying the cosmic battle in each individual and deciding its outcome in favor of the gods, Hawthorne, Mayo believed, lost the real flesh and blood that drove narrative.

ON MONUMENT MOUNTAIN

The critical and relative popular success of *The Scarlet Letter* ushered in a very creative period in Hawthorne's life, to which his chance meeting with another successful young author, Herman Melville, contributed. In the spring of 1850, flush from the excitement of publishing *The Scarlet Letter*, Hawthorne had moved his family to a cottage in the town of Lenox, Massachusetts, in the Berkshire Mountains, overlooking the beautiful lake known as the Stockbridge Bowl.

That August David Dudley Field, a Berkshire County historian, issued invitations for a climb of and picnic on nearby Monument Mountain. In addition to Field and his daughter Jenny, the party consisted of a number of friends and visitors: James T. Fields, Hawthorne's publisher, and his wife; Evert Duyckinck; Cornelius Mathews; Henry Sedgwick, a student of Longfellow's at Harvard; Oliver Wendell Holmes; and Herman Melville, a young novelist riding a wave of success since his first work, *Typee*, and now at work on his sixth, about the sperm whale fishery. A sudden thunderstorm overtook the group, forcing them to take cover under a ledge, where they drank iced champagne and listened to Mathews recite William Cullen Bryant's poem "Monument Mountain." When they attained the summit, there were more antics. Melville ventured on a high ledge to show how sailors hauled in canvas, and even Hawthorne entered the fun, playing at looking for "the great carbuncle," the subject of one of his best-known stories.[40] It was a memorable and spirited day.

Melville was staying at his cousin Robert Melvill's summer boardinghouse in Pittsfield and by September had decided to buy Arrowhead, a farm in the same town, a purchase made possible by a loan from his father-in-law. Before long he moved his family—his wife, Elizabeth, their son, Malcolm, his mother, and three unmarried sisters—to Arrowhead, where he started renovations and continued to toil at what became *Moby-Dick* (1851). Hawthorne's presence was exhilarating, and his influence on Melville pivotal. The two visited each other as family and work schedules allowed, usually at Melville's instigation but never seemingly often enough to satisfy him. Within two weeks of their meeting, Melville published in Duyckinck's *Literary World* a deeply appreciative essay titled "Hawthorne and His Mosses," in which he announced that Hawthorne was nothing less than Shakespeare's equal and that his new friend had "dropped germinous [*sic*] seeds" deep into his soul.

The chief product of Hawthorne's Berkshire County sojourn was *The House of the Seven Gables*. Because it followed so closely on the heels of *The Scarlet Letter*, reviewers welcomed it as a less gloomy and relentless depiction of sin and guilt. The Boston writer Henry T. Tuckerman stressed Hawthorne's appeal to "consciousness" and observed that what the use of lenses in the telescope and microscope had done for the scientist "the psychological writer does in relation to our own nature," using stories to make the reader aware of "mysteries within and around individual life." If one were obliged to describe Hawthorne's writing in a single word, Tuckerman ventured, it would be "metaphysical" or "soulful." As the earth and sky blend at the horizon, the reviewer concluded, where "things seen and unseen, the actual and the spiritual, mind and matter, what is within and what is without our consciousness, have a line of union," there Hawthorne "delights to hover."[41]

But Duyckinck thought that the novel was a step backward, for it was too "semi-allegorical," the house of the seven gables itself—"one [gable] for each deadly sin"—an "adumbration of the corrupted soul of man."[42] For all of its detailed depiction of such genuine New England characters as Hepzibah, Clifford, and Jaffrey Pyncheon, said another reviewer, the book "did not have the same force, precision, and certainty of handling" of *The Scarlet Letter*. Hawthorne's "intensely meditative cast of mind[,]" by which he views persons in relation to general laws," clotted the prose and caused him to "lose his hold upon characters."[43]

THE REVERIES OF MILES COVERDALE

After the publication of *The House of the Seven Gables*, Ticknor asked Hawthorne for another volume of stories, and he obliged with *The Snow-Image and Other Twice-Told Tales* (1852). He also completed a collection of retellings of classical myths for children, *A Wonder-Book for Girls and Boys* (1852), but he had another novel in mind. To his friend Horatio Bridge he wrote in the summer of 1851, "I know not what I will write next," but "should it be a romance," he continued, he meant "to put an extra touch of the devil in it."[44] The result was salutary, for some critics declared this next work, *The Blithedale Romance*, Hawthorne's "*chef-d'œuvre*," as a reviewer in the well-regarded *North British Review* put it, "the best novel of America, and one of the best of the present age."[45] Among novels published in the early 1850s, a time of great experimentation within the form, *The Blithedale Romance* is indeed a seminal work because of the ways in which Hawthorne, influenced by his friends and neighbors among the Transcendentalists, examined the interior life in a character remarkably similar to Ik Marvel, though one whose reveries brought him beyond melancholy.

Despite his pointed disclaimer in the book's preface, Hawthorne drew much from his several months' stay in 1841 at Brook Farm. In the novel, Hawthorne explored the individual's obligations to self and society. As sentimental authors like Warner and Cummins promulgated an ethic of self-regulation or self-negation—the development of character for the benefit of something larger than the self—Hawthorne, even as he borrowed some conventions from the sentimental genre, addressed the inevitable conflict between this ethos and one that celebrated the uniqueness of personality and, by extension, the self-centeredness that Transcendentalism implicitly encouraged. His *Blithedale Romance* was one of the best examples of this growing tendency, for the novel is about both psychology and sociology. Setting his fiction at a socialist community, Hawthorne confronted the reasons why such utopian experiments were established on this side of the Atlantic—that for all its rhetoric of equality, the United States was not yet a true democracy. In so doing, he also presented a memorably inventive portrait of the interior life.

Hawthorne accurately represented Ripley's original intentions for Brook Farm, particularly his attempt to level differences among different classes and engender in each member a concern for the whole. For once, the narrator, Miles Coverdale, explains, "we had divorced ourselves from Pride, and were striving to supply its place with familiar love," in an attempt to eliminate the social conflict endemic to free market capitalism. The reformers also wished "to lessen the laboring man's toil, by performing our due share of it," as intellectuals took turns in the fields and at various crafts, demonstrating that labor was not something performed only by the lower classes. They sought their profit "by mutual aid, instead of wresting it by the strong hand from an enemy, or filching it craftily from those less shrewd than ourselves, . . . or winning it by selfish competition with a neighbor." In short, Coverdale concluded, "we purposed to offer up the earnest toil of our bodies, as a prayer, no less than an effort, for the advancement of our race."[46]

At Blithedale, however, the chief characters, noble as their original intentions are, quickly succumb to the very "Pride" that the community was established to eradicate. At the outset, the reader incongruously finds the beautiful, magnetic women's rights advocate, Zenobia, in domestic work, acting as the gracious hostess the first evening at the farm. And when she soon shows herself to be imperious, rash, and willing to sacrifice the community, it is for another domestic ideal: a man's love.

The object of her affection, Hollingsworth, a blacksmith turned social reformer, appears at the farmhouse door in a snowstorm carrying a teenage girl, Priscilla, who needs their protection, and thus seems the epitome of the man of feeling. But he soon shows his true self, too; for him, Blithedale is only a stepping-stone to establish a new kind of reformatory for criminals.

Coverdale, a bachelor who "once had faith and force enough to form generous hopes of the world's destiny," says he is willing to do what he can for the greater good. But he qualifies his commitment. If going to Blithedale means "quitting a warm fireside, flinging away a freshly lighted cigar, and travelling far beyond the strike of the city-clocks, through a drifting snowstorm," he is on board, but his elision of anything more taxing suggests that he has given little consideration to the sacrifice Ripley had in mind.[47] When psychological tensions increase, Coverdale simply leaves Blithedale, retreating to bachelor's rooms in Boston, too selfish to realize that he might do something to avert impending tragedy. Despite Coverdale's assertion that he has made "but a poor and dim figure in [his] own narrative, establishing no separate interest," he becomes Hawthorne's main focus, just as Ik Marvel was Mitchell's. Or rather, the vexed relation between Coverdale's mind and will is Hawthorne's main focus. The entire book is Coverdale's attempt to recover and understand events that happened twelve years earlier—events filtered through not only his consciousness but also his memory—and what to do about them now.

Hawthorne, sensitive to his competitors and the market, may have wished to capitalize on *The Reveries of a Bachelor*'s considerable success. Coverdale is a twenty-six-year-old bachelor when the action begins and remains a bachelor at thirty-eight, when he narrates his story. Even more striking, Hawthorne constantly evokes fireplaces, their dancing flames or dying embers signaling Coverdale's varying moods. He begins his story with the memory of the "cheery blaze upon the heart" that he found at Blithedale after he trudged there through a mid-April snowstorm. "Vividly does that fireside recreate itself," Coverdale writes, "as I rake away the ashes from the embers in my memory, and blow them up with a sigh, for lack of more inspiring breath." The fire burns vividly but only for an instant, its oak logs long ago spent. Their "genial glow must be represented by the merest phosphoric glimmer, like that which eludes, rather than shines, from the damp fragments of decayed trees, deluding the benighted wanderer through a forest."[48]

This is the reader's first warning of Coverdale's potential unreliability; conjuring his memories before an artificial fire, he sees through a glass darkly. Try as he might—"the pleasant firelight! I must keep harping on it," he says a few pages later—all that has happened at Blithedale still is not clear to him.[49] Later, after he has left the farm because of a conflict with Hollingsworth, he sits quietly in his hotel room "in the laziest manner possible, in a rocking chair, inhaling the fragrance of a series of cigars," refusing just yet to plunge again "into the muddy tide of human activity and pastime" that has ruffled his serenity.[50]

Like Mitchell, Hawthorne explores why his main character has remained a bachelor. Coverdale fears the potential pitfalls and tragedy that can beset a married man and so is unable to act on his half-acknowledged desires. Thus, an almost pathological aversion to personal risk compounds his neurotic self-doubt. His insecurity takes its most tragicomic form in his relations with Zenobia, whom he cannot keep his eyes off of. From the moment he first sees her, he is struck by her "bloom, health, and vigor, which she possesse[s] in such overflow that a man might well have fallen in love with her for their sake only."[51] When Zenobia subsequently jokes that its being so cold in the group's newly founded paradise she could not assume "the garb of Eden" until spring, Coverdale can hardly control his thoughts. "Assuredly, Zenobia could not have intended it," he writes, and thus "the fault must have been entirely in my imagination—but these last words, together with something in her manner, irresistibly brought up a picture of that fine, perfectly developed figure, in Eve's earliest garment. I almost fancied myself," Coverdale recalls, "actually beholding it."[52]

No stranger to men's attention, Zenobia avers that she has "been exposed to a great deal of eye-shot in the few years of [her] mixing in the world" but never of the kind Coverdale casts on her. "What are you seeking to discover in me?" she asks him. Caught off guard, Coverdale blurts out, "The mystery of your life. And you will never tell me." Zenobia calls his bluff. Bending her head toward his, she looks into his eyes, as if challenging Coverdale to drop "a plummet-line" into the depths of her consciousness. "I see nothing," he says, closing his eyes, "unless it be the face of a sprite, laughing at me from the bottom of a deep well." Coverdale is afraid to look directly at the source of her attraction, her blatant sexuality. The whole episode so upsets him that he begins to wish that she would leave him alone. Suppressing his carnal feelings, he declares petulantly, like a boy whistling in the dark, that he would not have fallen in love with her "under any circumstances."[53]

Frightened by Zenobia's passion, Coverdale falls in love with her opposite, the unthreatening, adolescent Priscilla. His tragedy is that he cannot speak this love, either, for more than a decade passes after the final events at Blithedale before he is able to mention it publicly. Early on, however, Hawthorne alerts the reader to the growing infatuation that leads to Coverdale's "writing" the whole book. Coverdale mentions that as time passes, "Priscilla had grown to be a very pretty girl, and still kept budding and blossoming, and daily putting on some new charm," as though "Nature [were] shaping out a woman before our very eyes." Her "imperfections and shortcomings" affected him with "a kind of playful pathos which was as absolutely bewitching a sensation as ever I experienced," a reverie worthy of Ik Marvel.[54]

But there is yet another whom Coverdale "loves": Hollingsworth, four years older, "a tenderness in his voice, eyes, and mouth, in his gesture, in every indescribable manifestation, which few men could resist and no women."[55] When Coverdale is ill, Hollingsworth provides "more than brotherly attendance," for there is "something of the woman molded into [his] great stalwart frame."[56] "I loved Hollingsworth," Coverdale later says, and Hollingsworth returns the affection.[57] He asks Coverdale to join his enterprise, offering "what you have told me, over and over again, that you most need"—a purpose in life "worthy of the extremest self-devotion." Tears come to Hollingsworth's eyes as he murmurs to Coverdale, "[T]here is not the man in this wide world, whom I can love as I could you. Do not forsake me!" As Coverdale remembers this scene "through the coldness and dimness" of the twelve years since it occurred, he still has the sensation "as if Hollingsworth had caught hold of my heart, and were pulling it towards him with an almost irresistible force . . .

Had I but touched his extended hand, Hollingsworth's magnetism would perhaps have penetrated me with his own conception of all these matters."[58] Coverdale refuses and "never said the word—and certainly can never have it to say, hereafter—that cost me a thousandth part so hard an effort as that one syllable."[59] If Coverdale's behavior had not affected others, his constitutional reticence would be excusable; but his actions, even though he does not fully realize it, contribute to the confusion and tragedy that strike those who genuinely are his friends.

FROM SELF-CONSCIOUSNESS TO SELFISHNESS

Hawthorne's use of an unreliable first-person narrator grew out of one of his preoccupations: the problem of selfishness. Blithedale's population, for example, was comprised of "persons of marked individuality, crooked sticks . . . not exactly the easiest to bind up into a faggot." So Coverdale opines that the bond at Blithedale "was not affirmative, but negative," for each in the past had found "one thing or another to quarrel with" in his or her life, even as he or she could not agree on anything but the "inexpediency of lumbering along with the old system any farther."[60] Further, like Zenobia and Coverdale, many early members were not economically dependent on the enterprise, and the fact that they had it within their power to leave when they wished could not but lessen their commitment. At one point Coverdale realizes that although they "saw fit to drink [their] tea out of earthen cups to-night, in earthen company, it was at [their] option to use pictured porcelain and handle silver forks again, tomorrow."[61]

Tellingly, the perversion of love by possessiveness that Fourier deemed a major failing in modern society brings tragedy—and an end—to the Blithedale experiment. Hollingsworth correctly argues that Fourier based his system on the gratification of each individual's needs; but at Blithedale he, Zenobia, and Coverdale all deny or repress what truly attracts them, poisoning their behavior. Hollingsworth pretends that he loves Zenobia to acquire her money; in so doing, he initially denies his true feelings for Priscilla. Zenobia suppresses her beliefs in women's equality and throws herself at the feet of a chauvinist, then, broken-hearted, kills herself. Coverdale hides any acknowledgment of his love for Priscilla, first from fear of rejection and later, for twelve lonely years, from disappointment and embarrassment. Zenobia's severe judgment of Hollingsworth when she learns the truth about whom he loves indicts them all. "It is all self!" she screams. "Nothing else; nothing but self, self, self!" His "disguise" with her is finally "a self-deception." In denying his love for Priscilla, Hollingsworth has "stifled down" his "inmost consciousness" and done a "deadly wrong" to his heart.[62] In the end, Zenobia dismisses the Blithedale experiment. She tells Coverdale,

> I am weary of this place, and sick to death of playing at philanthropy and progress. Of all varieties of mock-life, we have surely blundered into the very emptiest mockery, in our effort to establish the one true system . . . It was, indeed, a foolish dream! Yet it gave us some pleasant summer days, and bright hopes, while they lasted.[63]

Eight years were to pass before Hawthorne's next and final novel, *The Marble Faun; or, The Romance of Monte Beni* (1860). Benefiting from his friendship with President Pierce, from 1853 to 1857 he served as the U.S. consul to Liverpool, like Mitchell, and then to Manchester. Relinquishing this position in 1858, Hawthorne traveled through France to Italy, where he lived for a year before returning to England. In Italy he wrote *The Marble Faun*, another story of the psychological wages of sin and guilt but one that suffers from both excessive length and Hawthorne's revived interest in allegory.

In these same years Hawthorne also worked on another manuscript he had begun in Italy, his "English" novel, but abandoned what was published posthumously as *Dr. Grimshawe's Secret* (1883). He then started a historical romance set at the time of the American Revolution. This, too, he failed to complete; it was published after his death as *Septimus Felton* (1872). Traveling through New Hampshire with his old classmate Pierce, whose party had abandoned him after one term and so had his own failures to consider, Hawthorne died at the Pemigewasset House in Plymouth in 1864. Another unfinished work, *The Dolliver Romance* (1876), about someone seeking the elixir of life, was among his papers.

TYPEE MAKES GOOD

Hawthorne exerted a decided, if wholly unplanned, influence upon Herman Melville. The latter's journey to that fateful day on Monument Mountain was circuitous. He was born in New York City in 1819, the son of the merchant Allan Melvill and Maria Gansevoort Melville, daughter of Peter Gansevoort, a Revolutionary War general. When Melville was eleven, his father's business failed, prompting the family to move to

Albany, the Gansevoorts' hometown. Two years later his father died, leaving the family in considerable debt. Although the young Melville attended Albany Academy for a year, college never seemed to be a real possibility. Between 1835 and 1837 he worked as a bookkeeper and clerk in Albany, and he also tried teaching. Lacking steady work and family money, at the age of twenty he followed the path of many in comparable straits: he went to sea. In the early summer of 1839 he left New York as a crew member on a London-bound merchant ship, an experience he later drew on in writing *Redburn* (1849).

In Bedford in the spring of 1841 he signed on to a whaling vessel, the *Acushnet*, bound for the largely unexplored South Seas. Disliking his captain, Melville and his friend Richard Tobias (Toby) Greene jumped ship at Nuku Hiva, the largest of the Marquesas Islands (in what now is French Polynesia). The two remained in the lush Taipi Valley for a month and then boarded an Australian whaler sailing for Tahiti, where the captain remanded them for mutiny. Melville escaped, worked on Tahiti, and in the autumn of 1842 boarded a Nantucket-based whaler. Then came a stint in the U.S. Navy aboard the frigate *United States*, which docked in Boston in the fall of 1844, finally returning Melville to his home country after four years of sailing the most exotic parts of the globe.

Before going to sea, Melville had published a few prose sketches in local papers and on his return decided to write a book-length novel based on his adventures in the Marquesas, hoping to repeat the success of Richard Henry Dana Jr.'s *Two Years Before the Mast* (1840). He worked on the manuscript through 1845, and after Harper & Brothers had rejected it because the editors doubted its veracity, through the good offices of his brother Gansevoort, a member of the American legation in London, Melville placed it with the English house of John Murray. Early in 1846 it appeared as *Narrative of a Four Months' Residence Among the Natives of a Valley of the Marquesas Islands*; a few months later the enterprising Wiley & Putnam issued it in New York as *Typee: A Peep at Polynesian Life*, part of its new series of American literature.

Presented as fiction but supposedly based on the author's own travels, *Typee* became a sensation and went through a second printing in late summer, albeit without passages critical of the work of Christian missionaries that some readers found offensive. Scenes like those in which the island's beautiful bare-breasted nymphs greeted the land- (and sex-) starved sailors also raised a few eyebrows but probably sold copies.

Despite the fact that its owners were strongly Methodist and supported their denomination's missionary activity, the next year Harper & Brothers snapped up *Typee*'s sequel, *Omoo*, though like its predecessor, it first appeared in London. There Murray included it in his Home and Colonial Library, guaranteeing sales throughout the British Empire. In *Omoo* Melville drew on his time on Tahiti. As with *Typee*, the novel was aimed at satisfying the public's yearning for first-person accounts of exotic regions just opened to European and American exploration.

By 1847, even though his books sold only a couple of thousand copies each and a few thousand more in their English editions, Melville was one of the country's brightest literary lights, widely and appreciatively reviewed. His personal life, too, appeared to take a turn for the better. In August, Melville married the well-to-do Elizabeth Shaw, daughter of the Massachusetts supreme court chief justice Lemuel Shaw. The Melvilles took up residence in a house on Fourth Avenue in Manhattan.

Because of his involvement in Young America, Melville spent much time with Evert Duyckinck and Cornelius Mathews and attending New York's literary salons. He heard constant calls for a pathbreaking American novel beyond what Cooper, Simms, Sedgwick, or Mathews had produced. He also read voraciously, buying a subscription to the New York Society Library, borrowing from Duyckinck's personal collection, and frequenting the city's secondhand bookstalls. He read Shakespeare, Montaigne, Rabelais, Sir Thomas Browne, Dante, Coleridge, and others. All this could not but affect the new book he was writing about his South Seas adventures, one, he told John Murray, that would "enter into scenes altogether new" and that would "possess more interest than the former [two novels]; which treated of subjects comparatively trite."[64] At twenty-eight, Melville had begun to entertain thoughts not just of commercial success but of literary greatness.

His irritation that his first two novels had not been regarded as based in fact also influenced this new work. Tired of "the reiterated imputation of being a romancer in disguise," this book would "show those who may take an interest in the matter, that a real romance of mine is no Typee or Omoo, & is made of different stuff altogether." This work was "no dish water nor its model borrowed from the Circulating Library," he explained to Murray. "It is something new I assure you, & original, if nothing more." He added, "Forbear to prejudge it," for while "it opens like a true narrative," the "romance & poetry of the thing thence grow continuously, till it becomes a story wild enough" but "with a meaning too."[65]

Murray passed, however, and Melville made arrangements to publish *Mardi: And a Voyage Thither* with Murray's chief rival, Richard Bentley, with Harper & Brothers again bringing out the American edition. The novel is ostensibly the story of Taji, who jumps ship in the archipelago of Mardi and becomes obsessed with finding the beautiful maiden Yillah. But this is only one strand of what is an abstruse political allegory, inspired by Melville's interest in national and European affairs that Young America had nurtured. With revolutionary fervor sweeping Europe and with the continuing debate over the United States' war with Mexico, Melville portrayed the islands in Mardi as representations of European nations and various states in the Union.

Reviewers were mystified. An English reviewer put it bluntly: the novel is "a 3 vol. metaphor into the applications of which we can only now and then catch a glimpse . . . We never," he continued in a telling phrase, "saw a book so like a kaleidoscope."[66] Some traced its stylistic lineage to Europe, with Jonathan Swift's *Gulliver's Travels* frequently mentioned, as well as the works of Sir Thomas Browne, Robert Burton, and Rabelais. Others invoked Transcendentalism, one writer noting wryly that Melville had been "drinking at the well of the 'English bewitched' of which Mr. Carlyle and Mr. Emerson are the priests."[67] An English journal termed *Mardi* "a compound of 'Robinson Crusoe' and 'Gulliver's Travels,' seasoned throughout with German metaphysics of the most transcendental school."[68]

Several reviewers, however, thought that even with its failings *Mardi* should be lauded for its ambition. Its purpose was "no less than the reconciling of the mind to the creation of an Utopia in the unknown latitudes of Pacific, to call into existence imaginary tribes and nations, to describe fabulous manners, and to glass them so distinctly in the fancy that they will appear to have been implanted there by memory," claimed one attentive reader.[69] The predictably sympathetic *United States Magazine and Democratic Review* chided skeptical readers for forgetting that *Mardi* might be the latest in a line of books that had changed the world. "Pilgrims Progress [*sic*] and Gulliver's Travels were written so long ago, that they seem to have dropped through the memory of critics," who have ceased "to think any reproduction or improvement of that sort of thing possible . . . Portions of Mardi are written with . . . divine impulse, and they thrill through every fibre of the reader with an electric force."[70]

But even if it provided glimpses of ambition and imagination not yet fully realized, *Mardi* was not Melville's breakout book. Most reviewers agreed with George Ripley, now working for Horace Greeley's *New-York Tribune*: Melville should have stayed in his "sphere, which is that of graphic, poetical narration" rather than launch "into the dim, shadowy, spectral, Mardian region of mystic speculation and wizard fancies ... Let the author return to the transparent narration of his own adventures," and he will be "everywhere welcomed as one of the most delightful of American writers."[71] Melville got the message, disappointed though he was to hear it. With a family to feed, he temporarily set aside his grand ambitions and within a year churned out two more novels, in the autobiographical vein that had made him famous.

By his own admission, Melville wrote *Redburn: His First Voyage* in less than two months, drawing on his first sea voyage, to Liverpool and London, a decade earlier. In *White-Jacket; or, The World in a Man-of-War* (1850), which took merely another two months, he re-created his fourteen months' experience in the U.S. Navy. He thought little of either novel, writing his father-in-law, "No reputation that is gratifying to me, can possibly be achieved by either of these books." They were, he continued to Chief Justice Shaw, "two *jobs*, which I have done for money—being forced to it as other men are to sawing wood."[72] *Redburn* and *White-Jacket* sold well as expected but also drew at least one prescient notice. "Keep your eye on Herman Melville," a critic wrote in a review of *White-Jacket*. "There is a humor, and sparkle of rhetoric in his writings, which, if he lives to be the man equal in years to Irving, Cooper, and Paulding, will rank as high on the chock-notch of fame as they."[73]

"A WICKED BOOK"

After returning from a trip to London to negotiate with Bentley for the English edition of *White-Jacket*, Melville mulled over his whaling voyage on the *Acushnet*, the one experience he had not yet used in his novels. In May 1850, he wrote to Richard Henry Dana that he was about "half way" into the "whaling voyage" story, which would make "a strange sort of a book ... blubber is blubber you know; tho' you may get oil out of it, the poetry runs as hard as sap from a forest maple tree;—& to cook the thing up, one must needs throw in a little fancy."[74]

The "fancy" came from many sources besides his visceral memories of his time in the whaling industry. His preliminary "Extracts" to the novel indicate his immersion in books about whales and whaling, but there were new chief literary and stylistic influences as well: the Old Testament, Shakespeare's *King Lear* and other plays, Milton's *Paradise Lost* and *Prometheus Bound*, Virgil's *Aeneid*, Laurence Sterne's *Tristram Shandy*, Robert Burton's *The Anatomy of Melancholy*, Pierre Bayle's *Dictionary*, Montaigne's *Essays*, as well as more recent works like William Beckford's *Vathek: An Arabian Tale*, Mary Shelley's *Frankenstein*, Carlyle's *Sartor Resartus* and *Heroes and Hero-Worship*, and De Quincey's *Confessions of an Opium-Eater*. As Melville told Hawthorne as he was completing *Moby-Dick*, "Until I was twenty-five, I had no development at all. From my twenty-fifth year I date my life. Three weeks have scarcely passed, at any time between then and now, that I have not unfolded within myself."[75]

In the same letter, however, Melville expressed a worry that he continued to be "pulled hither and thither by circumstances . . . Dollars damn me," he lamented. "What I feel most moved to write, that is banned,—it will not pay. Yet, altogether, write the *other* way I cannot. So the product is a final hash."[76] To another friend, he issued this warning about the book: "Don't you buy it—don't you read it, when it does come out, because it is by no means the sort of book for you . . . It is not a piece of fine feminine Spitalfields silk . . . but it is of the horrible texture of a fabric that should be woven of ships' cables & hausers [*sic*] . . . Warn all gentle fastidious people from so much as peeping into the book."[77] "I have written a wicked book," he wrote Hawthorne after his friend had read and praised it, "and feel spotless as the lamb."[78]

Moby-Dick's themes have been explored to near exhaustion: the nature of good and evil, the personal and general havoc wrought by hubristic behavior, the failure of good intentions to halt ongoing tragedy, the ambiguity of symbol, the relativism this ambiguity breeds, and many others. Melville's use of Romantic notions of the self-willed personality has been less commented on. Struggling to explain Captain Ahab's obsession with vengeance on what his first mate, Starbuck, calls "a dumb brute . . . that simply smote thee from blindest instinct," Melville created new ways of presenting the complexity of self-knowledge and warned of the dangers of self-absorption that by then were seemingly an inextricable part of American national character.[79]

Because Ishmael narrates the story, his spiritual and psychological growth best indicates Melville's purpose. Much of Ishmael's soul-searching comes from his watching, listening, and trying to fathom Captain Ahab, who, from his first appearance on the quarterdeck, is the novel's magnetic center, drawing all toward him, no matter how fierce their initial resistance. Ishmael, presented from the first page as a seeker, succumbs like the rest to his captain's spell. The hunt for Moby Dick forces Ishmael into experiences of sympathetic identity, not unlike Sheppard Lee's metempsychotic travels. Ishmael enters the lives of many individuals, from a son of South Seas royalty from the island Kokovoko like Queequeg; to a monomaniac Nantucket Quaker of "greatly superior natural force, with a globular brain and a ponderous heart," named after a biblical king whose blood the dogs licked as had been prophesied; to an African American cabin boy frightened out of his wits by the sea's immensity.[80]

For a young man, Ishmael also has a precocious sense of the perils of self-absorption. In the first chapter, drawing on the story of Narcissus, he declares that humanity sees itself "in all rivers and oceans," and what is mirrored there "is the image of the ungraspable phantom of life": this is "the key to it all."[81] Ahab, by contrast, believes that he has seen and touched that phantom and as a result is arrogance and free will personified. Successful in swaying the crew to his purpose, Ahab declares, "What I've dared, I've willed, and what I've willed I'll do!" His hubris knows no bounds. Yes, he has lost his leg according to a prophecy, but he now prophesies that he will "dismember" his "dismemberer." "Now, then, be the prophet and the fulfiller one. That's more than ye, ye great gods, ever were!"[82]

A short while later, as Ishmael ponders the white whale, he begins to comprehend the crazed old man. After his injury, the captain, who had "been in colleges, as well as 'mong the cannibals," has linked the creature not only to "all his bodily woes, but all his intellectual and spiritual exasperations," the "monomaniac incarnation of all those malicious agencies which some deep men feel eating at them."[83] And yet Ishmael understands that knowing this, he has only begun to plumb Ahab's self. "This is much," he concludes, "yet Ahab's larger, darker, deeper part remains unknown."[84] Why, for example, did the crew so readily respond "to the old man's ire"? By what evil magic did he possess their souls, "so that at times his hate seemed almost theirs"?[85] The reason, Ishmael begins to understand, lies in the fact that Ahab's quest is also humanity's, and the young crewman struggles not to be driven mad by it. Ishmael meditates on the safety of land and the danger of the immense, unknowable sea and perceives "a strange analogy" to something in man. "For as the appalling ocean surrounds the verdant land, so in the soul of man there lies one insular Tahiti, full of peace and joy, but encompassed by all the horrors of the half known life . . . Push not off from that isle; thou canst never return!"[86] Ahab, for one, has pushed off to challenge the gods, and he has taken an entire ship's crew with him.

The central question Ahab's behavior poses for Ishmael was the same that occupied many contemporary theologians as well as Melville's new friend Hawthorne: the extent of man's free will. Ishmael's meditation while weaving rattan mats with Queequeg suggests his still-unfinished answer. He describes their work as reminding him of "the Loom of Time" and himself as a shuttle "mechanically weaving and weaving away at the Fates." The fixed threads of the warp, just loose enough to "admit the crosswise interblending of other threads with its own," seemed "necessity," or fate. In his own hand Ishmael held the shuttle, the woof, and wove his destiny "into these unalterable threads." Meanwhile, Queequeg used a wooden "sword" to hit the woof and tighten it; he did this "slantingly, or crookedly, or weakly, as the case might be," and by this difference gave the weave its final shape. Queequeg thus represents "chance." "Aye," Ishmael concludes, "chance, free will, and necessity—no wise incompatible—all interweavingly working together."

> The straight warp of necessity, not to be swerved from its ultimate course—its every alternating vibration, indeed, only tending to that; free will still free to ply her shuttle between the threads; and chance, though restrained in its play within the right lines of necessity, and sideways in its motions modified by free will, though thus prescribed to by both, chance by turn rules either, and has the last featuring blow at events.[87]

Acknowledging divine Providence, granting man free will to make choices within his sphere of action, yet allowing for the fickle goddess Fortuna: this is Ishmael's understanding of man's destiny, a formulation tested by Ahab's insistence on the utter supremacy of free will.

Ahab wants the impossible: to know what Providence intends for him, a knowledge Melville associates with the unfathomable depths of the sea.

When one of the captured sperm whales has been butchered and Ahab sees its head hanging from the hawsers, he addresses it: "Speak, mighty head, and tell us the secret thing that is in thee. Of all divers, thou hast dived the deepest . . . O head! Thou hast seen enough to split the planets and make an infidel of Abraham, and not one syllable is thine!"[88] The "Sphinx" remains silent, and Ahab hastens to his appointed meeting with his fate.

One person on board knows these metaphorical depths, however, and is marked forever. Several times the African American cabin boy, Pip, frightened by being so close to a whale, jumps from the whaleboat. Finally, in the heat of a chase, his mates forget him, and Pip is left behind, a mile from any craft. They eventually retrieve him, but fearing that he is forever lost, Pip has experienced the "intense concentration of self in the middle of such a heartless immensity" and "an awful lonesomeness." After Pip is among the crew again, he prattles on incoherently. They think that he has lost his mind, for "the sea had jeeringly kept his finite body up, but drowned the infinite of his soul." He has been carried down alive, "to wondrous depths, where strange shapes of the unwarped primal world glided to and fro before his passive eyes." Pip has seen "God's foot upon the treadle of the loom, and spake [hailed] it," and therefore his "shipmates called him mad." Pondering the poor boy, Ishmael concludes, "So man's insanity is heaven's sense . . . wandering from all mortal reason, man comes at last to that celestial thought, which, to reason, is absurd and frantic."[89] To learn what Pip now knows is to accept, without wish or will to change, God's plan. But this knowledge demands a radical alienation.

The subsequent chapter provides the alternative to Pip's story and shows that such alienation can be countered through selfless love. Ishmael, Queequeg, and others sit around a tub of ambergris, an aromatic and valuable substance produced in the digestive tracts of whales and used in perfumery, and squeeze the soft globules to release their liquid. This simple labor, akin to crushing grapes to make wine, leads Ishmael to forget the oath that he had sworn to Ahab.

Squeeze! Squeeze! Squeeze! All the morning long; I squeezed that sperm till I myself almost melted into it; I squeezed that sperm till a strange sort of insanity came over me; and I found myself unwittingly squeezing my co-laborers' hands in it, mistaking their hands for the gentle globules. Such an abounding, affectionate, friendly, loving feeling did this avocation beget; that at last I was continually squeezing their hands, and looking up into their eyes sentimentally; as much as to say—Oh! my dear fellow beings, why should we any longer cherish any social acerbities, or know the slightest ill-humor or envy! Come; let us squeeze hands all round; nay, let us all squeeze ourselves into each other; let us squeeze ourselves universally into the very milk and sperm of human kindness.[90]

This scene of subconscious affection, itself the mark of a striking utopian vision, has the power to break Ahab's satanic oath. In the middle of that "heartless immensity," Pip loses human contact; Ishmael's mystical vision of brotherhood is the antidote to Ahab's hubris and self-absorption.

Even Ahab eventually becomes aware of the transformative power of affection, and ironically, this knowledge comes through Pip. When a crew member tries to shoo the boy from some of the sailors' work, Ahab explodes: "Hands off that holiness!" Pip then breaks into one of his nonsensical monologues, and Ahab realizes that he speaks this way as a result of his having seen the secrets of the deep. The captain decides to adopt him, telling Pip that now he will stay with him in his quarters. "Thou touchest my inmost centre, boy," Ahab says; "thou are tied to me by chords woven of my heart-strings." Pip then touches Ahab's hand. "What's this?" Pip asks. "Here's velvet shark-skin . . . Ah, now, had poor Pip but felt so kind a thing as this, perhaps he had ne'er been lost! This seems to me, sir, as a man-rope, something that weak souls may hold by."[91] This powerful, reciprocal relationship soon threatens to negate the hatred Ahab feels for Moby Dick. He tells Pip that when it is time to hunt the white whale, he must remain on the ship. "There is that in thee, poor lad, which I feel too curing to my malady . . . Do thou abide here below," he insists, "where they shall serve thee, as if thou wert the captain."[92]

Affection later surfaces again. One beautiful peaceful morning, Ahab asks Starbuck to stand closer to him. "Let me look into a human eye; it is better than to gaze into sea or sky, better than to gaze upon God . . . This is the magic glass [mirror], man; I see my wife and my child in thine eye." He then tells Starbuck that he, too, must not man a boat for the dangerous whale because he has a family back in Nantucket. Moved, Starbuck begs him to turn the ship and head for port, so that they both can see their wives and children; but Ahab, against all love and reason, refuses.

What is it, what nameless, inscrutable, unearthly thing is it; what cozening, hidden lord and master, and cruel, remorseless emperor commands me; that against all natural lovings and longings, I so keep pushing, and crowding, and jamming myself on all the time; recklessly making me ready to do what in my own proper, natural heart, I durst not so much as dare? Is Ahab, Ahab? Is it I, God, or who, that lifts this arm? . . . how then can this one small heart beat; this one small brain think thoughts; unless God does that beating, does that thinking, does that living, and not I. By heaven, man, we are turned round and round in this world, like yonder windlass, and Fate is the handspike."[93]

It is a crucial turning point. Ahab now understands that he can do nothing to stop himself because as he says after the second day of the chase, "This whole act's immutably decreed. 'T was rehearsed by thee and me a billion years before this ocean rolled. Fool! I am the Fates' lieutenant. I act under orders."[94] Again, as in so many early American novels from *Wieland* on, free will is negated.

Why does Ishmael alone escape to tell the tale? Though he has sworn to Ahab's oath, he embraces sympathy and brotherhood. His close association with Queequeg, a man of a different race yet a member, as Ishmael tells the dubious Captain Peleg, of "the great and everlasting First Congregation of this whole worshipping world," to which all humanity belongs, saves him.[95] As Ishmael comes to know Queequeg, he feels "a melting" in himself. "No more my splintered heart and maddened hand were against the wolfish world," for "this savage had redeemed it."[96]

Later, with Queequeg safely tied to him by a "monkey-rope" as he descends to cut into the whale, Ishmael realizes that his destiny is linked to his friend's, for "usage and honor" demanded that if Queequeg slipped, his belayer must not cut the cord but go down with him. "So strongly and metaphysically" did Ishmael conceive this that he "seemed distinctly to perceive that [his] own individuality was now merged in a joint stock company of two," that his "free will had received a mortal blow." In contrast, when Ahab's ivory leg splinters and he has to ask the ship's carpenter to fashion a new one, he exclaims, "Here I am, proud as a Greek god, and yet standing debtor to this blockhead for a bone to stand on! Cursed be that mortal inter-indebtedness which will not do away with ledgers. I would be free as air, and I'm down in the whole world's books."[97]

Watching the unfolding capaciousness of Ishmael's mind, as in "The Doubloon" chapter when he observes as each of the chief characters looks upon a coin and interprets it differently, the reader understands that Ishmael's salvation lies in sympathetic relativism. When Pip stares at the coin and babbles, "I look, you look, he looks; we look, ye look, they look," he is not reciting, as Stubb thinks, Lindley Murray's popular school *Grammar*.[98] Rather, Pip's newly acquired wisdom has granted him access to truth about truth itself. All "readings" are equally valid, for no one has a monopoly on truth. Allowing Ishmael's survival, Melville rejects the gospel of selfishness that emanates from Ahab to animate the rest of the crew; he rejects the reduction of "transcendent" ego into the mere egotism that is personified in Ahab's delusionary quest.

"HERMAN MELVILLE CRAZY"

In October 1851, a month before its American incarnation, *Moby-Dick* appeared in England as *The Whale*, in three volumes, but unfortunately in botched form. Inexplicably, Richard Bentley issued the work without the "Epilogue" that describes Ishmael's survival. English readers thus read a novel in which everyone perishes, so it was unclear how the story could be known. Despite this gaffe, however, British reviewers generally praised the work. Unfortunately, owing to the time it took for British papers to arrive in the United States, the first reviews Melville read were in American periodicals, and these were discouraging.

The English reviewers lauded Melville's ambition. A critic for London's *John-Bull* said that *The Whale* was "out and out the most extraordinary" of all of Melville's "extraordinary books," as far beyond "the level of an ordinary work of fiction" as one could imagine. He opined that it did not unfold a mere adventure story "but a whole philosophy of life."[99] "There are people who delight in mulligatawny," another reviewer wrote wittily. "They love curry at its warmest point," and "ginger cannot be too hot in the mouth for them." Such people "constitute the admirers of Herman Melville," for in trying to fathom the distance between God and man, he "spices up his narrative with uncommon courage."[100]

Melville's countrymen, however, largely disapproved of the novel. Some disliked its supposed impiety, one reviewer observing that "profanity and indecency" were always "shooting up through all the strata of

[Melville's] writings, and nowhere more so than in *Moby-Dick*."[101] A critic for what should have been the sympathetic *United States Magazine and Democratic Review* complained that Melville was evidently trying to ascertain how far the public's "gullibility and patience" could be imposed upon and encouraged any reader who sought a plenitude of examples of "bad rhetoric, involved syntax, stilted sentiment and incoherent English" to purchase the novel.[102] *The Southern Quarterly Review*'s critic's notice prompted readers to consider that the real link between Pip and Ahab was their mutual insanity. Ahab's "ravings, and the ravings of some of the tributary characters, and the ravings of Mr. Melville himself" were "such as would justify a writ de lunatico [to inquire whether a person is insane] against all the parties."[103]

A few American notices were kinder. After observing that in books like *Typee* and *Omoo* Melville did for the South Seas what Mayo had done for North Africa in *Kaloolah*, William Butler noted that in *Moby-Dick* Melville had "a strange power to reach the sinuosities of a thought" and delineated character in a way that was "actually Shakespearean."[104] The Transcendentalist George Ripley, working for the *Tribune* after the demise of Brook Farm, called the book a "Whaliad" and thought it "the best production which has yet come from [Melville's] seething brain."[105]

Undeterred by this mixed response to *Moby-Dick*, Melville quickly began to labor on another novel. He promised Sophia Hawthorne "a rural bowl of milk," not another of "salt water," for the new work was set in the Berkshires, not at sea or in far-off places. To her husband Melville revealed more about his ambition for the work. "Lord, when shall we be done growing?" he asked Hawthorne. "As long as we have anything more to do, we have done nothing. So, now, let us add Moby Dick to our blessing[s?], and step from that. Leviathan is not the biggest fish;—I have heard of Krakens" (an immense sea creature in Scandinavian folklore).[106]

But if the new book was to treat an even larger "monster" than the white whale, Melville had in mind something more financially economical than *Moby-Dick*, for he negotiated with Harper & Brothers for a volume of only about 360 pages, his shortest since *Omoo*. As he had confided to Sophia, it was not another seafaring novel but more engaged with the sentimental aspects of rural life epitomized in Mitchell's later works from Edgewood. The Harpers, remembering *Mardi*'s failure, were not as enthusiastic about the manuscript and were unwilling to issue a contract on any terms advantageous to Melville, offering royalties of only twenty cents (instead of the usual fifty) on the dollar, after publication costs.

Miffed, Melville shopped the manuscript elsewhere, unsuccessfully, and reluctantly accepted the Harpers' offer. Before he handed in the manuscript, however, Melville added 160 spiteful pages about the central character Pierre's trials as a young author struggling against his publishers, who are unwilling to support unconventional books. This diatribe swelled the book, and when published *Pierre; or, The Ambiguities* was as long as its predecessor. Its reception was even more disastrous.

The book's eponymous "hero," Pierre Glendinning, is an aristocratic young man raised by his widowed mother on the family's hereditary lands, Saddle Meadows, in western Massachusetts. At fifty, Mrs. Glendinning is still attractive. Haughty yet respected, the neighborhood's patroness is revered in part because of Pierre's grandfather, a Revolutionary War officer and hero. She dotes on her only child, and he happily returns her affection; the two affectionately call each other brother and sister. Pierre is engaged to a blond-haired, blue-eyed beauty, Lucy Tartan, a betrothal Mrs. Glendinning welcomes because of Lucy's docility as well as her family's good standing.

Storms begin to darken this idyll when at a local sewing society meeting, Pierre encounters a mysterious, attractive workingwoman—dark-haired and dark-eyed, Lucy's physical opposite—who faints when he is announced to the gathering. Soon after, she contacts him surreptitiously for a meeting. Fascinated by her unorthodox yet magnetic beauty, he consents, only to hear her identify herself as Isabel Banford, supposedly his unknown half sister. She believes herself the child of his youthful father's indiscretion with an attractive French émigrée who fled to the United States after the French Revolution. Isabel explains that working as a dairymaid on a neighboring farm, she accidentally learned of her patrimony, for which though she has no actual proof, there is compelling circumstantial evidence.

The effect of this revelation, conveyed in two interviews at her tiny house on the outskirts of town, shatters Pierre's comfortable world. It destroys his memory of his father as model husband, gentleman, and Christian, for in addition to having withheld knowledge of Isabel from his wife, he left his daughter essentially an orphan, deprived of familial love and protection. His father's actions place a great moral burden on

Pierre, whom Christian duty compels to acknowledge his sibling and assist her, even at the risk that by so doing he will crush his mother and destroy both the family name and his engagement to Lucy.

But Pierre, taken with Isabel's story and smitten by her beauty, is willing to risk all. He decides to announce to all concerned that the two have been secretly married, so shocking a ruse that Mrs. Glendinning puts him out of the house. Eventually, from her grief and anger, she goes insane (Melville hints that there is a hereditary disposition to insanity on both sides of Pierre's family) and dies. The first half of the narrative, driven by a Byronic hero's rash impulses, ends with Isabel, Pierre, and their maid, Delly Ulver (ostracized from the community because she is pregnant out of wedlock), leaving the countryside for crowded, anonymous New York City.

They find lodging in a crowded boardinghouse, the Church of the Apostles, filled with all sorts of artists, philosophers, and other impoverished souls. After his small amount of money is exhausted, Pierre attempts to resume his career (hitherto not mentioned, for this is the section Melville added to the original manuscript) as a popular author to pay for rent and food. In a bizarre twist, lovelorn Lucy writes that she wishes to come to serve Isabel and him; she is willing to give art lessons to add to their income, as long as she can be near him. This plan, which Pierre perversely welcomes, provokes Isabel's jealousy, even as her feelings for Pierre are supposedly only sisterly, and moral confusion in Delly, who knows (as Isabel does not) of Pierre's previous engagement to Lucy.

In their garret, as Pierre struggles to write a book based on his experiences, the quartet's situation becomes dire. After his cousin Glen Stanly, who pressed his suit on Lucy after Pierre's departure and who has inherited the Glendinning lands, tries to retrieve her, Pierre shoots and kills him. The story ends in the Tombs, New York's notorious prison, where Lucy and Isabel visit Pierre, incarcerated for murder. Learning that Isabel is his sister and believing that they are indeed "married," Lucy drops dead. Pierre and then Isabel commit suicide by poisoning themselves, ending this strange, twisted, family romance in which Melville mixed elements of the gothic as well as an extended parody of sentimental tropes.

HERMAN MELVILLE CRAZY, read the headline in the New York *Day Book*, its reviewer writing that the book appeared "to be composed of the ravings and reveries of a madman."[107] "The annals of Bedlam," another wrote, "might be defied to produce such another collection of lunatics as the hero, his mother, his sister, and the heroine."[108] William Gilmore Simms, in *The Southern Literary Messenger*, opined that Melville had succumbed to the predictable fate of many authors whose first books were unmitigated successes and so had "written themselves out."[109]

Others criticized the novel on stylistic grounds, particularly its extravagant language and diction, one calling Melville a "copyist of Carlyle" but without his "redeeming qualities," another compiling a list of Melville's neologisms and complaining about how often he added "est" or "ness" to words that already carried the intended significance.[110] A critic for *Godey's Lady's Book* parodied Melville's stylistic infelicities. He had sympathetically listened to the novel's "insignificant significances of that deftly-stealing and wonderfully-serpentining melodiousness" but found only "an infinite, unbounded, inexpressible mysteriousness of nothingness."[111]

A small number of reviewers saw Melville's intentions more clearly. "The style is a strange one," a writer for the *Hartford Courant* observed, "not at all natural and too much in the mystic transcendental vein of affection that characterizes some of our best writers." Such writing, however, "belong[s] to the new era of progress, and so we must submit to it."[112] Another sympathetic reviewer also linked the novel to Emerson and his cohort and said that "with all its transcendentalism, there is much earnest and original thought in this book."[113] Even the man-about-town and erstwhile editor Nathaniel Parker Willis saw the book's value. *Pierre*, he noted, "is psychologically suggestive. It is subtle," he continued, "metaphysical, often profound, and has passages of bewildering intensity."[114]

Duyckinck's take was incisive, even though he intended his criticism negatively. The central character, he wrote in the *Literary World*, is "a psychological curiosity, a moral and intellectual phenomenon . . . The most immoral moral of the story, if it has any moral at all, seems to be the impracticability of virtue," and this "leering demoniacal spectre" peers at the reader through "the dim obscure of this dark book, and mock[s] us with this dismal falsehood." If the book had any meaning at all, he ventured, it was "that virtue and religion are only for gods and not to be attempted by man."[115]

This is one of the keys to Melville's career after *Moby-Dick*. In that novel there are redemptive figures, including Ishmael, who survives and so is entrusted to tell the tale. But in subsequent works, Melville derided the shallow pieties of his countrymen—their optimistic philosophies, their faith in the marketplace, their political liberalism, a theology of a God of love rather than of redemption—and his vision darkened. Nowhere was this vision more apparent than in *The Confidence Man*.

"MORE REALITY, THAN REAL LIFE ITSELF CAN SHOW"

Following the disaster of *Pierre*, Melville wrote a short novel, *Israel Potter* (1855), based on the adventures of a Revolutionary War veteran who had fought at the battle of Bunker Hill. The book did not carry the philosophical weight of his two previous novels and, though respectfully reviewed, did nothing to boost his income or reputation. Melville's subsequent work appeared primarily in *Putnam's Monthly Magazine*, and in 1856 he collected some of these tales, including the well-known "Bartleby the Scrivener" and "Benito Cereno," in *The Piazza Tales*. By that time his relations with Putnam were so vexed that another firm, Dix, Edwards, & Company, issued the volume.

Melville's penultimate lengthy fiction and the last published during his lifetime was *The Confidence Man: His Masquerade* (1857). Set on a steamboat ironically named the *Fidèle* (Faith), on the Father of Waters, the Mississippi River, on April Fool's Day, the novel tells the story of a confidence man who gulls virtually every person he marks, asking each to place faith in him by giving him money or providing a service. This trickster impersonates a wide range of well-known figures, and the astute reader recognizes incarnations of Jesus, P. T. Barnum, Emerson, Thoreau, and Theodore Parker, as well as archetypal American confidence men: an herb doctor selling "Samaritan Pain Dissuader," a philanthropist, a stock-jobber for the Black Rapids Coal Company, an agent for a Seminole widow and orphan asylum, another for the "Philosophical Intelligence Office," and so on. The satire is extensive and the intent clear. The United States has become a country where the almighty dollar reigns. "Confidence is the indisputable basis of all sorts of business transactions," the trickster declares, for "without it, commerce between man and man, as between country and country, would, like a watch, run down and stop."[116]

The "cosmopolitan," the confidence man's last incarnation, flourishes in this environment, for he is "a catholic man; who, being such, ties himself to no narrow tailor or teacher. But federates, in his heart as in his costume, something of the various gallantries of men under various suns." He understands that "life is a pic-nic *en costume*" in which "one must take a part, assume a character, stand ready in a sensible way to play the fool."[117]

The Confidence Man is a mature novelist's commentary on the form itself. Regarding a reader's search for and value of consistency in characters, the narrator asks, "[I]s it not a fact that, in real life, a consistent character is a *rara avis*?" That a reader dislikes truly realistic characters "from perplexity as to understanding them?"[118] Yet the greatest writers "challenge astonishment at the tangled web of some character" and "then raise admiration still greater at the satisfactory unraveling of it," something at which "psychological novelists" are particularly adept.[119] Thus, in "books of fiction," a serious reader "look[s] not only for more entertainment, but, at bottom, even for more reality, than real life itself can show." Melville writes, "It is with fiction as with religion: it should present another world, and yet one to which we feel the tie."[120] Nowhere is this more striking than when one passenger calls another "a true original," for where does a novelist find the inspiration for such a creation? "For the most part, in town, to be sure," he replies, for "in nearly all original characters, loosely accounted as such in works of invention, there is discernible something prevailingly local, or of the age." Depicted convincingly, such a character functions "like a revolving Drummond light, raying away from itself all around it—everything is lit by it, everything starts up to it."[121] The cosmopolitan is that light.

Melville's central character evinces disdain at the country's unbounded optimism, its citizens' willingness—indeed, predilection—always to view things in the best light, a lack of a tragic sense which made it as so different from Europe. The confidence man tells one of his targets that "whatever our lot, we should read serene and cheery books, fitted to inspire love and trust."[122] Melville's United States, rushing headlong toward the tragedy of civil war, was populated, quite simply, by rubes. "You fools!" cries one of the only men who refuses to be taken in by the titular main character. "You flock of fools, under this captain of fools, in this ship of fools!"[123]

Fittingly, Melville ends this dark novel with the cosmopolitan offering an old man a stool that holds a half-filled chamber pot and extinguishing the light over him as he strains to read his Bible. In that book, the trickster reminds him, if he searches hard, he will find the words "Jehovah shall be thy confidence." But that seems of little consolation on board this riverboat in the heart of the country. The light going out, the only thing that one can be sure of is: "Something further may follow of this Masquerade."[124] Samuel Bowles, editor of the local *Springfield Republi-*

can, pithily and correctly observed that *The Confidence Man* seemed "like the work of one not in love or sympathy with his kind."[125]

Melville was one of those young men—he was only thirty-eight when he published *The Confidence Man*—whom Emerson described as having knives in their brains, a tendency to introspection. What the Concord sage did not say or perhaps understand was that this cohort had sharpened their tools on the very philosophical idealism that he himself best represented. But Melville's interest in dissecting human character, as much as it received an initial impetus from his discovery of Hawthorne's "power of blackness," also owed much to his realization that subscribing to Transcendentalist egotism required abandoning the principles of good citizenship and the commonwealth upon which the nation had been founded.

The new feeling in the culture that the ego should be given free rein became openly visible in popular writers like Mitchell and was broached by Hawthorne, when he did not succumb to his allegorical tendencies. But in the early 1850s it was in Melville's *Moby-Dick* and *Pierre* that the dark side of free will was most clearly delineated. Ironically, it was left to a cadre of women novelists still partially wedded to the culture of sentiment that Melville had so viciously parodied in *Pierre* to further his exploration of self-consciousness and motivation. They would continue to sound the alarm, as he had done in *The Confidence Man*, about the nation's descent into self-indulgence.

PART III } Toward the 1870s

7 } A *Neglected* Tradition

Women novelists who took up the Romantic notion of genius to which Hawthorne, Melville, Emerson, and other men subscribed were responsible for the final important development in the early American novel. Just a few short years after Warner, Cummins, and Fanny Fern, they created their own distinct vision of authorship. They were aided by a second great expansion of the national literary culture, again, as in the 1840s, based in and abetted by the appearance of new and influential cultural journals that welcomed writers of both sexes and writing in a variety of genres, not just the sentimental.

In the 1850s, for the first time, authors chose whether to publish in middlebrow journals that catered to an increasingly national readership or in those that primarily served a sophisticated urban audience. The first type was exemplified by *Harper's New Monthly Magazine*, which Harper & Brothers founded in 1850, in large measure to tout its own publications. Owing to its emphasis on illustrations, its frequent reprinting of British writers, and its focus on travelogues and adventure narratives, within a decade the magazine boasted a remarkable circulation of more than two hundred thousand.

Another New York publisher's periodical, *Putnam's Monthly Magazine*, sought to reach a more sophisticated readership, but it foundered in the deep recession of 1857. Yet another periodical started that same year, albeit in another city, was established along the same lines. With support from the Boston-centered authors Ralph Waldo Emerson, James Russell Lowell, and Oliver Wendell Holmes, and from the literary critic Edward Percy Whipple, and with the clerk of the state senate and self-educated literary enthusiast

Francis H. Underwood leading the way, in 1856 John J. Jewett and Company, publishers of *Uncle Tom's Cabin*, backed the new venture. A year later, however, the firm went bankrupt. Underwood, who had taken a job as a reader for Phillips, Sampson, & Company, then successfully convinced that firm to publish the proposed journal; the first issue of *The Atlantic Monthly* appeared in November 1857. Lowell edited it until 1861 and was succeeded by James T. Fields, whose firm Ticknor and Fields had purchased the journal in 1859, when Phillips, Sampson no longer could support it.[1]

The Atlantic Monthly committed itself to publishing the best American literature as well as essays on the other arts and on politics and, despite its bias toward New England writers, lived up to this expansive vision. Moreover, although Lowell never aimed to match *Harper's New Monthly Magazine*'s circulation, within a decade the new magazine reached a respectable thirty thousand subscribers and, as the founders had wished, had subscribers throughout the country. Lowell tried to recruit writers from all over, inviting contributions (without success) from the New Yorkers Herman Melville and George William Curtis; publishing their friend Richard Henry Stoddard; and signing the former Fourierist Parke Godwin to a regular column on politics, a particularly important position in the late 1850s.

Lowell also encouraged women writers, who contributed half the content of the first issue. In *The Atlantic Monthly*'s early years he and his successor were astute enough to publish Harriet Beecher Stowe, still immensely popular, as well as an emergent group, typified by Rose Terry Cooke and Harriet Prescott Spofford, who took New England as their subject. *The Atlantic Monthly* truly was open to whatever came over the transom. Lowell, for example, published the New York writer Elizabeth Stoddard's first story, in 1860, and Ticknor had the foresight to publish a young unknown West Virginian, Rebecca Harding Davis, whose remarkable "Life in the Iron Mills" appeared in 1861. At the start of the Civil War, the ambitious woman writer who sought literary fame as well as fortune thus had an important new outlet for serious literature. Within a few years she even had choices, with New York's *The Nation* (1865) and *The Galaxy* (1866) joining *The Atlantic Monthly* as organs of high culture. By the 1870s the group of regular women contributors to *The Atlantic Monthly* included, in addition to Stowe, Spofford, and Cooke, Celia Thaxter, Louisa May Alcott, Gail Hamilton, Elizabeth Stuart Phelps, and Lucy Larcom.

The fight for the extension of women's rights, a cause often invoked alongside abolition, influenced many of these women. Their models were European: Madame de Staël, Elizabeth Barrett Browning, Emily Brontë, George Eliot, and George Sand, who each wrestled with the assumption that artistic genius was a masculine trait and with the skepticism ambitious women met. Striving to be artists, these transatlantic sisters were regarded as unfeminine, egotistic, or even licentious for claiming the same creative powers as men. As a consequence, their fiction did not so much resemble that of Warner, Cummins, or E.D.E.N. Southworth, with their strong emphasis on Christian forbearance and self-control, but instead portrayed women caught in and continually frustrated by their status as second-class citizens and yearning to exercise the free will that defined their husbands' and brothers' lives.

Further, though these authors often criticized religion, they just as frequently simply had no use for it to begin with, particularly in its organized form. They often presented more secular visions, the biggest change from their sentimental predecessors. But philosophical issues and untraditional, liberal religion, from German idealism to Unitarianism and Transcendentalism—particularly Emerson's emphasis on the interior life—continued to fertilize their literary imaginations. Ultimately, the quality that distinguishes them most from their predecessors and that sent the American novel in new directions was their radical skepticism of all creeds and assumptions—religious, social, and political—in American life.

For all their willingness to think untraditionally, however, because they moved in overwhelmingly male coteries, many of these women still sought approval from their male peers. As a "member of the literary race," Stoddard wrote in an essay in 1871, "*Recognition* is the thing." She labored, she continued, for "praise" as well as "for money," and she did not mean the praise of the general public but of those who knew good literature.[2] The tepid reception of most of her and her cohort's novels, particularly in comparison to the glowing accolades bestowed upon women who continued to mine the sentimental vein, recalls the cause of the dismal second half of Melville's career: a stubborn belief in art over commerce.

ISHMAEL'S MOTHER

Though she did not regard herself as such, Alice Cary was a member of this vanguard of woman's genius. Nothing in her background indicated that by the time she was in her thirties she would be one of the country's best-known writers. Cary was born in 1820 on a farm eight miles north of Cincinnati; her father was one of the city's pioneer settlers. The family was large, and because of her household responsibilities, she had little time for formal education, even at the nearby district schoolhouse. "We hungered and thirsted for knowledge," she said of herself and her siblings, "but there were not a dozen books on our daily shelf, not a library within our reach." Those books included the Bible and a few other religious titles, for the family regularly attended services, most commonly of the Universalists, which marked them as religious liberals and social progressives. Another book on that shelf was Rowson's *Charlotte Temple*, still at the height of its popularity.[3]

The Carys lost two of their children when Alice was still young, and her mother died when she was in her teens. Her father remarried, but neither she nor her sister Phoebe, four years younger, grew close to him; to deal with their loss, both began to write poetry that unsurprisingly brimmed with sadness and mourning. Cary placed her first verse in local newspapers and Universalist periodicals. Encouraged by seeing her work in print, she solicited national periodicals. Soon she had the thrill and pleasure of seeing her poems appearing in Boston's *The Ladies' Repository*, *Graham's Magazine* of Philadelphia, and, after 1847, *The National Era* of Washington, D.C., which also published her fiction. The critic and anthologist Rufus Griswold included both Cary sisters in his pioneering collection *The Female Poets of America* (1848), assuring their prominence. Soon papers and periodicals throughout the United States began reprinting Alice's work.

In 1849, the *New-York Tribune* editor Horace Greeley stopped at the sisters' home during a trip through the West. His talk of publishing opportunities in the East may have contributed to Alice's decision the following year to move to New York. Personal disappointment may have been a factor as well: the well-to-do parents of a man whom she loved, and who she thought loved her equally, convinced him not to wed so rustic and poor a woman. Heartbroken, Alice was never to marry. In 1851, Phoebe and another, younger sister, Elmina, joined Alice in her New York boardinghouse quarters. As Greeley recalled, "They hired two or three modest rooms, in an unfashionable neighborhood, and set to work resolutely to earn a living by the pen." Within a few years, though, supporting herself through her writing and living frugally, Cary was able to purchase a house on Twentieth Street that soon became the meeting place of the city's premier literary salons. Every Sunday for almost two decades such luminaries as Greeley, George Ripley, Fanny Fern's publisher, Robert Bonner, the writers Richard and Elizabeth Stoddard, William Lloyd Garrison, Robert Dale Owen, Elizabeth Cady Stanton, and even P. T. Barnum could be found at the Carys' home. After one of these soirées, one "merely fashionable woman," the Carys' biographer recounted, exclaimed, "What queer people you do see at the Carys'! It is as good as a show!"[4]

Although the Cary sisters thought of themselves as poets first, Alice also began to try her hand at prose. In 1852 *Clovernook; or, Recollections of Our Neighborhood in the West*, a realistic portrayal of the joys and hardships of her country upbringing, met with success in the United States and England. She soon wrote two sequels, one for children. Her novel *Hagar: A Story of To-Day* was published in 1852 and was followed four years later by another lengthy fiction, *Married, Not Mated; or, How They Lived at Woodside and Throckmorton Hall*. By decade's end Cary was regularly publishing both poetry and stories in *The Atlantic Monthly*, *Harper's New Monthly Magazine*, the *New York Ledger*, and elsewhere, despite the fact that by the 1870s her always frail health had tolled to Phoebe's essentially becoming her caretaker.

Alice Cary's biographer Mary Clemmer wrote that Cary was deeply touched by "the record of past suffering" and "the shadow of many vanished dreams." Describing what could have been a character in one of Cummins's sentimental novels, Clemmer also noted that Cary had "conquered her own spirit" and, "alone and unassisted, through the mastery of her own will, has wrought out from the harshest and most adverse conditions, a pure, sweet, and noble life."[5] But Cary did not let the struggles—primarily against the inferior status and ill-treatment of women—that so affected her go unremarked. Her fiction gained its power in proportion to what she believed she had missed in her own life.

Her interest in the "woman question" led to her friendships with Stanton, Owen, and, later, Susan B. Anthony and became the subject of *Hagar*, her first novel. But upon its publication *Hagar* went unnoticed, and it remains misunderstood. Her biographer thought that this was because when the author tried to portray "the faults and passions of men and women," it proved unsuccessful, her "rudest work."[6] *The Una*, a women's rights journal that should have been sympathetic, claimed that *Hagar* had "no purpose but to give utterance to sickly, morbid fantasies."[7] Even twentieth-century feminist critics committed to recovering women's writing have had trouble praising her work. Judith Fetterley, in a reprint of *Clovernook*, claims that Cary's longer fictions "suffer from incoherence in both plot and character," and Nina Baym dismisses Cary's novels as "so badly written as to read like parody."[8]

But *Hagar* deserves better. First serialized in the *Cincinnati Dollar Weekly Commercial*, the novel is a dark, suggestive tale of adultery rooted in its author's experience with the losses and disappointments women suffered. The book is indebted to *The Scarlet Letter*, for the central character, the teenage Elsie, becomes pregnant by Nathaniel Warburton, a handsome young minister from New York City. She is in love with him, won over by "his handsome person, intellectual endowments, and persuasive eloquence." But he does not reciprocate this depth of feeling. After promising to see her as often as he can, Warburton leaves for the city, never to return, worried about what his parishioners and others would say if he married such a poor, uneducated girl.[9] It is not difficult to read Cary's own disappointment in love in this situation, but there is one major difference: Warburton leaves Elsie carrying his child.

Joseph Arnold and his friend Frederick Wurth, "a harmless slip of the moneyed aristocracy," whose wife, Catharine, dies after a grievous illness, leaving him with their young child, constitute another strand of the plot.[10] Arnold is from a poor family on the prairie but has left home and considers himself a "metropolitan," cocksure, cynical, and always ready for the next adventure.[11] After Catharine's death, he convinces Wurth to travel with him to the outskirts of Cincinnati to visit his family. There Wurth becomes enamored of Arnold's sister Eunice, who is obsessed with "civilizing" Native Americans and whom, despite her lower social status, he rather thoughtlessly marries. The new Mrs. Wurth turns out to be a termagant, lacking the grace of his first wife. She puts on upper-class airs, and treats her stepdaughter, Catharine (named for her mother), poorly. Soon enough Eunice has a child. For a nanny she eventually hires a twenty-year-old named Hagar, a woman fallen on hard times who carries a dark box under her arm.

In the meantime, Arnold glimpses Warburton in a tavern after his final visit to Elsie and finds him suspicious, "his sweet, low tone, and gliding step" appearing to Arnold not those of "an honest man."[12] Intrigued, he decides to track the clergyman to his city quarters but, after speaking with him, is taken with Warburton's religious views, so much so that after a short while he decides to enter the ministry. Fifteen years later, on a visit to the Wurths, he hears of and then meets Hagar, who has become something of an angel of mercy to the community. She lives (like Hester Prynne) by the graveyard on the outskirts of town, where she has buried a small coffin. Though she is shy and avoids intimacy, he persists in his advances. Eventually, he proposes, and after much imploring, she consents, to his and the town's great joy. The morning of the wedding, however, Hagar has disappeared, her cottage empty save for a lengthy missive left for Arnold.

In the letter, she explains her sadness and isolation, for the reader learns that, in a trope that speaks of the still-deep sentimental roots of fiction in this period, Hagar is none other than Elsie. She describes her simple rural upbringing; the accidental death of her father and the hardship it brought upon the family; her subsequent seven years' service to her uncle, during which time she rarely saw her mother; and, finally, her mother's good fortune in receiving a small inheritance, enabling her to buy a cottage about fifty miles from New York. There Elsie met the Reverend Nathaniel Warburton. Seeing her daughter's infatuation with the young man, Elsie's mother urges her to throw away her "idle fancies" and think instead about marrying John Dale, a local farm boy. Forbidden to see Warburton, Elsie meets him clandestinely in the forest, where, presumably, she becomes pregnant. Concerned for his career, Warburton soon abandons her.[13] Desperate to see her lover, Elsie fabricates a reason for leaving home for a short while and follows him to the city.

When finally ushered into his presence, she expects a joyous reunion. Instead, he is embarrassed, barely acknowledges her, and wonders what his friends will say about this "rustic girl" who has come looking for him. He fears "some dark and premature ending to his own career."[14] "What an ordeal awaited me!" Elsie writes. "Shame, confusion, self-reproach, utter despair, and, over all, the cold cruelty, the calm decision, the unconcealed anger and probable abandonment of him for whom I had bartered every hope."[15] Warburton tells her that an immediate marriage is impossible and installs her on the fourth floor of a boardinghouse in one of the worst parts of the city, where he occasionally visits her.

Elsie finds these quarters a "wretched prison" and spends hours tracing her own name on "a dark panel at the head and the foot of the bed" and writing "records of sin and suffering, fearful death-beds, and terrible judgments."[16] She dreams of going abroad with Warburton as his wife; but he keeps avoiding the question, urging her to forget herself in her work, trying to mollify her with talk of her "bright destiny" as an artist. A fellow boarder, a young grocer, John, befriends her; but fearing that she will reveal her secret to this new acquaintance, Warburton forbids her seeing him. Shortly after the birth of their baby, a boy, Warburton has a change of heart and tells her that he will indeed marry her. But he discovers a note that she has written John to thank him for a present for the baby and, angered that she has disobeyed him, snatches the child and leaves Elsie for good.

Years later, when Hagar is still with the Wurth family and Catharine Wurth is grown, Warburton, who has left the ministry and now is a well-known author, meets Catharine in society and marries her, even though he is twice her age. Hagar, who does not acknowledge him, assists in her ward's bridal preparations and later becomes a maid in the newlyweds' home. Warburton does not recognize her, though her voice and laugh inexplicably disturb him. She overhears him tell his new wife that his study is sacred to him and that she must never open a large, locked drawer about which she has asked and that made him turn pale and stammer about some "old letters" inside. Convinced that the drawer holds secrets to his and Hagar's affair, one day when the couple is out, Hagar finds a key and opens the drawer.

The reviewer for *The Una* said that Cary must have descended "into one of Dante's hells to get her inspiration for her last chapter of horrors."[17] Hagar does find letters, but that's not all. There also is a portrait of herself, and more horrifically, "in a case of black and polished wood," a coffin, "decayed, as if it had been buried many years." She removes the lid to see "a skeleton," which she "instinctively" recognizes as her child's. At this moment, Warburton enters the room and realizes who she is. In an agitated state, he tells her that he has always loved her and urges her to "fly" with him, far from New York, and "in each other's embrace defy what we cannot evade."

After briefly lapsing into her old infatuation, Hagar comes to her senses. "Murderer!" she screams at him as she snatches the coffin and flees. Two days later, as she passes a mental institution, she sees approaching a wagon, barred like a cage. "Looking intently as it passed," inside she "saw a white face pressed against the bars, and eyes glaring like fire—it was Mr. Warburton, on his way to the mad-house!"[18] Finishing the letter, now Joseph understands why she has taken her new name and why she has turned "from the fountain, and the white of innocence, to wander thirsty and alone in the desert" (an echo of Isaiah 55:1).[19]

With this sad tale, indebted not only to Hawthorne but to Rowson's *Charlotte Temple*, whose main character was similarly deserted and left to her fate, Cary posed questions about a woman's still-subordinate place in the new nation. And unlike *The Scarlet Letter*, which is set in the distant past, *Hagar* is a story of "to-day," in a world in which Warburton's duplicity and selfishness are commonplace and go punished. *Hagar* also is a story about the futility of faith. Nathaniel asks Elsie to believe that he will return to her as promised, but she misplaces her confidence. Warburton betrays her because his outward success is more important than sincerity, a particularly ironic sentiment in a man of the cloth.

Cary knew that her story had no easy moral. There is no redemption, spiritual or otherwise, as there is in *The Scarlet Letter* when Dimmesdale finally reveals his guilt to the assembled crowd at the novel's end. Nor is there a sparkling little Pearl to bring happiness to a mother's broken heart; Elsie's unnamed child is dead and carried around by its father as a totem of his suffering. Admittedly, as his talk with Arnold indicated, after getting Elsie pregnant, Warburton genuinely struggled with whether to remain in the ministry. Thus, when in their discussions Arnold asks him to speak to Christ's goodness in the face of persecution, and Warburton replies, "But when, overcome by temptation, we seal our doom, what motive have we to do good any more," Arnold thinks that he spoke "as one might who felt himself lost."[20]

Similarly, when Hagar reads to a young Catharine from a book that Warburton has written, she feels as though he has spoken directly to her. He writes,

> We may put on a fair outside, and assume the gloss of truth, til we make ourselves never so fair; we may cry out Peace when peace is broken, and Courage when our bosoms shake with fear; with a lie we may deceive the world, winning hearts to us all along the journey of life; but we cannot deceive ourselves. And, after all, perhaps the bitterest of our punishment is, that the world thinks better of us than we are.[21]

"What am I?" he continues. "[W]hat have I been? And what shall I be?"[22] Yet Warburton prolongs this self-torture because he cannot subdue his ego. The lure of public approval is too strong. Praying for strength to get through his troubles, he realizes that he has only been "goaded by con-science to recite a formula."[23]

Elsie's fate is likewise problematic. Her love for Warburton is deep and only shattered when she realizes, virtually simultaneously, that he always has loved her and that their child is dead. Yet Elsie is not a martyr as Hester Prynne is. She has neither pride nor a sense of possible redemp-tion. Arnold genuinely offers what she sought with her first lover, but Hagar cannot accept it because of her self-imposed atonement. "I am alone," she tells him, true to her new name, "an outcast from the world, seeking, in continual prayer and penitence, to atone for my sin."[24]

Among the previous generation of women writers, submission and ac-ceptance of one's place constituted the highest calling, but Cary under-stood that the result of pious resignation could just as easily be tragedy rather than grace. She inhabited a Christian world riddled with doubt and disgrace rather than certainty and peace. In her depiction of War-burton's inner conflict, she empathetically touched on the growing tension in American life between religious piety and self-serving individual-ism, one that could lead to stories like Hagar's. In her address in 1868 to the assembled members of Sorosis, a new women's club of which she was the first president, she declared that women were still "weighed down with shame and humiliation, and impelled, while we are about it, to make full confession of all our wild and guilty fantasies."[25] *Hagar* was Cary's full confession, a testament that she knew of what she spoke.

THE BELLE OF NEW HAVEN

Though Cary depicted passion, like the majority of her contemporaries, she was averse to, if not incapable of, writing about sex even in the guarded (though suggestive) way that Melville did in *Pierre*. But not so Lillie Dev-ereux Umsted Blake, another novelist who emerged in the late 1850s and later in life found a place in the women's rights movement. Her first two novels, *Southwold: A Novel* (1859) and *Rockford; or, Sunshine and Storm* (1863), brought forward such hitherto repressed topics as women's sexual-ity and yearning for psychological as well as economic equality.

From an early age Blake knew firsthand about love and loss.[26] She was born in 1833 in Raleigh, North Carolina, but her roots were in coastal Connecticut. Her father, George Pollock Devereux, was the son of a southern plantation owner who sent his boys to Yale; he met Lillie's mother, Sarah Elizabeth Johnson, a great-granddaughter of Jonathan

Edwards's, in New Haven. Devereux also studied law at Tapping Reeve's famous school in Litchfield and was admitted to the bar in 1818. Nine years later, following a five-year tour of Europe, Devereux married Johnson. As a wedding present his father gave them a plantation, Runeroi, on the Roanoke River in his home state. The family made annual visits to Connecticut, and on one of these journeys in 1837, in Suffolk, Virginia, Devereux died from a stomach hemorrhage. His widow, pregnant with another child, hastened back to New England, as her dying husband had urged, and settled near her family in New Haven.

After a suitable period of mourning, Blake's mother, who had received a considerable inheritance and did not need to remarry, became the town's best-known hostess. She raised her daughters in a cultured home, Maple Cottage, that was near campus and as a result constantly filled with highly educated and often well-known visitors. The elegant residence was large enough for Mrs. Devereux to hold frequent parties as well as summer and winter balls, attended by Yale professors, their guests, and Yale students who brought letters of introduction to their hostess. (She was a woman of high social principle; she refused to entertain an English author, Charles Dickens, on his American tour because he did not provide such a letter.) Blake attended a young ladies' academy in New Haven and, from the age of fifteen, with a divinity student as her tutor, studied what amounted to the Yale curriculum. She was reputedly the most sought-after young woman in the town, never lacking for attention from hopeful admirers.

One suitor caused her some embarrassment. In the winter of 1853–1854, William Barnes proposed to her. Still in her teens, she rejected his suit and then left to see relatives in the South. Upon her return, she found that the embittered Yale senior had twisted the story to save face. When another student reportedly told Barnes that he was going to propose to Blake, Barnes warned him off by claiming that when he learned of her frequent "intimacies" with a number of their classmates, *he* had ended his engagement with her, also saying that she had seduced him with her "artful temptations" so that marriage was the only way "to wipe away the stain." The new suitor went to the Devereux family with this story, and Barnes was hauled before the college's disciplinary committee for defaming Blake's name. He stuck to his story, hoping that the family would back off from worry that his version of the events would spread even further. But the faculty committee examined Barnes, found him guilty of impugning the prominent young woman (Blake's cousin was the college president, Theodore Dwight Woolsey), and expelled him, in the last term of his senior year. Still, rumors of Blake's "looseness" spread—indeed, persisted until the twenty-first century—even though she was guilty of nothing but flirtation with eligible young men. She learned a harsh lesson about how even callow men could control a woman's reputation.

A few months later, during one of her trips to the South, Blake met Frank Umsted, a Philadelphia attorney. After a short courtship—he came to New Haven twice—they married in the summer of 1855. Strangely, and despite their rush into marriage, Blake did not love Umsted. Later in life, she wrote cryptically that to her the marriage was "the result rather of circumstances than of that strong and passionate love which alone should unite two beings." Because of Umsted's devotion, however, she eventually developed sincere affection for him.[27] Following a wedding trip through the West, the young couple settled in St. Louis, where they lived off the sizable inheritance she had received from her paternal grandmother. Two years later, with a baby daughter in tow, they moved to New York City, where Umsted hoped to establish a practice. Blake, pregnant again but somehow managing to find time to write, published stories in *Harper's New Monthly Magazine* and *The Knickerbocker*. Late in the summer of 1858, three weeks after the birth of her second daughter, she began to write a novel.

The couple needed the income from its publication, for Umsted had mismanaged her sizable inheritance and lost most of it in the Panic of 1857, forcing them to move from an elegant home on Lexington Avenue to hotels and a boardinghouse. Early in 1859 Harper & Brothers accepted the completed manuscript of *Southwold: A Novel*, but because it said that it could not publish the book for several more months, Umsted shopped it to other firms, then settled on Rudd & Carleton, which issued it in February. The novel was widely noticed and reprinted twice within a month. Its publication and generally positive reception lifted the couple's mood.

But there was more difficulty ahead. Early in the morning on May 10, Blake heard a muffled noise, ran from the bed where her husband had just left her with a kiss, and found him slumped in an armchair, a bullet in his head. The coroner's report was inconclusive, and Blake always maintained that her husband's death had been accidental. It seems likely, however, that despairing of their financial condition and embarrassed by his role in ruining their prospects, he had killed himself. He left Blake and their two small children almost penniless, save for her royalties.

Blake returned to her mother in New Haven. Admirers once again came to Maple Cottage, but Blake surprised her mother by rejecting several marriage offers and deciding instead to try to make her own living as a writer. Her experience with marriage and motherhood, albeit brief, had convinced her that a woman should be allowed to find meaningful work so as not to be "reduced to the degrading necessity of marrying for a support—that is, selling herself because she sees with despair that, as society is presently constituted, and from the defects of her education, there is no hope of earning an honest livelihood."[28] Before long, she placed stories in *Harper's New Monthly Magazine* and *The Atlantic Monthly*, among other journals, and, in 1863, brought out her second novel, *Rockford; or, Sunshine and Storm*. During the Civil War she expanded her ambitions into journalism; she moved to Washington, D.C., and worked as a correspondent for New York newspapers.

In the spring of 1864 she fell in love with and married Grinfill Blake, a businessman seven years her junior. The couple settled in New York, where Blake was drawn deeper into work for women's rights and became the associate of such prominent suffragists as Stanton, Anthony, Victoria Woodhull, and others. In this period, she published her best-known novel, *Fettered for Life; or, Lord and Master* (1874), explicitly about women's issues. Until his death, in 1897, her husband generously supported her activism and her writing, and she continued to work for national women's rights organizations until about 1905, when declining health forced her to retire. She lived another eight years, but not long enough to witness the passage of the Nineteenth Amendment.

"A VOLCANO OF RAGE AND SCORN"

Even before her first marriage, Blake experienced frequent bouts of despair, which were only amplified by her first husband's terrible death and the financial straits in which it left her. Thus, it is not surprising that her first two novels explored the dependent state of women and the problematic connection between marriage and wealth.

The central figure in *Southwold* is Medora Fielding, nineteen years old when the story begins, "in all the power and glory of perfect health and magnificent beauty."[29] She is a much sought-after belle, a smart, savvy young woman who knows her power over men and is unafraid to use it to her advantage. She is, in other words, a consummate coquette. Named after a romantic heroine in Byron's poem "The Corsair" (1814), Medora is nearly perfect. "Her mind," Blake writes, "had a rare breadth and scope . . . almost masculine in its depth of thought and capability of analytical inquiry."[30] She has only one perceived deficiency. Her mother, another great belle in her own time, had married a dashing soldier who had died at a distant post, too young to leave her any meaningful pension. The Fieldings had therefore always struggled on the edge of respectability, even though they have come to expect it as their due.

Medora is very much taken with the unfortunately impecunious Walter Lascelles, who is equally entranced with her. Not without regret he instead marries Lucy Wentworth, whom he does not love but who carries a considerable fortune. Jilted, the madly jealous Medora decides that before the Lascelleses return from their wedding trip to Europe, she, too, will marry a man of great wealth, if only to prove her own worth to Lascelles.

Another central character, Floyd Southwold, lives with his widowed mother on the Connecticut shore. His father lost his wealth in the Panic of 1837 and died shortly thereafter, leaving the family with few resources. At Floyd's birth, his father's brother asked that the child be named after him and if someday he might adopt him. The parents granted the first request but not the second. After his brother's death, the elder Floyd Southwold, whose wise investments allowed him to escape financial ruin and who lived a country gentleman's life on the Hudson River in an estate named after the family, has kept the offer open. Thus, when the younger Floyd reaches manhood, with his mother's blessing he accepts an invitation to spend time at Southwold. On his way out of the city, he chances upon the Lascelleses' wedding and sees a strikingly beautiful woman. It is Medora, still incensed that Lascelles has rejected her. "No one could have guessed," Blake observed, "that the calm indifference of her manner" with other guests "concealed a volcano of rage and scorn."[31]

At Southwold, Floyd luxuriates in the cultured world of his uncle, who so greatly enjoys his nephew that he intends to will the entire estate to him. Before long, Floyd also learns the name of the mysterious woman he has seen in the city. A neighbor, Mrs. Clarkson, recognizes his description of the belle and mentions that she will soon be her guest. When Medora meets Floyd and learns of his prospects, she quickly sets her sights on him. At first, all goes according to her plan, though she regrets her calculating ways, for she genuinely likes him. She muses, "If I had only known him sooner . . . so honest, so amiable, so devoted, I might have loved him once! It seems scarcely right to give in exchange for his warm true heart only the ashes of a burnt-out passion" (presumably for Lascelles), a thought she abruptly dismisses with a "bah!"[32]

But there is a hitch in her plans. When Floyd asks his uncle's approval to marry her, his uncle voices no objections but says that the couple cannot live there with him, nor will he forward Floyd any money against his eventual inheritance. The elder Southwold treasures his bachelor's existence; he loves Floyd as a guest but selfishly has no intention of allowing women or children to be permanent residents. What Floyd does not anticipate, however, is Medora's disappointment when she hears about Southwold's stipulation, for he does not think that the delay, however long, can ruin their love. She anticipates what would lie ahead, though, if she married him under those circumstances: "the tedious waiting for an old man's death, the false position that must always arise from slender means and great expectations, and the possibility of wasting the last years of her life, in the same struggle against circumstances of which she already was so weary."[33]

Thus, Medora rejects Floyd's suit and returns to the city, where she identifies the wealthy Claude Hamilton as her new target, even as she learns that the Lascelleses have returned from Europe prematurely because Lucy's father has had a stroke. Moreover, their first year of marriage has not gone well because Walter has spent much time and money with new friends while paying little attention to his new wife. He is soon unable to stop himself from pursuing Medora again, even when Lucy suspects his infidelity. Before long, Hamilton notices Lascelles's interest in Medora, and when he catches the couple in a compromising situation, he breaks off from her, derailing her plans once again. Discouraged at this latest turn, when Floyd reappears, Medora decides to accept his proposal after all. They announce their engagement; but the elder Southwold, who suspects Medora's true character, tries to show his nephew what an unworthy match she is. He gets his chance when Lascelles appears at Southwold.

After a dinner at Southwold that includes Medora, Lascelles, and Floyd, some of the guests decide to take walks in the countryside. Floyd and Medora find their way to the top of a deep gorge through which a railroad runs and across which the elder Southwold is walking. A train approaches, and Southwold, angered at technology's invasion of his land, grows agitated and accidentally tumbles down the bank and onto the tracks. He screams to Floyd for help. But Medora, "full of an exultant joy," realizes that "the only obstacle between herself and fortune" is about to be removed. With "a sudden revengeful desperation" she winds her arms around her lover and whispers in his ear: "Let him die!" At Southwold's next scream for help, she still holds back Floyd "in the clinging grasp of those strong white arms." "Let me go, murderess! Let me go!"[34] He breaks free but too late to run down the bank to save Southwold from the speeding train. Floyd irrevocably ends the engagement.

Tragedy strikes in the city as well. The equally unscrupulous Lascelles, himself driven to desperation, watches over his sickly wife and child but does not have their welfare in mind. Instead, he worries that if the infant does not survive the mother, he will lose control of her wealth, for the fortune will go to other relatives. But if the infant survives, even for the shortest time, he would inherit it from the child. His insistent questions about the baby alert Margaret, the family's domestic, to the true motive for his concern. As Lucy dies, Margaret sits in another room by the fire, cradling the bundled baby, and, when the nurse comes for her, insists on holding her a bit longer because she has just dropped off to sleep. The child is dead, but knowing Walter's wishes, Margaret makes it seem as though the baby has outlived her mother. Margaret later testifies that the child outlived her mother by half an hour; in fact she died two hours earlier. The wily domestic then extorts money from Lascelles and, after traveling to England, again sells her knowledge, this time to a distant relative of the Wentworths, who, armed with this information, successfully wrests the inheritance from Lascelles.

Medora, meanwhile, wastes away, subject to increasing moodiness and hallucinations. She wonders if she is losing her mind. From her concerned mother she learns that insanity runs in the family, and a doctor confirms that it is likely that Medora has inherited the trait. Increasingly despondent, she drinks a vial of poison to escape what she thinks will be forty years in a "lunatic asylum." Meanwhile, Floyd, still a bachelor, lives on the estate he inherited, wondering if he will ever achieve the happiness he imagined he would have with Medora.[35]

Throughout the novel Blake is of two minds about Medora, whose favorite poet is the mercurial Byron, as Floyd's is the Puritan Milton.[36] Medora embodies many of the attributes that Blake wanted to be recognized in women: intelligence, independence, a desire to control their own financial and sexual lives, resilience in the face of setbacks. And, with

Hawthorne's Hester Prynne and Melville's Isabel, Medora is one of the most compelling women characters of the 1850s because she acknowledges her sexual desire. But doing so, she has lost all sense of virtue. All of Medora's considerable gifts are put to the service of self and are further compromised by the social system in which she finds herself, one in which marriage is a woman's only chance at success, even as she takes the blame for any failings in her spouse. "No man ever does anything wrong or foolish," Medora says at a dinner party at Southwold, "that people do not blame either his wife or mother."[37] Moreover, men are obtuse and do not realize that their pleasant young wives realize and seethe over their plight. Good Christian women, like the heroines of Warner's and Cummins's novels, suppress all outward signs of feeling so that even the most penetrating man does not "suspect the thoughts that are surging under the placid surface of a fair face."[38]

But Blake worried about the tendency of a woman of beauty, intelligence, and ambition to stray from goodness, particularly if she lacks traditional religious belief, for Medora is agnostic at best. At one point, Medora shocks Floyd with the cynicism of her sophisticated philosophical arguments against Christianity. A student of world religions and mythology, she tells Southwold that she much prefers the belief of the ancient "Scandinavians," whose religion did not denigrate women as Christianity does. "They regarded their wives as companions to be consulted on important occasions," as opposed to the perverted notions of the sexuality that the "Christian enthusiasts" subsequently codified.[39] At the same time, Blake implies that Medora's guile grows from her agnosticism. Lacking Christianity, she lacks as well a moral compass. Floyd never loses his faith and at the end is the character that the reader trusts most.

Blake's second novel, *Rockford; or, Sunshine and Shadow*, completed a few years after her husband's suicide, is a more mature and daring book. The plot is controlled, the characters' explosive passions remain covered by a veneer of respectability, and the tone is understated. Once more, Blake describes the joie de vivre and flirtatiousness of young women, consumed as they are with evening visits, dances, and discussions of the suitability of various beaux. Her ear for dialogue is acute, and her reproduction of a social milieu convincing. But the tale itself is as dark as *Southwold*.

The novel opens in another New England coastal town, at the funeral of George Sandys, a onetime resident who recently returned with his wife and daughter, Mabel. At the gravesite another townsperson, Claudia

Rockford, cries out and faints, causing a knowing titter among the assembled. Her husband, fifteen years older, is away on business, and when he returns that evening, he hears of his wife's behavior. But it does not surprise him, either, for he has long suspected what many in town do, that his son, Vinton, in fact is Sandys's child.

Soon Vinton and Mabel grow close. They declare their engagement, but when Mrs. Rockford, who has become ill, hears of it, she begs her son not to marry the girl. She refuses to explain why, even as she insists on the prohibition even after her death. Her husband, trying to make Claudia admit what he intuitively knows, perversely encourages his "son" in his suit; but Vinton, deeply affected by his mother's illness, honors her unexplained wish. Her concerns are twofold: she must prevent an incestuous relationship, and she must protect Vinton's inheritance.

Vinton tells his cousin the Reverend Haughton about his mother's seemingly irrational demand, and when Haughton visits her, he, too, attempts to learn its motivation. He suggests that by revealing her reasons, she can clear her conscience before she dies. But like Hester Prynne when the Puritan magistrates ask her to name Pearl's father, Claudia does not speak. Like Medora, she doubts the efficacy of Christianity. The consolations of Haughton's religion are useless to her. "I cannot repair the injury I inflicted. I will not make the reparation in my power—I do not even repent," presumably because she does not regret what she did.[40] Thus, Blake does not condemn the sexual act itself or the veil of secrecy that Claudia has thrown over it to ensure Vinton's happiness and inheritance. In this complex situation there are no easy moral judgments; Mrs. Rockford can be read as having acted from love for Sandys and then from love for her son. Blake includes subplots in which villains—southerners who set their sights on New England women—are readily apparent and ultimately foiled, but she never depicts adulterers in the same light.

As Mrs. Rockford's health fails, she asks to be buried in the same graveyard where her beloved Sandys lies. She summons Haughton to make him promise never to let Vinton marry Mabel. He cannot, however, for he himself loves her, and to grant Mrs. Rockford's wish would be to betray Vinton for his own gain. Struggling against time, Mrs. Rockford surreptitiously pens an account of her life that includes her long-kept secret. She realizes that only when Vinton knows the truth will he do what she wishes. After her funeral, he reads her lengthy confession, hidden in her keepsake box and, per her wishes expressed within the document, subsequently destroys it.

In his last encounter with Mabel, Vinton tells her that as much as he loves her, he will not ever marry her and that she is free to give her affections to whomever she wishes. He leaves, perhaps permanently, for Europe, but the ship on which he sails from New York is lost at sea, with no survivors. Mabel later marries Haughton, and Mr. Rockford, stricken by this turn of events, dies soon afterward, never learning the truth for sure.

Blake wrote several more novels, including *Fettered for Life*, now considered the best nineteenth-century American novel about women's rights and the only one of her works to have a modern reprint. By the time of the novel's first publication, she had become a major figure in the movement, and probably because of this, compared with *Southwold* and *Rockford*, this novel's politics are more overt, even propagandistic. In *Fettered for Life*, she sacrificed the psychological and moral complexity of her earlier novels, which allowed readers to imagine the welter of emotions that push people to act against their best interests. For in its long sequestration of a secret that holds the key to a character's actions—indeed, life—*Rockford* not only recalls *The Blithedale Romance* but similarly demonstrates its author's attempt to steer the reader into an interior realm where the line between rationality and its opposite blurs.

"MRS. R. H. STODDARD"

In the advertisements bound in after the conclusion to *Rockford*, Blake's publisher also listed *The Morgesons* (1862), by "Mrs. R. H. Stoddard," a "clever novel of American life." This terse description does little to capture what is arguably one of the most sophisticated psychological novels of the period. *The Morgesons* pulls the reader into a jumbled interior world that brought a new level of self-consciousness to American fiction. For an epigraph to her third novel, *Temple House*, Stoddard uses an appropriate and admonitory line from Emerson's "Experience": "Let us treat the men and women well: treat them as if they were real: perhaps they are." Indeed, her characters, often lost in their own thoughts, struggle to credit the subjectivity of others.

Elizabeth Barstow Stoddard was born in 1823 in a seaside town, Mattapoisett, Massachusetts, southwest of Cape Cod. In the antebellum years Mattapoisett was best known for shipbuilding, and Wilson Barstow was a master of that craft, a builder of whaling vessels (including the *Acushnet*, on which young Herman Melville sailed to the Marquesas). The economic vagaries of the business periodically resulted in financial uncertainty for the Barstow family, and Wilson Barstow never recovered from the double blow of the Panic of 1857 and the Civil War, when his business failed. There were other, more personal tragedies, too. Stoddard's favorite sister, Jane, died of consumption in 1848, and her mother, Betsy Drew Barstow, passed away a year later. Around that time, Stoddard's brother, Wilson, Jr., moved to New York, where she frequently visited him. She found that the city stimulated her artistic ambition, even as she always enjoyed returning for a time to the slower pace of her hometown and the comfort of the nearby sea.

In New York, at the behest of a friend she began to attend the Saturday evening soiree of Anne Lynch Botta, a salon whose only rival was that of the Cary sisters and where Elizabeth Barstow rubbed shoulders with Nathaniel P. Willis, William Cullen Bryant, George Ripley, Charles A. Dana, and Horace Greeley. At the salon she met an aspiring young writer with New England roots, Richard Henry Stoddard, and late in 1852, after much indecision, married him. The couple decided to live in New York, to pursue their ambitions.[41] They also attended Alice and Susan Cary's Sunday night gatherings, where they met the litterateurs Edward P. Whipple, Thomas Bailey Aldrich, Richard Watson Gilder, and others as well as the women's rights people and other reformers.

The Stoddards' closest friends were two other authors. One was the increasingly well-known Pennsylvania Quaker Bayard Taylor, a poet manqué who found success as a travel writer for Greeley's *New-York Tribune*, eventually reporting from Europe and the Middle and Far East and collecting his letters into bestselling books.[42] The other was George Boker, another Pennsylvania poet who had gravitated to New York; he was the scion of a wealthy family who, unlike his impecunious New England friends, never had to worry about money. Genuinely devoted to the young couple and increasingly well connected, Taylor and Boker did much to boost both their careers.

Stoddard's first publications, in the mid-1850s, were poems, but she soon turned to journalism. In the autumn of 1856 the San Francisco paper *Daily Alta California* hired her as its New York "Lady Correspondent," to keep forty-niners abreast of the East's cultural and social scene. She continued this work until early 1858, when she turned her attention to short fiction, publishing her first "sketch," "Our Christmas Party," in *Harper's New Monthly Magazine* in January 1859.

Some of her columns in the *Daily Alta California* and her correspondence with the editor of *The Atlantic Monthly*, James Russell Lowell, reveal the nature of her ambition and in particular how she distinguished herself from other popular women writers. In October 1854, in her first column for the *Daily Alta California*, she said that she had debated how to appear most effectively, "whether to represent myself as a genuine original, or adopt some great example in style," then adding tongue in cheek, like "the pugilism of Fanny Fern, the pathetics [*sic*] of Minnie Myrtle, or the abandon of Cassie Cauliflower."[43] Almost two years later, in a report to her western readers on bestsellers in the East, she again lampooned certain successful female writers who continued to trade on the profitable sentimental. "You can form no idea of the balderdash in our bookstores," she wrote. "One of our publishers has the run of three lunatic asylums, [and] another collects the 'compositions' of seventeen female boarding schools . . . Five new Minnie Myrtles have appeared since the date of my last, and three young Fanny Ferns, all warranted as good as the originals."[44] She had a particularly personal (though unspecified) animus against Fern, whom she called "a female Ishmael."[45]

As a result, her female contemporaries, Stoddard complained, wrote frothy prose and depicted unrealistic characters. "Why will writers, especially female writers," she asked, "make their heroines so indifferent to good eating, so careless about taking cold, and so impervious to all the creature comforts?" Distinguishing herself like Blake from many previous women authors, she complained about the "eternal preachment about self-denial, moral self-denial." In reading a book based in such pieties, she said, "I am reminded of what I have thought my mission was: a crusade against Duty—not the duty that is revealed to every man and woman of us by the circumstances of daily life, but that which is cut and fashioned for us by minds totally ignorant of our idiosyncrasies and necessities."[46]

Stoddard's response to James Russell Lowell's criticism of the first story she submitted to *The Atlantic Monthly* is equally revealing. Presumably because of her frankness about women's sexual desire, he was worried that she was "going near the edge" of respectability. "Must I create from whose, or what standard?" she replied testily. "Do I disturb your artistic sense by my lack of refinement? I must own that I am coarse by nature" and "at times" have "an overwhelming perception of the back side of truth. I see the rough laths behind the fine mortar—the body within its purple and fine linen—the mood of the man and the woman in the dark of the light of his or her mind when alone."[47] But Lowell's criticism genuinely worried her. To her friend the literary critic and anthologist Edmund Clarence Stedman, she wrote, "In me [Lowell] detects a tendency towards the *edge of things* and warns me against it . . . Alas, I am coarse and literal by nature, [so] what shall I do? My sensual perceptions react on my brain."[48]

She also told Stedman that she was working on a long story, which would become her first novel. She explained, "I am as yet incapable of wrestling my conceptions from my brain, they present themselves, to speak obstetrically, head and feet together—or I perceive that they are misshapen." Thus, she had "to labor hard to give them grace and expression," a particularly personal metaphor because within the last year she had given birth to a second child, who was born deformed and died a short while later.[49] She labored on the novel for almost two years, and in the fall of 1861, the Civil War erupting around her, she signed a contract with Rudd & Carleton for *The Morgesons*. Her celebration was brief, however. Within a month she had more tragedy. The Stoddards' six-year-old, Willy, died of scarlet fever. As she awaited her novel's publication, she experienced a breakdown and was confined to bed. "Nervous prostration the Dr. calls it," she wrote Stedman. "I call it *Life*."[50]

"TATTOOED"

In its own way, *The Morgesons* is as unusual a book as *Moby-Dick*, difficult to categorize and stylistically distinctive. Its subject is Cassandra Morgeson's psychological growth, from her youth to her early twenties, when she marries. The novel is a remembrance, and proceeds elliptically and often without logical explanations for important events. *The Morgesons* bore little relation to the sort of didactic fiction many readers expected, particularly from women authors. An anonymous reviewer in the *New York World* offered an accurate characterization of the novel. Its narrative, he wrote, is "simply a natural and truthful succession of incidents and outward circumstances, whereon hinge naturally the human characters and passions thereby formed or exhibited."[51]

Much like Fanny Fern in her novels, in *The Morgesons* Stoddard drew from her own life and, like Blake, sought to unearth subterranean emotions. But Stoddard probed deeper, by following the twists and turns of Cassandra's interior life. And if *Southwold* was about a young woman's discovery and expression of her sexual identity, *The Morgesons* was about its discovery and regulation.[52] Not surprisingly, given its novelty on this account, it attracted more attention than any novel of the season.[53]

Stoddard picks up the thread of Cassandra's life when she is ten years old, living in the old New England seacoast village of Surrey (patently, Mattapoisett). Her father, Locke Morgeson, owns a flourishing shipyard, which has brought the family both wealth and respectability. Her mother, Mary, seems conventional enough, wrapping herself in a mantle of simple, pious religion and hoping that she can raise her children in the same faith. She has one other child, Veronica, the largest influence on Cassandra but very different. A few years younger than Cassandra, Veronica is frequently ill and needs much care; she is a mysterious girl and frequently challenges her older sister for their mother's attention.

From the first line, when her aunt Mercy (also known as Merce) describes Cassandra as "possessed," it is clear that she is a rebellious child.[54] She is disciplined for mocking her schoolteacher and for upsetting one of her mother's tea parties. In her mid-teens she is sent to a school for girls at Barmouth (Fairhaven, Massachusetts), where she lives with her aunt and her grandfather Warren. As a newcomer and outsider at the academy, she is teased and bullied by her peers, one of whom causes an accident on a teeter-totter that injures Cassandra badly enough that she has to return home. At this point, a hitherto unknown cousin, Charles Morgeson, visits Surrey and takes advantage of the family's hospitality. Before he leaves, he invites Cassandra to live with his family at Rosville and attend its well-known academy. Her family allows it; once again, Veronica is left at home.

Charles has ulterior motives, though. Languishing in a marriage to a woman he considers dull and conventional, he is immensely attracted to Cassandra. To her surprise, she finds herself affected by his attention and begins to discover herself as a sexual being. Meanwhile, she meets Ben Somers, another distant relation (from a wealthy family living more on its past glory than its present assets), who unfortunately has inherited the family curse of alcoholism. Ben recognizes Charles's power over Cassandra and tries, unsuccessfully, to derail their relationship. He also visits Surrey and falls in love with Veronica, leaving Cassandra in an increasingly dangerous situation with her magnetic, imperious cousin.

Their chaste yet passionate affair ends tragically. One day Charles takes Cassandra driving behind a new stallion, even though his wife has warned him that the horse seems out of sorts. The animal indeed is not well; it has a fit and veers wildly off the road, overturning the carriage. Trying to save Cassandra, Charles is killed instantly. She survives but with facial scars; she is "tattooed," she says. During her recuperation, she admits to Charles's wife what she had suspected, that Cassandra and Charles were in love, though they had not consummated it.

Cassandra completes her recovery in Surrey, where Ben Somers eventually appears and asks her to come with him to Belem (Salem) to meet his family. He wants them to approve his love for her sister, who is too pathologically shy to make such a visit. In Belem, Cassandra learns that drunkenness runs in the family yet falls in love with Ben's brother Desmond, who also has inherited the family's curse. She returns to Surrey, pondering both Desmond's pledge that he will reform and Ben's warning that the marriage would be a disaster.

Cassandra's life begins to unravel. On her return, she tries to surprise her mother but finds the old woman in her chair, dead from a stroke. Before long, her father reveals that he is bankrupt. Ben returns and marries Veronica, isolating Cassandra even more. Her father is impressed with Alice Morgeson's considerable business acumen—Charles's widow has been running his factories—and marries her. Cassandra is shocked and tells her father about Charles's and her abortive love. She also tells her parent that she cannot remain in the same house with Alice.

Locke moves to Rosville with his new wife, leaving Cassandra in the homestead, alone with her memories and the ever-present sea, near which she retreats for solace. To make matters worse, Ben has begun drinking again. Desmond fares better. He returns from two years in Europe and, sober, marries Cassandra. In the novel's last scene, Veronica holds her baby, which appears sickly. The reader learns that several months earlier Ben had died in delirium tremens.[55] The newly married couple enjoys a degree of comfort because around the time that Ben married Veronica, the two boys came into their inheritance. At the novel's end it is not clear what is next for Cassandra, a woman of twenty-five who already has experienced her share of tragedy. Her thoughtfulness is auspicious, of course: she has bravely played the hand that she had been dealt. She has been "tattooed," though is not ashamed of it. Her life, seemingly mired in traces of the sentimental, in fact becomes a struggle between her personal power and that which pushes against it—her own history, linked as it is to her mother's youthful indiscretions and the curse of alcoholism that marks Desmond's family. The novel's last words, spoken by Desmond as he and Cassandra find Ben dead, indicates just the religious conundrum that for Stoddard defined the age. "God is the ruler," he exclaims. "Otherwise let this mad world crush us now."

THE EFFECT OF "REALITY"

American readers had not seen such a novel. *The Morgesons* is rife with gaps and ambiguities. It contains none of the preaching and moral lessons common to domestic tales, even though the book ends with a marriage. Religion is marginal; when a revival sweeps through the school Cassandra attends at Barmouth, it leaves her untouched. Nor does the novel feature a heroine who denies her passion by subduing her will, as Gerty does in *The Lamplighter*. If anything, Cassandra prevails because of her strong-mindedness; "possessed," she is not made for Surrey, or for nineteenth-century New England for that matter. She is a creature of intellect in addition to passion. In contrast with the almost preliterate Isabel in *Pierre*, who never acquired language as children normally do and communicates best through her guitar playing, Cassandra is precociously smart and self-aware. Her faith is in herself.

Because of the Stoddards' connections, *The Morgesons* was widely reviewed. Though the novel rapidly disappeared from the cultural scene, the notices were generally positive, particularly in their invocation of comparable European novelists. The genteel Boston essayist Henry T. Tuckerman compared the novel to the emerging realist movement in Europe: Stoddard's book was "a realistic Balzacian study of American life."[56] Others thought it closer to Charlotte Brontë and George Eliot.[57] Reviewers were alive to Stoddard's innovative characterizations. Most characters in contemporary novels, Boker wrote, were one-dimensional and showed little of the "fearful moral struggles by which the promptings of passion are subdued." Stoddard's were different. "The best of them have their imperfections, their bad tendencies, and their indulged weaknesses," and the worst of them, "their small virtues, their moments of repentance, and sufficient latent strength to preserve them against positive crime." The effect on a reader's mind, he concluded, "is that of reality."[58]

Stedman also emphasized how successfully Stoddard anatomized passion. "Forms of passion break out all the more impetuously for the pressure which strives to keep them down."[59] George Ripley concurred. One of the nation's most astute reviewers, he wrote in his *New-York Tribune*, "The aim of the book, in fact, is to analyze passion rather than to delineate personalities." In order to write such a book, the author had to be accustomed to brood over the mysteries of life "with a remorseless habit of stripping the veil from the softest illusions, and cherishing an inexorable sense of reality."[60]

One way that Stoddard conjured her realism was by emphasizing the determinative power of class and wealth in mid-nineteenth-century New England, putatively a democratic milieu. Cassandra tells the reader that her mother, née Mary Warren, was "poor, and without connection," the daughter of a tailor in a nearby town, and that every member of Locke's family save his grandfather opposed the marriage because even though she was beautiful, her background and prospects were undistinguished. When Cassandra attends school at Miss Black's in Barmouth, the fact that her father is the wealthiest man in Surrey is of no account, for most of her classmates had the "fulcrum" of inherited wealth and thought of her as a mere "parvenu."[61] Ben and Desmond Somers, cut from the august, if now threadbare, Pickersgill cloth, are obsessed with the prospect of their inheritance, though it will not be divided until the youngest of five children is twenty-one, an event for which they are "impatient."[62] When their mother unexpectedly has another baby, the men in the family, especially Desmond, fall into a funk.

Cassandra gradually comes to understand that her mother may have once been different from how she now appears, and why other members of the family, when Veronica acts in some untoward way, "smiled significantly and asked: 'Do you think she is like her mother?' "[63] Mary Morgeson remains "beautiful, with an indescribable air of individuality," but, as a married woman, has subdued herself. "I make no attempt to analyze her character," Cassandra says. "I describe her as she appeared, and as my memory now holds her. I never understood her."[64] Cassandra realizes that she may owe her passionate and unruly nature to her mother. "Hidden among the Powers That Be, which rule New England," Cassandra says, always "lurks the Deity of the Illicit," and it is that with which Cassandra must learn to live, reminded as she is of it each day by her "tattoos."[65]

What is it that has been hidden in her mother's life? Not surprisingly, it has to do with unfulfilled passion. Cassandra's schoolmate Charlotte Alden seems particularly eager to taunt her. Aunt Merce counsels Cassandra,

"[N]ever mind her if she says anything unpleasant."[66] One day after Cassandra has expressed her anger at Charlotte for her incessant teasing, the latter says, "Who are you to be angry? We have heard about your mother, when she was in love, poor thing." Cassandra, uncomprehending, strikes her. Hearing of this, Aunt Merce "turned pale, and said she knew what Charlotte Alden meant, and that perhaps mother would tell me in good time." "We had a good many troubles in our young days, Cassy," she adds.[67]

It is, however, Cassandra's father who reveals all. She learns from him that Charlotte's uncle once had "paid his addresses" to Mary, and there "might have been an engagement." But whether or not there was, "the influence of his family had broken the acquaintance," presumably because of Mary's plebeian roots. When Cassandra seems surprised, Locke says, "Are you so young still as to believe that only those who love marry? Or that those who marry have never loved, except each other?" He does not realize that Cassandra does indeed know of such things, for his words come after her involvement with her cousin Charles. She only answers, "I am afraid that Love, like Theology, if examined, makes one skeptical."[68]

The Morgesons's critique of religion runs deeper than Cassandra's profession of skepticism, though. As in the *The Scarlet Letter* and *Hagar*, clergymen do not live up to their professed values. The local minister, Mr. Park, has a habit of visiting with Mary. Veronica "mysteriously" tells her sister that he "likes mother." When Cassandra professes disbelief, Veronica replies: "He watches her so when she holds Arthur," the infant in the family. On another visit, when Mr. Park talks of the last week's sermon, Cassandra observes that Mary "listened with a vague, respectful attention," her hand pressed against her breast, "as if she were repressing an inward voice which claimed her attention." None of Stoddard's characters are immune to the temptations of the flesh. From the top of society to the bottom, and across families and towns, her characters are driven by passion, so that passion is the norm and the person who lives a controlled, pious life is the outlier. Is there something between the clergyman and Mrs. Morgeson? Is the child Mr. Park's?

Locke Morgeson's emotional life also surprises Cassandra, nowhere more so than when impressed as he is with Alice's business skills, he marries her. When Ben warns Cassandra that a wedding might be in the offing, the news floors her: "A devil ripped open my heart; its fragments flew all over me, blinding and deafening me." "I wanted to tell you," she says to her parent, "that Charles Morgeson loved me from the first, and you remember that I stayed by him to the last." When her father asks if Alice knew, Cassandra replies, "All." He stuns her with his next words: "We were married two days ago."[69]

But the Deity of the Illicit is most evident in the love between Charles and Cassandra. From an early age, Cassandra displayed her contrarian nature and strong will; as a youth she lived in sensation more than reflection. At Miss Black's school, she "concealed nothing; the desires and emotions which are usually kept as a private fund I displayed and exhausted." She notes, "My candor was called anything but truthfulness," and her classmates called it "sarcasm, cunning, coarseness, or tact," even as they emulated her.[70]

At first, Charles's gaze discomfits, but she soon begins, at first only half-consciously, to return his stare. "I fell into the habit of guessing each day whether I was to offend or please him, and then into that of intending to please," only half fathoming why, she recalled. "An intangible, silent, magnetic feeling existed between us, changing and developing according to its own mysterious law."[71] One day, when "he raised his intense, strange eyes" to hers, "a blinding, intelligent light flowed from them which I could not defy nor resist, a light which filled my veins with torrents of fire."[72]

The tension culminates at an evening entertainment, when Charles and Ben, who has been drinking, argue over her. "Somers," the former says, "behave like a man, and let us alone; I love this girl." When Cassandra refuses to leave with him, Ben knows that she in turn loves Charles. But she implores Charles, "Never say those frightful words again. Never, never."[73] Whatever it is they have together will not be spoken but acted. When in her recovery Cassandra asks Alice if she loved her husband, Alice replies, "Did *you* love him?" Cassandra replies, "[Y]ou may or may not forgive me, but I was strangely bound to him. And I must tell you that I hunger now for the kiss he never gave me."[74]

"SMOULDERING INSTINCTS OF PASSION AND RACE"
In the war years the Stoddards lived in a boardinghouse on Tenth Street run by a Miss Swift—herself an eccentric and outspoken intellectual—and presided over their own salon on Saturday evenings. At any given meal, however, Miss Smith tended a bevy of "authors, actors, artists, musicians, mathematicians, professors, journalists, critics, and essayists."

Among this impressive company, Elizabeth Stoddard stood out. A regular, Lillian Aldrich, wife of the writer Thomas Bailey Aldrich, claimed that she knew

> of no prototype of Mrs. Stoddard, this singular woman, who possessed so strongly the ability to sway all men who came within her influence. Brilliant and fascinating, she needed neither beauty nor youth, her power was so much beyond such aids. On every variety of subject she talked with originality and ready wit; with impassioned speech expressing an individuality and insight most unusual and rare.

Aldrich recalled that a summons to Stoddard's abode was "what a ribbon is to a soldier, and prized accordingly."[75] Indeed, the war loomed over the salon's discussions, and it touched Stoddard particularly closely. One of her brothers, Wilson Barstow, served as an officer on Gen. John Adams Dix's staff, and in the fall of 1862 another brother, Zaccheus, was killed in battle near New Bern, North Carolina. Unlike many of the people they knew, the Stoddards were Democrats; Richard had not voted for Lincoln in 1860. In some of her short fiction of 1861–1865, Elizabeth wrote explicitly about the war. Even though her next novel, *Two Men* (1865), appeared to have little to do with it, her depiction of a house divided called to mind the greater conflict. If war pitted brother against brother, in this novel Stoddard pitted members of the same family against one another. Dispiritingly, her characters fought not for a greater cause but merely to satisfy their passions.

As Harriet Wilson's *Our Nig* indicates, while there was much talk in New England of African Americans in the context of slavery and abolition, it was rare to find free blacks portrayed as realistic characters in fiction. But in *Two Men* Stoddard attempted to do just that. The novel, if not as psychologically acute as *The Morgesons*, was more radical in its cultural politics. Set in Crest, another town Stoddard based on her memories of Mattapoisett, the novel concerns twenty-year-old Jason Auster, a carpenter's apprentice. Auster has arrived in the small community intent on making his way in the world after fleeing a tyrannical father. He finds work building a new church and meets one of the parishioners, Sarah Parke, granddaughter of Squire Parke, the town's patriarch. "The Parkes are next to the Lord, in this country," one resident tells Auster. "One of 'em knocked off his heel cap on Plymouth Rock the day the Pilgrims came ashore; one of 'em was a governor; one of 'em settled here—cheated the Indians, I guess, out of the pine woods that still belong to the old Squire."[76]

Soon enough Jason courts her, and they marry, though they seem worlds apart: moody and drawn to the forest, he spouts theories of "Socialism, Abolitionism, and Teetotalism." Among his few belongings is a copy of "Man's Social Destiny," no doubt a stand-in for Albert Brisbane's Fourierist work *The Social Destiny of Man* and as such a testament to his egalitarian ethos.[77] By contrast, Sarah represents the inherited social privilege Jason believes is at the root of the country's problems.

The elder Parke is a widower twice over, and all his children are dead, making Sarah his ward. Osmond Luce, another grandchild and Sarah's half cousin, is the only other member of the family. A few years before Sarah's marriage to Jason, he left Crest for Venezuela, where he worked on the pampas and threw himself into the new nation's volatile politics. Stoddard makes clear that there once was something between Osmond and Sarah, the two heirs. Barring his return, Jason and Sarah's son, Parke Auster, will take over the family's business interests when he comes of age.

The domineering Sarah wears down Jason's idealism; he spends much time wandering outdoors. The two become estranged, though devoted to their son, they continue to live together in the family home. After Squire Parke's death, Jason, possessing a good mind for business, directs the estate, while Sarah's main interest becomes ensuring that their son eventually will inherit it all. But things are not that simple. Twelve years after his departure, Osmond returns with a young daughter, Philippa, "a strange-looking little girl," whom he wants to leave with the Austers while he continues his adventures. He assumes she will share the family fortune with Parke.[78] Although Stoddard leaves it ambiguous, it is likely that Philippa is mixed race, the offspring of Osmond's dalliance with a woman in South America; there is no mention of her mother, but the reader learns that the girl has been raised as a Catholic.[79] Sarah is unsettled by Philippa's arrival—indeed, by her very existence—for she, too, is an heir. Sarah's relationship with Osmond, in which "hatred and love were equally probable passions between such temperaments, and equally fatal," is tense.[80] Soon enough he leaves once again for South America, and Sarah subjects Philippa to harsh discipline while indulging Parke.

Nine years later, both children have returned from out-of-town schooling, and Philippa finds herself attracted to Parke. When her schoolmate Theresa Bond visits and also finds him of interest, Philippa warns her off.

Meanwhile, Jason, middle-aged, morose, and distant, still feeling like an outsider among the Parkes, questions his relationship to his wife. "Why did we ever marry, Sarah?" he asks. "I was neither handsome nor rich— only a stupid, green boy, just as I *have been*—a stupid, ignorant man."[81] To heighten tensions in the home, an attractive woman, Mrs. Lang, and her two teenage daughters arrive in Crest from Savannah, their passage paid by a Georgia plantation owner.

On the Langs' arrival, it is quickly apparent to all who see them that "the glitter of negro blood was in [Mrs. Lang's] eyes," and "the negro modulation" in her voice. "Her manners reflected the hut, the boudoir, and the Methodist gatherings of plantation slaves."[82] Mrs. Lang's daughters are even more striking: sixteen-year-old Charlotte, with "a brilliant swarthy complexion, shining, curly, black hair, large black eyes, with a vindictive sparkle, and manners which were a mixture of the sulky and vivacious," and eighteen-year-old Clarice, tall and willowy, "her lips always parted, her wistful light-blue eyes widely opened, and her straight, silky chestnut hair disordered."[83] It is not clear if the Langs are freed slaves or were born free in the South, but in a pique of anger Clarice screams at Mrs. Lang that she had "a white husband."[84]

Even though she has many suitors, Philippa is still set on Parke. "He makes devotion easy," Jason says of Parke to Sarah. "Besides, [Philippa] has grown up with him, and affection between them is a habit."[85] Sarah detests the girl, who threatens Parke's inheritance. Jason's feelings are more complicated. When he realizes that Philippa loves Parke, a "wave of anguish dashed over him, followed by a host of roaring, crawling, cruel emotions, that rent him asunder . . . as if his soul and body were parting," for he harbors an unusual, if not unnatural, desire for her.[86]

Parke attempts to help the Langs begin a friendly relationship with the white townspeople and invites the girls to a cotillion planned by him and his friend Sam Rogers; all Parke wants is "to have them treated like human beings."[87] But the whole evening, beautiful as they are, they stand apart. Raised in another slaveholding country, Philippa "had heard the sound of the lash on shoulders as lovely as Charlotte's" and thus knows what the Lang girls might have endured before they were sent North.[88] Parke's feelings are of an entirely different sort, for "he felt that a sure, irresistible, slow current was setting towards [Charlotte]," even as his friend Sam is disgusted by her. "I wish the yellow cook of the Unicorn [a ship] was here," he says to Parke; "I'd introduce him to those wenches." " 'I am almost sorry,' he said, 'that we have undertaken these parties; there is such a mess here—cabin and forecastle mixed'"—in the argot of sailors, a way of saying that these people should not be consorting.[89]

Soon Parke and Charlotte are in a secret romance; only Sam knows about it. Charlotte becomes pregnant, and when Parke tells Sam that he is going to marry Charlotte, his friend grows angry. "Now by God, Parke, you shall not do it! You must not, cannot do it! Nature is against it!"[90] The entire town, except for the Auster-Parke clan, learns of the pregnancy. Eventually, the Austers' servants hear of it, and inevitably one of them tells Philippa, who confronts Parke. As she leaves him, "she struck him so violently in the face that he was blinded." She then asks Charlotte why she went out of her "place" with him, not being "his equal." "He came after me, remember," she replies. "Why didn't you keep him away from me?" Deeply hurt and embarrassed by this challenge, Philippa exclaims, "Insensible, heartless, beastly African!"[91]

When Parke tells his mother that he is going to marry Charlotte (a course of action to which Jason, sensing an opening with Philippa, does not object), she is at first uncomprehending, then livid. She falls mortally ill. Returning from her burial services, the family discovers that Osmond is back and has learned from the servants that there soon is to be another mixed-race family member. But virtually simultaneously with the disappearance of Sarah's "dominant, exacting, forcible presence," Charlotte falls seriously ill and dies in childbirth, as does the baby. Parke is loyal to the end, insisting that she and their child be interred in his family's lot.

"Link by link," Stoddard writes, "the family chain was parting."[92] Osmond plans to return to Venezuela, where he intends to resume his life as a cowboy as well as lend support to Gen. José Antonio Páez's freedom fighters, and asks Parke to accompany him. Osmond wants Philippa to join them and thus to leave the Parke legacy behind her. She cannot, though. "How can I tell," she says, "whether I could bear the license of your life? I succumb to tradition and custom because I love them."[93]

Still adoring Philippa, Jason asks her to marry him. Incredulous, she refuses. Jason tries to commit suicide, recovers, and leaves for the West, where he wanders aimlessly for several months. At the novel's conclusion, Osmond and Parke are on a ranch in Venezuela, the latter pining for Philippa. Osmond wagers that when Parke returns to the United States, he will probably find her married. "To whom?" he asks. When Osmond says, "Jason Auster," he replies, "Never! It is impossible."[94] But it isn't: the two outsiders—one of mixed blood—have indeed married and control the Parke fortune.

Reviewers recognized the daring of *Two Men*. In the *New York Post*, Stedman observed that Stoddard captured men's complexity as much as she had women's in her first novel. She wanted, he averred, "to show her men and women as they are—to divide the real from the seeming—to mark the perpetual triumph of kind and individuality in their unending contest with conventional life—to prove what little strength even the force of New England's repression has to stifle the smouldering instincts of passion and race."

Stedman also astutely noted her similarity to Hawthorne in her attempt both to pull back "the rigid veil which hides the inner New England life" and to break "the ice which covers fervid and turbulent under-currents of soul and sense." Their methods, however, could not have been more different. While Hawthorne evoked "a misty host of weird superstitions" and offered his own authorial ruminations, Stoddard studied "the instincts of her modern personages, as involved with the experiences of family and social life." She moved, Stedman continued, "in the domain of tangible facts and events, the awe and mystery of common things." Finally, like certain European writers, she did not choose "repulsive or disagreeable" subjects; she was thus "the first of the American realist school."[95]

William Dean Howells, recently arrived in Boston from the Midwest and a new player in the nation's literary politics, to Stoddard's credit similarly invoked Hawthorne, who after his untimely death in 1864 came to be seen as the best novelist the nation had yet produced. Stoddard's forte, Howells thought, was her ability to present her ideas through action and dialogue and thus to eschew pontification. She "seldom vouchsafes a word of comment or explanation on anything that her people do or say," he wrote in *The Nation*, "and yet from their brief speeches and dramatic action, you have the same knowledge of motive which you acquire from the philosophization [*sic*] of some such subjective romance as *The Scarlet Letter*."

Although Howells disliked its contrived ending, he still found *Two Men* "one of the most original books written by an American woman." Even Stoddard's faults were original; they were "not Miss Shepherd's, as in the works of Miss [Harriet] Prescott [Spofford], nor Charlotte

Brontë's, as in the works of Miss [Rebecca] Harding [Davis]," referring to two emerging American writers who championed a new, more realistic kind of fiction but whose novels lacked Stoddard's psychological insight.[96] Ripley, in the *New-York Tribune*, concurred, ending his review by noting that "in a day of exuberant demonstration, and reckless imagery, especially among popular female writers, it is a refreshment to find a woman self-possessed as the Sybil."[97]

Stoddard calmly took apart the masks most people wore. At a crucial point in *Two Men*, Parke asks Philippa if she has ever thought of the "strangeness" of his mother's character (presumably because she so despises Philippa). "Such revelations [about people] come so unexpectedly," he continues, "from those who are the nearest of all. There is something appalling behind the screen of every-day life, countenance, custom, clothes. What is it?" he asks. "It is *us*," Philippa answers.[98] Thwarted ambition and love; hateful pride and covetousness of "outsiders"; twisted fixation on wealth and inheritance; thoughts of incest and, in some cases, actions that border on it; irrational fear of miscegenation or, as it then was more commonly termed, amalgamation: these are the things that Stoddard found underneath the polished veneer of New England life.

To explore this subterranean world of gesture, nuance, or silence, Stoddard developed her unique narrative style, based on the half-spoken, the elliptic, and the enigmatic. Howells, who came to know her well, accurately assessed why her novels did not become more popular. Her tales and novels had in them a foretaste of realism, he noted at the turn of the century, a diet "too strange for the palate of the day . . . But in whatever she did," he continued, "she left the stamp of a talent like no other, and of a personality disdainful of literary environment. In a time when most of us wrote like Tennyson, or Longfellow, or Browning, she never would write like anyone but herself."[99]

In this way, Stoddard was akin to an equally difficult writer, Emily Dickinson. No wonder that when the editor of *The Atlantic Monthly* Thomas Wentworth Higginson sat down to write his wife about his first visit to the Dickinson household in Amherst, Massachusetts, he had a ready analogy. "If you had read Mrs. Stoddard's novels," he observed, "you could understand a house where each member runs his or her own selves [*sic*]."[100] The Parke-Auster family's "individual independence" was what struck Theresa Bond when she visited them. "Apparently no member of it involved another in any pursuit, opinion, or interest."[101] The characters in *The Morgesons* as well as in *Two Men* exhibited this kind of passionate self-absorption, to the consternation and confusion of everyone around them.

Stoddard published her last novel, *Temple House*, with Carleton's in 1867, but despite Howell's praise, it did not do well and essentially ended her career as a novelist. She continued to publish short stories in the nation's better periodicals through the 1880s. Early in that decade Stedman, the writer Julian Hawthorne (Nathaniel Hawthorne's son), and a few others called for the republication of her novels. Finally, in 1888 and 1889, the British firm Cassell and Company reprinted them, with prefaces (Stedman supplied one for *Two Men*). In 1901, the Philadelphia publisher Henry T. Coates & Co. reissued them again.

Even so, before the end of the twentieth century few appreciated the pioneering subjectivity of Stoddard's fiction. In *The Bookman* in 1902, the critic Mary Moss summed up the prevalent opinion, concluding that Stoddard's books "form no link in the chain of literature."[102] Ripley, however, put her uniqueness in a more positive light, a judgment posterity is beginning to echo. He admired that Stoddard "may sometimes suggest the style of a great author, but she takes no one for a model . . . She accepts no authority, trades in the footsteps of no other, follows only her own nature, and is always herself."[103]

THE "TERRIBLE QUESTION"

Emerson's influence on Stoddard was extensive, as her use of the lines from his essay "Experience" in an epigraph to *Two Men* indicates. His emphasis on individual self-knowledge as a source of self-confidence fueled Stoddard's own ambition and that of her characters. To her friend Margaret Sweat she wrote that she liked Emerson because "he is a wonderful spurer [*sic*] on to self-culture."[104]

But not everyone was in thrall to Emerson and the movement with which he was identified. William B. Greene, a young liberal minister influenced by the fiery reformer and former Transcendentalist Orestes Brownson, worried about the egocentrism he saw in Emerson's writing and complained that Emerson's notion that each individual soul "creates all things" might end in the identification of God with man. "The reason of God and the universe are not to be found in man," he wrote in an assessment of Transcendentalism. Anyone who thought that they were is a "sort of human Pantheis[t]."[105]

Similarly, Elizabeth Palmer Peabody, a member of the Boston-Concord intellectual coterie who immersed herself in practical issues of reform, from childhood education to Native American rights, also criticized Emerson's encouragement of what she termed "ego-theism"—that is, his championing of the self-reliant man for whom conscience is the highest law. Emerson's followers "deified their own conceptions" so much that they had no faith in anything larger than themselves. But "Man," she saw, "proves but a melancholy God" in comparison to the divine being whom she still worshipped.[106]

Another individual who found Transcendentalist ideas problematic was the novelist Rebecca Harding Davis. She launched her career in Fields's *Atlantic Monthly* in 1861 and pioneered fiction that, while indebted to the sentimental novel as well as European models, anticipated not only the social realism of Howells and Henry James but also the literary "naturalists" Hamlin Garland and Frank Norris. In Davis's work, in which workingwomen often were central characters, private emotions, usually confined to the domestic sphere and exemplified in Stoddard's depiction of Cassandra Morgeson, collide head-on with the increasingly complex world defined and controlled by impersonal social and economic forces.

In 1862, at the encouragement of Hawthorne and of James and Annie Fields, Davis visited Boston, and long afterward, in her autobiographical fragments, *Bits of Gossip* (1904), described her still-vivid impressions of the intellectuals who hosted her. But Davis reacted against their emphasis on self-culture and credited her experience among them for strengthening her commitment to a literature that, like the novels of Émile Zola she admired, opened windows on worlds too many Transcendentalist fellow travelers left unexamined. Recalling one conversation with Alcott and Emerson at Hawthorne's home, she noted: "You heard much sound philosophy and sublime guesses at the eternal verities," but "the discussion left you with a vague, uneasy sense that something was lacking, some back-bone of fact."[107] She was particularly incensed by what she took as the group's seemingly cavalier way of speaking about the Civil War, the horrific effects of which she already had witnessed firsthand. "They had much to say of it," she remembered, "and all used the same strained high note of exaltation," particularly Alcott, who "chanted paeans to the war."

I had just come up from the border where I had seen the actual war, the filthy spewings of it; the political jobbery in Union and Confederate camps; the malignant personal hatreds wearing patriotic masks, and glutted by burning homes and outraged women; the chances in it for brutish men to grow more brutish, and for honorable men to degenerate into thieves and sots.

The Transcendentalists she encountered, blinded by their idealism, had no sense of "the actual war."[108]

Davis also lamented how Emerson allowed himself to become the object of hero-worship. "There were vast outlying provinces of intelligence where he reigned," she wrote, "as absolutely as does the unseen Grand Llama over his adoring votaries." New England swarmed "with weak-brained, imitative folk" who had studied books with "more or less zeal, and who knew nothing of actual life . . . They had revolted from Puritanism, not to enter any other live church, but to fall into a dull disgust, a nausea with all religion" that they cured by going to Concord. "To them came this new prophet with his discovery of the God within themselves," and they hailed him and his ideas with "acclamation."[109]

While not completely rejecting Transcendentalism—when she met Emerson, her "body literally grew stiff and [her] tongue dry with awe"—Davis found its best expression in such outer-directed members of the group as George Ripley and Theodore Parker. Her intellectual foundation, too, was in German philosophy; she had been tutored in it by her brother Wilse. Like Ripley, whose disenchantment with the organization of labor pushed him to found Brook Farm, and Parker, who fought incessantly for society's disenfranchised—the impoverished, the enslaved, the incarcerated—Davis challenged readers to acknowledge and lessen the suffering of others. If Melville, Stoddard, and others had brought subjectivity into the American novel, she wanted to make sure that selves in the aggregate nevertheless remained the novelist's chief subject.

"THIS VULGAR AMERICAN LIFE"

Davis was born in 1831 in Washington, Pennsylvania, just south of the booming new city of Pittsburgh. Soon after her birth she moved with her parents, Richard W. Harding, a recent emigrant from England, and Rachel Leet Wilson, to Big Springs (now Huntsville), Alabama, an area of large cotton plantations. The family moved again when she was five, to Wheeling, Virginia, a town on the Ohio River and a transportation hub between North and South that became, in 1863, part of a new free state, West

Virginia. In these same years, industry, particularly steel manufacturing, developed in Wheeling. Richard Harding entered several (not very successful) business partnerships and was actively involved in the growing city's civic life.

At fourteen Davis began to attend Washington Female Seminary in the town where she was born and where many members of her mother's family lived. Having graduated as valedictorian, she returned to Wheeling and began to assist her mother with domestic chores. Always an avid reader and an eager student, she soon began to write reviews, poems, and editorials for a local paper. At twenty-nine, she sent a story titled "Life in the Iron Mills" to Fields at *The Atlantic Monthly*. A month later she opened his reply, which included a fifty-dollar check; the story appeared in the April 1861 issue and launched her career.

The Atlantic Monthly's readers were likely unprepared for Davis's grim story of the plight of Hugh Wolfe. An impoverished Irish immigrant and ironworker, Wolfe and his cousin Deb live in a fictitious town based on the Wheeling of thirty years earlier, when owners of the mills were building their fortunes on the backs of immigrant laborers with no concern for their welfare. Years later the novelist Elizabeth Stuart Phelps, by that time better known than Davis, recalled the story's impact. Encountering it "was a distinct crisis at the point where intellect and the moral nature meet." After reading "Life in the Iron Mills," "one could never say again that one did not understand" the difficult lives of the working class.[110]

Addressing her genteel readers in a deliberately ironic style, Davis opened the story with these lines: "I want you to hear this story. There is a secret down here, in this nightmare fog, that has lain dumb for centuries: I want to make it a real thing for you. You, Egoist, Pantheist, or Arminian, busy in making straight paths for your feet in the hills, do not see it clearly,—this terrible question which men here have gone mad and died trying to answer."[111] The story that follows is essentially a description of the physical and psychological toll of working in an iron mill. Davis's is the language of suffering so common to earlier sentimental fiction, but she deployed it to spur her readers to anger and political action, rather than sympathetic tears.

Hugh has a remarkable artistic gift for sculpting human forms from korl, an end product of the smelting process. But unable to rise from his impoverishment, he turns to drinking. Imprisoned after Deb steals money for him from a wealthy visitor to the mill, Hugh dies from consumption he contracted at the mill, and his great gift perishes with him. At the end, the narrator, looking at one of Hugh's remarkable works, says, "Its pale lips seem to tremble with a terrible question. 'Is this the end?' they say, 'nothing beyond?—no more?' "[112] For the next three decades, in a variety of fictions that featured factory workers, freed slaves, immigrants, and others trapped at society's lower rungs, Davis continued to ask such difficult questions.

She did so most powerfully in *Margret Howth: A Story of To-Day*, her first novel, published the same year as *The Morgesons*. It could not have been more different from Stoddard's novel and signaled another crucial turn in American fiction. Rather than end in the hyperindividuality of Pierre Glendenning or Cassandra Morgeson, Davis's characters turn toward social awareness and commitment. In *Margret Howth*, self-consciousness leads to connections to other people across class, racial, and gender lines. Further, Davis eschews the sensationalism of Lippard, Thompson, or even Stowe, for she saw that the evils on which the social and economic systems are built are most often found in quotidian aspects of life—the paltry meal and pint of beer of the ironworker, for example—rather than just in the exceptional and lurid.

Margret Howth began as a short story. After the publication of "Life in the Iron Mills," Fields asked for more contributions. She sent him one titled "A Story of To-Day," a long fiction that he asked her to revise because he found it too "gloomy" for readers already depressed over the course of the war. She went back and forth about how precisely to change things, asking at one point if he had any objection to her characterization of Stephen Holmes, who in her story perverts Emersonian self-reliance into mere self-interest. "Would the character of Holmes be distasteful," Davis writes, "to your readers? I mean—the development of a common vulgar life of the Fichtian [*sic*] philosophy and its effect upon a self made man, as I view it?" She was alluding to the German philosopher Johann Gottlieb Fichte's insistence that the perpetual striving for self-development is the essential truth of human existence, an idea that influenced many Transcendentalists.[113] Still unsure of herself as a writer, Davis acquiesced to his suggestions and made alterations, particularly to the ending of *Margret Howth*, that resulted in a more optimistic book but that to some degree compromised the larger message toward which its earlier pages pushed the reader.

When she finally sent Fields a new version of "A Story of To-Day," he serialized it. Before gathering together its parts to publish as a novel, he toyed with it more, calling it *Margret Howth: A Story of To-Day*, a change he made without consultation. Davis pointedly told him that she did not like the title because Margret "is the completest [*sic*] failure in the story, beside *not* being the nucleus of it." Rather, at its center is Holmes, the consummate subjective idealist.[114] In the novel itself Davis responded to Fields's observation that the story lacked an easily discernible moral. Fiction no longer should be written as it had been a century earlier, the narrator explains, when people had no trouble "in seeing which were sheep and which were goats." By now there was no longer any use for didactic plots and representative characters. "I only mean to say I was never there [that is, alive at an earlier time]." She lived now, "in the commonplace," and had never seen "a full-blooded saint or sinner in [her] life."[115] The reader expects to see "idylls delicately tinted; passion-veined hearts, cut bare for curious eyes; prophetic utterances, concrete and clear," something to lift him from "this crowded, tobacco-stained commonplace." But "I want you to dig into the commonplace," the narrator explains, "this vulgar American life, and see what it is."[116]

Davis set *Margret Howth* in an Indiana factory town in December 1860, with the Civil War on the horizon. On her twentieth birthday the eponymous character has started a job as a bookkeeper in a factory owned by Dr. Knowles, "an old man, overgrown, looking like a huge misshapen mass of flesh," and an idealist who hopes to help the poor by creating a new community based on Charles Fourier's socialist theories. To finance his projected utopian community, he plans to sell the factory to Stephen Holmes, a very different type of idealist, who once was in love with Margret. Holmes threw her over, though, for a rich woman whose fortune will enable him to buy the factory. Margret's family lacks such means. Her father is a schoolteacher who can no longer work because of failing eyesight. One of his few joys is debating philosophy and history with Knowles; old Howth often baits Knowles by presenting himself as a skeptic of social reform.

Industry has brought many changes to the town. "Progress" is transforming the rural landscape; when Margret walks home after her first day on the job, she sees "trade everywhere—on the earth and under it." The river has been diverted to power the mills, the hills have been stripped of wood and grass, and along the road gape "the black mouths of coal pits."[117] Meanwhile, Mr. Howth ridicules Knowles's idealistic plans to base a community on truly democratic principles, given that to which the matters have come. "The world's a failure," he exclaims. "All the great old dreams are dead. Your own phantom, your Republic, your experiment to prove that all men are born free and equal—what is it to-day? . . . You talk of To-Day . . . Here is its type and history," he says, lifting a newspaper. "A fair type, with its cant, and bigotry, and weight of uncomprehended fact." And at the heart of the corrupt system there is only one thing: "Bargain and sale, it taints our religion, our brains, our flags."[118]

Another major character is an African American, Lois Yare, the "crippled" daughter of Joe Yare, who worked in the mill until he was imprisoned for a felony. After Yare serves his time, Knowles gives him another chance and finds that he is "as ready a stoker as any on the furnace-rooms."[119] Lois, who has a "child's face" on an "old and stunted body," sells produce from the countryside in town and is loved for her goodness and buoyant spirit. She has worked in the mill, too, starting when she was only seven and already suffering from rickets, and she remained until she was sixteen, while the disease ravaged her body.[120] She tells Margret that she thinks the factory is the cause of her deformity. "Over the years it seemed to me like I was part o' th' engines somehow," she says. "Th' air used to be thick in my mouth, black wi' smoke 'n' wool 'n' smells." Margret "listened, waked reluctantly to the sense of a different pain in the world from her own,—lower deeps from which women like herself draw delicately back, lifting their gauzy dresses."[121] Because of Margret's capacity for empathy, Knowles has long planned to include her in his work with the poor; but that now seems out of the question, for the pittance that she earns at the factory is all her family has.

As the negotiations between Knowles and Holmes proceed, the townspeople learn of Knowles's utopian vision. They are skeptical of his "Communist fraternity," having heard of the failure of similar schemes. "There's two ways for 'em to end," offers one citizen. "If they're made out of the top of society, they get so refined, so idealized, that every particle flies off on its own special path to the sun [as at Blithedale], and the Community's broke." And "if they're made of the lower mud [as Knowles's will be], they keep going down, down together,—they live to drink and eat, and make themselves as near the brutes as they can."[122] A farmer ridicules the doctor's plans:

He spends his days now hunting out the gallows-birds out of the dens [slumlike neighborhoods] in town here, and they're all to be transported into the country to start a new Arcadia. A few men and women like himself, but the bulk is from the dens, I tell you. All start fair, level ground, perpetual celibacy, mutual trust, honour, rise according to the stuff that's in them,—pah! It makes me sick![123]

Another man offers an explanation for why Knowles ventures such absurdities: "Blood, Sir. His mother was a half-blood Creek."[124] What rationale does Davis provide? Like Melville's Ahab, Knowles is "sick in soul from some pain that I dare not tell you of," for he had "looked into the depths of human loss with a mad desire to set it right."[125]

On the day before the property transfer is to occur, Holmes and Knowles meet in the countryside to look over the contract one final time. They have a philosophical discussion about Lois. The "self" in such people, Knowles offers, is "starved and humbled" but is still able to see God clearly. Holmes, drawing on Fichte, disagrees: the self is "so starved and blind that it cannot recognize itself as God." "So that's your creed!" Knowles replies. "Not Pantheism" but *Ego sum* [I am]." "And this wretched huckster [Lois] carries her deity about her . . . ? How, in God's name, is her life to be set free?" Even though he is wed to socialism, Knowles insists that "there *is* a God higher than we" and that thinking only of himself as he does, Holmes will learn this the hard way: "You'll find the Something above yourself, if it's only to curse Him and die."[126]

Later Holmes thinks about how he has "set apart the coming three or four years of his life to make money in," even though "money, or place, or even power, was nothing to him"; all this work was toward "the development of himself." "To tell the truth," the narrator says, "you will find no fairer exponent than this Stephen Holmes of the great idea of American sociology,—that the object of life is *to grow* . . . All men around him were doing the same—thrusting and jostling and struggling, up, up. It was the American motto, Go ahead" that fathers taught to their children. But Holmes's goal was to "lift this self up into a higher range of being when it had done with the uses of this."[127]

Such a man has no use for compromise, and soon enough a friend, Mr. Cox, asks him to do just that. Joe Yare is back at work but out of desperation has committed a forgery. Cox tells Holmes but asks him to keep it quiet, for if revealed, Joe will be sent back to prison for life. "He's old, and he's tryin'," Cox says, to which Holmes replies, smiling, "We did n't make the law he broke. Justice before mercy."[128] To complicate matters, the same day Holmes sees Margret, to whom he admits that he really does not love Miss Herne, his fiancée, whose father will sign the factory papers with him. "Her money," he explains, "will help me to become what I ought to be." He states, "There is no such thing as love in real life," to Margret, who loves him deeply.[129]

That evening Knowles takes Margret to the poorer area of town, to try to recruit her for his new work. "I want to show you a bit of hell," he tells her. He claims to be the inhabitants' "minister," because the regular clergy are too busy "measuring God's truth by the States-Rights doctrine"—that is, arguing whether southern states have the right to secede.[130] He asks her to consider that the loss of "that mass of selfishness" Holmes is nothing compared with what she will see. "Go back, will you, and drone out your life whimpering over your lost dream, and go to Shakespeare for your tragedy when you want it? Tragedy! Come hear,—let me hear what you call this."[131] He takes her into a room crowded with slatternly and drunken women. "Women as fair and pure as you have come into dens like this,—and never gone away. Does it make your delicate breath faint?" he asks sarcastically. "And you a follower of the meek and lowly Jesus!" In the back of one room he shows her "a heap of half-clothed blacks," on their way to Canada on the Underground Railroad. "Did I call it a bit of hell? It's only a glimpse of the underlife of America,—God help us!—where all men are born free and equal."[132] "Give yourself to these people," he implores her. "God calls you to it. There is none to help them."[133]

Things unravel quickly. Holmes encounters Joe and Lois, and Joe brings up Holmes's knowledge of his recent crime. "Have done with this," Holmes replies. "Whoever breaks law abides by it. It is no affair of mine."[134] He tells Joe that he will see him the next day and that he should not try to escape. That evening, after Holmes returns to the mill to sleep, Joe sets fire to the building, intending to kill Holmes. Lois comes upon the result of her father's act: "a live monster now,—in one swift instant, alive with fire,—quick, greedy fire, leaping like serpents' tongues out of its hundred jaws, hungry sheets of flame maddening and writhing to-wards her, and under a dull and hollow roar that shook the night." [135] Lois saves Holmes from the blaze but is now slowly dying from the burning copperas she inhaled. Still, she visits Holmes every day as he slowly recuperates.

Holmes has encountered circumstances that contest, and best, his self-reliance. As Knowles puts it, trying to forget his disappointment over the loss of his factory, where is "the strength of [Holmes's] self-existent soul now? . . . stopped in its growth by chance, this omnipotent deity,— the chance burning of a mill!"[136] Indeed, Holmes experiences a conversion after the fire. On Christmas Day, when he is released from the hospital, he visits Lois at her home and encounters Joe, who tearfully tells him that he set fire to the factory so that he could remain with his daughter. Holmes, knowing how ill Lois is, washes his hands of the "old scoundrel." "Have I his life in my hands?" he asks Lois rhetorically. "I put it into yours,—so, child."[137] Although he does not yet realize it, someday he will "know the subtile [sic] instincts" that drew him out of his self-reliance "by the hand of the child that loved him to the Love beyond, that was man and died for him, as well as she."[138]

Knowles, having lost his factory before the sale was finalized, plans to move to the poorer section of town to establish a "House of Refuge." Margret consents to work with him for five years. Davis's editor, Fields, heavily influenced the conclusion of the novel. Visiting Margret, Holmes admits, "When you loved me long ago, selfish, erring as I was, you fulfilled the law of your nature," but when "you put that love out of your heart, you make your duty a tawdry sham, and your life a lie." In her anger and disappointment, Margret realizes that "casing herself in her pride, her conscious righteousness, hugging her new-found philanthropy close, [she] had sunk to a depth of niggardly selfishness."[139] In the story's original version, Davis had Holmes killed on the bloody fields at Manassas.[140] Yet Fields prevailed on her to go with a happy ending, and in the published novel Holmes and Margret marry. Even more surprising, given Davis's animus against industry, the Howths' slave Joel discovers oil on their property. Was this meant to be God's reward to Margret for her finally realizing Holmes's love for her? The ending that her editor, Fields, thus urged on Davis mitigates Margret's commitment to the larger good, but the wholesale criticism of the nation's rampant acquisitiveness remains.

Margret Howth is precisely the kind of transitional fiction that one would expect at the onset of the Civil War. Like Cary, Blake, and Stoddard, Davis had not quite relinquished the sentimental mode, but all four authors brought a new and robust skepticism of religion and the market to American fiction a few decades before their male peers moved in similar directions. As women, barred from the clergy and the pursuit of wealth, they were in a perfect position to do so. Their critiques of American life were as trenchant as those of Hawthorne and Melville, but as self-conscious as their fiction often was, they did not succumb to allegory or to gloomy, self-absorbed nihilism. Rather, in showing the obstacles that real women routinely faced, they suggested an alternative to the status quo. And in their critique of selfishness, they offered as alternatives love for family and community, though not necessarily based in religion. In *Margret Howth*, Holmes's move from amoral, destructive hyperindividualism to love exemplifies a comparable shift in the trajectory of the American novel, from a Transcendentalist-infused liberalism ascendant since the 1820s to an ethic of fellow feeling. But as the nation entered the Gilded Age, the question was whether the former had already won.

8 From a Theology of the Feelings to an Ethic of Love

On every Sunday in 1865, three thousand people crammed into the Plymouth Congregational Church in Brooklyn Heights for the weekly service. Visitors had to arrive more than an hour early to have any hope of gallery seating; the floor was reserved for pew-holding members. This middle-class congregation had formed in 1847 to accommodate the many businessmen and their families who found Brooklyn's environment more welcoming than the metropolis across the East River, to which many men traveled to work daily on the Fulton Ferry. In 1847, this church, influenced by the merchants and philanthropists Henry C. Bowen and W. T. Cutter, called as its first minister a young New Englander then preaching in Indianapolis. He accepted a generous offer of fifteen hundred dollars for his first year and received periodic increases until in 1870 he was making an astonishing twenty thousand dollars a year. This clergyman made Plymouth Church the best-known church in the country and became the nation's most famous minister.

As a preacher Henry Ward Beecher, Harriet Beecher Stowe's brother, was an iconoclast.[1] He never dressed the part, eschewing ties and appearing in open-necked shirts that resembled Walt Whitman (whom he knew and admired), dressing like his working-class friends. Beecher's preaching, though, was overwhelming, "like the Falls of Niagara," reported one listener. It was electrifying, animated, extemporaneous, based in his experiences and common sense rather than in book learning, all of which made Beecher the polar opposite of ministers like Nathaniel William Taylor, who spent his career splitting the metaphysical hairs of the New Divinity. Rather than scholasticism and elitism, Beecher was given to dramatic gestures; not for nothing was he termed "the Shakespeare of the pulpit." Once he appeared with the chains that he claimed had held John Brown, rattling and slamming them to the floor to make his case for abolition. On another occasion, he brought to his service an enslaved child whom he "sold" to the congregation—that is, the congregation purchased her freedom.

An aesthete who patronized classical music and art, Beecher kept jewels in his pocket and stuffed hummingbirds in his study for inspiration. Although not handsome, with his large frame and thick lips he radiated a sensuality that women parishioners found irresistible. Master of the straight-faced joke, he wanted to (and often did) please everyone, taking as much time with neighborhood children or visitors who crossed the river on the so-called Beecher boats to hear his sermons as with his pew-renting congregants. Nor did his considerable gifts benefit only Plymouth Church. For several decades, Beecher was a regular on the lyceum circuit and a frequent columnist for papers like Robert Bonner's *New York Ledger* and Bowen's *Independent*. At the height of his career in the 1860s, Beecher's income from lecturing and writing added fifteen thousand dollars per year to his clerical salary. Never quite eclipsing his sister Harriet's fame, he still was an extraordinary individual, a veritable force of nature for religious and social reform.

Born, like Harriet, in Litchfield, Connecticut, Beecher was not an overly promising student and so was sent first to Mount Pleasant Academy in Amherst, Massachusetts, and then to Amherst College rather than to Yale, where his brothers matriculated. Lyman Beecher, his own generation's best-known clergyman, thought that Henry might do better at the smaller, less competitive but still religiously conservative school. He was correct, for while there, although undistinguished as a scholar, Henry flourished, particularly after he discovered his oratorical gifts in debating and acting. After graduation he accompanied his parents and a number of his siblings (including Harriet) to Cincinnati, where Lyman had become president of the new Lane Theological Seminary. He decided to follow in his parent's footsteps as a minister; his father and Harriet's husband, Calvin Stowe, ordained the young man. Beecher's first pastorate was in Lawrenceburgh, Indiana, but he soon moved to a larger church in Indianapolis, where he stayed for eight years. W. T. Cutter, a Brooklyn businessman there on business, heard him preach and came away very much impressed.

Around the same time as Cutter's visit in 1846, Beecher broke from

Calvinism and moved toward what Edwards Amasa Park called a theology of the feelings, which historians later termed evangelical liberalism.[2] Beecher's timing was propitious, for his new religion, based, as it was, in an affective response to Scripture, was precisely what Americans were looking for. Like his sisters Harriet and Catharine, he dismissed calls for religious revival, believing that rather than instantaneous, miraculous conversion, people needed something akin to what Horace Bushnell, in a book by the title, called Christian nurture.

After arriving at Plymouth Church, Beecher's writing began to appear in Bonner's *New York Ledger*. Beecher collected and issued his columns in such popular books as *Star Papers; or, Experiences of Art and Nature* (1856) and *Eyes and Ears* (1862). In the spring of 1865 Bonner, the *New York Ledger*'s savvy editor, decided to take a chance similar to the one he had taken with Fanny Fern: he offered Beecher twenty-four thousand dollars to write a serial novel, for later publication as a book. In need of cash to support his conspicuous consumption, which included the purchase of a summer home outside the city, Beecher accepted. The first installment of the work appeared in May 1867, and later that year Bonner issued the whole book. He also contributed his usual advertising blitz, whipping up so much excitement that one enterprising dramatist, Augustin Daly, brought the novel to the stage before it even hit stores.[3]

The novel's title, *Norwood; or, Village Life in New England*, does not serve it well, for it is not a conventional reminiscence. "I propose to make a story," he told Bonner, "which shall turn not so much on outward action" as "on certain mental or inward questions."[4] Surprisingly for a first-time novelist, Beecher produced precisely that: a full-blown philosophical novel that became a bestseller.

He set the novel in a small New England town much like Litchfield or Lenox, Massachusetts, where in the mid-1850s he had purchased Blossom Farm, the summer home where he and his family escaped the city's heat. Structurally, the book is uncomplicated, for as Beecher promised, the clash of ideas constitutes the drama. *Norwood* begins with the genealogy of several families—the Cathcarts, the Wentworths, the Buells, and the Davises. The story proper centers on the young college graduate Basil Cathcart, the son of hardworking middle-class farmers, who has had his faith shaken and tries to regain it. As it was beginning to do to so many other Christians, his exposure to the evolutionary science presented in Charles Darwin's *Origin of Species* (1859) initiates a crisis of faith.

Cathcart courts Rose, the daughter of Reuben Wentworth, the town's Boston-born, Harvard-educated, European-trained doctor. Despite Rose's pedigree, however, she resembles a sophisticated version of Sylvester Judd's Margaret, her spiritual life originating in her relation to the natural world and extending to Christ's gospel of love. Basil knows that he must regain confidence in his faith before he can hope to win the pious Rose, who is also being courted by two others: Frank Esel, a spoiled, spendthrift artist, and Tom Haywood, a southerner. Before the story's end all three suitors will be caught up in the Civil War.

Beecher drives his narrative through theological and philosophical discussion. Dr. Wentworth debates with Judge Bacon, the town's skeptical rationalist, and Parson Buell, a Yale-educated clergyman whose beliefs bear a strong likeness to Beecher's. At a crucial point, the young Cathcart experiences a moment of spiritual transcendence in the natural world and visits Dr. Wentworth to discuss its implications for his Christian faith. Wentworth delivers Cathcart to the doorstep of the evangelical liberalism that was becoming a major force in American Protestantism.

The debates have their drama and irony. For all his intelligence, for example, Judge Bacon, a hardened cynic, offers little beyond an emotionless, scientific understanding of the world. He has no use for religion because it is scientifically unverifiable. As Wentworth puts it, the judge has "no *ideality*."[5] Likewise Parson Buell offers Cathcart little comfort, for he has been trained in the logic chopping that characterized Yale under the influence first of Lyman Beecher's colleague Timothy Dwight and later of Nathaniel William Taylor and his phalanx of New Divinity men. Buell's knowledge of Scripture, deep as it flows, has never truly warmed his heart. He apprehends the distant logic of the gospel plan and each soul's part in it—a theology of the intellect—but he is a stranger to the theology of the feelings.

In short, both Bacon and Buell, different as they seem, are united by their belief in the supremacy of logic. As Dr. Wentworth puts it, addressing Buell, each of you "may differ in regard to facts and convictions," yet both of you "insist upon reducing all truth to some material equivalent before you are subject to conviction." To Bacon and Buell, "a truth that does not admit of a logical statement" seems a fantasy. "You believe not upon any evidence in your spirit," Wentworth continues, "but upon the semi-material form which language and philosophical statements give to thought." "Imagination," the doctor declares to the doubting Bacon, "is the very marrow of faith."[6] "Man does not live in a book." Rather, his savior is "in Nature, in human life, in my own experiences as well as in the recorded fragments of His history."[7]

Dr. Wentworth lifts Cathcart's gloom by counseling a faith based in experience and imagination, one that essentially combines Emerson's *Nature* (1836) with the metaphoric understanding of the Gospels that Bushnell championed in *God in Christ* (1849). Thus, Wentworth begins to ground his religious belief in his experience of nature, which he believes mirrors the spiritual world. In a crucial passage, he asks Buell to look at some beautiful hollyhocks as light falls on them. "They are transfigured!" he exclaims, for "the light seems to palpitate upon them, and on the crimson blossom it fairly trembles! Is that materialism? Is there no moral ground in them?" He thinks of the questions as rhetorical, but Buell thinks them heretical. "You don't mean," Buell says, "that a hollyhock is a moral and accountable being?" Wentworth does. "Does it not send sheets of light to my eyes?"

> Does not that raise up a thousand fancies and yearnings? Do I not, in its exquisite effects, almost see through matter and onto the other life? And is not that clump [of flowers], with its atmosphere of light, the instrument producing such effects? And when God created light and flowers, did he not know what power it was possible that they could exert upon human souls, and design that they should do it?

"They have a moral function," he concludes, "even if they have no moral nature."[8]

In his account of Cathcart's struggle with doubt, Beecher also invokes Emerson's notion that one needs to leave behind the past in order to move forward with self-reliance. As Emerson puts it, "Why should not we also enjoy an original relation to the universe? Why should not we have a poetry and philosophy of insight and not of tradition, and a religion by revelation to us, and not the history of theirs?"[9] The echoes in *Norwood* are direct. For Cathcart, that past is most present in his inherited religion, the religion of Buell that no longer makes sense to the young graduate. Like Wentworth, he feels a spiritual attachment to nature. Cathcart responds to the natural world with both his understanding (the logical, ratiocinative faculty) and his reason (the spiritual, intuitive faculty). As he progresses in his studies, Cathcart's "[r]eason was asserting its sovereignty." "Should he believe," he wonders, "because his parents and teachers did? . . . Was a man to be superscribed by his parents, like a letter, and sent to this or that church?"[10]

Soon enough he realizes that God is in the universe around him, not in Scripture or the church; this makes him a stronger Christian, not a skeptical deist. For Beecher, a direct, experiential relation with God no longer meant, as it had when he began preaching, that the deity had broken through the natural order of things. Rather, grace meant awareness of or insight into the world in all its beauty and led one instinctively to right moral action. Rose, whom Wentworth has raised to understand nature's grammar and poetry, is the lovely fruit of his beliefs.

Thus, the inconsistencies in the Bible pointed out by the higher critics do not affect the larger truth it contains, what the Transcendentalist minister Theodore Parker terms the difference between the "transient" and the "permanent" in Christianity.[11] The Bible is not composed of logical arguments on points of doctrine but of imaginative language that has to be interpreted symbolically, as Bushnell argues in his "Preliminary Dissertation on Language" preface to *God in Christ*. So Wentworth patiently tells Buell that "[t]he Bible cannot contain the truth itself, only the *word-forms*, the lettered symbols" of divine truth. Words themselves have no signification, he explains. They "mean whatever they have the power to make us think of when we look on them," a function, that is, of experience and imagination.[12]

Beecher also brought to judgment another pillar of his father's religion, belief in a wrathful God. American Protestants had gradually been moving toward a God of love. As adumbrated in *Christian Nurture* (1847), *God in Christ*, and *The Vicarious Sacrifice* (1866), Bushnell's theology tended in this direction, as did Edwards Amasa Park's notion (borrowed from Friedrich Schleiermacher) of religion as an affectionate response to the world's beauty. In *Norwood*, Beecher explores love's many incarnations, including man's love for woman, a mother's love for her family, and God's love for mankind. "That mystic Law with which God has bound to himself his infinite realm," Beecher calls it, "the law of Love!"[13]

Cathcart comes to understand the law of love at his moment of conversion, which here derives from Wentworth's counsel on how to understand and appreciate the natural world. Cathcart recalls falling "into one of those balanced states of mind" that eventuate in a remarkable "calm." Hearing a robin call for its mate, Cathcart says, "a call of loneliness for company, of love *for* love . . . I almost ceased to be conscious of my body . . . I did not *think*. It was *seeing*[,] rather," that the heavens were full of "ineffable gentleness," an echo of Emerson's famous characterization of himself as a "transparent eyeball" who could see "all" when he experienced transcendence. For the first time in his life, Cathcart had "a conception of *infinite* love."[14]

The beauty of Beecher's faith—like that of Judd in his utopian Mons Christi—was that it did not require overturning society in order to renovate it. People could go about their business just as they always had, as long as they expressed their affection for everyone else in their world, from ragamuffins at their doors in Brooklyn Heights to shackled slaves on a Carolina plantation. Ever the reformer, Beecher wanted Americans to embrace this ethic to knit together a torn nation. His faith-based love would end the hatred between North and South; lessen the isolation of men locked in faceless economic combat; combat the natural selfishness of people living in a liberal society; mitigate the feelings of helplessness that resulted from scientific inquiry; and promise the reform of corrupt politics. Love was what a shell-shocked country needed, and Beecher became wealthy and famous proclaiming it.

And shell-shocked it was, which explains Beecher's inclusion of the war in his narrative. Although in the preface to *Norwood* he claimed to have never studied "the mystery of [fiction's] construction"—"plot and counterplot, the due proportion of parts, the whole machinery of a novel"—he holds the reader's attention by showing how none of the chief characters could escape the national conflagration. The Virginian Haywood, a supporter of the southern right to nullification, is present at South Carolina's attack on Fort Sumter and killed on the fields of Gettysburg. Cathcart, having quickly risen to a position of command in the Union army, is severely wounded in the same battle, captured by the Confederates, but eventually reunited with Rose, who received word that he had died. Rose and Cathcart's sister Alice, who loves Haywood and sees his body amid the carnage at Gettysburg, serve as nurses at the front. Even Dr. Wentworth is pulled into the fray, serving as a surgeon for the Union.

A combination of current events and national soul-searching over a suitable faith for the postwar nation, *Norwood* was very popular, even though the reviews were mixed. In *The Atlantic Monthly* Howells wrote that he abhorred "the ruthlessness with which the author preaches."[15]

Orestes Brownson, by now immersed wholly in the Church of Rome, aimed his barbs at what he took as Beecher's dilution of Christianity. Not accepting that Wentworth's understanding of nature leads back to Christ, "Beecherism," he huffed, only reduces "the Christian law of perfection into the natural law of the physicists . . . The persons and personages of his book are only so many points in the arguments which he is carrying on against Calvinistic orthodoxy for pure naturalism."[16] With a new century's perspective, though, the historian of American religion William McLoughlin draws an accurate bead on the novel. *Norwood*, he argues, is the "first fully developed statement of Liberal Protestantism to appear in book form," a "long-neglected key to a significant transition in the American religious mind."[17]

AMATIVENESS RUN AMOK

By 1870 word had spread that Beecher was applying his ethic of love a little too indiscriminately, in ways that could embarrass his ministry and perhaps even end it. People began to notice that he and his parishioner Elizabeth Tilton were spending a lot of time together, particularly during the months he was writing *Norwood*, for which, his most recent biographer claims, she served as something of muse.[18] Elizabeth was the wife of Theodore Tilton, before the Civil War Bowen's right-hand man at the *Independent*. During Reconstruction he became its editor as well as a major player in reformist politics, particularly as an advocate of women's rights.

Bowen had heard rumors of Beecher's infidelity, and not only with Mrs. Tilton. For his part, Tilton had long suspected an affair, but Elizabeth usually was able to explain away his accusations, even when evidence of the liaison seemed quite convincing; moreover, he admired Beecher and spent much time with him, even transcribing his lecture notes for publication as the "Star" columns for the *New York Ledger*. Eventually, worn down by innuendo and guilt, Elizabeth confessed, telling her husband that her minister had convinced her that "their love was proper and not wrong, therefore it followed that any expression of that love, whether by the shake of a hand or the kiss of the lips, or even bodily intercourse" was not only perfectly understandable but right.

Tilton tried to forgive her and control his outrage, but paranoia ensued. He accused Elizabeth of seeing other men, began to believe that one of their four children was not his, and spread ugly rumors about her infidelity to family and friends. At Bowen's urging, he demanded the minister's resignation. After much hand-wringing, Beecher convinced Tilton to keep the mess quiet; but after he became embroiled with the notorious free love advocate Victoria Woodhull, and she (without his permission) broke the story in her *Woodhull & Claflin's Weekly* at the same time that Beecher was celebrating his twenty-fifth anniversary at the Plymouth congregation, all hell broke loose.

Accusations flew in public. After a church committee, before which Beecher had confessed errors in judgment but not outright seduction, found insufficient reason to dismiss him, Tilton sued Beecher in civil court, for "criminal conversation." The trial was a media circus, with newspapers from all over the country sending correspondents to file daily reports; the proceedings occupied the nation for six months. But the jury deadlocked (with a sizable majority supporting Beecher), and the unfortunate result of Beecher's broad interpretation of Christian love was Elizabeth Tilton's excommunication from the Plymouth Church, for slandering her pastor, even as Beecher was exonerated.

One fact about Beecher may help explain, though not excuse, his behavior. Since college he had been a strong believer in and advocate of the "science" of phrenology, which posited that an individual's character could be determined by analyzing the bumps and indentations of his or her head.[19] Particularly before the Civil War, phrenology fitted with America's optative mood, for the accurate identification of one's traits and propensities might serve as a starting point on the path to personal betterment. Once the patient understood his traits, he could cultivate and improve those that were positive and rein in any with potentially negative consequences, thereby achieving harmony. Phrenology thus jibed with the age's belief in individual free will and in nurture over nature.

The traits a phrenologist examined included ideality, ambition, sociability, modesty, anger, and firmness, as well as "amativeness" and "adhesiveness." Amativeness is sexual feeling between men and women; adhesiveness is more akin to deep friendship and can occur with someone of the same sex. Beecher thus could rationalize and excuse his indiscretions with Elizabeth Tilton as owing to his "enlarged" propensity toward amativeness. He embraced phrenology because he believed it helped him understand himself, particularly his habits and obsessions, as well as his passions. Although he does not mention phrenology directly in *Norwood*, he viewed it as another of those sharp "knives" that one could use to dissect self-consciousness and thus a way to learn about the unexplored corners of the mind that had been a focus of American fiction since Charles Brockden Brown's *Wieland*.

THE SNAKE-WOMAN'S STORY

But phrenology was not everyone's tool of choice for exploring the mind. Oliver Wendell Holmes, Sr., progenitor of the "genteel tradition" and responsible for terming Boston "the hub of the universe," was a medical doctor who dismissed phrenology as balderdash. He had different notions of motivation and explored them in *Elsie Venner: A Romance of Destiny* (1861).

In particular, he understood that the triumph of Darwin's principles of evolution and natural selection could not help but affect an individual's understanding of good citizenship, for in Darwin's amoral world, a person's obligations to his fellow men and women came into question. This was particularly true for those who adopted the sociologist Herbert Spencer's notion of the survival of the fittest to describe competition between individuals for limited resources. Social Darwinism, as this was sometimes erroneously termed, thus became the perfect faith for those who espoused the laissez-faire capitalism that exploded in the post–Civil War years, affecting all aspects of American life.[20]

In *Elsie Venner*, Bernard Langdon, a young medical student turned schoolmaster, is caught between science and religion. He encounters an odd, aloof, yet magnetically attractive seventeen-year-old student, Elsie Venner, the only child of the wealthy Dudley Venner. From her youngest years, she has been happiest in nature, often wandering off to roam through fields and woods, returning with "a nest, a flower, or even a more questionable trophy of her ramble."[21] Elsie's moods change with the weather and the seasons. She luxuriates in the noonday July heat, when she is at her most attractive but also quick to anger, and she becomes torpid and withdrawn in the depths of winter. Strange and private as she is, this young woman becomes interested in Langdon, signaling her attention through disconcerting stares and then surreptitiously placing in one of his books a rare flower from the crags on The Mountain, where she has a retreat. Fascinated by her, Langdon decides to find her remote playground in the mountains but gets into trouble. Entering a cave where he hopes to find her, he instead encounters a huge rattlesnake, about to strike. Luckily, Elsie arrives and stares into the snake's eyes, which surprisingly "shrunk [*sic*] and faded under the stronger enchantment of her own."[22] The deadly reptile slithers away.

After this terrifying experience, Langdon interrogates the town physician, Dr. Kittredge, about Elsie's seeming power over the wild creature. Kittredge hems and haws and finally cryptically explains that only love can save Elsie from her destructive urges. At the same time, when he hears that Elsie seems drawn to Langdon, Kittredge warns him away from her. Undeterred, Langdon seeks to learn about her past from her nurse, Old Sophy, an African American whose mother was a slave in the family and who has been with the young woman since her birth. He learns that, much like another insufficiently socialized woman, Isabel Banford in *Pierre*, Elsie has difficulty putting her thoughts into words. One day, however, she tells Sophy the reason for her despair. "Nobody loves me. I cannot love anybody. What is love, Sophy?" she asks her plaintively.[23]

Elsie's infatuation with Langdon persists, and in a crucial moment, she asks him to love her. When he tells her that he loves Ellen Darley, his fellow instructor at the academy, and can treat Elsie only as a friend, her health begins to decline. While ministering to her, Ellen learns her secret from Old Sophy. When Elsie's mother was pregnant, a rattlesnake bit her, and she perished a month later from complications from the wound. Strangely Elsie was born with a birthmark in the same spot where her mother was bitten, which she always covers with a golden necklace. Old Sophy believes, as does Dudley Venner, that the snake's venom transferred the creature's traits to the baby, accounting for her alternating moods, seemingly controlled by the warmth or cold of the seasons.

As Elsie languishes, surrounded by her father, Old Sophy, and Ellen, her nature becomes gentler, her visage more like her mother's than ever seemed possible. Before she dies, she tells her father that she loves him, and later, when Sophy prepares the body for burial, she sees that the birthmark has disappeared. Could Langdon have "saved" her with his love? If he was so attracted to her beauty and vitality, why did he eventually choose another, safer love, Miss Letty, Wentworth's granddaughter?

Holmes, like Beecher in *Norwood*, has a range of New England characters discuss philosophical and theological matters, in this case, the mysterious girl's implications for traditional belief. The debaters include Langdon; the conservative minister Reverend Pierrepont Honeywood; the liberal minister Reverend Chauncy Fairweather; the village physician Kittredge, who has been studying Elsie since her birth; and Langdon's medical school professor.

After his experience in the cave, the young man asks this last: "Do you think there may be predispositions, inherited or ingrafted, but at any rate constitutional, which shall take out certain apparently voluntary determinations from the control of the will, and leave them as free from moral responsibility as the instincts of the lower animals?" More simply: "Do you not think there may be a crime which is not a sin?"[24] Such questions, his mentor replies, "belong to that middle region between science and poetry"—as Hawthorne might say, a region where the "Actual" and the "Imaginary" meet and influence each other.[25]

The professor states his belief that no one, except the phrenologists, has ever properly studied the thorny question of the will, "the limits of human responsibility." Although overall a pseudoscience, phrenology had the virtue of having "melted the world's conscience in its crucible, and cast it in a new mould" by its proof that "there are fixed relations between organization and mind and character."[26] That said, in his judgment, "nine tenths" of people's "perversity" still derived from the environment in which they had been raised or still live—"outside influences, drunken ancestors, abuse in childhood, [and] bad company."[27] Nurture, in other words, trumped nature, the same lesson Beecher wished to teach.

Like his predecessors, Holmes was trying to ascertain the relationship between fate, free will, and the wages of sin. In his preface he wrote that through the "disguise of fiction," he wished to present for consideration "a grave scientific doctrine"—the possible inheritance of traits that mark one as evil—without pledging absolute belief in it. He had adopted the notion "as a convenient medium of truth rather than as an accepted scientific conclusion" and wanted readers to consider it, too, particularly as it affected their notions of free will and culpability.[28] The critical difference between Holmes and his predecessors and a sign of how far the American novel—and American culture generally—had come was that he answered such inquiries through science rather than Scripture.

To discover more about Elsie's condition, Langdon writes his medical school professor, who cites various authorities going back to Aetius and Paulus (on the cognate subject of lycanthropy—that is, men acting as wolves), the seventeenth-century savant Sir Kenelm Digby, the homoeopathist Dr. Hering of Surinam, the orientalist Claude-Étienne Savary in his *Letters on Egypt*, and even John Keats's *Lamia*.[29] Theological explanations—most obviously, the inheritance of sin from Adam—hover in the background, while Langdon puts most trust in experimentation and observation, going so far as to observe rattlesnakes in captivity for clues to the girl's condition.[30] Holmes's world is Charles Darwin's, and he, unlike many orthodox clergymen, was not afraid of what he might find.

"LIFE IS MORAL RESPONSIBILITY"

In her autobiography, published late in life, Elizabeth Stuart Phelps (1844–1911) defended her belief that fiction of any merit ought to have an ethical purpose. "Fear less to seem 'Puritan' than to be inadequate. Fear more to be superficial than to seem 'deep,'" for where "'the taste' is developed at the expense of 'the conscience,' the artist is incomplete." In a word, she continued, "the province of the artist is to portray life as it is; and life is moral responsibility."[31] No wonder that her idol was Harriet Beecher Stowe and that she claimed help from angels in writing her runaway bestseller *The Gates Ajar* (1868). As she saw it, the United States was engaged in a great moral struggle, and she would not shirk her part in it.

Phelps was born to the clerical purple. Her maternal grandfather was none other than Moses Stuart (1780–1852), the redoubtable professor of sacred literature at Andover Theological Seminary, bastion of Calvinist orthodoxy, where he taught for more than forty years and she spent much of her girlhood. He died when his granddaughter was only eight, but she felt his influence for years. Her mother, Elizabeth Stuart's oldest daughter and a writer in her own right, married Austin Phelps, a Congregational minister and son of the Reverend Eliakim Phelps, who in addition to pastoral duties devoted much time to the movement for Sunday schools and later served as secretary of the American Education Society, which trained pious men for the ministry. Austin, too, proved an important scholar and eventually became the professor of sacred rhetoric and homiletics at Andover. Before that, he worked at Boston's Pine Street Church, where the family's first daughter, Mary Gray (later renamed Elizabeth Stuart in honor of her mother) lived for the first six years of her life.

Phelps did not reject her orthodox Protestant upbringing as forcefully as the Beecher children did, even though she was exposed to English Romantics as well as to German philosophers and theologians whose works gave fits to the Andover faculty. She did gravitate toward a more liberal faith but never gave up her belief in the historical Jesus. Like the liberal Unitarians whom Andover was founded to combat, she believed that each individual was a personification of the divine and that each life was a voyage of self-development and fulfillment. This was especially so for women, who for too long had been prevented from pursuing intellectual and spiritual growth. She devoted her novels like *Hedged In* (1870), *The Silent Partner* (1871), and *The Story of Avis* (1877), as well as much in her voluminous short fiction, to this premise, even as she understood that a woman's place in society was inextricably linked to economics.[32]

A true polymath, and convinced of the existence of a spirit world by personal experiences with hypnotism, séances, and the like, Phelps was enamored with spiritualism. In 1889, she addressed the subject of paranormal experience in an essay titled "The Psychical Opportunity." Praising the newly formed Society of Psychical Research in London, which aimed to investigate "mesmeric, psychical, and spiritualistic" phenomena, Phelps welcomed the scientific community's interest in that "which is hidden, not in desert islands, or in cuneiform inscriptions, but in human experience."[33] Scientists needed to address the question of such spiritual manifestations with the same seriousness with which they investigated geology or evolution, to establish "the scientific basis of thought and action."[34] Beginning to map the physical attributes of the brain, they now had to explore the nature of consciousness itself. "The Darwin of the science of soul," she wrote, "is yet to be."[35]

One of the seminal early explorers was William James, whose *The Principles of Psychology* (1890) almost single-handedly invented the science for which Phelps called. Indeed, James brought a novelist's feel for language and experience to his *The Varieties of Religious Experience* (1902). In a sense, James, who coined the term "stream of thought" or "consciousness," bridged fiction and science, and not only because of his supple prose style. Starting in the 1850s, American novelists had begun to depict rich and distinctive human personalities. James did the same in his own writing, but his subjects (including, famously, himself) were actual people. If science followed fiction in taking up the study of interiority, it never took it over. Within two decades, modernist novelists—James Joyce, Virginia Woolf, and Marcel Proust among the Europeans, Henry James, Gertrude Stein, and William Faulkner among the Americans—began to embody consciousness in an array of new and startling ways.

Phelps's work represented another significant strain of postbellum fiction, though, for Darwin was not the only giant stalking the intellectual and cultural landscape of the late nineteenth century. He shared the stage with the French scientist and philosopher Auguste Comte, who in his writings on positivism developed a systematic and predictive science of society, focusing on groups rather than on the individual. His influence on nineteenth-century thinkers like Karl Marx, John Stuart Mill, and Herbert Spencer was immense. Like Comte, Phelps and her contemporary Rebecca Harding Davis saw where the West's culture of individualism and self-reliance led. Instead of focusing on the idiosyncrasies of individuals, they took a broader view of human life and saw mostly trouble—specifically, a sickness of the soul resulting from the conditions of modern life. The remedy lay where it had at least since the 1790s, in brotherhood and selfless commitment to the commonwealth that in ways both explicit and subtle had informed the development of the American novel.

CODA

From the late eighteenth century through 1870 many American novelists made a conversation about the nation's values the subject of their work. This conversation began and ended in religious sensibility, specifically with the implications in a new century (and then after the Civil War) of the still-influential synthesis of Jonathan Edwards's theology. The question of the nature of true virtue that Edwards had explored so brilliantly in the mid-eighteenth century took on new meaning, for the democratic ideals that the colonial patriots unleashed could not help but affect moral behavior as well as religious belief, as the nation became defined more and more by an individualistic ethos and a rapidly expanding market economy. The cultural synthesis that emerged in the early nineteenth century included a belief that good citizenship entailed sympathetic identification with those in need, be they orphans, the working poor, chattel slaves, or women economically, legally, and psychologically enchained in a patriarchy from which there seemed little hope of escape.

The country's deification of individualism led to significant shifts in theological reasoning as well as in civic behavior, the result most visible in a virtually wholesale acceptance of personal agency as well as in the momentous shift from a theology of intellect to one of feeling. Methodist itinerants, Presbyterian revivalists, Freewill Baptist proselytizers—these and others embraced free will and a religion of the heart, with emotion the centerpiece of faith. Their emphasis on self-development—and its corollary, self-control toward that end—received an added boost from the selective adoption of European Romantic thought by influential intellectual groups like the New England Transcendentalists, who championed the notion of self-reliant individuals who believed, as Emerson counseled, that they could build their own worlds.

Some, however, novelists and readers both, began to question these forces of political and cultural liberalism, realizing how they frequently led to callousness about the fate of others and thus to an unhealthy division between individual well-being and the good of society as a whole. Many American novelists creatively addressed this growing bifurcation, first evident in the merger of Protestant evangelicalism with a culture of sentiment. They pointed out the sin of egotism and the self-serving nature of the self-regulation counseled by religious groups like the Methodists and others. In doing so, these writers also addressed the nation's failures of sympathetic identification: its seemingly blind eye to the persistence of slavery and racism, the denial of equal rights to women, exploitation of the laboring classes, the hypocrisy and tribalism of religion.

Crucially, some writers also offered alternative visions of the good society. Dissecting individual character and motivation and often placing them in religious or philosophical frameworks, through their novels they contributed to a particular dialectic that subsequently marked American culture and, more specifically, the response to what came to be called modernism. This dialectic led not only to William James's "stream of thought" and his philosophical pragmatism but also to Walter Rauschenberg's and Washington Gladden's Social Gospel; to John Dewey's concern with society's influence on the development of personality; to Jacob Riis's and Lincoln Steffens's "muckraking" investigations of the country's labor and financial institutions; and to Jane Addams's redemptive work at Hull-House.

American novelists in the first half of the nineteenth century, many of them still little known, produced remarkable, and remarkably complex, fiction. But the harsh truth is that even after the cataclysm of the Civil War, the United States remained unique among countries in a schizophrenic emphasis on the individual and his feelings as well as on the commonwealth and one's obligation to it. That Americans still debate precisely the relation of the individual to society does not imply that these writers failed to frame the debate properly or to argue their positions cogently, but that despite their searching criticism and moral correctives, the nation continues to believe in the virtue of democratic liberalism, even in view of its often destructive results.

Yet the ghost of Jonathan Edwards and his conception of the nature of true virtue will not be put to rest. Making the mind aware of itself is not enough; it must become aware of and concerned with others. Trying to encourage such awareness and concern was the burden of American fiction in its first century. It remains ours.

Notes

Acknowledgments

Index

Notes

PREFACE

1. This crucial period has been the subject of recent synthetic histories. See Charles Sellers, *The Market Revolution: Jacksonian America, 1815–1846* (New York: Oxford University Press, 1991); Sean Wilentz, *The Rise of American Democracy: Jefferson to Lincoln* (New York: W. W. Norton, 2005); Daniel Walker Howe, *What Hath God Wrought: The Transformation of America, 1815–1848* (New York: Oxford University Press, 2007); and David Reynolds, *Waking Giant: America in the Age of Jackson* (New York: HarperCollins, 2008). In addition, this period saw a flowering of American literature, particularly of the novel, in which these momentous changes were treated as constitutive of a new kind of democratic selfhood. In the first half of the twentieth century, some scholars sought to assess the period's impact on and in American literature as well as on evolving American democracy. Lewis Mumford's *The Golden Day: A Study in American Experience and Culture* (New York: Boni and Liveright, 1926), Vernon Louis Parrington's *Main Currents in American Thought: An Interpretation in American Literature from the Beginnings to 1920*, 3 vols. (New York: Harcourt Brace, 1927–1930), and F. O. Matthiessen's *American Renaissance: Art and Expression in the Age of Melville and Whitman* (New York: Oxford University Press, 1941) immediately come to mind. Matthiessen's work is very selective. A broad study of American fiction on the scale of the recent work is Alexander Cowie, *The Rise of the American Novel* (New York: American Book Company, 1948), and one even more influential, Richard Chase's *The American Novel and Its Tradition* (Garden City, NY: Doubleday, 1957). Emerson's quotation is from his "Historic Notes of Life and Letters in New England," *Works of Ralph Waldo Emerson*, 14 vols. (Boston: Houghton, Mifflin and Company, 1883), 10:308.

2. I take this movement from Richard Rabinowitz's seminal *The Spiritual Self in Everyday Life: The Transformation of Religious Experience in Nineteenth-Century New England* (Boston: Northeastern University Press, 1989). Rabinowitz restricts his study to the praxis of religious experience but suggests that such shifts in consciousness indelibly stamped the antebellum years. "More than the ink and paper" that American writers used, he says, "[more than] the publishers and audiences they needed, or even the sources of their stories they told," writers drew on "the common language of religious life among their contemporaries" (30).

3. *Graham's Magazine* 44 (April 1854), 452.

4. *Putnam's Monthly Magazine* 3 (October 1854), 396.

5. Hugh Frank Foster, *The Life of Edwards Amasa Park* (New York: Fleming H. Revell Co., 1911); Anthony C. Cecil, Jr., *The Theological Development of Edwards Amasa Park: Last of the "Consistent Calvinists"* (Missoula, MT: American Academy of Religion and Scholars' Press, Dissertation Series no. 1, 1974); and Joseph Conforti, "The Creation and Collapse of the New England Theology: Edwards A. Park and Andover Seminary, 1840–1881," in *Jonathan Edwards, Religious Tradition, and American Culture* (Chapel Hill: University of North Carolina Press, 1995), 108–44.

6. See Philip F. Gura, *American Transcendentalism: A History* (New York: Hill and Wang, 2007), 101–16.

7. Schleiermacher particularly influenced John Weiss, one of Theodore Parker's acolytes; see Gura, *American Transcendentalism*, 277–80. As early as the 1820s, Park's colleague Moses Stuart, Professor of Sacred Literature, introduced his students to the new "higher criticism" of Scripture. He used it to defend conservative Trinitarian views, but some students found his conclusions inconsistent and their faith shaken.

8. Edwards Amasa Park, *The Theology of the Intellect and That of the Feelings* (Boston: Perkins and Whipple, 1850), 8.

9. Edwards's words, in one historian's assessment, gave nothing less than "a new and powerful pulse, which continued to be felt for almost a century"—one powered, however, in good measure by an understanding not just of logic but also of the affective nature of doctrine. See Joseph Haroutunian, *Piety Versus Moralism: The Passing of the New England Theology* (New York: H. Holt and Co., 1932), xxii.

10. See Conforti, *Jonathan Edwards, Religious Tradition, and American Culture*, 62–86.

11. Herman Melville, *Pierre; or, The Ambiguities* ([1852] Evanston, IL: Northwestern University Press, 1971), 212.

12. Harriet Beecher Stowe, *The Minister's Wooing*, in *Three Novels* (New York: Library of America, 1991), 728.

13. Henry Ward Beecher, *Norwood; or, Village Life in New England* ([1867] New York: Fords, Howard and Hulbert, 1887), 133–34. Until about 1820, as the literary historian Ann Douglas has noted, this complex Edwardsian theological tradition was "a chief, perhaps the chief, vehicle of intellectual and cultural activity in American life" (*The Feminization of American Culture* [New York: Knopf, 1977], 6). The literary critic Lawrence Buell agrees, adding that we should envisage nothing less than an intricate and extensive "network of Calvinist literary culture" right to the Civil War (*New England Literary Culture from Revolution Through Renaissance* [New York: Cambridge University Press, 1986], 50).

14. Charles G. Finney, *The Memoirs of Charles G. Finney [1868]: The Complete Restored Text*, ed. Garth M. Tosell and Richard A. G. Dupuis (Grand Rapids, MI: Zondervan Publishing House, 1989), 57.

15. Edmund Wilson, *Patriotic Gore: Studies in the Literature of the American Civil War* (New York: Oxford University Press, 1962), and Daniel Aaron, *The Unwritten War: American Writers and the Civil War* (New York: Knopf, 1973).

16. Alan Heimert, *Religion and the American Mind, from the Great Awakening to the Revolution* (Cambridge: Harvard University Press, 1966), 11.

I. BEGINNINGS

1. Richard Schlatter reprinted it in 1946, hyperbolically calling the book "the best allegory written in colonial America, or even in America before the days of Hawthorne and Melville." Joseph Morgan, *History of the Kingdom of Basaruah* (Cambridge: Harvard University Press, 1946), 42.

2. As David D. Hall has pointed out, such allegories (as well as "Providence tales" that

revealed God's will at work in the world) were the kinds of stories most Christians knew and recited for centuries. As he puts it, these texts tell a common story: the progress of the soul to Christ. It was, he continues, "a story rich in dramatic possibilities, as in the terrifying moments when the soul seemed on the 'brink of hell' or the Devil beckoned with a tempting offer of release from sin." Reading and relating to such stories that were as much a part of folk tradition as of Christian history, seventeenth-century colonists "learned that no matter how routine or humble someone's situation seemed, the real meaning of existence was far greater." See *Worlds of Wonder, Days of Judgment: Popular Religious Belief in Early New England* (New York: Knopf, 1986), 120–21.

3. Royall Tyler, *The Algerine Captive; or, The Life and Adventures of Doctor Updike Underhill* (Walpole, NH: D. Carlisle, 1797), preface.

4. William Hill Brown, *The Power of Sympathy* ([1789] New York: Penguin, 1986), 53.

5. Cathy S. Davidson, for one, so argues, for the book was "written in America, by an author born in America, published first in America, set in America, concerned with issues that are specifically grounded in the new country" (*Revolution and the Word: The Rise of the Novel in America* [New York: Oxford University Press, 1984], 85). Admittedly, a few lengthy fictions had appeared previously in American periodicals. The New Hampshire historian Jeremy Belknap, for example, issued his *The Foresters*, a political satire, in *The Columbian Magazine* from 1787 to 1788 but did not publish it separately until 1792. Similarly, Anna Eliza Bleeker wrote *The History of Maria Kittle*, the earliest fiction based on Indian captivity, in 1779, first published it in *The New-York Magazine* in 1790 and 1791, but only issued it separately in 1797. Brown's work thus rightly claims a certain priority as the first book-length fiction by an American published in that format.

6. For biographical details, see Henri Petter, *The Early American Novel* (Columbus: Ohio State University Press, 1971), 243–51, and Carla Mulford's introduction to the 1986 Penguin edition.

7. The same year, for example, Thomas also published Brown's play *The Better Sort; or, The Girl of Spirit*, which mockingly alluded to the same Boston scandal.

8. *Herald of Freedom*, October 9, 1788. The scandal rocked proper Bostonians, but they soon closed ranks to protect their own. The future president John Adams and the former governor of Massachusetts James Bowdoin, who reviewed an investigation by a "Jury of Inquiry" into the "late unhappy event," concluded that the accusations against Apthorp were not "in any degree supported," so that there was "just ground for the restoration of peace and harmony" between the parties.

9. Brown, *Power of Sympathy*, 39.

10. Ibid., 86.

11. Ibid., 63.

12. Ibid., 77.

13. Ibid., 89.

14. Ibid., 92.

15. Ibid., 11.

16. Gordon S. Wood, *The Radicalism of the American Revolution* (New York: Knopf, 1992), 341.

17. Biographical information gleaned from Elias Nason, *A Memoir of Mrs. Susanna Rowson, with Elegant and Illustrative Extracts from Her Writing in Prose and Poetry* (Albany, NY: Joel Munsell, 1870); Patricia Parker, *Susanna Rowson* (Boston: Twayne Publishers, 1986); Dorothy Weil, *In Defense of Women: Susanna Rowson* (State College: Pennsylvania State University Press, 1976); and Marion Rust, *Charlotte Temple: Authoritative Text, Contexts, and Criticism* (New York: W. W. Norton, 2011) and *Prodigal Daughters: Susanna Rowson's Early American Women* (Chapel Hill: University of North Carolina Press, 2008).

18. "Obituary Notice of Mrs. Rowson," *Boston Commercial Gazette,* March 11, 1824, 2.

19. Peter Force, *American Archives,* 4th series (Washington, D.C.: M. St. Clair Clarke and Peter Force, 1834), 4:1282.

20. Susanna Rowson, *Charlotte Temple and Lucy Temple,* ed. Ann Douglas (New York: Penguin, 1991), 46.

21. Rowson, *Charlotte Temple,* 36.

22. Ibid., 37.

23. Ibid., 23.

24. Timothy Dwight, *The Nature and Danger of Infidel Philosophy* (New Haven: George Bunce, 1798), 50.

25. Rowson, *Charlotte Temple,* 23.

26. Ibid., 132.

27. Ibid., 108.

28. Timothy Dwight, *The Duty of Americans, at the Present Crisis* (New Haven: Thomas and Samuel Green, 1798), 20–21.

29. Eliza Lanesford Cushing wrote *Saratoga: A Tale of the Revolution* (1824) and *Yorktown: An Historical Romance* (1826) and also coedited the annual *The Literary Garland.* Harriet Vaughan Cheney authored *A Peep at the Pilgrims in 1636* (1824) and *The Rivals of Acadia* (1827).

30. Foster's position as the town's doyenne, however, eventually became vexed, for soon after the disestablishment of the Congregational Church in Massachusetts in 1826, the Brighton church split into two separate congregations, the First Parish Church and the Evangelical Congregational Society. This ecclesiastical fracture took an emotional toll on Foster's husband, who resigned shortly thereafter.

31. William B. Sprague, *Annals of the American Pulpit,* 9 vols. (New York: Robert Carter & Brothers, 1857–1865), 1:315.

32. Although some do not accept the identification, during the late eighteenth and nineteenth centuries Pierpont was generally thought the villain. For those who do, his rejection to be seated in the Congress of 1790 after winning a seat during a heated campaign suggests embarrassment about what was coming out about his past. The term "adulterer" was in fact then used against him, even though at the time of the purported affair he was married with eleven children.

33. Hannah W. Foster, *The Coquette,* ed. Jane E. Locke (Ithaca, NY: Mack, Andrus, and Co., 1855), 10, 12–16.

34. Ibid., 19–20.

35. Hannah W. Foster, *The Coquette*, ed. Cathy S. Davidson (New York: Oxford University Press, 1986), 7.

36. Ibid., 13.

37. Ibid., 14.

38. Ibid., 15.

39. Ibid., 18.

40. Ibid., 20.

41. Ibid., 22.

42. Ibid., 26.

43. Ibid., 26, 28.

44. Ibid., 53.

45. Ibid., 55.

46. Ibid., 56.

47. Ibid., 70.

48. Ibid., 105–106.

49. Ibid., 107.

50. Ibid., 108.

51. Ibid., 121.

52. Ibid., 123.

53. Ibid., 133.

54. Ibid., 40.

55. Sukey Vickery, *Edith Hamilton* ([1803] Lincoln: University of Nebraska Press, 2009), 97–98.

56. Evert A. and George L. Duyckinck, *Cyclopedia of American Literature*, 2 vols. (New York: Scribner, 1855), 1:504.

57. Tabitha Tenney, *Female Quixotism, Exhibited in the Romantic Opinions and Extravagant Adventures of Dorcasina Sheldon*, eds. Jean Nienkamp and Andrea Collins ([1801] New York: Oxford University Press, 1992), preface.

58. Ibid., 325.

59. Such tropes, Karen Weyler argues, "indicate loci of cultural anxiety and energy, heuristics developed by and within the early novel as a means of mapping and reforming social relations" (*Intricate Relations: Sexual and Economic Desire in American Fiction, 1789–1814* [Iowa City: University of Iowa Press, 2004], 2).

60. John Adams to William Cunningham, Quincy, Massachusetts, March 15, 1804.

61. Margaret Fuller, "American Literature: Its Position in the Present Time, and Prospects for the Future," *Papers on Literature and Art, Part II* (New York: Wiley and Putnam, 1846), 146–50.

62. Anon., "Memoir of Charles Brockden Brown," in *The Novels of Charles Brockden Brown: Wieland, Ormond, Arthur Mervyn, Edgar Huntly, Clara Howard, Jane Talbot*, 6 vols. (Boston: S. G. Goodrich, 1827), 1:xii–xiii.

63. John Neal, *American Writers: A Series of Papers Contributed to Blackwood's Magazine (1824–1825)*, ed. Fred Louis Patee (Durham, NC: Duke University Press, 1937), 65–66. The most thorough early biography is William Dunlap, *The Life of Charles Brockden Brown:*

Together with Selections from the Rarest of His Printed Works, from His Original Letters, and from His Manuscripts Before Unpublished, 2 vols. (Philadelphia: James P. Parks, 1815).

64. William H. Prescott, "Life of Charles Brockden Brown," *Library of American Biography*, ed. Jared Sparks (Boston: Hilliard Gray & Co., 1834), 131.

65. *American Daily Advertiser*, February 27, 1810.

66. The publication of Dunlap's *Life of Brown* initiated a second wave of notices. A reviewer in the weighty *North American Review* presciently described what continues to hold the twenty-first-century reader's attention. Brown, he wrote, "selects minds that are strangely gifted or influenced, as if for the pleasure of exploring some secret principles of our nature, disclosing new motives of conduct, or old ones operating in a new direction . . . as if he had discovered springs of action which could not be understood in the usual way." Brown's novels, he continued, show "the mind's perfect consciousness of all that is passing within" but not merely toward the end of some obvious moral lesson, as most contemporary novelists did. Rather, the author was "perfectly satisfied" in such analysis itself. Finally, this reviewer thought that although Brown was "chiefly occupied with the mind," for him the question was not "how much of this has happened or is about to happen" but "how is it felt" (Anon., "The Life of Charles Brockden Brown," 24 and 58–77 passim). One of the most interesting appraisals appeared in 1824 in *Blackwood's Edinburgh Magazine*. There John Neal, in one of a series of essays on "American Writers," opined that Brown's work had no poetry, no pathos, no wit, no humor, no pleasantry, no playfulness, no passion, little or no eloquence, and no imagination. Yet, Neal admitted, Brown had the remarkable facility "to impress his pictures upon the human heart with such unexampled vivacity, that no time can obliterate them; and withal, to fasten himself with such tremendous power, upon a common incident, as to hold the spectator breathless." *Wieland* particularly struck Neal, for it left the reader "in a tense—a sort of uncomfortable, fidgeting, angry perplexity—ashamed of the concern that [he has] shown—and quite in a huff with him—very much as if [he] had been running [himself to death]—in a hot wind—after a catastrophe—with the tail soaped" (Anon., "On the Writings of Charles Brockden Brown and Washington Irving," *Blackwood's Edinburgh Magazine* [February 1820], 554–55). Reprinted in Neal, *American Writers*.

67. *The New-York Weekly Magazine; or Miscellaneous Repository* 2 (July 20): 20 and (July 27): 28 (1796).

68. Charles Brockden Brown, *Wieland*, ed. Jay Fliegelman ([1798] New York: Penguin, 1991), 14.

69. Ibid., 20.

70. Ibid., 21.

71. Ibid., 29.

72. Ibid., 36–37.

73. Ibid., 39.

74. Ibid., 52.

75. Ibid., 57–59.

76. Ibid., 174–75, 123.

77. Ibid., 223–24.

78. Ibid., 235.

79. Ibid., 249.

80. Ibid., 261–62.

81. Ibid., 278.

82. Ibid., 3–4.

83. On these groups, see Stephen A. Marini, *Revolutionary Sects of Revolutionary New England* (Cambridge: Harvard University Press, 1982).

84. Brown, *Wieland*, 23.

85. Ibid., 24.

86. Ibid., 96.

87. Ibid., 99.

88. Ibid., 99.

89. Ibid., 101.

90. Ibid., 5, 167.

91. Ibid., 204–205.

92. Ibid., 214.

93. Prescott, "Life of Brown," 176.

2. GLIMMERINGS OF CHANGE

1. See, for example, Nathan O. Hatch, *The Democratization of American Christianity* (New Haven: Yale University Press, 1989), passim. Neal finally is getting some modern attention; see the essays in Edward Watts and David J. Carlson, eds., *John Neal and Nineteenth-Century American Literature and Culture* (Lewisburg, PA: Bucknell University Press, 2012).

2. James Brooks, "Letters from the East—John Neal," *New-York Mirror* 11 (1833–1834): 69.

3. John Neal, *American Writers: A Series of Papers Contributed to Blackwood's Magazine (1824–1825)*, ed. Fred Louis Patee (Durham, NC: Duke University Press, 1937), 29.

4. Ibid., 63.

5. Ibid., 68.

6. Ibid., 70, 208.

7. Ibid.,167–68; Walt Whitman, *American Primer* (Boston: Small, Maynard and Co., 1904), 4.

8. John Neal tells the reader that is what he was going to call it. *Keep Cool: Written in Hot Weather* (Baltimore: Joseph Cushing, 1817), 31.

9. Neal, *American Writers*, 169.

10. Benjamin Lease, *That Wild Fellow John Neal and the American Literary Revolution* (Chicago: University of Chicago Press, 1972), 41, from *The Columbian Observer*, clipping in Neal scrapbook.

11. John Neal, *Wandering Recollections of a Somewhat Busy Life* (Boston: Roberts Brothers, 1869), 229.

12. John Neal, *Errata; or, The Works of Will. Adams, a Tale*, 2 vols. (New York: For the Proprietors, 1823), 1:265–67.

13. Edgar Allan Poe, *Marginalia* (1849), in *Poe: Essays and Reviews* (New York: Library

of America, 1984), 1448. Poe thought enough of the writer to dedicate the poem "Tamerlane" to him when he republished it in a collection in 1829.

14. Nathaniel Hawthorne, "P's Correspondence," in Hawthorne, *Tales and Sketches* (New York: Library of America, 1982), 1020.

15. Julian Hawthorne, *Nathaniel Hawthorne and His Wife*, 2 vols. (Boston: J. R. Osgood, 1885), 1:145.

16. See Hatch, *Democratization*, passim.

17. David Paul Nord, *Faith in Reading: Religious Publishing and the Birth of Mass Media in America* (New York: Oxford University Press, 2004), 7.

18. See Thomas B. Lovell, "Separate Spheres and Extensive Circles: Sarah Savage's *The Factory Girl* and the Celebration of Industry in Early Nineteenth-Century America," *Early American Literature*, 31 (1996): 1–24, and Margaret B. Moore, "Sarah Savage of Salem: A Forgotten Writer," *Essex Institute Historical Collections*, 127 (1991): 240–59. Also Sylvia Jenkins Cook, *Working Women, Literary Ladies: The Industrial Revolution and Female Aspiration* (New York: Oxford University Press, 2008), chap. 1.

19. [Sarah Savage], *Trial and Self-Discipline* (Boston and Cambridge: James Munroe and Co., 1835), 67.

20. There is no full-scale modern biography of Sedgwick, but see Edward Halsey Foster, *Catharine Maria Sedgwick* (New York: Twayne Publishers, 1974) and [Catharine Maria Sedgwick], *The Power of Her Sympathy: The Autobiography and Journal of Catharine Maria Sedgwick*, ed. with intro. by Mary Kelley (Boston: Massachusetts Historical Society, 1993). Still invaluable is Mary E. Dewey, ed., *Life and Letters of Catharine M. Sedgwick* (New York: Harpers, 1872).

21. *Power of Her Sympathy*, ed. Kelley, 36–37.

22. Dewey, ed., *Life and Letters*, 150–51, 153.

23. Catharine Maria Sedgwick, *A New-England Tale; or, Sketches of New-England Characters and Manners*, ed. Victoria Clements ([1822] New York: Oxford University Press, 1995), 7.

24. Ibid., 131.

25. Catharine Maria Sedgwick, *Redwood: A Tale* ([1824] New York: George P. Putnam, 1850), vii, ix.

26. Dewey, ed., *Life and Letters*, 172.

27. Sedgwick, *Redwood*, ix.

28. Dewey, ed., *Life and Letters*, 168–69.

29. *North American Review* 20 (April 1825): 245–46.

30. Dewey, ed., *Life and Letters*, 187.

31. Caroline Karcher, "Introduction" to Catharine Maria Sedgwick, *Hope Leslie* ([1827] New York: Penguin, 1998), ix.

32. Dewey, ed., *Life and Letters*, 129–30.

33. Sedgwick, *Hope Leslie*, 49–51.

34. Ibid., 52–53.

35. Ibid., 55.

36. Ibid., 359.

37. Ibid., 349.

38. Ibid., 292.

39. Bryant's encomium at the end of his lengthy notice in the *North American Review* can stand for the whole. "We pray [Sedgwick] to go on in the path in which she must excel and has excelled, and which she ought to make her peculiar one," he wrote. "We pray her to go on soon . . . for the public's sake, and for the honor of our youthful literature." William Cullen Bryant, *North American Review*, 26 (April 1828): 420.

40. Review of John Lothrop Motley, "Merry-Mount," *North American Review*, 68 (January 1849): 205.

41. Donald Grant Mitchell, *American Lands and Letters* (New York: Chas. Scribner's Sons, 1899), 254.

42. In the winter of 1834 Ware wrote her to see if she would contribute to a new project he was sponsoring, "a series of narratives, between a formal tale and a common tract," to illustrate "the practical character and influences of Christianity." Dewey, ed., *Life and Letters*, 239.

43. Catharine Maria Sedgwick, *Married or Single?* (New York: Harper, 1857), vi.

44. *Cooper Memorial,* 70.

45. Poe, "William Gilmore Simms" (1846), in *Poe: Essays and Reviews*, 904.

46. See, for example, Daniel Cohen, *Pillars of Salt, Monuments of Grace: New England Crime Literature and the Origins of American Popular Culture, 1674–1860* (New York: Oxford University Press, 1993).

47. William Gilmore Simms, *Martin Faber: The Story of a Criminal* ([1833] Fayetteville: University of Arkansas Press, 2005), 1–3.

48. Ibid., 24–25.

49. Ibid., 40.

50. *Arcturus* 1, no. 28 (January 1841): 90.

51. On Kennedy, see Charles H. Bohner, *John Pendleton Kennedy: Gentleman from Baltimore* (Baltimore: Johns Hopkins University Press, 1961).

52. This ancient belief, the transmigration of souls as a means of purification and penance, had gained currency in the late-eighteenth- and early-nineteenth-century Western world with the translation of Hindu sacred texts into German, French, and eventually English. It also derived in part from ancient Greek belief, primarily through Pythagoras, who adopted it into his philosophy. Plotinus, in particular, believed that heavenly souls passed not only into earthly bodies but also from earthly bodies to other ones. Its presence in nineteenth-century American literature is attested to particularly in the works of Poe, whose tales of lost love, "Ligeia" and "Morella," depend on it.

53. John Pendleton Kennedy, *Sheppard Lee, Written by Himself* ([1836] New York: New York Review of Books, 2008), 7.

54. Ibid., 7.

55. Ibid., 8–9.

56. Ibid., 9–10.

57. Ibid., 11.

58. Ibid., 22–24.

59. Ibid., 47.

60. Ibid., 50–52.

61. Ibid., 415.

62. Ibid., 344.

63. Ibid., 341.

3. PREPARING THE GROUND

1. See Michael Winship, "Manufacturing and Book Production," in *A History of the Book in America: The Industrial Book, 1840–1880*, eds. Scott Casper et al. (Chapel Hill: University of North Carolina Press, 2007), 40–69, and "Distribution and the Trade," ibid., 117–29.

2. See Edward L. Widmer, *Young America: The Flowering of Democracy in New York City* (New York: Oxford University Press, 1999), 104, and Ezra Greenspan, *George Palmer Putnam: Representative American Publisher* (University Park: Pennsylvania State University Press, 2000), 111. "I had long," Putnam later wrote, "had an eye on the trade and written many schemes for them on the empty air when Mr[.] Wiley applied to me for counsel—so the apple had not ripened in a day though it was ready for shaking." Greenspan, "A Publisher's Legacy: The George Palmer Putnam Correspondence at Princeton," *Princeton University Library Chronicle* 40, no. 1 (Autumn 1992): 50.

3. Widmer, *Young America*, 105.

4. Nathaniel Hawthorne to George Duyckinck, July 1, 1845, in Hawthorne, *Letters, 1843–1853* (Columbus: Ohio State University Press, 1985), 106.

5. See Perry Miller, *The Raven and the Whale: The War of Works and Wits in the Era of Poe and Melville* (New York: Harcourt, Brace, 1956), passim.

6. David Dowling, *The Business of Literary Circles in Nineteenth-Century America* (New York and London: Palgrave Macmillan, 2011).

7. As one historian puts it, these New Yorkers "lived in a hyperpolitical time, when every question was probed for its relevance to the great party struggle taking place" (Widmer, *Young America*, 26).

8. Miller, *Raven and the Whale*, 12.

9. Widmer, *Young America*, 62.

10. Ibid., 40–41. "O'Sullivan's conception of democracy as a 'creed' not only lent it a spiritual hue, but more specifically, invested it with a collective sense of philanthropy, a disinterested benevolence toward all humankind, in contrast to the Whig philosophy of individual self-betterment." Further, in championing "America," he encouraged a very large understanding of the term, to include Canada, South and Central America, and even the period of pre-Columbian settlement.

11. *Democratic Review*, 1 (October 1837): 14.

12. Miller, *Raven and the Whale*, 80, where Miller notes that Mathews was someone who "excited among his contemporaries a frenzy of loathing beyond the limits of rationality."

13. Keeping to a higher road than most competitors, *Arcturus* was well regarded and even considered remarkable during its three years of existence. Poe thought it "decidedly the very best magazine in many respects ever published in the United States" (Edgar Allan Poe, "The

Literati of New York City" (1846) in *Poe: Essays and Reviews* [New York: Library of America, 1984], 1161). James Russell Lowell, who eventually grew to dislike Mathews's arrogance, paid it a backhanded compliment by saying that it was "as transcendental as Gotham can be." James Russell Lowell, *The Letters of James Russell Lowell*, 2 vols. (New York: Harper and Brothers, 1894), 1:62.

14. Cornelius Mathews, *The True Aims of Life* (New York: Wiley and Putnam, 1839), 23, 37–38.

15. *Arcturus* 2, no. 12 (November 1844): 366–67.

16. On Lippard, see David S. Reynolds, *George Lippard* (New York: Twayne Publishers, 1982).

17. Charles Chauncey Burr, introduction to George Lippard, *Washington and His Generals; or, Legends of the Revolution* (Philadelphia: G. B. Ziever and Co., 1847), vi.

18. See Samuel Otter, *Philadelphia Stories: America's Literature of Race and Freedom* (New York: Oxford University Press, 2010), 170.

19. Published as an epilogue to George Lippard's *Herbert Tracy; or, The Legend of the Black Rangers* (Philadelphia: R. G. Berford, 1844).

20. *Quaker City Weekly* (October 29, 1849), 1.

21. The brotherhood, one historian notes, synthesized various causes in which Lippard long had had an interest: "land reform, Fourierism, co-operation, election reform, and subversive anticapitalism." See George Lippard, *The Quaker City; or, The Monks of Monk Hall: A Romance of Philadelphia Life, Mystery, and Crime*, ed. David S. Reynolds ([1844] Amherst: University of Massachusetts Press, 1995), 20.

22. Ibid.

23. Ibid., 21. The editor and author Burr wrote in 1847 that Lippard had a "determinate, unmovable self-reliance." Moreover, he was "not a pipe for Fortune's finger (or anyone else's finger) to play what stop she pleases on; if it come to the matter of playing, he will be likely to play his own tunes, to his own time." Burr, in Lippard, *Washington and His Generals*, xxv.

24. Theodore Parker, *Massachusetts Quarterly Review* 1, no. 1 (December 1847): 125.

25. George Lippard, "The Heart-Broken," *The Nineteenth-Century* (1848), in *George Lippard, Prophet of Protest: Writings of an American Radical, 1822–1854*, ed. David S. Reynolds (New York: Peter Lang, 1986), 270.

26. *Quaker City Weekly* (June 2, 1849), ibid., 279.

27. Lippard, *Quaker City*, 84.

28. Ibid., 305–306.

29. *Quaker City Weekly* (March 16, 1850), in *George Lippard, Prophet of Protest*, ed. Reynolds, 47.

30. George Lippard, *New York: Its Upper Ten and Lower Million* (1853), ibid., 46.

31. *Quaker City Weekly* (July 21, 1849), ibid., 173, 175.

32. Lippard, *Quaker City*, vii.

33. Burr in Lippard, *Washington and His Generals*, xiv.

34. See Donna Dennis, *Licentious Gotham: Erotic Publishing in Nineteenth-Century New York* (Cambridge: Harvard University Press, 2009).

35. George Thompson, *Venus in Boston and Other Tales of Nineteenth-Century Life*, eds. David S. Reynolds and Kimberly R. Gladman (Amherst: University of Massachusetts Press, 2002), 47.

36. Ibid., 37.

37. Ibid., 3.

38. Edwin Percy Whipple, "The Romance of Rascality," *Essays and Reviews*, 2 vols. (Boston: Ticknor and Fields, 1848), 2:107.

39. Writing approvingly of Sue's work, Greeley criticized those in the United States who censored passages that indicated his reformist zeal. "To chronicle the horrors and suppress their moral," he wrote, to "omit the very passages that can alone excuse such exhibition—is the wrong way entirely" (*New-York Tribune*, November 24, 1843). In the 1850s Thompson's novels, pornographic by contemporary definition, ran afoul of the law. A series of prosecutions in New York against the publishers of the sporting papers drove such literature underground; see Dennis, *Licentious Gotham* and Patricia Cline Cohen et al., eds., *The Flash Press: Sporting Male Weeklies in 1840s New York* (Chicago: University of Chicago Press, 2008).

40. Arethusa Hall, *Life and Character of the Rev. Sylvester Judd* (Boston: Crosby, Nichols and Co., 1854), 74, 77–78. Also see Richard D. Hathaway, *Sylvester Judd's New England* (University Park: Pennsylvania State University Press, 1981).

41. Hall, *Judd*, 80–103.

42. Ibid., 354.

43. Margaret Fuller, *Writings from the New-York Tribune 1844–1846* (New York: Columbia University Press, 2000), 210, 335–36.

44. *Christian Examiner*, 39 (November 1845): 418–20.

45. James Russell Lowell, in *National Anti-Slavery Standard* 10, no. 35 (January 24, 1850).

46. George Ripley, in Perry Miller, *The Transcendentalists: An Anthology* (Cambridge: Harvard University Press, 1950), 152.

47. On Fourier's American disciples and implementations of his utopian scheme, see Carl Guarneri, *The Utopian Alternative: Fourierism in Nineteenth-Century America* (Ithaca, NY: Cornell University Press, 1991).

48. [Anonymous], *Henry Russell; or, The Year of Our Lord Two Thousand* (New York: William Graham, 1846), 37. Also see "Radical Freelance," *The Philosophers of Foufouville* (New York: G. W. Carleton, 1868), based at the North American Phalanx in Red Bank, New Jersey.

49. Ibid.

50. George Lippard, *New York: Its Upper Ten and Lower Million* ([1853] New York: Ranney, 1854), 284.

51. W. S. Mayo, *Kaloolah; or, The Journeyings to the Djébel Kumri: An Autobiography of Jonathan Romer* (New York: Putnam's, 1849), 461–65.

52. Ibid., 465–66.

53. Ibid., 465.

54. Ibid., 420–21.

55. He wrote three novels that treated this agitation: *The Chainbearers* (1845), *Satanstoe* (1845), and *The Redskins* (1846), known as the "Littlepage Trilogy."

56. James Fenimore Cooper, *The Crater; or Vulcan's Peak*, ed. Thomas Philbrick ([1847]; Cambridge: Harvard University Press, 1962), 139.

57. Ibid., 233.

58. Ibid., 299–300.

59. Ibid., 431.

60. Ibid., 438.

61. Ibid., 387.

62. Ibid., 455–56.

63. Ibid., 459.

4. THE CONVENTIONS OF SENTIMENT

1. Anna Warner, *Susan Warner ("Elizabeth Wetherell")* (New York: G. P. Putnam's, 1909), 283. This biography of Susan remains the most useful. Also see Olivia Stokes, *Life and Memories of Susan and Anna Bartlett Warner* (New York: G. P. Putnam's, 1925).

2. J. C. Derby, *Fifty Years Among Authors, Books and Publishers* (New York: G. W. Carleton and Co., 1884), 304–305.

3. Warner, *Susan Warner*, 305. Nina Baym, who has done more than any other to make available and help the modern reader make sense of early American women's writing, has argued that "if critics ever permit the woman's novel to join the main body of 'American literature,' then all our theories about American fiction ... will have to be radically revised" (*Woman's Fiction: A Guide to Novels by and About Women, 1820–1870* [Urbana: University of Illinois Press, 1993], 36–37).

4. Nathaniel Hawthorne to William D. Ticknor, January 19, 1855, in Nathaniel Hawthorne, *Letters, 1853–1856* (Columbus: Ohio State University Press, 1987), 304.

5. On the sentimental and the American novel, see especially Elizabeth Barnes, *States of Sympathy: Seduction and Democracy in the American Novel* (New York: Columbia University Press, 1997); Julia Stern, *The Plight of Feeling: Sympathy and Dissent in the American Novel* (Chicago: University of Chicago Press, 1997); and Shirley Samuels, ed., *The Culture of Sentiment: Race, Gender, and Sentimentality in Nineteenth-Century America* (New York: Oxford University Press, 1992).

6. See Richard Rabinowitz, *The Spiritual Self in Everyday Life: The Transformation of Religious Experience in Nineteenth-Century New England* (Boston: Northeastern University Press, 1989), 85–137.

7. For as literary critic Jane Tompkins has argued, modern readers too often have failed to perceive what to Warner's contemporaries was everywhere apparent: that "the great subject" of sentimental fiction was "preeminently ... the nature of power," a topic all the more significant because women novelists like Warner "lived in a society that celebrated free enterprise and democratic government" yet had as central characters in their novels women excluded from participating in these and other of the age's defining institutions (*Sensational Designs: The Cultural Work of American Fiction, 1790–1860* [New York: Oxford University Press, 1986], 160).

8. Elizabeth Wetherell (Susan Warner), *The Wide, Wide World* (Leipzig: Tauchnitz, 1854), 509.

9. Thomas Harvey Skinner and Edward Beecher, *Hints, Designed to Aid Christians in Their Efforts to Convert to God* (Philadelphia: French and Perkins, 1832), 42.

10. Thomas Harvey Skinner, *The Religion of the Bible, in Select Discourses* (New York: John S. Taylor, 1839), 14–15.

11. Ibid., 183, 185.

12. Horace Bushnell, *Christian Nurture*, ([1847] New Haven: Yale University Press, 1916), 208.

13. John S. Hart, *Female Prose Writers of America* ([1852] Philadelphia: E. H. Butler and Co., 1866), 421. A reviewer in *Holden's Dollar Magazine* (so named because a dollar purchased a year's subscription), although complaining of Ellen's "incessant blubbering" and counseling Warner to make her next book contain "less dry logic and more dry land," still found it "wholly and unmistakably good" as "moral and religious instruction," emphasizing, as many reviewers did, its importance as a religious text (March 8, 1851, 136–37).

14. Caroline Kirkland, "Novels and Novelists," *North American Review* 76 (January 1853): 104.

15. Ibid., 105.

16. Ibid., 106.

17. Ibid., 112–13.

18. Ibid., 121–22.

19. As the southern novelist Virginia Terhune put it, within a year *The Lamplighter* "was in every home, and gossip of the personality [it was published pseudonymously] of the author was seized upon greedily by press and readers" ([Virginia Terhune,] *Marion Harland's Autobiography: The Story of a Long Life* [New York: Harper & Brothers, 1910], 285).

20. Maria Cummins, *The Lamplighter*, ed. Nina Baym ([1854] New Brunswick, NJ: Rutgers University Press, 1988), 99.

21. Ibid., 117.

22. Ibid., 143.

23. Charles Dickens, *American Notes for General Circulation* (New York: Wilson and Company, 1842), 26–29.

24. *Lowell Offering* 1 (August 1841), 169–70.

25. *Olive Leaf and New England Operative* 1 (September 2, 1843).

26. Lucy Larcom, *A New England Girlhood, Outlined from Memory* (Boston: Houghton, Mifflin and Company, 1889), 181–82.

27. Factory Tracts #1, in Philip Foner, ed., *The Factory Girls* (Urbana: University of Illinois Press, 1977), 133–34.

28. Amos Blanchard, "Introduction," in Dorus Clarke, *Lectures to Young People in Manufacturing Villages* (Boston: Perkins and Marvin, 1836), ix–xi.

29. See Patricia Caldwell's modern edition of *Fall River* ([1834] New York: Oxford University Press, 1993), with its brief but informative introduction.

30. Martha W. Tyler, *A Book Without a Title: or, Thrilling Events in the Life of Mira Dana* (Boston, MA: Printed for the Author, 1855), 9.

31. Ibid., 13.

32. Ibid., 15.

33. Ibid., 18.

34. Ibid., v.

35. Ibid., vi.

36. Harriet Beecher Stowe, in Fanny Fern, *Ruth Hall and Other Writings*, ed. Joyce W. Warren (New Brunswick, NJ: Rutgers University Press, 1986), xii, from Stowe's letters at the Sophia Smith Collection, Smith College.

37. Cited in Joyce W. Warren, *Fanny Fern: An Independent Woman* (New Brunswick, NJ: Rutgers University Press, 1992), 93. This is the standard biography.

38. "Notices of New Books," *New York Times*, December 20, 1854.

39. Susan Belasco Smith, in Fanny Fern (Sara Willis Parton), *Ruth Hall*, ed. Susan Belaso Smith ([1854] New York: Penguin, 1997), xxxv.

40. Ibid., "To the Reader."

41. Ibid., 19.

42. Ibid., 47.

43. Ibid., 63.

44. Ibid., 66.

45. Ibid., 87.

46. Ibid., 141.

47. Ibid., 155.

48. Ibid., 170.

49. Ibid., 213.

50. Ibid., 225.

51. Ibid., 227.

52. Ibid., 264.

53. Ibid., 272.

54. *Southern Quarterly Review* 22 (April 1855): 438–50.

55. *The Pioneer* 3, no. 6 (June 1855): 363.

56. Ibid.

57. *The Knickerbocker* 45, no. 1 (January 1855): 84.

58. *The Una* 3 (February 1855): 29–30.

59. From *Harper's New Monthly Magazine*, cited in Hart, *Female Prose Writers*, 512. The best modern assessment of her is James Machor, *Reading Fiction in Antebellum America: Informed Responses and Reception Histories, 1820–1865* (Baltimore: Johns Hopkins University Press, 2011), 256–98. Also see his *Reading Fiction in Antebellum America: Informed Response and Reception Histories, 1820–1865* (Baltimore: Johns Hopkins University Press, 2011).

60. *The Knickerbocker* 44 (September 1856): 303.

61. Caroline Chesebro', *Isa, a Pilgrimage* (New York: Redfield, 1852), 35.

62. Ibid., 44.

63. Ibid., 131.

64. Ibid., 46.

65. Ibid., 294.

66. Ibid., 132–33.

67. Ibid., 219–20.

68. Ibid., 317.

69. *American Whig Review* 16.1 (July 1852): 94.

70. From *Harper's New Monthly Magazine*, in Hart, *Female Prose Writers*, 512.

71. Chesebro', *Isa*, 112.

72. Hart, *Female Prose Writers*, 513.

73. George Ripley, *New-York Tribune*, April 17, 1852.

74. Jean L. Silver-Isenstadt, *Shameless: The Visionary Life of Mary Gove Nichols* (Baltimore: Johns Hopkins University Press, 1992), 139.

75. Mary Gove Nichols, *Mary Lyndon; or Revelations of a Life: An Autobiography* (New York: Stringer and Townsend, 1855), 14.

76. Ibid., 119.

77. Ibid., 135.

78. Ibid., 166–67.

79. Ibid., 188–89.

80. Ibid., 200.

81. Ibid., 198.

82. Ibid., 204–208.

83. Ibid., 312.

84. Ibid., 385.

5. ON THE COLOR LINE

1. Henry James, *A Small Boy and Others* (New York: Scribners, 1913), 158–59.

2. See David S. Reynolds, *Mightier than the Sword: "Uncle Tom's Cabin" and the Battle for America* (New York: W. W. Norton, 2011) for a description of the book's remarkable influence.

3. The story may be apocryphal but was first published by Annie Fields in *The Atlantic Monthly* 78 (August 1896): 148. It also appeared in Fields's biography of Stowe, published a year later, making Fields the first Stowe biographer to print Lincoln's greeting. Annie T. Fields, *The Life and Letters of Harriet Beecher Stowe* (Boston: Houghton, Mifflin and Company, 1897), 269.

4. Joan Hedrick, *Harriet Beecher Stowe: A Life* (New York: Oxford University Press, 1994) is now the standard biography.

5. See Emily Noyes Vanderpoel, *Chronicles of a Pioneer School from 1792 to 1833, Being the History of Miss Sarah Pierce and Her Litchfield School* (Cambridge, MA: The University Press, 1903).

6. See Marian C. McKenna, *Tapping Reeve and the Litchfield Law School* (New York: Oceana, 1986).

7. On the Second Great Awakening, see David Kling, *A Field of Divine Wonders: The New Divinity and Village Revivals in Northwestern Connecticut, 1792–1822* (State College: Pennsylvania State University Press, 1993).

8. Isabella Beecher, cited in Hedrick, *Stowe*, 145.

9. An 1879 edition. This was not some sort of evangelical hubris, for others concurred in its purportedly divine sanction. Delegates to the Colored National Convention in Rochester, New York, in 1853, for example, hailed the novel as nothing less than "a work plainly marked by the finger of God." "Proceedings of the Colored National Convention Held in

Rochester, July 6th, 7th, and 8th, 1853," in Howard Holman Bell, ed., *Minutes of the National Negro Conventions, 1830–1864* (New York: Arno Press, 1969), 40.

10. *New York Daily Times*, September 18, 1852.

11. Thus, the literary critic Jane Tompkins's designation of *Uncle Tom's Cabin* as "the *summa theologica* of America's religion of domesticity" is apt (*Sensational Designs: The Cultural Work of American Fiction* [New York: Oxford University Press, 1986], 125).

12. Harriet Beecher Stowe, *Uncle Tom's Cabin*, ed. Ann Douglas ([1852] New York: Penguin, 1986), 290.

13. Ibid., 261.

14. Ibid., 388–89.

15. Ibid., 392.

16. Ibid., 412.

17. This did not necessarily detract from her characterizations' power, however, for as the literary critic Philip Fisher has observed, "The political content of sentimentality is democratic in that it experiments with the extension of full and complete humanity to classes of figures from whom it has been socially withheld" (*Hard Facts: Setting and Form in the American Novel* [New York: Oxford University Press, 1985], 99).

18. William Edward Farrison, *William Wells Brown: Author and Reformer* (Chicago: University of Chicago Press, 1969) is the standard biography.

19. Ibid., 112–13.

20. William Wells Brown, *Clotel; or, The President's Daughter: A Narrative of Slave Life in the United States* ([1853]; New York: Carol Publishing Group, 1995), 46.

21. Ibid., 46–47.

22. Ibid., 46.

23. *Literary Gazette and Journal of Belles Lettres, Arts, and Sciences* (December 31, 1853): 1263.

24. *The Athenaeum: Journal of Literature, Science, and the Fine Arts* (January 21, 1854): 86.

25. Farrison, *Brown*, 220.

26. Grace Greenwood (Sarah Jane Lippincott), *Poems* (Boston: Ticknor and Fields: 1851), 80–82.

27. Farrison, *Brown*, 222.

28. A runaway slave advertisement that Norcom placed in the Norfolk, Virginia, *Daily Beacon* (ironically, on July 4, 1835) provides a detailed portrait of her. She was "a light mulatto, 21 years of age," he wrote, "about 5 feet four inches high, of a thick and corpulent habit, having on her head a thick covering of black hair that curls naturally but which can be easily combed straight. She speaks easily and fluently," he continued, "and has an agreeable carriage and address." She "has been accustomed to dress well," he added, "has a variety of fine clothes, made in the prevailing fashion, and will probably appear, if abroad, tricked out in gay and fashionable finery."

29. Child's role was minimal, for by that time Jacobs was an accomplished writer. Child explained, "I abridged, and struck out superfluous words sometimes" but did not alter "fifty words in the whole volume." See Jane Fagan Yellin, "Introduction," Harriet Jacobs, *Incidents in the Life of a Slave Girl* ([1861]; Cambridge: Harvard University Press, 2000), xii.

30. Child solicited the Boston firm Thayer and Eldridge, which offered Jacobs a 10 percent royalty. Because Child also assured the firm that the Anti-Slavery Society was going to

peddle the volume, Thayer and Eldridge took the unusual step, for a new author, of having the plates stereotyped, so that more copies than the two thousand planned could be printed on short notice. After Thayer and Eldridge had the plates made, however, it fell into financial difficulties and went bankrupt. Presumably with the aid of others, Jacobs bought the stereotyped plates and contracted with a Boston printer to issue the book "for the author," marking it a commodity with less prestige than one backed by a prominent publishing house. There is no record of how many copies Jacobs initially had printed.

31. *The Liberator* (February 8, 1861).

32. *National Anti-Slavery Standard* (February 16, 1861).

33. Jacobs, *Incidents*, 27.

34. Ibid., 53.

35. Ibid., 154–55.

36. Ibid., 55.

37. Harriet Jacobs to Amy Post, June 21, [1857], cited in Yellin, "Introduction," xiii.

38. Webb later indicated that his wife was from New Bedford, Massachusetts, the daughter of a runaway full-blooded African slave woman from Virginia and "a Spanish gentleman of wealth" who tried (unsuccessfully) to buy his "wife" and who continued to support the mother and child. See Frank J. Webb, "Biographical Sketch of Mary E. Webb," in Frank J. Webb, *Fiction, Essays, Poetry*, ed. Werner Sollors (New Milford, CT: Toby, 2004), 425.

39. Ibid., 427.

40. Sollors, in Webb, *Fiction*, 2.

41. *Frederick Douglass' Paper* (December 1857).

42. Webb, "Biographical Sketch," 426, 428.

43. Harriet Beecher Stowe, in Frank J. Webb, *The Garies and Their Friends* ([1857] New York: Arno Press, 1969), v.

44. Samuel Otter, *Philadelphia Stories: America's Literature of Race and Freedom* (New York: Oxford University Press, 2010), 240.

45. Webb, *The Garies*, 14.

46. Ibid., 41.

47. Ibid., 121–22.

48. Ibid., 133.

49. Ibid., 129, 137.

50. Ibid., 166.

51. Ibid., 229.

52. Ibid., 226.

53. Ibid., 233.

54. Ibid., 260.

55. Ibid., 275–76.

56. Ibid., 354.

57. Ibid., 378.

58. Ibid., 63.

59. Sarah Josepha Hale, *Liberia, or, Mr. Peyton's Experiments* (New York: Harper & Brothers, 1853), 67.

60. Ibid., 224.

61. See Charles Henry Brown, *Agents of Manifest Destiny: The Lives and Times of the Fili-busters* (Chapel Hill: University of North Carolina Press, 1980) and Amy S. Greenberg, *Manifest Manhood and the Antebellum American Empire* (New York: Cambridge University Press, 2005).

62. Martin Robison Delany, *Blake; or, the Huts of America, a Novel* (Boston: Beacon Press, 1970), 260–61.

63. Ibid., 290.

64. Ibid., 262.

65. Ibid., 126.

66. Harriet E. Wilson, *Our Nig; or, Sketches from the Life of a Free Black*, ed. Henry Louis Gates ([1859] New York: Vintage, 2002), 138–39. Subsequent citations in the text are to this edition.

67. Ibid., 133.

68. Ibid., 139.

69. Henry Louis Gates, "Introduction," ibid., xxiv.

70. Wilson, ibid., 3.

71. Ibid., 5.

72. Ibid., 6.

73. Ibid., 8–9.

74. Ibid., 11.

75. Ibid., 13.

76. Ibid., 16.

77. Ibid., 21.

78. Ibid., 25–26.

79. Ibid., 30.

80. Ibid., 31.

81. Ibid., 41.

82. Ibid., 35.

83. Ibid., 33–34.

84. Ibid., 47.

85. Ibid., 61, 68.

86. Ibid., 74–75.

87. Ibid., 86.

88. Ibid., 88.

89. Ibid., 95.

90. Ibid., 105.

91. Ibid., 122.

92. Ibid., 129.

6. DISCOVERING SELF-CONSCIOUSNESS

1. "Novels: Their Meaning and Mission," *Putnam's Monthly Magazine* 4, no. 2 (October 1854): 395.

2. Philip F. Gura, *American Transcendentalism: A History* (New York: Hill & Wang, 2007), 46–69.

3. "Novels," 396.

4. Henry James, *Hawthorne* ([1879] Ithaca: Cornell University Press, 1997), 51.

5. "Novels," 391.

6. Here I am indebted to Richard Rabinowitz's *The Spiritual Self in Everyday Life: The Transformation of Religious Experience in Nineteenth-Century New England* (Boston: Northeastern University Press, 1989), especially 166–77.

7. Waldo Hilary Dunn, *Life of Donald G. Mitchell, Ik Marvel* (New York: Scribner's, 1922), 225, 232. This is the standard biography, but see also Wayne R. Kime, *Donald G. Mitchell* (Boston: Twayne, 1985).

8. See, for example, Maura D'Amore, "'A Man's Sense of Domesticity': Donald Grant Mitchell's Suburban Vision," *ESQ: A Journal of the American Renaissance* 56, no. 2 (2010): 135–62.

9. *American Whig Review* 13, no. 37 (January 1851): 74.

10. "Our Young Authors," *Putnam's Monthly Magazine* 1, no. 1 (January 1853): 74.

11. Ik Marvel (Donald G. Mitchell), *Reveries of a Bachelor; or, A Book of the Heart* (New York: Baker and Scribner, 1850), in Paul C. Gutjahr, *Popular American Literature of the Nineteenth Century* (New York: Oxford University Press, 2001), v.

12. "Our Young Authors," 77.

13. Marvel, *Reveries*, 478.

14. See Vincent J. Bertolini, "The Erotics of Sentimental Bachelorhood in the 1850s," in *Sentimental Men: Masculinity and the Politics of Affect in American Culture*, ed. Mary Chapman and Glenn Hendler (Berkeley: University of California Press, 1999), 19–42, and passim.

15. Marvel, *Reveries*, 482.

16. Ibid., 484.

17. Ibid., 527.

18. Ibid., 551.

19. Ibid., 557.

20. Ibid., 564.

21. Ibid., 567.

22. Ibid., 584.

23. Emily Dickinson to Susan Gilbert, October 9, 1851, in *The Letters of Emily Dickinson*, ed. Thomas H. Johnson, 3 vols. (Cambridge: Harvard University Press, 1965), 1:144.

24. Nathaniel Hawthorne, *The Scarlet Letter* ([1850]; New York, Penguin, 1983), 13.

25. *Boston Weekly Messenger* 18 (November 13, 1828); [J. T. Buckingham], *The New-England Galaxy* 9, no. 577 (October 31, 1828).

26. Nathaniel Hawthorne, *Tales and Sketches* (New York: Library of America, 1982), 1150.

27. *North American Review* 45 (July 1837): 59.

28. Edgar Allan Poe, "Twice-Told Tales" (1842), in *Poe: Essays and Reviews* (New York: Library of America, 1984), 570.

29. *The Knickerbocker* 19 (March 1842): 282.

30. *Boston Miscellany* 1 (1842): 92.

31. *Godey's Lady's Book* 35 (November 1847), 252–56.

32. Nathaniel Hawthorne, "Rappaccini's Daughter" (1844), in *Hawthorne: Tales and Sketches* (New York: Library of America, 1982), 975.

33. *Democratic Review* 16 (April 1845): 380.

34. Herman Melville, "Hawthorne and His Mosses," *Literary World* (August 17 and 24, 1850).

35. Sterling F. Delano, *Brook Farm: The Dark Side of Utopia* (Cambridge: Harvard University Press, 2004) is the standard history.

36. Amory Dwight Mayo, "Nathaniel Hawthorne," *Universalist Quarterly and General Review* 7 (July 1851): 272–93.

37. Ibid., 276, 278.

38. Ibid., 276.

39. Ibid., 290.

40. See the description in Hershel Parker, *Herman Melville: A Biography, 1819–1851* (Baltimore: Johns Hopkins University Press, 1996), 745–48.

41. Henry T. Tuckerman, "Nathaniel Hawthorne," *Southern Literary Messenger* 17 (June 1851): 344, 346, 349.

42. Evert Duyckinck, "The House of the Seven Gables," *Literary World* 8 (April 26, 1851): 333.

43. Edwin Percy Whipple, "Review of New Books," *Graham's Magazine* 38 (May 1851): 467.

44. Nathaniel Hawthorne to Horatio Bridge, July 22, 1851, in Hawthorne, *Letters, 1843–1853*, 461–62.

45. *North British Review* 20, no. 39 (1853–1854): 49, 52.

46. Nathaniel Hawthorne, *The Blithedale Romance*, ed. Annette Kolodry [1852] in *Hawthorne: Novels* (New York: Library of America, 1995), 648.

47. Ibid., 641.

48. Ibid., 639.

49. Ibid., 652.

50. Ibid., 760–61.

51. Ibid., 645.

52. Ibid., 646.

53. Ibid., 672.

54. Ibid., 695.

55. Ibid., 656–57.

56. Ibid., 667.

57. Ibid., 692.

58. Ibid., 749–50.

59. Ibid., 751.

60. Ibid., 686.

61. Ibid., 653.

62. Ibid., 822–23.

63. Ibid., 830.

64. Melville to John Murray, October 29, 1847, Herman Melville, *Correspondence* (Evanston, IL: Northwestern University Press, 1993), 98.

65. Melville to John Murray, March 25, 1848, ibid., 106.

66. [London] *Literary Gazette*, March 24, 1849, in Parker, *Melville*, vol. 1, 628.

67. *Athenaeum*, March 24, 1849, in Brian Higgins and Hershel Parker, *Herman Melville: The Contemporary Reviews* (Cambridge: Cambridge University Press, 1995), 193.

68. [London] *Atlas*, March 24, 1849, in Higgins and Parker, *Reviews*, 194.

69. *Bentley's Magazine* 25 (April 1849), ibid., 201.

70. *United States Magazine and Democratic Review* 25 (July 1849), in ibid., 238.

71. *New-York Tribune*, May 10, 1849, in ibid., 226.

72. Melville to Lemuel Shaw, October 6, 1849, in Melville, *Correspondence*, 138.

73. [New Orleans] *Commercial Bulletin*, April 9, 1850, in Higgins and Parker, *Reviews*, 319.

74. Melville to Richard Henry Dana, Jr., May 1, 1850, in Melville, *Correspondence*, 162.

75. Melville to Nathaniel Hawthorne, [June 1?] 1851, ibid., 193.

76. Ibid., 191.

77. Melville to Sarah Huyler Morewood, September [12 or 19], 1851, ibid., 206. Morewood was a neighbor who, with her husband, had bought Robert Melvill's farmhouse in Pittsfield, Massachusetts, known as "Broadhall."

78. Melville to Nathaniel Hawthorne, November [17], 1851, in Melville, ibid., 212.

79. Herman Melville, *Moby-Dick*, ed. Andrew Delbanco ([1851] New York: Penguin, 1992), 178.

80. Ibid., 82.

81. Ibid., 5.

82. Ibid., 183.

83. Ibid., 88.

84. Ibid., 201–203.

85. Ibid., 203.

86. Ibid., 299.

87. Ibid., 233–34.

88. Ibid., 339–40.

89. Ibid., 453–54.

90. Ibid., 455–56.

91. Ibid., 567–68.

92. Ibid., 380.

93. Ibid., 591–92.

94. Ibid., 611.

95. Ibid., 97.

96. Ibid., 57.

97. Ibid., 512.

98. Ibid., 475.

99. *John-Bull*, October 25, 1851, in Higgins and Parker, *Reviews*, 357–58.

100. *News of the World*, November 2, 1851, ibid., 365.

101. *Independent*, November 20, 1851, ibid., 380.

102. *United States Magazine and Democratic Review*, January 30, 1852, ibid., 410.

103. *Southern Quarterly Review*, new series 5, January 5, 1852, ibid., 412.

104. *National Intelligencer*, December 16, 1851, ibid., 399–400.

105. *New-York Tribune*, November 22, 1851, ibid., 383–84.

106. Melville to Sophia Hawthorne, January 8, 1852, in Melville, *Correspondence*, 219; and Melville to Nathaniel Hawthorne, [17?] November 1851, ibid., 213.

107. [New York] *Day Book* 7 (September 1852), in Higgins and Parker, *Reviews*, 436.

108. *Boston Daily Times,* August 5, 1852, ibid., 422.

109. *Southern Literary Messenger* 18 (September 1852), 574, ibid., 434.

110. *American Whig Review* 16 (November 1852), 446–54, ibid., 448.

111. *Godey's Lady's Book* 45 (October 1852), 390, ibid., 440.

112. *Hartford Courant* 4 (August 1852), ibid., 420.

113. *Philadelphia Evening Post*, August 14, 1852, ibid., 425.

114. *New York Home Journal*, September 4, 1852, ibid., 436.

115. *Literary World* 290 (August 21, 1852), ibid., 430.

116. Herman Melville, *The Confidence Man: His Masquerade*, ed. John Bryant ([1857] New York: Penguin, 1991), 155.

117. Ibid., 160–61.

118. Ibid., 84.

119. Ibid., 85–86.

120. Ibid., 217–18.

121. Ibid., 282. Drummond light—limelight—was used in theaters in Melville's day for spotlighting.

122. Ibid., 35.

123. Ibid., 21.

124. Ibid., 298.

125. [Springfield (MA)] *Republican*, May 16, 1857, in Higgins and Parker, *Reviews*, 501.

7. A NEGLECTED TRADITION

1. See Ellery Sedgwick, *The "Atlantic Monthly," 1857–1909: Yankee Humanism at High Tide and Ebb* (Amherst: University of Massachusetts Press, 1994), chap. 1 and 2.

2. "A Literary Whim," *Appleton's Journal* 6 (October 14, 1871): 441.

3. Mary Clemmer, *A Memorial of Alice and Phoebe Cary* (Boston: Houghton, Mifflin and Company, 1872), 19.

4. Ibid., 32–34, 59–69.

5. Ibid., 71.

6. Ibid., 122.

7. *The Una* 1 (May 2, 1853).

8. Judith Fetterley, "Introduction," Alice Cary, *Clovernook Sketches and Other Stories* (New Brunswick, NJ: Rutgers University Press, 1987), xx. Nina Baym, *Woman's Fiction: A Guide to Novels by and About Women, 1820–1870* (Urbana: University of Illinois Press, 1978), 262.

9. Alice Cary, *Hagar: A Tale of To-day* (New York: Redfield, 1852), 255.

10. Ibid., 25.

11. Ibid., 27.

12. Ibid., 29.

13. Ibid., 256.

14. Ibid., 263.

15. Ibid., 256–57.

16. Ibid., 260.

17. *The Una* 1 (May 2, 1853).

18. Carey, *Hagar*, 299–300.

19. Ibid., 300.

20. Ibid., 74.

21. Ibid., 172.

22. Ibid., 173.

23. Ibid., 93.

24. Ibid., 210.

25. Clemmer, *Memorial*, 79.

26. Biographical details are from Grace Farrell's indispensable *Lillie Devereux Blake: Retracing a Life Erased* (Amherst: University of Massachusetts Press, 2002) and Katherine Devereux Blake, *Champion of Women: A Life of Lillie Devereux Blake* (New York: Fleming Revell, [1943]).

27. Cited in Farrell, *Blake*, 41.

28. "The Social Condition of Woman," *The Knickerbocker* 61 (May 1863): 23.

29. Lillie Devereux Blake, *Southwold: A Novel* (New York: Rudd & Carleton, 1859), 10.

30. Ibid., 18.

31. Ibid., 47.

32. Ibid., 86.

33. Ibid., 105.

34. Ibid., 194–95.

35. Ibid., 257.

36. Ibid., 80.

37. Ibid., 191.

38. Ibid., 192.

39. Ibid., 172–73.

40. Lillie Devereux Blake, *Rockford* (New York: Rudd & Carleton, 1862), 204.

41. Richard Henry Stoddard, *Recollections, Personal and Literary* (New York: A. S. Barnes and Co., 1903) offers glimpses of their married life. See particularly 106–15.

42. See the section on Taylor in Larzer Ziff, *Return Passages: Great American Travel Writing, 1780–1919* (New Haven: Yale University Press, 2000), 118–69.

43. *Daily Alta California*, October 8, 1854.

44. Ibid., July 19, 1856.

45. Ibid., January 29, 1855.

46. Ibid., December 3, 1856.

47. Elizabeth Stoddard to James Russell Lowell, May 5, 1859, in James Matlack, "The Literary Career of Elizabeth Barstow Stoddard" (Ph.D. dissertation, Yale University, 1968), 185.

48. Elizabeth Stoddard to Clarence Stedman, May 21, 1860, in ibid., 185a.

49. Ibid.

50. Elizabeth Stoddard to Clarence Stedman, June 22, 1862, ibid., 216.

51. *New York World*, July 4, 1862. If Stoddard errs, the reviewer continues, she does so "on the side of economy and paucity of language. No word is superfluous," even as this sometimes causes the reader to lose "a thread of development from the lack of fullness of expression or the exceeding condensation or reticence of speech and style." The remedy, he urges, is to read more carefully, for quite simply, "there is nothing to skip."

52. Alfred Habegger, *Henry James and the "Woman Business"* (New York: Cambridge University Press, 1989), 96.

53. "Personal," *The Round Table* 2 (October 7, 1865): 70.

54. Elizabeth Stoddard, *The Morgesons*, eds. *Lawrence Buell and Sandra Zagarell* ([1862] New York: Penguin, 1997), 1.

55. In the few changes she made to later editions of the book, she omitted this phrase but still left enough clues for the reader to suppose Ben's drinking killed him.

56. Richard Stoddard to Manton Marble, June 26, 1862, quoting a review in the New York *Transcript*, cited in Matlack, *Stoddard*, 219.

57. *New York World*, July 4, 1862.

58. [Philadelphia] *North American and United States Gazette*, June 28, 1862.

59. [Philadelphia] *Evening Bulletin*, June 24, 1862.

60. *New-York Tribune*, July 19, 1862.

61. Stoddard, *The Morgesons*, 34.

62. Ibid., 97.

63. Ibid., 13.

64. Ibid., 17.

65. Ibid., 23.

66. Ibid., 37.

67. Ibid., 40–41.

68. Ibid., 137.

69. Ibid., 245.

70. Ibid., 58–59.

71. Ibid., 74.

72. Ibid., 86.

73. Ibid., 109.

74. Ibid., 123.

75. Lillian Woodman Aldrich, *Crowding Memories* (Boston: Houghton, Mifflin and Company, 1922), 14–15.

76. Elizabeth Stoddard: *Two Men* ([1865] Lincoln: University of Nebraska Press, 2008), 3.

77. Ibid., 2.

78. Ibid., 21.

79. Ibid., 51.

80. Ibid., 33.

81. Ibid., 90–91.

82. Ibid., 96–97.

83. Ibid., 97.

84. Ibid., 130.

85. Ibid., 110.

86. Ibid., 114.

87. Ibid., 125.

88. Ibid., 124.

89. Ibid., 125.

90. Ibid., 150.

91. Ibid., 161.

92. Ibid., 191.

93. Ibid., 200.

94. Ibid., 261.

95. *New York Post*, October 17, 1865.

96. *The Nation* 1 (October 26, 1865): 537.

97. *New-York Tribune*, November 16, 1865.

98. Stoddard, *Two Men*, 172.

99. William Dean Howells, *Literary Friends and Acquaintances: A Personal Retrospect of American Authorship* (New York: Harper & Brothers, 1900), 87.

100. Thomas Wentworth Higginson, "To Mary Channing Higginson," n.d., letter 342a, *The Letters of Emily Dickinson*, 3 vols., ed. Thomas H. Johnson (Cambridge: Harvard University Press, 1958), 2: 473–76.

101. Stoddard, *Two Men*, 64.

102. *The Bookman* 16, no. 3 (November 1902): 260.

103. *New-York Tribune*, January 27, 1868.

104. Elizabeth Stoddard to Margaret Sweat, April 14, [1852], cited in Anne E. Boyd, *Writing for Immortality: Women and the Emergence of High Literary Culture in America* (Baltimore: Johns Hopkins University Press, 2004), 23.

105. William B. Greene, *Transcendentalism* (West Brookfield, MA: O. S. Cooke, 1849), 12–14.

106. Elizabeth Palmer Peabody, *Reminiscences of the Rev. William Ellery Channing, D.D.* (Boston: Roberts Brothers, 1980), 373, and "Egotheism, The Atheism of To-day" (1858), reprinted in *Last Evening with Allston and Other Papers* (Boston: D. Lothrop, 1886), 245.

107. Rebecca Harding Davis, *Bits of Gossip* (New York: Houghton, Mifflin and Company, 1904), 36.

108. Ibid., 36.

109. Ibid., 45–46.

110. Elizabeth Stuart Phelps, "Stories that Stay," *The Century* 81 (1910): 120.

111. Rebecca Harding Davis, "Life in the Iron Mills" (1861), in *Norton Anthology of American Literature*, 8th ed., ed. Nina Baym et al. (New York: W. W. Norton, 2012), B: 1707.

112. Ibid., 1732.

113. Stoddard to James T. Fields, cited in Sharon M. Harris, *Rebecca Harding Davis and American Realism* (Philadelphia: University of Pennsylvania Press, 1991), 62. On Fichte, see J. D. Morrell, *An Historical and Critical View of Modern Philosophy in Europe* (New York: Robert Carter and Brothers, 1872), 490 ff.

114. Cited in Harris, *Rebecca Harding Davis*, 64. This and Jean Pfaelzer's *Parlor Radical: Rebecca Harding Davis and the Beginnings of American Social Realism* (Pittsburgh: University of Pittsburgh Press, 1996) are the best modern studies.

115. Rebecca Harding Davis, *Margret Howth: A Story of To-day* (Boston: Ticknor and Fields, 1862), 101–102.

116. Ibid., 6.

117. Ibid., 18.

118. Ibid., 34–35.

119. Ibid., 57.

120. Ibid., 68.

121. Ibid., 70–71.

122. Ibid., 83–84.

123. Ibid., 84–85.

124. Ibid., 84–85.

125. Ibid., 90.

126. Ibid., 111–13.

127. Ibid., 120–21.

128. Ibid., 131–32.

129. Ibid., 142–43.

130. Ibid., 150.

131. Ibid., 152.

132. Ibid., 151–52.

133. Ibid., 154.

134. Ibid., 165.

135. Ibid., 171.

136. Ibid., 184.

137. Ibid., 211.

138. Ibid., 212.

139. Ibid., 233.

140. See Pfaelzer, *Parlor Radical*, 74, quoting from the James T. Fields and Rebecca Harding Davis correspondence.

8. FROM A THEOLOGY OF THE FEELINGS TO AN ETHIC OF LOVE

1. Debbie Applegate, *The Most Famous Man in America: The Biography of Henry Ward Beecher* (New York: Doubleday, 2006) is the best biography.

2. See Clifford E. Clark, Jr., *Henry Ward Beecher: Spokesman for a Middle-Class America* (Urbana: University of Illinois Press, 1978), 187–94.

3. Marvin Felheim, "Two Views of the State, or the Theory and Practice of Henry Ward Beecher," *New England Quarterly* 25 (September 1951): 314–26.

4. Letter published in preface to Henry Ward Beecher, *Norwood* ([1867] New York: Fords, Howard, 1887).

5. Henry Ward Beecher, *Norwood; or, Village Life in New England* ([1867] New York: Scribner, 1868), 52.

6. Ibid., 51–52.

7. Ibid., 59–60.

8. Ibid., 53.

9. Ralph Waldo Emerson, *Nature* (1836), in *Essays and Lectures* (New York: Library of America, 1983), 7.

10. Beecher, *Norwood*, 266.

11. See Philip F. Gura, *American Transcendentalism: A History* (New York: Hill & Wang, 2007), 145–49.

12. Beecher, *Norwood*, 59.

13. Ibid., 10.

14. Ibid., 272.

15. [William Dean Howells] *The Atlantic Monthly* 21 (June 1868): 761–64.

16. *The Nation* 6 (April 2, 1868): 274–75; *Catholic World* 10, no. 57 (1869): 399–400.

17. William G. McLoughlin, *The Meaning of Henry Ward Beecher: An Essay on the Shifting Values of Mid-Victorian America, 1840–1870* (New York: Knopf, 1970), 56, 63.

18. The story is best told in Richard Wightman Fox, *Trials of Intimacy: Love and Loss in the Beecher-Tilton Scandal* (Chicago: University of Chicago Press, 1999).

19. See John Davies, *Phrenology: Fad and Science; a Nineteenth-Century Crusade* (New Haven: Yale University Press, 1955) and Charles Colbert, *A Measure of Perfection: Phrenology and the Fine Arts in America* (Chapel Hill: University of North Carolina Press, 1998).

20. See Richard Hofstadter, *Social Darwinism in American Thought* (Philadelphia: University of Pennsylvania Press, 1944).

21. Oliver Wendell Holmes, *Elsie Venner: A Romance of Destiny* ([1861] New York: Doubleday and Company, [no date]), 128–29.

22. Ibid., 165.

23. Ibid., 343.

24. Ibid., 188.

25. Nathaniel Hawthorne, *The Scarlet Letter* ([1850] New York: Penguin, 1983), 35.

26. Holmes, *Elsie Venner*, 193.

27. Ibid., 194.

28. Ibid., 7.

29. Ibid., 190–92.

30. Ibid., 177–79.

31. Elizabeth Stuart Phelps, *Chapters from a Life* (Boston: Houghton, Mifflin and Company, 1896), 262–63.

32. See, for example, Charlotte Perkins Gilman, *Women and Economics: A Study of the Economic Relation Between Men and Women as a Factor in Social Evolution* (Boston: Small, Maynard, 1900).

33. Elizabeth Stuart Phelps, *The Struggle for Immortality* (Boston: Houghton, Mifflin and Company, 1889), 199–200.

34. Ibid., 206.

35. Ibid., 222.

Acknowledgments

Like my previous book on American Transcendentalism, this one derives from decades of thinking and teaching its subject; but again like the former, it owes much, though I did not realize it until later in my career, to Warner Berthoff. For years at Harvard he offered a course in what one might call neglected American novels from the entire nineteenth century. It included not only the "secondary" works of, say, Cooper and Melville but also the fiction of John Pendleton Kennedy and Robert Montgomery Bird from the antebellum years and John Hay's *The Breadwinners*, Henry Adams's *Democracy*, and Louisa May Alcott's *Work* and *Moods*. His suggested reading list comprised two single-spaced, typed pages, from which each student could pick and choose on which novels to write. The course was a revelation, as is Professor Berthoff's example as an elegant stylist.

At the urging of my mentor and constant inspiration (as I write, the centenarian) Daniel Aaron, I explored most of his good friend Edmund Wilson's work and here have been influenced particularly by *Patriotic Gore*. The economy and justness of his writing most strikes me, as does his ability to capture in a trenchant essay the entire life and œuvre of each subject. The chapters therein on Mary Chesnutt and General Grant epitomize his labor and his gift. I have striven, admittedly without his success, at a comparable economy in my descriptions of this book's subjects and their work.

The long shadow of Perry Miller hangs over this work, as it does over most of what I have written. His Ahab-like will to know and understand each of the subjects with which he grappled has been a constant challenge. Like many others, I am not satisfied with *The Raven and the Whale*, and here one sees part of my engagement with it. But also important to me is his unfinished *The Life of the Mind in America*, with its insistence that, along with law and science, religion remained formative in nineteenth-century American literature and culture. When I consider that I now am older than he was when he died in 1963, his work incomplete and yet so much more enduring and significant than mine, or that of most of my contemporaries, I am humbled.

I thank Ellen Dunlap, president of the American Antiquarian Society, for supporting me in the initial stages of this work and the Society's entire staff for their unflinching dedication to the preservation and dissemination of America's printed archive. As usual, too, I am greatly indebted to the inspiration of my friend David D. Hall, whom I got to know under the Society's "generous dome."

At Farrar, Straus and Giroux, Thomas LeBien first encouraged my ambitious project, and Daniel Gerstle did heroic service to put the manuscript in order. My thanks to both.

Finally, the book's dedication to longtime friend Lawrence Buell bespeaks my acknowledgment of both his mastery of one of my chosen fields and the strength of his moral example to attempt to correct what is wrong in the often strange and unsettling world of academia. I offer this work to him as a gift on his retirement after an exemplary career at Oberlin and Harvard.

Index

Franklin, Benjamin, 4, 90; *Autobiography*, xiii, 68

Frederick Douglass' Paper, 162

free blacks, 145, 158, 161–77, 247–51; emigration, 167–72

Freedmen's Bureau, 171

free love, 138, 273

Freeman, Mary E. Wilkins, 147

Freemasons, 86, 132

free will, xii, 5, 21, 50, 108, 117, 207, 215, 221, 273, 279; Nathaniel Hawthorne on, 185–97; Oliver Wendell Holmes on, 274–77; Herman Melville on, 197–215

Freewill Baptists, 33, 279

frontier life, 39–40, 72, 77; Robert Montgomery Bird on, 72–73; James Fenimore Cooper on, 39–40, 43–44; John Neal on, 43–44, 46; Catharine Maria Sedgwick on, 54–59. *See also* West

Fugitive Slave Law, 145, 162

fugitive slave narratives, 144, 150, 151–61

Fuller, Margaret, 24, 62, 65, 76, 79, 96, 135; *Papers on Literature and Art*, 77; *Woman in the Nineteenth Century*, 135

Galaxy, The, 220

gambling, 60

Gamesters, The, 36

Garland, Hamlin, 254

Garrison, William Lloyd, 154, 223

gay sex, 91

gentlemen's clubs, 87

Germany, 29, 60, 63, 79, 95, 145; literature, 5, 79, 81

Gilded Age, 263

Gilder, Richard Watson, 238

Gladden, Washington, 280

Godey's Lady's Book, 138, 140, 168, 212

Godwin, Parke, 220

Godwin, William, 25, 65, 93; *The Adventures of Caleb Williams*, 35, 37, 179

Goethe, Johann Wolfgang von, 81, 179; *The Sorrows of Young Werther*, 5

Gothic novels, xvi, 25, 36, 65; by Charles Brockden Brown, 27–37

Graham, Sylvester, 136

Graham's Magazine, xii, 84, 132, 222

Greeley, Horace, 76, 96, 125, 135, 137, 159, 201, 222–23, 238

Greene, William B., 253

Greenwood, Grace, 124, 133; "The Leap from the Long Bridge: An Incident at Washington," 157

Griswold, Rufus, *The Female Poets of America*, 222

Haiti, 36–37, 164

Hale, Edward Everett, 95

Hale, Nathan, Jr., 187

Hale, Sarah Josepha, 167–69; background of, 168; *Liberia*, 167, 168–69

Hall, James, *The Wilderness and the Warpath*, 77

Hamilton, Gail, 220

Hancock, John, 61

Harper, Frances Ellen Watkins, *Iola Leroy*, 167

Harper & Brothers, 64, 75, 137, 168, 198, 199, 209–10, 219

Harper's New Monthly Magazine, 135, 181, 219, 220, 223, 230, 231, 239

Hart, John S., *The Female Prose Writers of America*, 62, 113

Hartford *Courant*, 212

Harvard Divinity School, 94–95

Harvard Medical School, 169

Haswell, William, 8, 9

Hawthorne, Julian, 253

Hawthorne, Nathaniel, xvii, 24, 35, 46, 76–77, 79, 80, 82, 108, 126, 130, 136, 179, 181, 185–97, 202, 204, 209, 215, 219, 251, 254, 263, 276; background of, 185–88; *The Blithedale Romance*, xvii, 97–98, 188, 191–97, 237; *Fanshawe*, 186; "The Fountain of Youth," 79; *The House of the Seven Gables*, 191; *The Marble Faun*, 197;

Prescott, William Hickling, 26

press, xii, 4, 26, 27, 54, 75, 161–62; abolitionist, 159, 160, 173; black, 169; of 1840s, 75–76, 84; of 1850s, 159, 208, 219–20. *See also* journals, literary; reviews, book; *specific publications*

prostitution, 8

Protestants, 33, 268, 270, 272, 277, 280

Proust, Marcel, 278

psychological novels, 179–263; by Lillie Devereux Blake, 228–37; by Alice Cary, 221–28; by Rebecca Harding Davis, 254–63; of 1850s, 179–235; of 1860s, 235–63; by Nathaniel Hawthorne, 185–97; by Herman Melville, 197–215; by Donald G. Mitchell, 180–85; by Elizabeth Stoddard, 237–53

publishing industry, xviii, 4; African American authors and, 157–59; of 1810s–1830s, 46–49, 64–65; of 1840s, 75–77, 78–83, 95, 99; of 1850s, 108, 124–25, 146, 157–59, 177, 181, 185, 198–200, 208–10, 219–20, 230; of 1860s, 240, 253, 267; religious tracts, 46–49, 51; turn of the century, 8, 10, 27. *See also specific publishers*

Puritanism, xv, 54–59, 186, 189; Catharine Maria Sedgwick on, 54–59

Putnam, George Palmer, 99, 107

Putnam's Monthly Magazine, xii, 76, 179, 213, 219–20

Quaker City Weekly, The, 85

Quakers, xv, 25, 52, 69, 72, 103, 136, 152, 159

Quincy, Edmund, 153

Rabelais, François, 199, 200

race, xv, xvi, 73, 143–77, 280; African American novelists on, 151–77; Robert Montgomery Bird on, 67–73; black emigration, 167–72; William Wells

Brown on, 151–57; Rebecca Harding Davis on, 259–61; Martin Delany on, 169–72; 1850s novels on, 143–77; Sarah Josepha Hale on, 167–69; interracial relationships, 43–44, 46, 55–59, 154–68, 172–77, 248–52; Harriet Jacobs on, 157–61; John Neal on, 43–44, 46; Catharine Maria Sedgwick on, 54–59; Elizabeth Stoddard on, 247–53; Harriet Beecher Stowe on, 143–51; Frank J. Webb on, 161–67; Harriet E. Wilson on, 172–77

Radcliffe, Ann, *The Mysteries of Udolpho,* 37

railroads, xi, 47, 75, 89, 118

rape, 44, 87, 157, 158

rationality, xiii, xiv, 7

Rauschenberg, Walter, 280

Reconstruction, 167, 272

Relf, Samuel, *Infidelity,* 24

religion, xi–xiv, xv–xvi, xvii, 3, 47, 180, 279–80; Henry Ward Beecher on, 265–74; Charles Brockden Brown on, 27–37; Alice Cary on, 227–28; Caroline Chesebro' on, 133–35; James Fenimore Cooper on, 102–104; Maria Cummins on, 115–18; of 1810s–1830s, 46–64, 72, 73; of 1840s, 78, 86, 87, 89–90, 94–97, 104; of 1850s, 107–14, 123, 131, 133–35, 141, 147, 154, 176–77, 180, 188–90, 221, 227–28, 235; of 1860s, 243, 245–46, 253–54, 262, 265–80; Nathaniel Hawthorne on, 188–90; Sylvester Judd on, 94–97; Mary Gove Nichols on, 136, 139; Sarah Savage on, 47–49; Catharine Maria Sedgwick on, 49–64; Elizabeth Stoddard on, 245–46; Harriet Beecher Stowe on, 147–51; tract societies, 46–49, 51, 61; turn of the society, 3, 27–37; utopian fiction and, 93–104; Susan Warner on, 107–14. *See also specific religions*

religious tract societies, literature of, 46–49, 51, 61

Mitchell, 180–85; by Mary Gove Nichols, 136–41; by Harriet Beecher Stowe, 143–51; turn of the century, 3–37; by Harriet E. Wilson, 172–77

sex, xvi, 8; Lillie Devereux Blake on, 228–37; William Hill Brown on, 4–8; Alice Cary on, 223–28; of 1810s–1830s, 43–46; of 1840s, 87–93; of 1850s, 121, 137, 138, 155, 158, 228–37; of 1860s, 239–51; Hannah Webster Foster on, 14–21; free love, 138, 273; Nathaniel Hawthorne on, 188–90, 195; interracial, 154–68, 172–77, 248–52; George Lippard on, 87–90; John Neal on, 43–46; Susanna Rowson on, 10–13; Elizabeth Stoddard on, 239–51; George Thompson on, 91–93; turn of the century, 4–24, 27–37

Shakers, 33, 53–54

Shakespeare, William, 199, 202

Shaw, Lemuel, 199, 201

Shays, Daniel, 4

Shelley, Mary, 25, 202

Shelley, Percy Bysshe, 25

Sigourney, Lydia, 123, 124

Simms, William Gilmore, xv, 64–66, 73, 104, 212; *Martin Faber: The Story of a Criminal*, 65–66; *The Partisan*, 64; *Views and Reviews in American Literature, History and Fiction*, 65, 77; *The Wigwam and the Cabin*, 77; *The Yemassee*, 64

sin and guilt, Hawthorne on, 185–97

Skinner, Thomas Harvey, 111–12; *The Religion of the Bible*, 111–12

slavery, xi, xvi, 36, 102, 247, 249, 266, 279, 280; Robert Montgomery Bird on, 67–73; border wars, 146–47; William Wells Brown on, 151–57; Martin Delany on, 169–72; end of, 162, 177; fugitive slave narratives, 144, 150, 151–61; Sarah Josepha Hale on, 167–69; Harriet Jacobs on, 157–61; Kansas/Nebraska Act, 146, 152; rebellions, 147, 156; runaway slaves, xvi, 147–61; Harriet Beecher Stowe on,

143–51; trade, 36, 152, 154–56; violence, 69–70, 147, 149, 156; Frank J. Webb on, 161–67

Smith, Elihu Hubbard, 26

Social Darwinism, 274–77

social realism, 254; by Rebecca Harding Davis, 254–63

society, 90, 104; of 1810s–1830s, 39–73; of 1840s, 75–104; of 1850s, 105–235; of 1860s, 235–74; turn of the century, 3–37; utopian, 93–104. *See also specific groups and concerns*

Society of Psychical Research, 278

somnambulism, 36

Sorosis, 228

South, xi, xvi, xvii, 146, 160; sectional crisis, 66; slavery, 96, 147–51. *See also specific states and cities*

South Carolina, 171

Southern Literary Messenger, The, 181, 212

Southern Quarterly Review, 130, 209

Southworth, E.D.E.N., 221

Spencer, Herbert, 274, 279

Spirit of the Times, The, 84

spiritualism, 278–79

Spofford, Mary Prescott, 147, 220

sporting magazines, 90–91

Staël, Madame de, 221

Stanton, Elizabeth Cady, 131, 135, 223, 231

steam power, xi, 47, 75, 89, 117, 152

Stedman, Edmund Clarence, 240, 243, 251, 253

Steffens, Lincoln, 280

Stein, Gertrude, 278

Stephens, Uriah S., 85

Sterne, Laurence, 45; *A Sentimental Journey*, xiv, 3; *Tristam Shandy*, 45, 202

Stockbridge, Massachusetts, 49–50

Stoddard, Elizabeth Barstow, 220, 221, 223, 237–53, 262; background of, 237–39; *The Morgesons*, xvii, 237, 240–47, 253, 254, 257; reviews on, 239, 240, 243–44, 251–53; *Temple House*, 237, 253; *Two Men*, 247–53